Accountability in American Higher Education

Education Policy

Series Editors

Lance Fusarelli, North Carolina State University
Frederick M. Hess, American Enterprise Institute
Martin West, Harvard University

This series addresses a variety of topics in the area of education policy. Volumes are solicited primarily from social scientists with expertise on education, in addition to policymakers or practitioners with hands-on experience in the field. Topics of particular focus include state and national policy, teacher recruitment, retention, and compensation, urban school reform, test-based accountability, choice-based reform, school finance, higher education costs and access, the quality instruction in higher education, leadership and administration in K-12 and higher education, teacher colleges, the role of the courts in education policymaking, and the relationship between education research and practice. The series serves as a venue for presenting stimulating new research findings, serious contributions to ongoing policy debates, and accessible volumes that illuminate important questions or synthesize existing research.

Series Editors

LANCE FUSARELLI is a Professor and Director of Graduate Programs in the Department of Leadership, Policy and Adult and Higher Education at North Carolina State University. He is co-author of *Better Policies, Better Schools* and co-editor of the *Handbook of Education Politics and Policy*.

FREDERICK M. HESS is Resident Scholar and Director of Education Policy Studies at the American Enterprise Institute. He is the author of *The Same Thing Over and Over: How School Reformers Get Stuck in Yesterday's Ideas*.

MARTIN WEST is an Assistant Professor of Education in the Graduate School of Education at Harvard University. He is an Executive Editor of *Education Next* and Deputy Director of Harvard's Program on Education Policy and Governance.

Ohio's Education Reform Challenges: Lessons from the Frontlines
   Chester E. Finn, Jr., Terry Ryan, and Michael B. Lafferty

Accountability in American Higher Education
   Edited by Kevin Carey and Mark Schneider

Education Reform: Coalitions and Conflicts (forthcoming)
   Alex Medler

Freedom and School Choice in American Education (forthcoming)
   Edited by Greg Forster and C. Bradley Thompson

Accountability in American Higher Education

Edited by

Kevin Carey

and

Mark Schneider

palgrave
macmillan

First published in 2010 by
PALGRAVE MACMILLAN®
in the United States—a division of St. Martin's Press LLC,
175 Fifth Avenue, New York, NY 10010.

Where this book is distributed in the UK, Europe and the rest of the world,
this is by Palgrave Macmillan, a division of Macmillan Publishers Limited,
registered in England, company number 785998, of Houndmills,
Basingstoke, Hampshire RG21 6XS.

Palgrave Macmillan is the global academic imprint of the above companies
and has companies and representatives throughout the world.

Palgrave® and Macmillan® are registered trademarks in the United States,
the United Kingdom, Europe and other countries.

ISBN: 978–0–230–11031–1

Library of Congress Cataloging-in-Publication Data

Accountability in American higher education / edited by
Kevin Carey and Mark Schneider.
    p. cm.
    ISBN 978–0–230–11031–1 (alk. paper)
    1. Educational accountability—United States. 2. Educational
productivity—United States. 3. Education, Higher—Political aspects—
United States. I. Carey, Kevin, 1970– II. Schneider, Mark, 1948–

LB2806.22.A2485 2010
379.1'58—dc22   2010023193

A catalogue record of the book is available from the British Library.

Design by Newgen Imaging Systems (P) Ltd., Chennai, India.

First edition: December 2010

10 9 8 7 6 5 4 3 2 1

Printed in the United States of America.

Contents

Acknowledgments

There are many individuals to whom we are indebted for their help in the creation of this volume. We'd be remiss if we did not first acknowledge the authors who wrote the conference papers that were presented at the American Enterprise Institute (AEI) in November 2009, and then edited them for contribution to this volume. We'd also like to thank the discussants who participated in that conference and gave thoughtful feedback on those initial papers. Many thanks go to the Bill & Melinda Gates Foundation for providing the financial backing that enabled us to gather such a talented group of individuals on such a pressing issue. Our deepest appreciation goes out to Frederick Hess and Andrew Kelly of AEI for providing invaluable support, both material and intellectual, in the development and production of the volume. Special thanks go to research assistant Raphael Gang of AEI for his management of this project. Finally, we would like to express our appreciation to our editor Burke Gerstenschlager and editorial assistant Samantha Hasey for the exceptional work they did at Palgrave Macmillan in turning the manuscript into this completed volume.

Introduction

Kevin Carey and Mark Schneider

Everyone knows that America has the greatest higher-education system in the world. From humble beginnings in the colonies, our colleges and universities exploded upward and outward in the late nineteenth and twentieth centuries, opening their doors to students whose parents never dreamed of college, while simultaneously building an unrivalled constellation of elite research institutions. The combination of excellence and egalitarianism was unmatched and remains so today.

But in recent years, a growing number of public officials, parents, and students have looked past the glitter of the system's crown jewels and become uneasy with what they see. Success in getting students into college has not been accompanied by a commensurate focus on helping them finish with a degree. The scant available evidence on student learning is deeply disturbing. And our colleges are world beating in another, less enviable way—no other system exacts such a financial toll on students and taxpayers alike. The cost of American higher education is enormous and growing by the year.

While these problems are complex, there is a common thread that runs between them: our higher education institutions are unorganized, each pursuing a vigorous self-interest. To be sure, this unruly arrangement has many benefits. Independence allowed many colleges to become diverse and strong. No one should want to put colleges under the yoke of bureaucracy and politicization. The possibility—some would say "threat"—of increased accountability has created much consternation in the academy, which rightly guards its freedom of action.

But the divergence between institutional and public interests is becoming untenable. Each college's narrow pursuit of status and money has created a collective indifference to the needs of the nation as a whole. Colleges care too much about the accumulation of wealth and status and too little about helping a diverse array of students achieve a high-quality degree at a reasonable price. The result is gradual public disinvestment, a trend that has been accelerated by the recent economic crisis. Colleges are in danger of being marginalized by a society that does not see its aspirations reflected in higher learning as it is presently practiced.

Accountability must be part of any solution. This means harnessing institutional self-interest by making what's good for colleges and what's good for society one and the same. With deft, sustained implementation, accountability can preserve institutional independence while helping to close the rift between the academy and the public at large.

This is a delicate and complicated task. Colleges are multidimensional. Large research universities in particular are less coherent organizations than loose collections of disparate and often warring interests and fiefdoms. Accountability requires information; an individual or organization can't be responsible for an outcome if there is no way to determine their success. Accountability also requires some plausible process for acting on information, for creating strong incentives that will guide institutional choices.

This volume is meant to provide solutions to these problems. Some chapters clarify how higher-education success can be fairly measured. Others offer a roadmap for translating those measures into incentives that will spur college improvement. The authors conceive of accountability broadly, looking well beyond the regulatory schemes that have proven controversial in K-12 education to a much broader set of policies and arrangements that influence the way greatness in higher education is defined, and thus, achieved. While each chapter addresses a distinct dimension of the challenge, they all acknowledge the inherent complexity of higher-education accountability and the critical importance of implementing it well.

Few would dispute, for example, that a primary purpose of higher education is helping students learn. But the question of measuring student learning has proven to be vexing. Jeff Steedle, a psychometrician employed by the Council for Aid to Education (a nonprofit organization formerly allied with the RAND Corporation) argues that measures of student learning, such as his organization's Collegiate Learning Assessment, can provide consistent and valuable information about how much progress groups of students at individual colleges make in acquiring higher-order thinking and communication skills between their freshmen and senior years. While acknowledging that no single measure can capture the totality of human learning or operate without error, Steedle provides evidence that assessments have advanced to the point where important signals about student learning can be found within the statistical noise.

Lawrence Martin, an anthropologist and dean of the Graduate School at SUNY Stony Brook, tackles the other great purpose of higher education: scholarship. Martin notes that most public accountability regimes focus on measures such as undergraduate-degree production, creating a danger that scholarship will be shortchanged. Fortunately, the newfound availability of vast electronic databases of publications, awards, and research grants allows for up-to-date, fine-grained measures of scholarly productivity at the individual faculty-member level. Martin shows how new measures of faculty scholarly productivity developed by Academic Analytics, a company he owns, can allow for fair comparisons of productivity in similar disciplines at different institutions. He also notes that productivity is not evenly distributed; the top 20 percent of faculty produce over half of the scholarly output, while the bottom 20 percent contribute virtually nothing. Even the best universities have some of the laggards, and even the worst have some of the stars.

Noted accountability expert Peter Ewell, vice president of the National Center for Higher Education Management Systems, also explores the way rapid advances in information technology are changing the accountability equation. In recent years all but eight of the fifty states have developed so-called unit-record data systems that can track individual students as they move from high school to college and into the workforce. Private philanthropies and the federal government have poured hundreds of millions of dollars into the effort to build out these systems. But states have barely begun to exploit the power of this data to measure higher-education success. Ewell describes a series of detailed student progression and attainment measures that states should implement while also exploring the potential of state data-sharing consortia to broaden our understanding of how increasingly mobile students progress through college across state lines.

Creating accountability measures is only the first step. The second is using them. Harvard economist Bridget Terry Long describes the challenges of using financial incentives to influence institutional behavior. There is a long history of such budgetary accountability policies, she notes, and most of them have had limited success. Cost data are often hard to come by while both positive and negative financial incentives create the possibility of unintended effects. Most state attempts to use money as an accountability lever have suffered from incomplete and inaccurate accountability information as well as inadequate and transitory funding. Only strong, sustained incentives, paired with accurate measures will succeed.

Existing accountability arrangements also demand greater scrutiny. Kevin Carey, coeditor of this volume and the policy director of the

Washington, DC think tank Education Sector, offers a case study of how the accreditation process failed to prevent a DC college from persisting for decades in obscurity, mediocrity, and intermittent corruption. Students dropped out and defaulted on loans in large numbers, yet it took the college's accreditor over thirty years to shut it down. Carey argues that traditional accreditors are ill suited to the tasks of reporting public information about college success and enforcing hard-edged regulatory standards, functions that should be transferred to a new federal commission on higher education.

Anne Neal, president of the American Council of Trustees and Alumni, tackles the governance dimension of accountability, asserting that university trustees have historically failed in their duty to provide strong institutional oversight because of a history of what she believes are misplaced concerns about academic freedom. As a result, some trustees micromanage the financial decisions over which they maintain some control, while others are little more than a rubber stamp. While acknowledging the importance of scholarly independence, Neal argues that such values are not inconsistent with trustees reasserting their role as strong stewards of the college or university as a whole.

The Kauffman Foundation's Ben Wildavsky, meanwhile, dives into one of the most controversial and high-profile higher-education debates: college rankings. Wildavsky, the former editor of the market-leading *U.S. News & World Report*'s annual guide, *America's Best Colleges*, describes how college rankings have become a worldwide phenomenon, with global rankings published in London and Shanghai driving national decision making and a growing number of national governments using nation-specific rankings for accountability purposes. College rankings are here to stay, he notes, and if properly designed can be both a valuable source of consumer information and a market-based tool for spurring institutional improvement.

Even if the right accountability measures can be developed and the right systems for using that information can be defined, there will still be numerous barriers to the development of robust, long-lasting, and effective accountability systems. Political scientist and volume coeditor Mark Schneider of the American Institutes of Research draws on his experience as the former commissioner of the National Center for Education Statistics to describe how higher-education interest groups can create powerful opposition to new accountability policies. Closely tied systems of organized interests, entrenched bureaucrats, and compliant legislators can thwart even the most modest and sensible reforms.

Sara Goldrick-Rab, a sociologist at the University of Wisconsin-Madison, comes at the implementation challenge from the perspective of individual institutions. Accountability, she notes, depends in large part on the consent of those being held to account. Institutions that view accountability as illegitimate will work to undermine the system. Goldrick-Rab suggests that community colleges—often neglected in higher-education policy discussions despite enrolling nearly half of all college freshmen—are likely to be most amenable to new accountability regimes. Their workforce training and transfer missions are more readily quantifiable, and as traditionally underresourced institutions, they have the most to gain from moving up to a new equilibrium of higher expectations and funding to match.

Former *Wall Street Journal* editor and affiliate scholar with the Institute for American Values Naomi Riley examines barriers to accountability within institutions, specifically, in terms of faculty tenure. In the end all accountability policies come down to creating incentives for institutions to act differently. But that supposes that institutional leaders have the ability to lead. Riley argues that tenure prevents them from doing so. Echoing Neal's critique of academic freedom, Riley recommends scaling back the number of professors who are granted permanent job security. Those whose academic focus is essentially vocational or reflects a preestablished political agenda don't need or deserve the absolute freedom of tenure, she argues, nor do those whose loyalty ultimately lies with the outside businesses that sponsor their research.

Finally, internet entrepreneur Burck Smith lays out a broad-reaching, postinstitutional vision of higher education and the accountability regimes that should govern it. Advances in information technology have created entirely new modes of teaching and learning that are rapidly growing in popularity. Preinformation age systems such as accreditation now serve as barriers to innovation by forcing new market entrants to conform to expensive and unworkable organizational models. Accountability should be agnostic on means and highly focused on ends, Smith says, with a multitude of providers competing in a system that evaluates success in terms of how much students learn.

The higher-education accountability problem is daunting. It is as complex as the process of creating and disseminating knowledge itself. It mirrors broader societal anxieties and challenges in giving all students the opportunity to receive the affordable high-quality education they need. But it is not a problem that can be walked away from. The nation's historic success in higher education will not necessarily last forever. Without fair, effective accountability systems that preserve the best of the existing system while marrying institutional and public interests, the great American higher-education system will increasingly become a thing more of the past than the future.

1

On the Foundations of Standardized Assessment of College Outcomes and Estimating Value Added

Jeffrey Steedle

The notion of holding institutions of higher education accountable for student learning resonates with many during these times of financial constraint and increasing global competition. As the commission appointed by former Secretary of Education Spellings stated, "parents and students have no solid evidence, comparable across institutions, of how much students learn in colleges or whether they learn more at one college than another. Similarly, policymakers need more comprehensive data to help them decide whether the national investment in higher education is paying off and how taxpayer dollars could be used more effectively."[1] Additionally, business leaders are calling for greater accountability in higher education to ensure that college graduates have the skills necessary to make contributions in the workplace. In part, these calls are motivated by the realization that economic growth in the United States will likely decelerate because of a shortfall of skilled workers in the next decade.[2]

In recognition of their responsibility to provide evidence of student learning, many colleges and universities have ramped up their institutional assessment programs and joined in collective efforts such as to the Voluntary System of Accountability (VSA) and the University and College Accountability Network to publicly share comparative data. As explained by the Association of American Colleges and Universities (AAC&U) and the Council for Higher Education Accreditation (CHEA), "We in higher education must constantly monitor the quality of student learning and development, and use the results both to improve achievement and to demonstrate the value of our work to the public."[3]

Toward these ends, many schools now administer standardized tests of general college outcomes. Indeed, rigorous efforts to improve student learning require direct and comparative measures of current student achievement and a process for tracking improvement. Standardized tests fulfill these requirements by indicating achievement on important college outcomes, signaling curricular strengths and weaknesses, and by virtue of standardization, providing benchmarks for performance and facilitating institutional comparisons based on contributions to learning. As the National Research Council Board on Testing and Assessment affirmed, "In many situations, standardized tests provide the most objective way to compare the performance of a large group of examinees across places and times."[4]

Current demands for direct measures of college outcomes are fueled by recognition that commonly used indicators of educational quality (e.g., persistence, degree attainment, *U.S. News and World Report* rankings) are correlated with educational inputs such as students' entering academic ability levels and institutional resources.[5] Directly measuring student learning (i.e., the "output" of education) seems to be a natural remedy to this problem, but test scores also tend to be highly correlated with entering academic ability. This is especially true when the school (rather than the student) is the unit of analysis, as is the case for many standardized testing programs in higher education.[6] Thus, scores on college outcomes tests may only provide yet another reflection of educational inputs, which tend to paint highly selective institutions in a positive light and discount the value of attending less selective institutions.

This difficulty manifests the general problem that student achievement is strongly related to prior achievement and a host of other factors such as parental education and income levels that are unrelated to institutional quality.[7] To address this difficulty, standardized testing programs in higher education have adopted value-added modeling, which provides scores indicating whether the learning that occurred at a school is commensurate with other institutions with similar educational inputs.[8] This affords recognition for schools whose students demonstrate significant learning, even if those students have not yet reached a desired level of proficiency.

Value-added modeling has unquestionable intuitive appeal, but many have expressed doubts about the statistical dependability of value-added scores. Mainly, critics assert that value-added scores cannot be estimated with sufficient precision to warrant valid interpretations as indicators of relative learning. At a more fundamental level, critics question the use of standardized testing, which is necessary for estimating institutional value-added scores. Their primary contention is that such tests cannot possibly capture the outcomes of higher education in a meaningful way because those outcomes are so numerous, complex, and inextricably tied to a field of study or curriculum.

This chapter supplies evidence supporting the statistical dependability of value-added scores derived from standardized test results. Analyses of data from recent administrations of the Collegiate Learning Assessment (CLA) demonstrate that value-added scores are substantially less prone to measurement error than critics claim, but there is room for improvement. Additional analyses show that the dependability and interpretability of value-added scores are improved using a new statistical model. This chapter concludes with recommendations for administering standardized tests and integrating them into comprehensive systems of accountability and improvement.

First, it is necessary to address the more fundamental concerns about the use of standardized tests of general college outcomes. This chapter provides some history of standardized testing in higher education, summarizes critiques of current standardized testing efforts, and presents arguments for the utility of standardized testing as a component of institutional assessment programs. It is argued here that postsecondary schools should be measuring higher-order skills such as critical thinking and writing because teaching those skills is central to their missions; standardized tests provide the capacity to gauge strengths and weaknesses on these skills, and standardized test results (and the tests themselves) have the potential to stimulate improvements in teaching and learning.

Standardized Testing in Higher Education

Measuring General College Outcomes

The contemporary history of measuring general college outcomes using standardized tests reaches back to the first half of the twentieth century.[9] Early highlights from this history include the Pennsylvania Study, which tracked thousands of students from their sophomore year in 1930 to their senior year in 1932 using an eight-hour battery of objective tests (i.e., multiple-choice, matching, and true/false) measuring "memory, judgment, and reasoning ability through simple recognition."[10] Students were tested on their knowledge of the natural sciences, social sciences, two foreign languages, the history of ancient and modern civilization, math, and English (the original 12-hour test battery administered to seniors in 1928 did not include math or English). The Pennsylvania Study provided evidence of large differences in achievement between the forty-five participating institutions, and also that the number of credit hours in the natural sciences as well as language, literature, and fine arts was strongly related to achievement in those domains (this was not true of social studies).

In the years to follow, tests were designed to assess greater depth of understanding at schools such as the University of Chicago, where multiple-choice and essay tests were used to measure students' abilities to apply knowledge, predict outcomes, and make decisions in unfamiliar situations.[11] Other early, standardized-testing efforts such as the Cooperative Study of General Education, which involved a consortium of schools dedicated to improving general education, were more holistic and included noncognitive outcomes such as life goals, social understanding, and health.[12]

In the 1930s the Graduate Record Exam (GRE) gained popularity as an objective test of verbal reasoning and of general education content knowledge in several disciplines (mathematics, physical science, social studies, literature and fine arts, and one foreign language) for students applying to graduate studies, and the GRE Advanced Tests were developed to assess high-level content in specific majors. Though, in the decades to follow, general reasoning supplanted content knowledge as the primary construct measured by the GRE.[13] In this vein, the GRE Aptitude test emerged in 1949 with the now-familiar verbal and quantitative reasoning sections, and GRE Area Tests were first administered in 1954 to measure students' abilities to reason with new information and draw valid inferences in the natural sciences, social sciences, and humanities.

Some standardized testing programs that surfaced in the 1970s resisted the pervasive preference for inexpensive, easy-to-administer, objective tests by employing open-ended tasks requiring students to demonstrate critical thinking, problem solving, and communication skills in real-world scenarios.[14] Early versions of the American College Test's (ACT) College Outcomes Measures Project (COMP) exemplified these efforts. COMP was originally a six-hour test including oral, written, and multiple-choice items related to fifteen simulated activities. For instance, one COMP task asked students to choose between two paintings that might adorn a public library in a rural town and to support that choice. Test results revealed that COMP scores tended to increase from freshman to senior year by an effect size of roughly 0.80 and that COMP could discriminate between college seniors and matched groups of students attending vocational or technical schools.[15]

In the late 1970s and early 1980s the notion of using standardized tests for institutional accountability arose in response to the widely held belief that education was the key to maintaining a global competitive edge and to growing recognition that improving education required measuring learning.[16] States mandated accountability testing, and some schools responded by administering off-the-shelf tests that were not designed for institutional assessment (e.g., the GRE and the ACT). At the time, COMP was the only test specifically designed to measure general college outcomes and to facilitate group-level inferences. COMP provided the distribution of scores for a reference sample of fifteen representative schools to serve as a consistent point for comparison when evaluating student achievement. For example, Ohio University saw its average senior COMP performance increase from the fiftieth percentile to the sixty-sixth percentile during the years following its implementation of new general education requirements.[17]

Institutional assessment efforts were largely supplanted by accreditation during the recession of the early 1990s,[18] but demands for accountability testing in higher education persisted. Recent calls for such testing originate chiefly from leaders in higher education, business, and government.[19] As in the past, most are motivated to ensure that college graduates in the United States have the skills necessary to maintain a competitive edge, but contemporary calls for measuring student outcomes are increasingly motivated by a desire to remedy social inequities. The idea is that accountability testing can inform curricular and pedagogical improvements that will help address the needs of college students coming from backgrounds lacking in educational opportunity, thereby narrowing historical gaps in achievement and degree attainment.

Contemporary Standardized Tests

Several standardized tests are currently employed to measure general outcomes in higher education. Prominent examples include the Collegiate Assessment of Academic Proficiency (CAAP) from ACT (the successor to COMP), the Proficiency Profile (formerly known as the Measure of Academic Proficiency and Progress) from ETS, and the CLA from the Council for Aid to Education (where the author is currently employed). CAAP and the Proficiency Profile are multiple-choice tests, each with an optional essay. CAAP is administered in forty-minute modules that assess students in reading, writing, essay writing, mathematics, science, and critical thinking. The Proficiency Profile is a two-hour test of reading, critical thinking, writing, and mathematics (a forty-minute version is also available). These tests provide student-level scores that may be employed for identifying an individual's strengths and weaknesses, and aggregated student scores from either tests may be interpreted as indicators of institutional performance.

The CLA employs a fully open-ended format. Students either take an analytic writing test, which involves developing and critiquing arguments, or a performance task, which presents students with a real-world problem, provides them with a library of relevant information, and asks them to propose and justify a course of action and suggest research to address unanswered questions. For example, one performance task asks students to evaluate proposals for reducing crime in "Jefferson," using information from documents such as newspaper articles, crime statistics, and research journal abstracts. The documents include a mix of credible and unreliable evidence that must be evaluated and synthesized in order to draw valid conclusions and make informed recommendations.

The CAAP and Proficiency Profile critical-thinking tests bear some resemblance to CLA tasks (especially the Critique-and-Argument task). These tests consist of several passages, each with associated multiple-choice questions. The passages commonly present an argument or opposing viewpoints such as one CAAP item that provides the transcript of a debate over deregulating the distribution of certain prescription medications. The associated questions ask students to identify assumptions and implications and to evaluate the strength of evidence and claims.

Unlike other tests, the CLA was designed exclusively for use in institutional assessment programs. CLA tasks are randomly distributed among participants, and students are allotted approximately ninety minutes to complete their essay responses. CLA scores are designed to reflect the integration of critical thinking, analytic reasoning, problem solving, and written communication skills. Students receive their CLA scores, but these scores cannot be used to compare students or to draw conclusions about their abilities. The reason is that, for individual students, CLA scores (and test scores reflecting performance on a small number of open-ended tasks in general) are typically more prone to measurement error than scores from well-designed multiple-choice tests incorporating a large number of items. Much of this unreliability is related to the interaction between students and tasks (i.e., students might have received different scores had they been assigned different CLA prompts). These measurement errors are substantially reduced at the aggregate level, making it sensible to interpret estimates of institutional performance on the CLA.[20]

Reporting Test Results

In a recent survey of AAC&U member institutions, roughly one quarter of schools reported that they administer "standardized national tests of general skills, such as critical thinking."[21] As noted previously, results from such tests are employed for two purposes: demonstrating student achievement and improving teaching and learning. Some schools only review test results internally, but other schools share results as part of a consortium, such as the thirty-three member institutions of the Council of Independent Colleges (CIC) that have administered the CLA since 2005.[22] At their most recent meeting, presenters shared curriculum reforms that were influenced by standardized test results, methods of engaging faculty in institutional assessment programs, classroom efforts to assess critical thinking and writing skills, and techniques for analyzing test data.[23]

Some schools, like those in the University of Texas system, are required by state accountability systems to report results publicly, but others do so voluntarily as part of efforts to demonstrate their commitments to assessment and improvement. The VSA, developed jointly by the Association of Public and Land-grant Universities (formerly NASULGC) and the American Association of State Colleges and Universities (AASCU), exemplifies voluntary collective efforts toward these ends.[24] As part of the VSA, nearly three hundred schools publish a College Portrait, based on a common template for sharing institutional information with prospective students and their parents. It includes a Student Learning Outcomes section that provides institutional scores on CAAP, the Performance Profile, or the CLA (some schools have yet to select an assessment or post results).

Christine Keller, Executive Director of the VSA, and John Hammang, Director of Special Projects at AASCU, reported that a "volatile mixture of technical matters, philosophical differences, and political fears" made the decision to include standardized test results in the College Portrait highly contentious.[25] Similar debates continue among testing experts and among faculty at institutions struggling to satisfy demands for greater accountability. The following sections explore the principal critiques of standardized testing in higher education and make the case that, despite their limitations, standardized tests can play an important role in institutional assessment programs.

Common Objections

Despite the nearly ubiquitous use of standardized tests in high-stakes admissions decisions, standardized tests of general college outcomes have yet to win widespread acceptance even when they are used for low-stakes purposes such as identifying academic strengths and weaknesses. Above all, critics argue that results from these tests cannot be interpreted as meaningful indicators of student learning. One aspect of this critique focuses on the context-specific nature of college learning. That is, college learning is so deep and so particular to a field of study that it would be grossly inadequate to measure that learning with a test so general that it can be administered to any student.

For instance, a test of college outcomes for history majors might involve critically analyzing historical documents, drawing conclusions about historical events, and communicating ideas effectively. If history majors are assessed on critical thinking and writing skills apart from the context of historical analyses, one may not observe the true depth of their learning. Moreover, their critical thinking and writing skills may not generalize to contexts other than historical analyses. Either way, results from tests of general outcomes would not adequately reflect student learning in the domain that matters most: their chosen field of study.

The other aspect of this critique focuses on the idea that there are many important outcomes of postsecondary education that are not measured by currently available standardized tests (e.g., ethical reasoning, civic engagement, and intercultural skills). Thus, test scores reflecting only a narrow range of outcomes cannot adequately convey the overall value of attending a particular institution. In this manner, the AAC&U and the CHEA, in a joint statement, affirmed the importance of gathering evidence of student learning and demonstrating educational value, but they stopped short of recommending that schools publicly share standardized test results because "standardized measures currently address only a small part of what matters in college."[26]

Critics also take issue with the utility of standardized test results. Aggregate scores, which are intended to support inferences about entire institutions (or programs within institutions), typically serve only as indicators that schools are doing something right or something wrong. Unfortunately, it is not apparent what that "something" is, especially when the test is not tied directly to the curriculum. In other words, standardized tests cannot diagnose the causes of specific academic strengths and weaknesses and therefore cannot prescribe ways to enhance learning at a school. For instance, standardized tests results cannot indicate that certain classes should be added to a school's general education requirements or that instructors need to improve some specific aspect of their pedagogy.

Other negative reactions to the use of standardized tests arise from faculty who, based on the principle of academic freedom, would resist any program that "interferes" with academic matters. As former Harvard University president Derek Bok explained, "The principle of academic freedom, originally conceived to safeguard a scholar's right to express unpopular ideas, has been stretched to protect individual professors from having to join any collaborative effort to improve the quality of teaching and learning."[27] Some faculty react negatively to accountability and assessment programs because of their associations with the federally mandated K-12 accountability system created by the No Child Left Behind Act of 2001.[28]

In sum, critics point out that standardized tests do not provide a complete solution to the challenges of institutional assessment, they do not measure depth of learning in students' respective fields of study, and they do not measure every important outcome of undergraduate education. Additionally, results from standardized tests do not diagnose the specific causes for academic strengths and weaknesses, and the introduction of standardized tests may interfere with the curriculum. Notwithstanding these limitations and concerns, standardized tests can still play an important role in institutional assessment and have the potential to foster improvements in teaching and learning.

Responding to Objections

Testing proponents (and testing agencies) should be quick to agree that standardized tests have limitations, but it is not fair to dismiss standardized testing for that reason alone. After all, other institutional assessment methods suffer from limitations that standardized tests do not. For example, student surveys (e.g., asking students how much they learned in college) do not measure learning directly. Portfolios provide direct evidence of academic development, but they cannot facilitate fair comparisons between students or institutions because they lack adjustments for task difficulty (even if a standardized evaluation rubric is employed).

By focusing on what tests do not measure, critics fail to give appropriate consideration to the relative importance of particular general outcomes measured by available standardized tests. These general outcomes transcend academic programs and institutions and therefore have the potential to be measured using standardized tests. Indeed, many postsecondary institutions have general education goals that could be measured using standardized tests. A recent survey found that a "large majority of AAC&U member institutions (78 percent) say that they have a common set of intended learning outcomes for *all* their undergraduate students...The skills most widely addressed are writing, critical thinking, quantitative reasoning, and oral communication skills."[29]

The importance of these skills is also widely recognized by leaders in business and government who regard critical thinking, writing, and other "higher-order" skills as essential for accessing and analyzing the information needed to address the complex, nonroutine challenges facing workers and citizens in the twenty-first century.[30] Along these lines, a full 95 percent of employers (and more than 90 percent of recent graduates) affirmed the importance of providing a four-year college education that includes domain-specific knowledge and skills as well as "intellectual and practical skills that span all areas of study, such as communication, analytical, and problem-solving skills, and a demonstrated ability to apply knowledge and skills in real-world settings."[31] In the same survey, nearly 75 percent of employers said that colleges should place greater emphasis on teaching critical thinking and communication skills.

At present, standardized testing seems like a sensible approach to measuring critical thinking and writing skills in particular because past research indicates that college education has a positive effect on these outcomes and that certain instructional practices are likely to promote the development of these skills.[32] Thus, growth in these skills is measurable, and guidance for improving instruction on these skills is available to underperforming schools.

Moreover, unlike some desirable general outcomes of higher education (e.g., preparedness for working in a global society), critical thinking and writing have operational definitions that are generally agreed upon,[33] and this allows for the development of tests that elicit responses many would accept as evidence of students' abilities in those domains. In the case of critical thinking, tests should be designed to elicit evidence that students can identify the strengths and weaknesses of multiple perspectives on an issue, recognize connected and conflicting information, evaluate evidence as credible or unreliable, detect flaws in logic and questionable assumptions, acknowledge the need for additional information in the face of uncertainty, and weigh evidence from multiple sources to make a decision. With regard to writing, tests should elicit evidence that students can communicate ideas clearly and accurately as part of an organized and logically cohesive argument and control the elements of standard written English. Note that available standardized tests do not measure dispositions to think critically nor can they reasonably evaluate students' skills related to drafting and revising text.

Institutional assessment focuses on the entire curriculum, and this broad scope explains why results from standardized tests of general college outcomes cannot diagnose the causes of academic strengths and weaknesses. However, much as blood pressure and cholesterol level serve as useful indicators of illness in medicine (but not of the exact underlying cause for the illness), standardized test scores indicate the presence (or absence) of potential problems in academic domains. Even critic Trudy Banta acknowledges that standardized tests of general skills are "appropriate for giving individual students and faculty ideas about strengths and weaknesses and areas of curriculum and instruction to improve."[34] If results are unacceptable, additional research is called for to determine which aspects of the learning environment might be improved. Alternatively, when test results are favorable, administrators might want to research what the school is doing right. One common approach involves interpreting test scores in light of results from student surveys such as the National Survey of Student Engagement (NSSE), a self-report measure that asks students about their behaviors inside and outside of the classroom that may be associated with academic and personal growth.

In fact, standardized test results (along with data from complementary research) have informed reevaluations of general education programs at many schools.[35] This includes reform efforts in the University of Texas system, where CLA results were used to identify and address deficiencies in writing skills. At Stonehill College, CLA and NSSE results led to questioning of the level of academic challenge. Subsequent discussions resulted in modifications of the course-credit model to provide additional opportunities to take challenging courses and to the development of first-year seminars focusing on critical thinking and writing skills. At Seton Hill University, disappointing CLA scores and NSSE results suggesting low levels of academic challenge contributed to the decision to implement biweekly professional development on teaching critical thinking as well as additional requirements for writing in each major. In another example, CLA results at Barton College revealed performance above statistical expectations, but below personal expectations.[36] As a result, Barton revised its general education curriculum to require courses that specifically target critical thinking and written communication skills and included CLA score targets as part of their reaccreditation "Quality Enhancement Plan."

Furthermore, if standardized tests set a good example for assessment, these tests can reinforce classroom teaching and assessment of higher-order skills. Consider that, given the importance of teaching critical thinking, instructors should infuse classroom assessments (and other instructional activities) with opportunities to practice and demonstrate critical thinking. To this end, critical thinking tasks such as those appearing in standardized tests can be tailored to the content and goals of courses in a broad spectrum of academic domains. One way to accomplish this is through professional development programs such as the CLA in the Classroom Academy, a two-day workshop designed to foster teaching and assessment practices that align with general education goals. Through the course of the workshop, participants learn to develop CLA-like performance tasks for use in their classrooms and to apply scoring rubrics that provide students with useful performance feedback. Evidence from workshop evaluations reveals that some reluctant participants have developed newfound enthusiasm for student assessment at the classroom and institution levels, and several schools now embed performance tasks in their general education programs as well as courses such as chemistry, quantitative methods, and linguistics.[37]

While these are commendable efforts to improve general education programs, as noted earlier, institutional test scores tend to be highly correlated with educational inputs, so test results, while providing useful information about the absolute level of student achievement, do not afford nonselective institutions the opportunity to demonstrate their educational efficacy for accountability purposes. Value-added modeling is an approach that is becoming increasingly popular to address this shortcoming.

Value-Added Modeling

Highly selective institutions typically rank favorably when compared with other schools using average test scores, but research suggests that an institution's selectivity provides little information about its actual contributions to learning.[38] With value-added modeling, each school's performance is compared to expectations established by the entering academic ability of its students. Thus, a nonselective school might perform poorly in an absolute sense, but it could obtain a high value-added score by performing much better than one would expect of a school admitting students of similar entering ability.

The dominant institutional value-added model currently used in higher education was first employed during the 2004–2005 CLA administration.[39] The basic idea behind this model is to compare the average difference in CLA scores between freshmen and seniors to the average difference one would expect based on their respective average entering academic ability (as measured by the SAT or ACT). When a school's average freshman–senior difference exceeds expectations, this indicates above-expected learning at the school, and the school obtains a high value-added score. This value-added approach has also been used recently by CAAP and MAPP for schools participating in VSA. This decision followed from research at ACT and ETS demonstrating the potential for using scores from their respective assessments for estimating value added using this model.[40]

While value-added modeling sounds like an appealing way to evaluate educational quality, value-added scores, like all inferential statistics, are estimates of unknown values and therefore have inherent uncertainty that arises primarily from the fact that value-added scores might have come out differently if schools tested different samples of students. The extent of this uncertainty is evaluated by estimating the *reliability* of the scores, which is indexed by a coefficient ranging from zero to one. For the purposes of this chapter, high reliability indicates that value-added scores are precisely estimated (i.e., contain little random error) and that schools would receive similar scores if they repeated testing with different but similarly representative student samples.

The major argument that critics levy against value-added modeling is that value-added scores are not nearly reliable enough to be interpreted validly as indicators of relative learning. Citing existing literature, Trudy Banta reported the reliability of value-added scores to be approximately 0.10.[41] In an analysis of longitudinal data from students taking the multiple-choice version of COMP, Gary Pike of Indiana University–Purdue University, Indianapolis estimated the reliability of gain scores as 0.14 and the reliability of residual scores as 0.17.[42] It must be noted, however, that these reliability coefficients are based on models that treat the student as the primary unit of analysis. Just as school means are more reliable than individual student scores, one might expect institutional value-added scores to be more reliable than student-gain scores or residual scores. On the other hand, high value-added score reliability may simply be an impossibility because nearly all of the score variation is within schools on collegiate measures such as NSSE, when between-school variation is required to obtain nonzero reliability.[43] As further reason to distrust value-added modeling, critics also point to evidence that different value-added models lead to different results.[44] In that case, it would not be clear which result to trust.

Several other criticisms of CLA value-added assessment not directly related to the statistical model (e.g., sampling issues and concerns about student motivation) are addressed elsewhere.[45] However, since this chapter may be serving as an introduction to value-added modeling for some readers, it is worth addressing a few common concerns associated with estimating value added using cross-sectional data (i.e., freshmen and seniors in the same academic year). First, some highly selective institutions may be reluctant to study value added because their students could be "topping out" on the test as freshmen and therefore have little room to improve their scores. Contrary to this idea, CLA data consistently show that highly selective schools gain as much, on average, as less selective schools. Furthermore, value-added scores are appropriately interpreted as conditional on the entering characteristics of students—that is, a value-added score reflects learning gains relative to other schools admitting students of similar entering academic ability (not all schools).

A second concern relates to selective attrition from college. Assuming that less able students tend to drop out at a higher rate, the difference in ability between freshmen and seniors (and consequently the difference in standardized test scores) will be greater at institutions with higher dropout rates, which could lead to inflated value-added scores. The original CLA value-added approach addresses this concern in a straightforward way by comparing the observed freshman-senior average CLA difference to the expected difference given the entering ability of participating freshmen and seniors separately. Schools with large selective attrition would have a higher expected difference, making it more difficult for them to obtain a high value-added score. The new CLA value-added approach (described below) gets around this issue by not directly comparing freshman and senior performance. Instead, it uses freshman CLA performance as information (in addition to average SAT or ACT scores) about the entering characteristics of students. Moreover, concerns about selective attrition fade away, assuming that similarly selective institutions have similar drop-out rates because, as noted previously, value-added scores should be interpreted as relative to similarly selective institutions. Of course, all of these concerns disappear when studying a cohort of students over time, which is why longitudinal analyses are regarded as the "gold standard." However, few schools currently commit the resources necessary to carry out such research.

Are Institutional Value-Added Scores Reliable?

Tests scores with a reliability of 0.80 or greater are commonly upheld as adequately reliable, but the true determination of adequacy depends heavily on the intended use of the test scores. If test scores are used to make high-stakes decisions about students, teachers, or schools, reliability greater than 0.80 might be called for. On the other hand, reliability less than 0.80 would likely suffice if test results are used for a relatively low-stakes purpose such as identifying academic strengths and weaknesses to help improve teaching and learning. In efforts to improve educational programs, it is also worth considering the relative reliability of various sources of information. As explained by Derek Bok, "The proper test for universities to apply is not whether their assessments meet the most rigorous scholarly standards, but whether they can provide more reliable information than the hunches, random experiences, and personal opinions that currently guide most faculty decisions about education."[46]

As large-scale efforts to compute institutional value-added scores in higher education are fairly recent, there has only been one study published thus far providing the reliability of value-added scores generated by the original CLA approach. In this study, Stephen Klein, Roger Benjamin, Richard Shavelson, and Roger Bolus, all staff members or consultants at CAE, made the case that value-added scores based on CLA results are reliable.[47] They employed a novel approach to estimating reliability that involved randomly splitting available data from each class (freshmen and seniors) in each school, estimating separate value-added scores for the two samples, and computing the correlation between them.

The reliability coefficient reported by Klein and his colleagues, 0.63, could be considered high enough to warrant interpretations of value-added scores for low-stakes purposes. Their analyses were recently extended by correcting for the use of half-size samples and by computing the mean of one thousand possible random splitting instead of just one.[48] These analyses were carried out using data from 99 schools that administered the CLA in the 2006–2007 academic year and 154 schools from 2007–2008. Value-added reliability computed using these methods was 0.73 for the 2006–2007 data and 0.64 for the 2007–2008 data. These values provide higher estimates of value-added score reliability, but room for improvement is still evident. One possible contributor to unreliability is that the original CLA approach depends on difference scores (i.e., the difference between freshman and senior mean CLA scores), which are known to be less reliable than the scores from which they are derived.

This unreliability may be manifested in low year-to-year consistency in value-added scores. In fact, some schools express puzzlement about seemingly unrealistic swings in value-added scores across years. Of course, one should not expect value-added scores to be the same every year (e.g., due to programmatic changes, major differences in sampling methods, or measurement error), but one should not expect them to change radically either. Using the data from seventy-one schools participating in both CLA administrations, the correlation between value-added scores across years was only 0.32, which suggests that sizable year-to-year fluctuations in value-added scores were fairly common. For instance, Allegheny College's change from "at expected" to "below expected" value added coincided with a change from administering the test during the first few weeks of classes to administering the test during orientation (when students were "burned out, overwhelmed, and had too much going on").[49] This sort of variability in value-added scores, which is not always easily explainable, does not bode well for institutional assessment programs that seek to measure small improvements in value added over time. In light of this, greater standardization of student sampling and test administration is preferable (if possible) and may have a positive impact on value-added score stability across years.

Briefly, with regard to concerns about between- and within-school variance, approximately 20 percent of the variance in CLA scores is between schools (compared to less than 5 percent on some NSSE scales). As the percentage of between-school variance approaches zero, one would expect the reliability of between-school comparisons to approach zero. With

20 percent between-school variance, the reliability of value-added scores is roughly 0.70 using the original CLA value-added model (and nearly 0.80 using the model described below). Thus, it seems that 20 percent between-school variance is sufficient to allow for reasonable value-added score reliability.

To sum up, critiques concerning the unreliability of institutional value-added scores are often overstated due to their orientation toward student-centered value-added models rather than models treating the school as the unit of analysis. Reliability analyses that treat the school as the unit of analysis reveal that value-added scores generated by the original CLA value-added model are reliable enough to serve as indicators of relative learning for low-stakes purposes, but not reliable enough to make high-stakes institutional comparisons or to measure small changes in value added over time.

An Alternative Value-Added Model

Recently, CAE researchers evaluated other possible value-added models and identified one model as particularly promising because it improved on the reliability of value-added scores and allowed for the calculation of institution-specific indicators of value-added score precision, which signal to each campus the uncertainty in its value-added score and therefore facilitate honest interpretations of the significance of differences between schools. The lack of these indicators was a drawback of the original CLA approach because, for example, a school testing a very small number of students would have a less precise value-added score estimate, but the original CLA value-added model could not quantify the degree of imprecision.

The alternative value-added estimation approach employs a hierarchical linear model (HLM) with two levels of analysis: a student level for modeling within-school CLA score variation and a school level for estimating institutional value-added scores.[50] Rather than computing value added based on difference scores (a possible source of unreliability), the new model works by comparing senior average CLA scores to expected CLA scores based on entering academic ability as measured by average SAT or ACT scores and average freshman CLA scores (serves as a control for selection effects not covered by the SAT or ACT). Although this model does not provide a direct measure of growth between freshman and senior year, it still works as a value-added model because, if one observes a group of seniors performing better than expected, it suggests that more learning took place at their school than at the typical school with students of comparable entering academic ability. Modeling within-school variance at the student level allows for computing standard errors of the value-added scores.

The same analyses described above were carried out using value-added scores derived from the HLM-based model. Results indicate that value-added score reliability increased to 0.81 in 2006–2007 and 0.75 in 2007–2008 with the new model, and the correlation between value-added scores across years increased from 0.32 to 0.58. These results suggest that value-added scores based on the new model are more sensible for use in comparing institutions and have more realistic stability across years. Still, any differences between value-added scores should be evaluated in light of their standard errors (explained below).

To address to concerns about different value-added models producing different results, correlations were computed between scores generated by the original CLA model and by the HLM-based model. The correlation was 0.80 in 2006–2007 and 0.72 in 2007–2008. These correlations reveal that the schools line up in similar but not identical ways based on the value-added scores derived from the two models. However, after disattenuating for unreliability (using the reliability coefficients provided above), the correlation was 1.00 in both years (rounded down from values slightly higher than 1.00), which suggests that the value-added scores would be identical apart from measurement error.

Additional evidence from a simulation study supports this conclusion. CLA and SAT data for two hundred simulated schools were generated using parameters from actual CLA schools (means, standard deviations, and covariance matrices). These data were used to estimate value-added scores under the condition that all schools tested all students (i.e., no sampling error). Using these full simulated data sets, the correlation between value-added scores was 1.00. Thus, if all schools tested all students, it would not matter which value-added model was used because results would be identical. However, since financial and practical constraints prevent this, it makes sense to choose the value-added model that provides more reliable scores for a given number of students tested. For this reason, the new, HLM-based model will be used for the CLA starting in the 2009–2010 administration.

In addition to improvements in reliability, the HLM-based model provides a standard error for each school's value-added score, which may be used to compute a 95 percent confidence interval. By providing confidence intervals, schools get a realistic sense of the variability in value-added scores they could expect if testing was repeated with different students. The intervals also provide a sense of which differences in value-added scores could be considered significant. Figure 1.1 shows the value-added

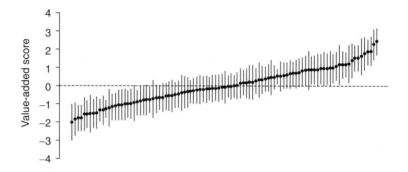

Figure 1.1   Value-added scores (shown as dots) and 95 percent confidence intervals (vertical lines) in 2006–2007.

estimates and 95 percent confidence intervals for schools in 2006–2007 in order of increasing value-added. The influence of sample size on confidence interval size is noticeable in this figure. (Schools testing the most students have the smallest confidence intervals.)

To further investigate value-added stability over time, value-added scores and corresponding 95 percent confidence intervals were computed for forty schools that participated in each of three recent CLA administrations. The ranges of their value-added scores were compared to the maximum of their 95 percent confidence intervals across the three administrations. Only 10 percent of schools had a range that exceeded the size of its maximum 95 percent confidence intervals, suggesting that the confidence intervals provide a realistic indicator of random variation in value-added scores. Regarding consistency across years, 40 percent of schools had low consistency (range greater than 1.5) across the three administrations under the original value-added model; 38 percent had moderate consistency (range between 0.75 and 1.5); and 23 percent had high consistency (range less than 0.75). With the new model, a much higher percentage of schools had moderate rather than low consistency (25 percent low, 55 percent moderate, and 20 percent high).

Since most schools have moderate to high consistency with the HLM-based model, value-added scores, despite their inherent uncertainty, appear to be capturing fairly stable characteristics of schools. This supports the interpretability of value-added scores as indicators of relative learning, but the degree of remaining uncertainty makes it difficult to reliably compare schools with similar value-added scores or to detect small changes in value-added scores over time. As an additional caution, it seem advisable to examine value-added scores across multiple years or to cross-validate value-added scores with other indicators of student learning to ensure that any consequential decisions are based on dependable information.

Conclusions and Recommendations

There are limitations to currently available standardized tests of general college outcomes, but there are still many reasons to administer them. Standardized tests measure some especially salient outcomes of higher education such as critical thinking and written communication skills; they provide signals of possible problems by indicating academic strengths and weaknesses, and they may positively affect teaching by setting a good example for classroom assessment.

With regard to value-added modeling, evidence indicates that value-added scores are significantly more reliable than critics have claimed. Furthermore, advances in institutional value-added modeling promise greater score reliability, more realistic consistency across years, and improved score interpretability. At this time, the statistical dependability of value-added scores is likely sufficient to allow for a rough ordering of schools by their contributions to student learning on outcomes measured by standardized tests. This ordering is rough in the sense that many schools have value-added scores that could not be considered significantly different from one another. This statistical uncertainty precludes the possibility of measuring small changes over time or using value-added scores to make high-stakes institutional comparisons.

In order to maximize the quality and interpretability of value-added scores, it is recommended that schools sample students randomly for testing if possible, meet sample-size guidelines, and consider in-depth sampling of subunits within institutions. This final recommendation is especially important for large schools where the most appropriate unit of analysis may be colleges within the university rather than the entire university.

As evidenced by the examples provided earlier, standardized tests seem to be providing data that schools can act upon, but they do not offer a complete solution to the challenges of institutional assessment. According to Lee Shulman, President of the Carnegie Foundation for the Advancement of Teaching, "nearly any goal of using the results of assessment for serious practical and policy guidelines should intentionally employ an array of instruments."[51] For example, evaluation programs in the University of Texas system include five components: "persistence and graduation rates, license exam pass rates in critical fields, postgraduate experience, student experience, and student learning assessments."[52] By combining evidence from a variety of sources, schools obtain a more complete picture of educational quality and help ensure that changes to general education programs are informed by robust information.

Standardized tests may also be supplemented with other direct measures of student learning such as electronic portfolios that allow students to upload and organize evidence of learning such as papers, presentations, artwork, videos, and audio recordings. It is unfortunate that standardized tests and portfolios are frequently pitted as arch nemeses (with proponents of each conveniently ignoring the shortcomings of their favored approach) because there is possibility for overlap. Technology exists that would allow for the inclusion of student responses to standardized open-ended tasks in portfolios with scores reported on a standard scale. This could benefit portfolios by adding a standardized component, which might improve the comparability of portfolios across students and schools.

Legislators should take note that while standardized testing may be imposed, this does not guarantee that schools with put forth the effort and resources required to administer the test properly or that results will be put to good use. It is unfortunate that at many schools student outcomes assessment is mostly a matter of "going through the motions" for state-mandated accountability programs or accreditation. Many faculty members have genuine misgivings about standardized testing, and some have gross misperceptions of the current state of assessments. Negative sentiment among faculty is passed along to students, and in some cases students have been told "this test doesn't matter." This would likely undermine any possibility of obtaining results that could be interpreted validly.

In order for standardized testing and value-added assessment to gain widespread acceptance in higher education, it seems that efforts to implement standardized tests must be accompanied by programs that engage faculty and help foster a culture of assessment and improvement. For any school considering a standardized test of general college outcomes, Trudy Banta offers sensible guidelines for involving faculty, staff, and students in the process of test selection.[53] These guidelines include ensuring that tests align with the general educational goals of the institution, having faculty and students take the test, publicizing the decision, and continually evaluating the usefulness of a test. Schools might take additional steps to establish buy-in from faculty through professional development programs such as the CLA in the Classroom Academy, described earlier.

Despite efforts to create a culture of evidence and assessment, there will be holdouts at many schools who dismiss standardized test results and other findings from institutional research efforts. One way to overcome this roadblock would be to provide the tools and resources needed to develop assessments that would allow faculty to demonstrate growth on the knowledge and skills they claim to teach and to carry out small-scale research on improving instruction. Faculty members are unlikely to persist in claiming to teach something without providing evidence of learning or to express concern about instructional quality without evaluating it. If many faculty members rise to these challenges, their work could stimulate interesting developments in classroom practice.

In the near future, standardized test providers should carry out the research needed to supply additional evidence that value-added scores can be interpreted validly as indicators of learning relative to expected. Specifically, it has yet to be demonstrated that cross-sectional and longitudinal data collections would produce similar results. Additionally, the relationships among institutional value-added scores, other school-level indicators of student learning, and institutional characteristics should be examined. This research could contribute to the validation of value-added scores, and it might help identify student behaviors and institutional characteristics that are associated with learning.

As for test development, there appears to be demand for major-specific standardized assessments that incorporate critical thinking and writing skills. Faculty in certain departments may be more inclined to take results from such assessments seriously because they would call upon students to demonstrate higher-order skills and apply content knowledge as a historian, an engineer, a social scientist, or a businessperson, to name a few possibilities. There is also room for standardized tests of the noncognitive, higher-order outcomes of higher education such as personal and social responsibility, creativity, leadership, teamwork skills, and others. However, substantial research is called for in order to establish consensus definitions of these constructs and to demonstrate that they can be measured reliably and validly.

To conclude, standardized testing and value-added scores provide valuable contributions to institutional assessment programs. With consideration paid to the statistical dependability of value-added scores, policymakers and leaders in higher education should focus their attention on the original (and arguably most important) purposes of administering standardized tests of general college outcomes: indicating areas of possible weakness in general education programs and stimulating discussions about improving instruction. A large number of schools have already taken advantage of the opportunities afforded by currently available tests. As other schools come to recognize the positive changes that have resulted from concerted efforts to measure and improve learning using standardized tests, these measures should gain wider acceptance and schools will take the steps necessary to ensure that results are put to good use.

Notes

1. U.S. Department of Education, *A Test of Leadership: Charting the Future of U.S. Higher Education* (Washington, DC: 2006), 14. http://www2.ed.gov/about/bdscomm/list/hiedfuture/reports/pre-pub-report.pdf.

2. Business-Higher Education Forum, *Public Accountability for Student Learning in Higher Education: Issues and Options* (Washington, DC: American Council on Education, 2004). http://www.bhef.com/publications/documents/public_accountability_04.pdf.

3. Association of American Colleges and Universities and the Council for Higher Education Accreditation, *New Leadership for Student Learning and Accountability: A Statement of Principles, Commitments to Action* (Washington, DC: AAC&U and CHEA, 2008), 1. http://www.chea.org/pdf/2008.01.30_New_Leadership_Statement.pdf.

4. National Research Council, Board on Testing and Assessment, *Lessons Learned about Testing: Ten Years of Work at the National Research Council* (Washington, DC: National Research Council, 2007). http://www7.nationalacademies.org/dbasse/Lessons_Learned_Brochure_PDF.pdf.

5. Thomas Webster, "A Principal Component Analysis of the *U.S. News & World Report* Tier Rankings of Colleges and Universities," *Economics of Education Review 20*, no. 3 (June 2001).

6. Stephen Klein, George Kuh, Marc Chun, Laura Hamilton, and Richard Shavelson, "An Approach to Measuring Cognitive Outcomes across Higher Education Institutions," *Research in Higher Education* 46, no. 3 (May 2005).

7. William Bowen, Matthew Chingos, and Michael McPherson, *Crossing the Finish Line: Completing College at America's Public Universities* (Princeton, NJ: Princeton University Press, 2009).

8. Robert Lissitz, ed., *Value Added Models in Education: Theory and Applications* (Maple Grove, MN: JAM Press, 2005).

9. Peter Ewell, "An Emerging Scholarship: A Brief History of Assessment," in *Building a Scholarship of Assessment*, ed. Trudy Banta and Associates (San Francisco: Jossey-Bass, 2002); C. Robert Pace, *Measuring Outcomes of College: Fifty Years of Findings and Recommendations for the Future* (San Francisco: Jossey-Bass, 1979); Richard Shavelson, *A Brief History of Student Learning Assessment: How We Got Where We Are and a Proposal for Where to Go Next* (Washington, DC: Association of American Colleges and Universities, 2007).

10. William Learned and Ben Wood, *The Student and His Knowledge: A Report to the Carnegie Foundation on the Results of the High School and College Examinations of 1928, 1930, and 1932* (Boston: Merrymount Press, 1938), 371.

11. Reuben Frodin, "Very Simple but Thoroughgoing," in *The Idea and Practice of General Education: An Account of the College of the University of Chicago by Present and Former Members of the Faculty*, ed. F. Champion Ward (Chicago: University of Chicago Press, 1950).

12. Executive Committee of the Cooperative Study in General Education, *Cooperation in General Education* (Washington, DC: American Council on Education, 1947).

13. Shavelson, *A Brief History of Student Learning Assessment*.

14. Ibid.

15. ACT, *College Outcome Measures Project Revised Summary Report of Research and Development 1976–1980* (Iowa City, IA: ACT, 1981). Ernest Pascarella and Patrick Terenzini, *How College Affects Students: A Third Decade of Research* (San Francisco: Jossey-Bass, 2005). Laura Underwood, Barbara Maes, Lisa Alstadt, and Michael Boivin, "Evaluating Changes in Social Attitudes, Character Traits, and Liberal-Arts Abilities During a Four-Year Program at a Christian College," *Research on Christian Higher Education* 3 (1996).

16. Ewell, *An Emerging Scholarship*.

17. Ohio University Office of Institutional Research, *General Education Outcomes: The College Outcomes Measures Program (COMP) at Ohio University 1981–1985* (Athens, OH: Ohio University, 1996). http://www.ohio.edu/instres/assessments/genedACTCOMP.pdf.

18. Peter Ewell, "Assessment and Accountability in America Today: Background and Context," in *Assessing and Accounting for Student Learning: Beyond the Spellings Commission: New Directions for Institutional Research, Assessment Supplement 2007*, ed. Victor Borden and Gary Pike (San Francisco: Jossey-Bass, 2008).

19. State Higher Education Executive Officers, *Accountability for Better Results: A National Imperative for Higher Education* (Boulder, CO: State Higher Education Executive Officers, 2005). http://www.sheeo.org/account/accountability.pdf.

20. Stephen Klein, Roger Benjamin, Richard Shavelson, and Roger Bolus, "The Collegiate Learning Assessment: Facts and Fantasies," *Evaluation Review* 31, no. 5 (October 2007).

21. Hart Research Associates, *Learning and Assessment: Trends in Undergraduate Education—A Survey among Members of the Association of American Colleges and Universities* (Washington, DC: Hart Research Associates, 2009), 9. http://www.aacu.org/membership/documents/2009MemberSurvey_Part1.pdf.

22. Council of Independent Colleges, *Evidence of Learning: Applying the Collegiate Learning Assessment to Improve Teaching and Learning in the Liberal Arts College Experience* (Washington, DC: Council of Independent Colleges, 2008). http://www.cic.org/publications/books_reports/CLAreport.pdf.

23. Council of Independent Colleges, *CIC/CLA Consortium Resources* (Washington, DC: Council of Independent Colleges, 2009), http://www.cic.edu/projects_services/coops/cla_resources/index.html

24. Peter McPherson and David Shulenburger, *Toward a Voluntary System of Accountability (VSA) for Public Universities and Colleges* (Washington, DC: National Association of State Universities and Land-grant Colleges, 2006). http://www.voluntarysystem.org/docs/background/DiscussionPaper3_Aug06.pdf.

25. Christine Keller and John Hammang, "The Voluntary System of Accountability for Accountability and Institutional Assessment" in *Assessing and Accounting for Student Learning: Beyond the Spellings Commission: New Directions for Institutional Research, Assessment Supplement 2007*, ed. Victor Borden and Gary Pike (San Francisco: Jossey-Bass, 2008), 45.

26. Association of American Colleges and Universities and the Council for Higher Education Accreditation, *New Leadership for Student Learning and Accountability*, 5.

27. Derek Bok, *Our Underachieving Colleges: A Candid Look at How Much Students Learn and Why They Should Be Learning More* (Princeton, NJ: Princeton University Press, 2006), 251. Also see the chapters by Naomi Reilly and Anne Neal in this volume.

28. Pedro Reyes and Roberta Rincon, "The Texas Experience with Accountability and Student Learning Assessment," in *Assessing and Accounting for Student Learning: Beyond the Spellings Commission: New Directions for Institutional Research, Assessment Supplement 2007*, ed. Victor Borden and Gary Pike (San Francisco: Jossey-Bass, 2008).

29. Hart Research Associates, *Learning and Assessment*, 2.

30. The New Commission on the Skills of the American Workforce, *Tough Choices or Tough Times* (Washington, DC: National Center on Education and the Economy, 2006). http://www.skillscommission.org/pdf/exec_sum/ToughChoices_EXECSUM.pdf; The Secretary's Commission on Achieving Necessary Skills, *What Work Requires of Schools: A Scans Report for America 2000* (Washington, DC: U.S. Department of Labor, 1991). http://wdr.doleta.gov/SCANS/whatwork/whatwork.pdf.

31. Hart Research Associates, *How Should Colleges Prepare Students to Succeed in Today's Global Economy?—Based on Surveys Among Employers and Recent College Graduates* (Washington, DC: Hart Research Associates, 2006). *How Should Colleges Prepare Students to Succeed in Today's Global Economy?—Based on Surveys Among Employers and Recent College Graduates*

32. Pascarella and Terenzini, *How College Affects Students*. Elizabeth Jones, Steven Hoffman, Lynn Moore, Gary Ratcliff, Stacy Tibbetts, and Benjamin Click, *National Assessment of College Student Learning: Identifying College Graduates Essential Skills in Writing, Speech and Listening, and Critical Thinking* (Washington, DC: National Center for Education Statistics, 1995). http://www.eric.ed.gov/PDFS/ED383255.pdf.

33. Jones, Hoffman, Moore, Ratcliff, Tibbetts, and Click, *National Assessment of College Student Learning*.

34. Trudy Banta, "Editor's Notes: Trying to Clothe the Emperor," *Assessment Update* 20, no. 2 (March–April 2008), 4.

35. Council of Independent Colleges. Richard Ekman and Stephen Pelletier, "Reevaluating Learning Assessment," *Change* 40, no. 4 (July–August 2008); Reyes and Rincon, "Texas Experience with Accountability and Student Learning Assessment."

36. Alan Lane and Kevin Pennington, *General Education, the QEP and the CLA: Barton College*, presented at the CIC/CLA Consortium Summer Meeting (Jersey City, NJ: 2009).

37. Kristy Miller, Gerald Kruse, Christopher LeCluyse, and Joel Frederickson, *CLA Performance Tasks*, presented at the CIC/CLA Consortium Summer Meeting (Jersey City, NJ: 2009).

38. Pascarella and Terenzini, *How College Affects Students*.

39. Klein, *The Collegiate Learning Assessment*.

40. ACT, *Voluntary System of Accountability Learning Gains Methodology* (Iowa City, IA: ACT, 2009), http://www.voluntarysystem.org/docs/cp/ACTReport_LearningGainsMethodology.pdf. Ou Lydia Liu, *Measuring Learning Outcomes in Higher Education Using the Measure of Academic Proficiency and Progress (MAPP)*, ETS RR-08–47 (Princeton, NJ: ETS, 2008), http://www.voluntarysystem.org/docs/cp/RR-08–47MeasuringLearningOutcomes UsingMAPP.pdf

41. Banta, "Editor's Notes: Trying to Clothe the Emperor."

42. Gary Pike, "Lies, Damn Lies, and Statistics Revisited: A Comparison of Three Methods of Representing Change," paper presented at the Annual Forum of the Association for Institutional Research (San Francisco, CA: 1992).

43. George Kuh, *Director's Message—Engaged Learning: Fostering Success for All Students* (Bloomington, IN: National Survey of Student Engagement, 2006). http://nsse.iub.edu/NSSE_2006_Annual_Report/docs/NSSE_2006_Annual_Report.pdf.

44. Trudy Banta and Gary Pike, "Revisiting the Blind Ally of Value Added," *Assessment Update* 19, no. 1 (January–February 2007).

45. Stephen Klein, David Freedman, Richard Shavelson, and Roger Bolus, "Assessing School Effectiveness," *Evaluation Review* 32, no. 6 (December 2008).

46. Bok, *Our Underachieving Colleges*, 320.

47. Klein, *Collegiate Learning Assessment*.

48. Jeffrey Steedle, *Advancing Institutional Value-Added Score Estimation (draft)* (New York: Council for Aid to Education, 2009), http://www.collegiatelearningassessment.org/files/AdvancingInstlValueAdded.pdf

49. Doug Lederman, "Private Colleges, Serious about Assessment," *Inside Higher Ed*, August 4, 2008, http://www.insidehighered.com/news/2008/08/04/cla.

50. Steedle, *Advancing Institutional Value-Added Score Estimation*.

51. Lee Shulman, *Principles for the Uses of Assessment in Policy and Practice: President's Report to the Board of Trustees of the Carnegie Foundation for the Advancement of Teaching* (Stanford, CA: Carnegie Foundation for the Advancement of Teaching, 2006), http://www.teaglefoundation.org/learning/pdf/2006_shulman_assessment.pdf.

52. Reyes and Rincon, "Texas Experience with Accountability and Student Learning Assessment," 51.

53. Banta, "Editor's Notes: Trying to Clothe the Emperor."

2

Faculty Scholarly Productivity at American Research Universities

Lawrence B. Martin

S tatement of interests: Lawrence Martin is the Founder of Academic Analytics, LLC and has a significant financial interest in the company.

Discussions of higher education accountability among policy makers have tended to focus on the value provided by universities and colleges in terms of human capital, specifically the number of graduates being produced. To the extent that research is considered, the discussion tends to focus on somewhat nebulous terms such as *innovation* and *new technologies*, usually with a link to ideas concerning economic development. The university research mission is, quite properly, much broader than that, and many of the great discoveries of the twentieth century that drive the economy today were the result of discoveries from basic research driven by the pursuit of knowledge rather than the search for a better product. If accountability policies continue to develop in a way that reflects the prevailing interest in degree production and narrowly defined research, the broader scholarly mission of higher education could be damaged. That being said, the greatest cost at American universities is for faculty salaries, and a substantial portion of this expenditure is incurred to enable the production of scholarship. Assessing the returns on this expenditure is thus an important component of accountability discussions.

America's research universities have come to be the envy of the world since their rapid expansion following World War II. Much of this stature results from the extraordinary contributions made by scholars based in the United States to the developing knowledge base, as evidenced by the quantity of research publications and citations of those publications. In recent years America's ability to continue to dominate the development of knowledge has been questioned as the result of rapidly improving universities in Asia and increased emphasis on research excellence at universities in Europe. Peter Magrath, past president of the National Association of Land-grant Universities and Colleges NASULGC (recently renamed the Association of Public and Land-grant Universities [APLU]) and Bob Berdahl, president of the Association of American Universities (AAU) have separately stated that they believe the United States can no longer afford as many research universities as it now has. The National Academies study, entitled *The Gathering Storm*, raised similar concerns about American competitiveness in science, technology, engineering, and mathematics (STEM) disciplines and recent reports in the *Chronicle of Higher Education* have suggested that the level of productivity of faculty at American universities has declined in the last decade.

The research mission of universities should not be exempt from assessment and accountability because it is both expensive and vital to national competitiveness. In turn, as fiscal pressure increases on America's research universities and as the society demands more accountability, accurately measuring research productivity will become ever more important. However, it is critical to employ fair, accurate, nuanced metrics of research productivity that provide a basis to compare and assess performance while recognizing the breadth of the scholarly enterprise. In particular, it is important to pay close attention to cross-disciplinary differences in performance that require more sophisticated data on performance within disciplines as the basis for assessment. In most cases, such metrics need to be standardized to permit comparisons among disciplines.

This chapter addresses the following questions:

1. How productive are faculty at American research universities?
2. How much variation in research productivity is there among faculty?
3. How much variation in productivity is there among disciplines?
4. How is scholarly productivity best measured and compared across disciplines?

Background to the Use of Faculty Scholarly Productivity Data to Evaluate Program Quality

In 1982 and again in 1995 the National Research Council (NRC) published an assessment of research doctorate (PhD) programs in the United States.

These studies contained information on faculty scholarship at the discipline level, but their results for ranking programs derived from surveys of faculty. In the 1995 study, faculty members were asked to rate programs in their own discipline on the basis of their assessment of the scholarly quality of the program faculty on a scale from zero (not sufficient for doctoral education) to five (distinguished). The average scores for programs were reported in a measure entitled "93Q." The fiercest critics of the use of "reputational," as opposed to "objective," metrics of quality were the late Hugh Graham and his collaborator Nancy Diamond who argued that few faculty had sufficient, accurate, and current knowledge of fifty programs in the country to assess their quality on the NRC's six-point scale. In their 1997 book, Graham and Diamond concluded that only per-capita metrics should be used when comparing programs made up of different numbers of faculty members. Graham and Diamond also analyzed data from the 1995 NRC study and concluded in their 2001 paper that the best single metric to measure quality for the program was the number of journal article citations per faculty member.

Beginning with the release of the last National Research Council report on research doctorate programs in the United States in 1995, I began to analyze data on faculty scholarship in relation to the perceived quality of PhD programs in the United States. These analyses led to the conclusion that some, but by no means all, of the metrics compiled by the NRC correlated well with the overall rating of programs using the NRC's summary statistic (93Q). Most importantly, aspects of scholarly performance on which most believe that academic quality and reputation is based (journal articles, citations of articles, federal research grants, and prestigious honors and awards) were shown to be useful metrics of quality. These have the advantage that they can be based on recent performance and thus avoid the issue of reputational inertia inherent in reputational assessments and the long lag time between reputational studies. Some programs had performance metrics that exceeded the perceived quality of the program (suggesting that their reputation might be expected to improve in the future), while others had lower performance measures than their reputation would suggest, and these programs might be vulnerable to a declining reputation in the future. An early conclusion of this work was that size-adjusted metrics, such as per capita measures and ratios, were much more useful in comparing programs than the raw numbers.[1]

Available discipline-level data were later supplemented by the NRC with the release of more complete data files made available in 1997. At this stage I was joined by Anthony Olejniczak, and together we developed an index of faculty scholarly productivity (FSP) that covered journal publications, citations, grants, and honors and awards for each of the forty-one disciplines in the 1995 NRC study.

The FSP results were of interest to many as a means to identify strong programs that had not yet achieved national recognition and programs whose reputation was unlikely to persist unless scholarly performance improved. The overall conclusions of our analyses of the 1995 NRC data were that, while there is agreement that scholarly performance in terms of journal articles, citations, grants, and honors and awards is well correlated with, and probably the underlying basis of academic quality assessments, performance in these areas must be measured in the appropriate way for the particular discipline, and per capita or other size-corrected measures have the most power to describe performance differences among programs. A methodology study was started by the NRC in 2002 and their report was published in 2004. The study itself commenced in 2005 and is still in progress, with an expected report in the summer of 2010. We also share the current view of the NRC Methodology Committee that assessments of scholarly performance in the humanities and other lettered disciplines that did not include data on books published were incomplete and unreliable.

Beginning in 2005 Academic Analytics, LLC (AA) began to build annually a national database on faculty scholarly productivity (FSP) in American research universities and data from AA's FSP 2008 database are used in this chapter. AA's data are proprietary, but the company has a policy of making data available to scholars of higher education for use in academic work. (Such requests may be directed to AA's CEO, Peter Maglione, pmaglione@academicanalytics.com.) The initial goal for the database was to include all elements of faculty scholarly productivity included in the 1995 NRC study, with the addition of authored and edited books and with an increased coverage of scholarly disciplines. This approach led to the adoption of a taxonomy of PhD disciplines that includes 172 disciplines. To facilitate comparisons of performance across universities employing different program groupings (for example, biomedical sciences as a general category in contrast with a finely divided set of disciplines), the disciplines are grouped into eleven broad fields that mirror the taxonomy commonly used by federal agencies, universities, and the NRC (for example, social and behavioral sciences, and biological and biomedical sciences). Following the NRC approach, AA assembled lists of faculty associated with PhD programs in the United States and used these lists to compile data on journal articles published, citations of those articles, books published, federal research grants awarded by the principal federal funding agencies, and prestigious honors and awards received.

Data on Faculty Scholarly Performance
Used in the Current Study

The following measures are used in this chapter, all of them contained in the FSP 2008 database. Data on journal articles and data on citations of those articles were obtained from Scopus, covering over 16,000 peer-reviewed journals from more than 4,000 publishers. Each year of journal article data represents a complete year's worth of scholarly activity captured by Scopus, amounting to more than 6.5 million journal articles per year. FSP 2008 includes journal publications from 2006, 2007, and 2008 that had been indexed by Scopus by May 2009. FSP 2008 includes four years of citations of journal articles that were published from 2005 to 2008. All authors are recorded for journal articles and for books.

FSP 2008 employs book publication data from Baker and Taylor, Inc. whose academic library service offers a comprehensive catalogue of titles. Each year of initial books data contains approximately 266,000 titles, for a total of approximately 1,328,500 books over five years. FSP 2008 contains data on books published in 2004, 2005, 2006, 2007, and 2008 in six of the broad fields (business; education; family, consumer, and human sciences; health professions sciences; humanities; and social and behavioral sciences). A title is included once per person, and all published works are weighted equally.

FSP 2008 includes three years (2006, 2007, and 2008) of data on new federal funding from the National Institutes of Health (NIH), National Science Foundation (NSF), Department of Education (DoED), National Oceanic and Atmospheric Association (NOAA), United States Department of Agriculture (USDA), Department of Energy (DOE), the National Aeronautics and Space Administration (NASA), and Department of Defense (DoD), except the Defense Advanced Research Projects Agency (DARPA). Only competitive awards are collected; noncompetitive grants or noncompetitive renewals are not included in FSP 2008. Only principal investigators (PI) are counted for grants awarded because this is the common element for all of the data sources currently obtained (NIH only added co-PIs in 2007).

FSP 2008 includes data for about 27,000 recipients of about 43,000 honorific awards, issued by about three hundred governing bodies held by faculty in 2008 (a complete list showing durations for which the data are compiled, which varies by award, may be obtained on request from Academic Analytics).[2]

For FSP 2008, faculty are grouped into disciplines based on their listing as faculty of a PhD program or a department that offers a PhD program. Data on faculty performance are combined for the individuals making up the faculty of a program and metrics of performance for the whole faculty are then added (percentage with a grant, etc.). For FSP 2009, faculty will be grouped by department and in subsequent releases of the database both departmental and PhD program views will be available.

The individual data elements available in FSP 2008 are:

1. The number of journal articles published by the faculty
2. The number of faculty who authored or coauthored a journal article
3. Journal articles per faculty
4. Journal articles per author
5. Authorship index (percentage of faculty who authored an article)
6. The number of citations of all journal articles
7. The number of faculty with a citation
8. The number of authors of journal articles with a citation
9. Citations per faculty
10. Citations per author
11. Citations per article
12. The number of books published by the faculty in the discipline
13. The number of authors of books among the faculty of the discipline
14. Books per faculty
15. Books per author
16. Authorship index (percentage of faculty who authored a book)
17. The number of new grants awarded
18. Average annualized funding for grants awarded
19. The number of faculty who are PIs of grants awarded
20. Grants per faculty
21. Grants per author
22. Research dollars per faculty
23. Research dollars per author
24. Research dollars per grant
25. The number of awards held
26. The number of faculty holding awards
27. Awards per faculty
28. Awarded faculty index (percentage of faculty holding an award or honor)

The Scale of Scholarly Endeavor in
American Research Universities

How many faculty members are involved?

In 2008 in the United States, 9,874 PhD programs at 385 accredited universities that award a PhD listed a total faculty membership of about 233,675. Programs that are delivered as distance programs and for which faculty lists are not available were not included (table 2.1).

Table 2.1   Grants by national, discipline quintile of the faculty

Discipline	Broad Field	No. of PhD program faculty, 2008–2009
Animal Sciences	Agricultural Sciences	1,380
Agronomy and Crop Science	Agricultural Sciences	955
Food Science	Agricultural Sciences	761
Agricultural Economics	Agricultural Sciences	678
Plant Sciences	Agricultural Sciences	629
Soil Science	Agricultural Sciences	629
Horticulture	Agricultural Sciences	563
Agriculture, various	Agricultural Sciences	231
	Agricultural Sciences Total Headcount	**5,160**
Neurobiology/Neuroscience	Biological and Biomedical Sciences	6,278
Molecular Biology	Biological and Biomedical Sciences	5,809
Biology/Biological Sciences, general	Biological and Biomedical Sciences	5,539
Cell Biology	Biological and Biomedical Sciences	5,009
Biochemistry	Biological and Biomedical Sciences	4,585
Biomedical Sciences, general	Biological and Biomedical Sciences	3,650
Microbiology	Biological and Biomedical Sciences	3,274
Physiology, general	Biological and Biomedical Sciences	2,833
Pharmacology	Biological and Biomedical Sciences	2,306
Genetics	Biological and Biomedical Sciences	2,270
Biophysics	Biological and Biomedical Sciences	2,159
Ecology	Biological and Biomedical Sciences	2,019
Pathology	Biological and Biomedical Sciences	1,951
Immunology	Biological and Biomedical Sciences	1,824

Continued

Table 2.1 Continued

Discipline	Broad Field	No. of PhD program faculty, 2008–2009
Developmental Biology	Biological and Biomedical Sciences	1,444
Pharmaceutical Sciences	Biological and Biomedical Sciences	1,424
Toxicology	Biological and Biomedical Sciences	1,399
Epidemiology	Biological and Biomedical Sciences	1,370
Evolutionary Biology	Biological and Biomedical Sciences	1,364
Bioinformatics and Computational Biology	Biological and Biomedical Sciences	1,344
Botany/Plant Biology	Biological and Biomedical Sciences	1,012
Biomedical Sciences, various	Biological and Biomedical Sciences	1,006
Oncology and Cancer Biology	Biological and Biomedical Sciences	955
Entomology	Biological and Biomedical Sciences	864
Molecular Genetics	Biological and Biomedical Sciences	805
Biological Sciences, various	Biological and Biomedical Sciences	752
Anatomy	Biological and Biomedical Sciences	724
Cognitive Science	Biological and Biomedical Sciences	720
Human and Medical Genetics	Biological and Biomedical Sciences	636
Plant Pathology	Biological and Biomedical Sciences	528
Molecular Pharmacology	Biological and Biomedical Sciences	480
Zoology	Biological and Biomedical Sciences	437
Structural Biology	Biological and Biomedical Sciences	319
Oral Biology and Craniofacial Science	Biological and Biomedical Sciences	300
	Biological and Biomedical Sciences Total Headcount	**41,786**
Business Administration	Business	3,214
Management	Business	1,950
Finance	Business	795
Business, various	Business	770
Marketing	Business	722
Accounting	Business	679
Management Information Systems	Business	586
	Business Total Headcount	**8,011**

Continued

Table 2.1 Continued

Discipline	Broad Field	No. of PhD program faculty, 2008–2009
Curriculum and Instruction	Education	1,820
Teacher-Education-Specific Subject Areas	Education	1,532
Educational Leadership and Administration	Education	1,324
Education, general	Education	1,104
Special Education	Education	716
Counselor Education	Education	451
Teacher-Education-Specific Levels	Education	408
Foundations of Education	Education	290
Educational Evaluation and Research	Education	272
Higher Education/Higher Education Administration	Education	252
Science Education	Education	235
Mathematics Education	Education	223
	Education Total Headcount	**7,935**
Electrical Engineering	Engineering	4,814
Mechanical Engineering	Engineering	3,688
Computer Engineering	Engineering	3,069
Civil Engineering	Engineering	2,673
Materials Science and Engineering	Engineering	2,140
Biomedical Engineering	Engineering	1,988
Chemical Engineering	Engineering	1,931
Environmental Engineering	Engineering	1,559
Engineering, various	Engineering	1,475
Agricultural/Biological Engineering and Bioengineering	Engineering	1,393
Aerospace Engineering	Engineering	1,280
Industrial Engineering	Engineering	988
Engineering Mechanics	Engineering	517

Continued

Table 2.1 Continued

Discipline	Broad Field	No. of PhD program faculty, 2008–2009
Engineering, general	Engineering	515
Operations Research	Engineering	487
Systems Engineering	Engineering	461
Nuclear Engineering	Engineering	324
Geological and Mining Engineering	Engineering	238
Materials Engineering	Engineering	224
	Engineering Total Headcount	**22,132**
Health Promotion, Kinesiology, Exercise Science, and Rehab	Family, Consumer, and Human Sciences	1,739
Communication and Communication Studies	Family, Consumer, and Human Sciences	1,327
Nutrition Sciences	Family, Consumer, and Human Sciences	1,197
Human Devel. and Family Studies, general	Family, Consumer, and Human Sciences	1,143
Mass Communications/ Media Studies	Family, Consumer, and Human Sciences	912
Urban and Regional Planning	Family, Consumer, and Human Sciences	554
Architecture, Design, Planning, various	Family, Consumer, and Human Sciences	471
Architecture	Family, Consumer, and Human Sciences	460
Health, Physical Education, Recreation	Family, Consumer, and Human Sciences	434
Family and Human Sciences, various	Family, Consumer, and Human Sciences	337
Consumer and Human Sciences, various	Family, Consumer, and Human Sciences	291
	Family, Consumer, and Human Sciences Total Headcount	**8,641**
Nursing	Health Professions Sciences	2,837
Medical Sciences, various	Health Professions Sciences	2,179
Public Health	Health Professions Sciences	1,228
Veterinary Medical Sciences	Health Professions Sciences	1,013
Health Professions, various	Health Professions Sciences	823

Continued

Table 2.1 Continued

Discipline	Broad Field	No. of PhD program faculty, 2008–2009
Environmental Health Sciences	Health Professions Sciences	571
Communication Disorders and Sciences	Health Professions Sciences	430
Speech and Hearing Sciences	Health Professions Sciences	416
Pharmacy	Health Professions Sciences	388
	Health Professions Sciences Total Headcount	**9,885**
History	Humanities	5,057
English Language and Literature	Humanities	4,891
Philosophy	Humanities	1,929
Comparative Literature	Humanities	1,114
Religion/Religious Studies	Humanities	1,069
Theology/Theological Studies	Humanities	1,037
Art History and Criticism	Humanities	1,002
Music, general	Humanities	908
Spanish Language and Literature	Humanities	845
Linguistics	Humanities	829
Humanities/Humanistic Studies, general	Humanities	793
Area and Ethnic Studies, various	Humanities	680
American Studies	Humanities	672
French Language and Literature	Humanities	623
Classics and Classical Languages	Humanities	613
Performing and Visual Arts, various	Humanities	560
Asian Studies	Humanities	539
Composition, Rhetoric, and Writing	Humanities	485

Continued

Table 2.1 Continued

Discipline	Broad Field	No. of PhD program faculty, 2008–2009
Gender Studies	Humanities	474
Germanic Languages and Literatures	Humanities	445
Languages, various	Humanities	437
Theatre Literature, History, and Criticism	Humanities	423
Music specialties	Humanities	401
Near and Middle Eastern Languages and Cultures	Humanities	374
Asian Languages	Humanities	353
Ancient Studies	Humanities	284
Slavic Languages and Literatures	Humanities	192
Italian Language and Literature	Humanities	117
European Studies	Humanities	110
	Humanities Total Headcount	**23,368**
Environmental Sciences	Natural Resources and Conservation	1,996
Natural Resources	Natural Resources and Conservation	1,603
Forest Resources/Forestry	Natural Resources and Conservation	808
Fisheries Science	Natural Resources and Conservation	475
Wildlife Science	Natural Resources and Conservation	452
	Natural Resources and Conservation Total Headcount	**4,676**
Mathematics	Physical and Mathematical Sciences	5,317
Physics, general	Physical and Mathematical Sciences	5,281
Chemistry	Physical and Mathematical Sciences	4,923
Computer Science	Physical and Mathematical Sciences	4,478
Geology/Earth Science, general	Physical and Mathematical Sciences	2,710
Astronomy and Astrophysics	Physical and Mathematical Sciences	1,603
Statistics	Physical and Mathematical Sciences	1,410
Applied Mathematics	Physical and Mathematical Sciences	1,339

Continued

Table 2.1 Continued

Discipline	Broad Field	No. of PhD program faculty, 2008–2009
Marine Sciences	Physical and Mathematical Sciences	1,304
Information Science/ Studies	Physical and Mathematical Sciences	989
Oceanography, Physical Sciences	Physical and Mathematical Sciences	986
Chemical Sciences, various	Physical and Mathematical Sciences	980
Applied Physics	Physical and Mathematical Sciences	877
Biostatistics	Physical and Mathematical Sciences	800
Computational Sciences	Physical and Mathematical Sciences	780
Atmospheric Sciences and Meteorology	Physical and Mathematical Sciences	767
Geophysics	Physical and Mathematical Sciences	448
Computer and Information Sciences, various	Physical and Mathematical Sciences	404
Info. Technology/ Information Systems	Physical and Mathematical Sciences	383
	Physical and Mathematical Sciences Total Headcount	**29,852**
Psychology, general	Social and Behavioral Sciences	4,025
Economics, general	Social and Behavioral Sciences	3,266
Political Science	Social and Behavioral Sciences	3,169
Sociology	Social and Behavioral Sciences	2,555
Anthropology	Social and Behavioral Sciences	2,194
Social Work/Social Welfare	Social and Behavioral Sciences	1,467
Psychology, various	Social and Behavioral Sciences	1,384
Public Policy	Social and Behavioral Sciences	1,332
Clinical Psychology	Social and Behavioral Sciences	1,186
Geography	Social and Behavioral Sciences	1,046
Educational Psychology	Social and Behavioral Sciences	791
Public Administration	Social and Behavioral Sciences	765
Criminal Justice and Criminology	Social and Behavioral Sciences	692
Social Sciences, various	Social and Behavioral Sciences	664

Continued

Table 2.1   Continued

Discipline	Broad Field	No. of PhD program faculty, 2008–2009
International Affairs and Development	Social and Behavioral Sciences	632
Counseling Psychology	Social and Behavioral Sciences	469
School Psychology	Social and Behavioral Sciences	322
Applied Economics	Social and Behavioral Sciences	275
	Social and Behavioral Sciences Total Headcount	**24,424**
	Grand Total Headcount	**165,091**

Because many faculty members belong to more than one PhD program, these faculty counts reduce to a total of 165,091 individual people. The impact of summing PhD program membership in terms of inflating total faculty counts is most marked in biological and biomedical sciences where the sum of program faculty lists is 1.61 greater than the total number of people involved. Engineering has a ratio of 1.34; physical and mathematical sciences, 1.20; humanities, 1.17; natural resources and conservation, 1.14; agricultural sciences,1.13; business, 1.09; education, 1.09; social and behavioral sciences, 1.07; family, consumer, and health sciences, 1.03; and health professions sciences, 1.00. It is tempting to suggest that this ratio may indicate the degree of interdisciplinarity involved in a field, but it seems likely that it is also heavily influenced by the robustness of the taxonomy of disciplines, which is least secure in biological and biomedical sciences.

In the FSP 2008 database each person listed counts fully in each program rather than being prorated across the various programs to which they belong. To avoid double counting of performance when comparing larger units (whole universities, broad fields of disciplines, etc.) faculty records are de-duplicated at each level of aggregation of disciplines. This means that a faculty member who appears in the list for both biochemistry and for genetics at a particular university will count as a single person in the data for each discipline but as a single person when biomedical sciences is considered as a broad field or when the performance of the entire university is measured. Table 2.1 shows the number of faculty members associated with each of the 172 disciplines and the eleven broad fields included in FSP 2008.

Publication of scholarly results

In the period under study 103,729 (63 percent) of these 165,091 scholars published 757,948 articles in journals indexed by Scopus during the three-year period from 2006 to 2008, which attracted a total of 6,592,887 citations, including self-citations.

Of the 103,729 faculty who authored a journal article in 2006 to 2008, over 9,500 did not receive a single citation during those three years. Because citations are often taken as a good indicator of the importance of a piece of knowledge to the field, it is surprising to find that almost 10 percent of the PhD program faculty who publish articles in journals are producing a body of work that attracts no citations whatever. In the lettered disciplines, publication of scholarship is more often in the form of a scholarly book and 18,148 (11 percent) of the 165,091 scholars authored or edited 34,994 books in the six-year period from 2003 to 2008. As some scholars publish both books and articles, the sum of these two numbers is an overestimate of the total number of faculty who disseminated the results of their scholarly work through books or journal articles, but the total count of 121,877 faculty members who published either a book or an article still represents only 74 percent of the PhD faculty in the United States.

It is possible that the more than 40,000 PhD program faculty members who did not produce any scholarly output measured in FSP 2008 were productive in other ways. Some may have recently changed their names or locations so that their productivity was not matched to them, though the impact of this is likely to be small. Others may have published in journals that are not included in the 16,000+ titles indexed by Scopus or may have published in books not included in the Baker and Taylor database. However, the per capita measures of books published per faculty member or per book author/editor and articles published per faculty member or per article author are impressively high, suggesting that FSP 2008 includes most of the scholarly output of the faculty. Some of these faculty may have been released from scholarly work by their universities to pursue administrative or service roles, or even to recover from medical problems, but again, those numbers are unlikely to have a big impact on the total of 43,214.

It seems clear that at least 20 percent of the faculty members in the USA who enjoyed PhD program faculty status (with its attendant teaching-load reductions and other privileges) in the period from 2008 to 2009 provided no measurable return to their university in terms of the dissemination of new scholarship.

Grants and Honorific Awards

In terms of federal research grants, 46,098 of the 165,091 faculty members held 95,292 grants with an annual value of over $18 billion from the main federal funding agencies. As this number only counts the PI (not co-PIs) on grants it is likely unfair to compare it to the number who might seek such external funding for their work (presumably, at minimum, the number of faculty publishing journal articles). Finally, 17,145 of these 165,091 scholars held 26,007 prestigious honors and awards.

The Costs of Released Time for Research

The contribution of American research university faculty to scholarship is substantial, but the costs to produce the scholarship are not fully documented or understood.

A significant component of the national investment in scholarship is the investment made by research universities in faculty resources to allow them to fulfill both teaching and scholarly commitments. As an initial estimate let's assume that at a typical four-year college a faculty member may teach six courses per year (3+3) in the sciences and eight courses per year (4+4) in the humanities and social sciences. At a research university, faculty will teach at most half of this load in the social sciences and humanities and perhaps one third of the load in the sciences. This means that at least half, and more likely about 60 percent of the costs associated with faculty at research universities are costs to allow them to be productive as scholars. If the average faculty member earns around $80,000 per year (all levels and all disciplines at four-year institutions[3] and more at research universities) then the universities' investment in scholarship amounts to somewhere in excess of $8.9 billion annually (185,876 x $80,000 x 60 percent) in addition to direct expenditures and to traditionally accounted indirect costs of research. This expenditure by research universities to release faculty from teaching is not currently reported as research and development expenditure in the NSF report on research expenditures but represents a major investment by the nation.

Because the salary assumption levels are low for research universities, these are the *lowest* likely costs for faculty effort. Given the current status of funding for higher education, these investments demand some assessment of the return that is being received.

Publishing in Scholarly Journals

The primary medium for dissemination of new knowledge in the sciences is the scholarly article in a peer-reviewed journal. The absolute number of such publications is obviously an important output measure but is less interesting for studying productivity than other standardized metrics because the number of faculty involved in producing the output varies so much among disciplines (table 2.1).

Table 2.2 shows information on journal publishing that is adjusted in three distinct ways to be independent of the number of faculty involved so as to enable comparison among disciplines. The table is ordered by broad field and then by the percentage of PhD program faculty who authored

Table 2.2   Grants dollars by national, discipline quintile of the faculty

Discipline	Broad Field	Percentage of faculty with at least one journal publication indexed by Scopus, 2006–2008	Journal pubs. per faculty member	Journal pubs. per journal article author
Agronomy and Crop Science	Agricultural Sciences	81	5.10	6.27
Horticulture	Agricultural Sciences	80	5.10	6.40
Food Science	Agricultural Sciences	79	6.39	8.05
Soil Science	Agricultural Sciences	78	6.22	7.99
Plant Sciences	Agricultural Sciences	78	4.97	6.39
Agriculture, various	Agricultural Sciences	76	5.96	7.83
Animal Sciences	Agricultural Sciences	76	5.14	6.76
Agricultural Economics	Agricultural Sciences	68	2.25	3.33
Human and Medical Genetics	Biological and Biomedical Sciences	93	11.68	12.51
Structural Biology	Biological and Biomedical Sciences	93	10.86	11.70
Immunology	Biological and Biomedical Sciences	92	10.15	11.05
Bioinformatics and Computational Biology	Biological and Biomedical Sciences	92	11.16	12.19
Genetics	Biological and Biomedical Sciences	91	8.38	9.21
Biophysics	Biological and Biomedical Sciences	90	10.53	11.64
Molecular Genetics	Biological and Biomedical Sciences	90	8.67	9.66

Continued

Table 2.2 Continued

Discipline	Broad Field	Percentage of faculty with at least one journal publication indexed by Scopus, 2006–2008	Journal pubs. per faculty member	Journal pubs. per journal article author
Ecology	Biological and Biomedical Sciences	89	7.56	8.50
Evolutionary Biology	Biological and Biomedical Sciences	89	7.58	8.54
Neurobiology/ Neuroscience	Biological and Biomedical Sciences	89	7.75	8.73
Molecular Biology	Biological and Biomedical Sciences	88	8.14	9.25
Cell Biology	Biological and Biomedical Sciences	88	8.06	9.16
Oncology and Cancer Biology	Biological and Biomedical Sciences	88	10.39	11.82
Developmental Biology	Biological and Biomedical Sciences	87	7.48	8.56
Toxicology	Biological and Biomedical Sciences	87	8.63	9.87
Microbiology	Biological and Biomedical Sciences	87	8.00	9.20
Biomedical Sciences, various	Biological and Biomedical Sciences	87	10.02	11.53
Pharmacology	Biological and Biomedical Sciences	87	8.55	9.85
Epidemiology	Biological and Biomedical Sciences	87	12.91	14.91
Zoology	Biological and Biomedical Sciences	86	6.03	6.97
Botany/Plant Biology	Biological and Biomedical Sciences	86	6.43	7.45
Physiology, general	Biological and Biomedical Sciences	86	7.58	8.79
Biochemistry	Biological and Biomedical Sciences	86	8.25	9.58
Pathology	Biological and Biomedical Sciences	86	8.70	10.10

Continued

Table 2.2 Continued

Discipline	Broad Field	Percentage of faculty with at least one journal publication indexed by Scopus, 2006–2008	Journal pubs. per faculty member	Journal pubs. per journal article author
Oral Biology and Craniofacial Science	Biological and Biomedical Sciences	85	7.61	8.91
Molecular Pharmacology	Biological and Biomedical Sciences	85	9.57	11.21
Biomedical Sciences, general	Biological and Biomedical Sciences	85	8.12	9.60
Biology/Biological Sciences, general	Biological and Biomedical Sciences	84	6.99	8.28
Biological Sciences, various	Biological and Biomedical Sciences	84	9.30	11.08
Cognitive Science	Biological and Biomedical Sciences	84	5.40	6.46
Plant Pathology	Biological and Biomedical Sciences	82	5.58	6.81
Entomology	Biological and Biomedical Sciences	78	5.32	6.83
Pharmaceutical Sciences	Biological and Biomedical Sciences	76	6.89	9.03
Anatomy	Biological and Biomedical Sciences	76	4.85	6.41
Management Information Systems	Business	65	2.79	4.30
Management	Business	61	1.92	3.16
Marketing	Business	59	1.50	2.52
Business, various	Business	58	1.61	2.79
Business Administration	Business	56	1.57	2.77
Finance	Business	52	1.10	2.11
Accounting	Business	41	0.92	2.24
Educational Evaluation and Research	Education	60	1.69	2.84
Science Education	Education	57	1.77	3.10

Continued

Table 2.2   Continued

Discipline	Broad Field	Percentage of faculty with at least one journal publication indexed by Scopus, 2006–2008	Journal pubs. per faculty member	Journal pubs. per journal article author
Mathematics Education	Education	48	1.43	2.98
Foundations of Education	Education	43	0.78	1.81
Special Education	Education	41	1.09	2.64
Education, General	Education	37	0.79	2.12
Curriculum and Instruction	Education	36	0.62	1.72
Counselor Education	Education	35	0.65	1.85
Educational Leadership and Administration	Education	33	0.58	1.78
Teacher-Education-Specific Levels	Education	33	0.83	2.54
Teacher-Education-Specific Subject Areas	Education	29	0.72	2.45
Higher Education/ Higher Education Administration	Education	28	0.41	1.50
Materials Science and Engineering	Engineering	90	14.57	16.14
Chemical Engineering	Engineering	89	11.75	13.28
Biomedical Engineering	Engineering	88	10.55	12.02
Computer Engineering	Engineering	87	11.65	13.40
Engineering Mechanics	Engineering	87	9.39	10.81
Agricultural/Biological Engineering and Bioengineering	Engineering	87	9.85	11.36
Electrical Engineering	Engineering	86	12.04	13.95
Nuclear Engineering	Engineering	86	9.25	10.72
Materials Engineering	Engineering	86	8.61	10.05

Continued

Table 2.2 Continued

Discipline	Broad Field	Percentage of faculty with at least one journal publication indexed by Scopus, 2006–2008	Journal pubs. per faculty member	Journal pubs. per journal article author
Aerospace Engineering	Engineering	85	9.21	10.78
Mechanical Engineering	Engineering	85	8.83	10.44
Systems Engineering	Engineering	84	7.41	8.82
Environmental Engineering	Engineering	84	6.76	8.08
Civil Engineering	Engineering	82	5.70	6.94
Industrial Engineering	Engineering	81	5.81	7.22
Operations Research	Engineering	80	5.51	6.89
Geological and Mining Engineering	Engineering	77	4.43	5.73
Engineering, general	Engineering	76	7.02	9.20
Engineering, various	Engineering	74	6.99	9.41
Nutrition Sciences	Family, Consumer, and Human Sciences	85	7.90	9.30
Family and Human Sciences, various	Family, Consumer, and Human Sciences	72	3.86	5.37
Health Promotion, Kinesiology, Exercise Science, and Rehab	Family, Consumer, and Human Sciences	68	4.45	6.56
Consumer and Human Sciences, various	Family, Consumer, and Human Sciences	63	3.27	5.17
Health, Physical Education, Recreation	Family, Consumer, and Human Sciences	60	3.00	4.97
Human Development and Family Studies, general	Family, Consumer, and Human Sciences	59	2.50	4.27
Urban and Regional Planning	Family, Consumer, and Human Sciences	57	2.07	3.62
Architecture, Design, Planning, various	Family, Consumer, and Human Sciences	47	1.85	3.96
Communication and Communication Studies	Family, Consumer, and Human Sciences	45	1.18	2.64

Continued

Table 2.2 Continued

Discipline	Broad Field	Percentage of faculty with at least one journal publication indexed by Scopus, 2006–2008	Journal pubs. per faculty member	Journal pubs. per journal article author
Mass Communications/ Media Studies	Family, Consumer, and Human Sciences	33	0.99	3.02
Architecture	Family, Consumer, and Human Sciences	32	1.23	3.80
Environmental Health Sciences	Health Professions Sciences	84	8.26	9.80
Veterinary Medical Sciences	Health Professions Sciences	83	5.79	6.99
Public Health	Health Professions Sciences	82	8.78	10.73
Health Professions, various	Health Professions Sciences	75	5.58	7.45
Pharmacy	Health Professions Sciences	74	7.27	9.83
Speech and Hearing Sciences	Health Professions Sciences	72	2.97	4.10
Communication Disorders and Sciences	Health Professions Sciences	66	2.77	4.22
Medical Sciences, various	Health Professions Sciences	57	6.44	11.25
Nursing	Health Professions Sciences	57	2.05	3.61
Linguistics	Humanities	49	1.07	2.19
Philosophy	Humanities	41	0.91	2.22
Area and Ethnic Studies, various	Humanities	30	1.00	3.31
Gender Studies	Humanities	28	0.56	1.99
Asian Studies	Humanities	23	0.50	2.16
Asian Languages	Humanities	21	0.46	2.25
Composition, Rhetoric, and Writing	Humanities	20	0.33	1.64
Religion/Religious Studies	Humanities	20	0.33	1.64
Ancient Studies	Humanities	19	0.37	1.93

Continued

Table 2.2 Continued

Discipline	Broad Field	Percentage of faculty with at least one journal publication indexed by Scopus, 2006–2008	Journal pubs. per faculty member	Journal pubs. per journal article author
History	Humanities	19	0.33	1.76
Slavic Languages and Literatures	Humanities	19	0.26	1.40
American Studies	Humanities	19	0.31	1.67
Near and Middle Eastern Languages and Cultures	Humanities	18	0.34	1.90
Humanities/Humanistic Studies, general	Humanities	17	0.27	1.58
Germanic Lang. and Lit.	Humanities	17	0.23	1.36
French Language and Literature	Humanities	16	0.19	1.20
Comparative Literature	Humanities	14	0.17	1.18
European Studies	Humanities	14	0.14	1.00
Theology/Theological Studies	Humanities	14	0.18	1.33
Classics and Classical Languages	Humanities	13	0.23	1.78
Italian Language and Literature	Humanities	13	0.19	1.47
Languages, various	Humanities	12	0.18	1.56
Art History and Criticism	Humanities	11	0.15	1.29
Performing and Visual Arts, various	Humanities	11	0.21	1.83
English Language and Literature	Humanities	10	0.14	1.41
Spanish Language and Literature	Humanities	10	0.18	1.79
Music, general	Humanities	10	0.20	2.01
Music specialties	Humanities	10	0.18	1.85
Theatre Literature, History, and Criticism	Humanities	5	0.09	2.00

Continued

Table 2.2 Continued

Discipline	Broad Field	Percentage of faculty with at least one journal publication indexed by Scopus, 2006–2008	Journal pubs. per faculty member	Journal pubs. per journal article author
Wildlife Science	Natural Resources and Conservation	82	5.42	6.62
Fisheries Science	Natural Resources and Conservation	82	5.52	6.75
Environmental Sciences	Natural Resources and Conservation	80	6.30	7.87
Forest Resources/ Forestry	Natural Resources and Conservation	79	4.64	5.85
Natural Resources	Natural Resources and Conservation	77	5.48	7.11
Chemical Sciences, various	Physical and Mathematical Sciences	91	14.00	15.44
Atmospheric Sciences and Meteorology	Physical and Mathematical Sciences	90	7.80	8.64
Oceanography, Physical Sciences	Physical and Mathematical Sciences	90	6.93	7.73
Astronomy and Astrophysics	Physical and Mathematical Sciences	90	13.07	14.59
Applied Physics	Physical and Mathematical Sciences	90	14.98	16.73
Biostatistics	Physical and Mathematical Sciences	88	10.68	12.07
Physics, general	Physical and Mathematical Sciences	87	14.38	16.50
Geophysics	Physical and Mathematical Sciences	87	6.06	6.96
Marine Sciences	Physical and Mathematical Sciences	86	5.99	6.93
Geology/Earth Science, general	Physical and Mathematical Sciences	85	6.48	7.60
Chemistry	Physical and Mathematical Sciences	85	10.71	12.65
Computational Sciences	Physical and Mathematical Sciences	84	8.64	10.25

Continued

Table 2.2 Continued

Discipline	Broad Field	Percentage of faculty with at least one journal publi-cation indexed by Scopus, 2006–2008	Journal pubs. per faculty member	Journal pubs. per journal article author
Statistics	Physical and Mathematical Sciences	83	5.22	6.31
Applied Mathematics	Physical and Mathematical Sciences	82	6.13	7.43
Computer Science	Physical and Mathematical Sciences	82	7.13	8.66
Information Technology/ Information Systems	Physical and Mathematical Sciences	78	5.58	7.16
Information Science/ Studies	Physical and Mathematical Sciences	73	4.84	6.67
Computer and Information Sciences, various	Physical and Mathematical Sciences	72	5.20	7.18
Mathematics	Physical and Mathematical Sciences	72	3.33	4.64
Psychology, general	Social and Behavioral Sciences	79	4.64	5.88
Geography	Social and Behavioral Sciences	75	3.68	4.90
Psychology, various	Social and Behavioral Sciences	71	3.32	4.69
Economics, general	Social and Behavioral Sciences	67	2.15	3.23
Clinical Psychology	Social and Behavioral Sciences	66	2.82	4.28
Applied Economics	Social and Behavioral Sciences	64	2.08	3.26
School Psychology	Social and Behavioral Sciences	62	1.87	3.01
Educational Psychology	Social and Behavioral Sciences	61	1.59	2.60
Sociology	Social and Behavioral Sciences	60	1.72	2.84

Continued

Table 2.2   Continued

Discipline	Broad Field	Percentage of faculty with at least one journal publication indexed by Scopus, 2006–2008	Journal pubs. per faculty member	Journal pubs. per journal article author
Social Work/Social Welfare	Social and Behavioral Sciences	58	1.73	2.97
Public Policy	Social and Behavioral Sciences	58	2.69	4.66
Social Sciences, various	Social and Behavioral Sciences	57	2.47	4.30
Counseling Psychology	Social and Behavioral Sciences	56	1.49	2.66
Anthropology	Social and Behavioral Sciences	55	1.78	3.25
Criminal Justice and Criminology	Social and Behavioral Sciences	54	1.59	2.92
Public Administration	Social and Behavioral Sciences	51	1.79	3.50
Political Science	Social and Behavioral Sciences	49	0.99	2.04
International Affairs and Development	Social and Behavioral Sciences	45	1.14	2.52

or coauthored at least one article during the three year period from 2006 to 2008. It is perhaps not surprising that no discipline has 100 percent of the faculty publishing, but it is quite surprising that so few approach this figure. Much of the variance appears to be patterned by discipline, but even within the eleven broad fields in the FSP taxonomy there is a considerable difference between the high and low publication rate across disciplines (table 2.2).

While differences among these broad fields are intriguing, some of them simply reflect the pattern of scholarly publishing so that humanists and social scientists may publish their work in books rather than journals. It is also the case that the Scopus database for this period did not include complete coverage of the humanities, arts, and social sciences. That said, the significant differences in publication rates within broad fields is striking as is the fact that over all broad fields (including those for which book publishing is the primary forum) only 70 percent of faculty publish an article in a three-year period. Even more surprising is the fact that in most fields for which journal publishing would be expected (omitting business, education, and humanities from the eleven broad fields listed above), fully 20 percent of the faculty associated with PhD training programs have not authored or coauthored a single journal article in one of the 16,000 journals indexed in a three-year period. These faculty members *may* have been productive in other areas, but one has to wonder how suitable they are to mentor the next generation of scholars, based on this low level of productivity, and how much universities are paying for research that they are not getting via reduced teaching time.

We can provide a rough estimate of these losses: If 20 percent of PhD faculty are not publishing as expected, this represents something close to $2 billion in university investments in scholarship for which the return seems to be nil.

Having considered how many faculty members are publishing *any* scholarly work, it is useful to look at two measures of how much scholarly work they produce. The first of these is the number of publications per faculty member, which also vary dramatically among disciplines (table 2.2). Because this metric could be affected by differences in the percentage of faculty who publish, a third metric—journal articles per journal-article author—is provided. This reduces the denominator to those faculty members who have published a journal article. The metric is useful when comparing disciplines for which some faculty may publish their scholarship in books while others publish in journals. Even with this correction there exist substantial differences among performance levels even within a relatively homogeneous broad field such as biological and biomedical sciences. It seems probable that highly productive scholars exist in all disciplines, so the differences among disciplinary means likely reflects disciplinary differences in terms of the standards for a publishable unit that are quite different even among disciplines that one would expect to behave in a similar manner—for example, physical sciences and mathematics. Whatever the reason, these results present a cautionary note for those who seek to compare or to evaluate performance levels in fields beyond those for which they have immediate expertise or appropriate comparative, discipline-level data. It is almost certainly a mistake to compare productivity levels among faculty members in different disciplines even within a broad field because this variance likely represents different patterns of scholarly output in different disciplines. These results present a cautionary tale for cross-disciplinary performance evaluation and thus for many college, school, or university-wide promotion and tenure committees.

Return on Investment of Federal Research Funding

In the sciences, great weight is placed on the ability to secure funding to support research. The federal government (and others) supports research in order to make discoveries and to disseminate new knowledge. Consequently, it seemed interesting also to look at the number of articles produced as the consequence of funding to support the production of scholarship. The broad fields of business, education, and humanities have been eliminated from this analysis because they are not areas for which a great deal of federal funding for research exists. It is important to remind readers at this point that some federal agencies are not yet included in the database (DoD's DARPA being the most critical). This means that comparisons among broad fields should be treated as preliminary at this point because the missing agencies are disproportionately involved in the funding of engineering and physical sciences whose costs per publication and per citation may thus be underestimated. The comparisons of return on investment among disciplines within each of the eight broad fields that are included should be much less affected and thus much more reliable. The results of this return-on-investment analysis are quite striking and full details are presented in table 2.3.

Table 2.3   Books by national, discipline quintile of the faculty

Discipline	Broad Field	Journal articles per million dollars of federal grants
Agricultural Economics	Agricultural Sciences	150
Food Science	Agricultural Sciences	147
Animal Sciences	Agricultural Sciences	121
Soil Science	Agricultural Sciences	115
Agriculture, various	Agricultural Sciences	103
Agronomy and Crop Science	Agricultural Sciences	103
Horticulture	Agricultural Sciences	77
Plant Sciences	Agricultural Sciences	52
Entomology	Biological and Biomedical Sciences	69
Plant Pathology	Biological and Biomedical Sciences	54
Zoology	Biological and Biomedical Sciences	53
Epidemiology	Biological and Biomedical Sciences	51
Ecology	Biological and Biomedical Sciences	50

Continued

Table 2.3 Continued

Discipline	Broad Field	Journal articles per million dollars of federal grants
Evolutionary Biology	Biological and Biomedical Sciences	48
Pharmaceutical Sciences	Biological and Biomedical Sciences	45
Toxicology	Biological and Biomedical Sciences	39
Bioinformatics and Computational Biology	Biological and Biomedical Sciences	39
Botany/Plant Biology	Biological and Biomedical Sciences	37
Pathology	Biological and Biomedical Sciences	35
Cognitive Science	Biological and Biomedical Sciences	34
Human and Medical Genetics	Biological and Biomedical Sciences	33
Anatomy	Biological and Biomedical Sciences	33
Biology/Biological Sciences, general	Biological and Biomedical Sciences	32
Biological Sciences, various	Biological and Biomedical Sciences	32
Oral Biology and Craniofacial Science	Biological and Biomedical Sciences	30
Structural Biology	Biological and Biomedical Sciences	30
Biomedical Sciences, general	Biological and Biomedical Sciences	30
Biomedical Sciences, various	Biological and Biomedical Sciences	29
Oncology and Cancer Biology	Biological and Biomedical Sciences	29
Pharmacology	Biological and Biomedical Sciences	29
Biophysics	Biological and Biomedical Sciences	28
Physiology, general	Biological and Biomedical Sciences	27
Immunology	Biological and Biomedical Sciences	27
Biochemistry	Biological and Biomedical Sciences	26
Microbiology	Biological and Biomedical Sciences	26
Genetics	Biological and Biomedical Sciences	25
Molecular Pharmacology	Biological and Biomedical Sciences	25
Neurobiology/Neuroscience	Biological and Biomedical Sciences	23
Molecular Biology	Biological and Biomedical Sciences	23
Cell Biology	Biological and Biomedical Sciences	23
Developmental Biology	Biological and Biomedical Sciences	21
Molecular Genetics	Biological and Biomedical Sciences	21
Aerospace Engineering	Engineering	163

Continued

Table 2.3 Continued

Discipline	Broad Field	Journal articles per million dollars of federal grants
Nuclear Engineering	Engineering	149
Geological and Mining Engineering	Engineering	135
Engineering, general	Engineering	129
Mechanical Engineering	Engineering	120
Electrical Engineering	Engineering	113
Materials Engineering	Engineering	113
Engineering, various	Engineering	105
Engineering Mechanics	Engineering	104
Materials Science and Engineering	Engineering	102
Computer Engineering	Engineering	98
Industrial Engineering	Engineering	93
Civil Engineering	Engineering	88
Systems Engineering	Engineering	84
Operations Research	Engineering	78
Chemical Engineering	Engineering	77
Environmental Engineering	Engineering	69
Agricultural/Biological Engineering and Bioengineering	Engineering	54
Biomedical Engineering	Engineering	44
Consumer and Human Sciences, various	Family, Consumer, and Human Sciences	186
Urban and Regional Planning	Family, Consumer, and Human Sciences	125
Health, Physical Education, Recreation	Family, Consumer, and Human Sciences	118
Architecture, Design, Planning, various	Family, Consumer, and Human Sciences	114
Architecture	Family, Consumer, and Human Sciences	106
Mass Communications/ Media Studies	Family, Consumer, and Human Sciences	65

Continued

Table 2.3 Continued

Discipline	Broad Field	Journal articles per million dollars of federal grants
Communication and Communication Studies	Family, Consumer, and Human Sciences	65
Family and Human Sciences, various	Family, Consumer, and Human Sciences	57
Health Promotion, Kinesiology, Exercise Science, and Rehab	Family, Consumer, and Human Sciences	57
Nutrition Sciences	Family, Consumer, and Human Sciences	51
Human Development and Family Studies, general	Family, Consumer, and Human Sciences	41
Health Professions, various	Health Professions Sciences	84
Veterinary Medical Sciences	Health Professions Sciences	67
Environmental Health Sciences	Health Professions Sciences	65
Pharmacy	Health Professions Sciences	52
Medical Sciences, various	Health Professions Sciences	51
Public Health	Health Professions Sciences	43
Nursing	Health Professions Sciences	39
Speech and Hearing Sciences	Health Professions Sciences	25
Communication Disorders and Sciences	Health Professions Sciences	19
Forest Resources/Forestry	Natural Resources and Conservation	201
Wildlife Science	Natural Resources and Conservation	110
Natural Resources	Natural Resources and Conservation	88
Environmental Sciences	Natural Resources and Conservation	68
Fisheries Science	Natural Resources and Conservation	67
Physics, general	Physical and Mathematical Sciences	114
Biostatistics	Physical and Mathematical Sciences	106
Applied Physics	Physical and Mathematical Sciences	98
Astronomy and Astrophysics	Physical and Mathematical Sciences	88
Statistics	Physical and Mathematical Sciences	73
Computational Sciences	Physical and Mathematical Sciences	60
Computer and Information Sciences, various	Physical and Mathematical Sciences	59
Applied Mathematics	Physical and Mathematical Sciences	58

Continued

Table 2.3 Continued

Discipline	Broad Field	Journal articles per million dollars of federal grants
Information Technology/ Information Systems	Physical and Mathematical Sciences	57
Mathematics	Physical and Mathematical Sciences	55
Information Science/Studies	Physical and Mathematical Sciences	53
Chemical Sciences, various	Physical and Mathematical Sciences	52
Geology/Earth Science, general	Physical and Mathematical Sciences	51
Computer Science	Physical and Mathematical Sciences	49
Chemistry	Physical and Mathematical Sciences	45
Atmospheric Sciences and Meteorology	Physical and Mathematical Sciences	34
Geophysics	Physical and Mathematical Sciences	33
Marine Sciences	Physical and Mathematical Sciences	27
Oceanography, Physical Sciences	Physical and Mathematical Sciences	22
Criminal Justice and Criminology	Social and Behavioral Sciences	136
Economics, general	Social and Behavioral Sciences	84
Applied Economics	Social and Behavioral Sciences	74
Political Science	Social and Behavioral Sciences	74
Public Policy	Social and Behavioral Sciences	67
Social Work/Social Welfare	Social and Behavioral Sciences	63
Geography	Social and Behavioral Sciences	62
International Affairs and Development	Social and Behavioral Sciences	62
Counseling Psychology	Social and Behavioral Sciences	59
Public Administration	Social and Behavioral Sciences	55
Social Sciences, various	Social and Behavioral Sciences	51
Anthropology	Social and Behavioral Sciences	49
Clinical Psychology	Social and Behavioral Sciences	42
Sociology	Social and Behavioral Sciences	36
Psychology, general	Social and Behavioral Sciences	35
Psychology, various	Social and Behavioral Sciences	30
School Psychology	Social and Behavioral Sciences	23
Educational Psychology	Social and Behavioral Sciences	17

It is the range of the variance, overall and within broad fields, that is so striking. The fact that $1 million of research funding in molecular genetics (the most expensive biomedical- science research field by this measure) results in 21 papers while the same amount produces 69 papers in Entomology and 201 in Forestry was not something that I expected! Some work is clearly much more expensive to do than others, but I have been surprised to see the scale of this effect with, for example, physicists who produce 114 journal articles per $1 million while biochemists produce 26.

The Impact of Journal Articles on the Field

Since the pioneering study by Cole and Cole in 1972,[4] citation analysis has become an important tool to understand the impact of journal publications. Most scholars can find some outlet for their work, so citation data provide an important counterbalance to raw counts of publication numbers when these are not weighted in terms of quality. The standard way to weight publications is to use the citation impact for the journal—that is, the average citation rate for the papers in that journal over a defined period. However, citation rates vary widely among papers in a single journal, and the use of average citation counts to weight the importance of articles obscures this variance. As FSP 2008 enables analysis of actual citation numbers per paper and per author, it provides a more independent assessment of publication quality than a weighted count of publications.

Raw counts of citations in Broad Fields show a huge discipline effect that has generally been ascribed to the number of scholars working in (and thus available to cite other work) a discipline. For that reason, the standard metric for citations used by the NRC in 1995[5] and by Graham and Diamond[6] in their analysis of NRC data has been citations per faculty member. Results for this metric, and for two others, are presented in table 2.4.

Within a tightly constrained discipline, citations per faculty member may be a good metric, but it is clearly influenced by some combination of the number of practitioners in the discipline, the number of papers in the discipline, and discipline-particular citation practices. An obvious impact occurs in the lettered disciplines, but the dramatic differences in values within the Broad Fields where journal articles are the norm demonstrate that this metric should only be used with great caution to make performance comparisons across disciplines. To enable comparison of performance across disciplines the data should be transformed to

Table 2.4 Journal articles by national, discipline of the faculty

Discipline	Broad Field	Citations per faculty member	Citations per author of a journal article	Citations per journal article
Plant Sciences	Agricultural Sciences	45	58	9
Soil Science	Agricultural Sciences	42	54	7
Horticulture	Agricultural Sciences	38	48	8
Agriculture, various	Agricultural Sciences	35	46	6
Food Science	Agricultural Sciences	35	44	5
Agronomy and Crop Science	Agricultural Sciences	35	43	7
Animal Sciences	Agricultural Sciences	30	40	6
Agricultural Economics	Agricultural Sciences	9	13	4
Structural Biology	Biological and Biomedical Sciences	212	228	20
Human and Medical Genetics	Biological and Biomedical Sciences	200	214	17
Oncology and Cancer Biology	Biological and Biomedical Sciences	187	212	18
Immunology	Biological and Biomedical Sciences	180	196	18
Epidemiology	Biological and Biomedical Sciences	169	195	13
Biological Sciences, various	Biological and Biomedical Sciences	159	189	17
Bioinformatics and Computational Biology	Biological and Biomedical Sciences	166	182	15
Biophysics	Biological and Biomedical Sciences	163	181	16
Biomedical Sciences, various	Biological and Biomedical Sciences	152	175	15
Molecular Pharmacology	Biological and Biomedical Sciences	148	173	15
Molecular Genetics	Biological and Biomedical Sciences	153	170	18
Biomedical Sciences, general	Biological and Biomedical Sciences	141	166	17

Continued

Table 2.4 Continued

Discipline	Broad Field	Citations per faculty member	Citations per author of a journal article	Citations per journal article
Cell Biology	Biological and Biomedical Sciences	136	155	17
Pathology	Biological and Biomedical Sciences	133	155	15
Genetics	Biological and Biomedical Sciences	141	155	17
Developmental Biology	Biological and Biomedical Sciences	132	151	18
Molecular Biology	Biological and Biomedical Sciences	133	151	16
Biochemistry	Biological and Biomedical Sciences	121	141	15
Pharmacology	Biological and Biomedical Sciences	119	137	14
Biology/Biological Sciences, general	Biological and Biomedical Sciences	115	137	17
Neurobiology/ Neuroscience	Biological and Biomedical Sciences	114	128	15
Microbiology	Biological and Biomedical Sciences	110	127	14
Physiology, general	Biological and Biomedical Sciences	94	109	12
Toxicology	Biological and Biomedical Sciences	93	107	11
Oral Biology and Craniofacial Science	Biological and Biomedical Sciences	91	106	12
Evolutionary Biology	Biological and Biomedical Sciences	84	95	11
Ecology	Biological and Biomedical Sciences	83	93	11
Botany/Plant Biology	Biological and Biomedical Sciences	77	90	12
Pharmaceutical Sciences	Biological and Biomedical Sciences	65	85	9
Anatomy	Biological and Biomedical Sciences	54	72	11

Continued

Table 2.4 Continued

Discipline	Broad Field	Citations per faculty member	Citations per author of a journal article	Citations per journal article
Plant Pathology	Biological and Biomedical Sciences	56	68	10
Zoology	Biological and Biomedical Sciences	50	58	8
Cognitive Science	Biological and Biomedical Sciences	47	56	9
Entomology	Biological and Biomedical Sciences	38	49	7
Management	Business	10	17	5
Management Information Systems	Business	11	16	4
Business Administration	Business	7	13	5
Business, various	Business	6	11	4
Marketing	Business	6	10	4
Accounting	Business	4	9	4
Finance	Business	5	9	4
Mathematics Education	Education	7	14	5
Science Education	Education	7	13	4
Teacher-Education-Specific Levels	Education	3	10	4
Educational Evaluation and Research	Education	6	10	3
Special Education	Education	4	9	3
Education, general	Education	3	8	4
Teacher-Education-Specific Subject Areas	Education	2	6	3
Foundations of Education	Education	2	6	3
Educational Leadership and Administration	Education	2	5	3
Counselor Education	Education	1	4	2
Curriculum and Instruction	Education	1	4	2

Continued

Table 2.4 Continued

Discipline	Broad Field	Citations per faculty member	Citations per author of a journal article	Citations per journal article
Higher Education/ Higher Education Administration	Education	1	3	2
Materials Science and Engineering	Engineering	94	104	6
Agricultural/ Biological Engineering and Bioengineering	Engineering	89	103	9
Biomedical Engineering	Engineering	87	99	8
Chemical Engineering	Engineering	86	98	7
Electrical Engineering	Engineering	45	53	4
Engineering Mechanics	Engineering	43	49	5
Computer Engineering	Engineering	41	48	4
Engineering, general	Engineering	36	47	5
Environmental Engineering	Engineering	39	46	6
Mechanical Engineering	Engineering	36	43	4
Engineering, various	Engineering	31	42	4
Materials Engineering	Engineering	35	41	4
Aerospace Engineering	Engineering	30	35	3
Nuclear Engineering	Engineering	28	32	3
Civil Engineering	Engineering	24	29	4
Systems Engineering	Engineering	23	27	3
Operations Research	Engineering	16	20	3
Geological and Mining Engineering	Engineering	15	19	3
Industrial Engineering	Engineering	14	18	2
Nutrition Sciences	Family, Consumer, and Human Sciences	82	97	10
Health Promotion, Kinesiology, Exercise Science, and Rehab	Family, Consumer, and Human Sciences	31	46	7

Continued

Table 2.4 Continued

Discipline	Broad Field	Citations per faculty member	Citations per author of a journal article	Citations per journal article
Family and Human Sciences, various	Family, Consumer, and Human Sciences	31	43	8
Consumer and Human Sciences, various	Family, Consumer, and Human Sciences	16	25	5
Health, Physical Education, Recreation	Family, Consumer, and Human Sciences	15	25	5
Human Development and Family Studies, general	Family, Consumer, and Human Sciences	14	24	6
Architecture	Family, Consumer, and Human Sciences	6	18	5
Urban and Regional Planning	Family, Consumer, and Human Sciences	10	17	5
Architecture, Design, Planning, various	Family, Consumer, and Human Sciences	6	13	3
Communication and Communication Studies	Family, Consumer, and Human Sciences	5	12	4
Mass Communications/ Media Studies	Family, Consumer, and Human Sciences	4	11	4
Medical Sciences, various	Health Professions Sciences	81	142	13
Public Health	Health Professions Sciences	111	136	13
Pharmacy	Health Professions Sciences	81	109	11
Environmental Health Sciences	Health Professions Sciences	83	98	10
Health Professions, various	Health Professions Sciences	51	68	9
Veterinary Medical Sciences	Health Professions Sciences	37	44	6
Communication Disorders and Sciences	Health Professions Sciences	15	23	5
Speech and Hearing Sciences	Health Professions Sciences	14	20	5

Continued

Table 2.4 Continued

Discipline	Broad Field	Citations per faculty member	Citations per author of a journal article	Citations per journal article
Nursing	Health Professions Sciences	10	17	5
Near and Middle Eastern Languages and Cultures	Humanities	5	26	14
Music specialties	Humanities	2	16	9
Area and Ethnic Studies, various	Humanities	5	15	5
Asian Studies	Humanities	3	14	7
Ancient Studies	Humanities	3	14	7
Asian Languages	Humanities	3	14	6
Classics and Classical Languages	Humanities	1	11	6
Performing and Visual Arts, various	Humanities	1	10	5
Music, general	Humanities	1	9	5
Religion/Religious Studies	Humanities	2	9	5
Gender Studies	Humanities	2	9	4
Linguistics	Humanities	4	8	4
American Studies	Humanities	1	8	5
English Language and Literature	Humanities	1	8	5
Theatre Literature, History, and Criticism	Humanities	0	7	4
History	Humanities	1	7	4
Languages, various	Humanities	1	7	4
Composition, Rhetoric, and Writing	Humanities	1	6	4
Philosophy	Humanities	2	6	3
Art History and Criticism	Humanities	1	5	4
Italian Language and Literature	Humanities	1	5	4

Continued

Table 2.4 Continued

Discipline	Broad Field	Citations per faculty member	Citations per author of a journal article	Citations per journal article
Humanities/ Humanistic Studies, general	Humanities	1	5	3
Spanish Language and Literature	Humanities	0	5	3
Germanic Languages and Literatures	Humanities	1	3	3
Comparative Literature	Humanities	0	3	3
Theology/ Theological Studies	Humanities	0	2	2
French Language and Literature	Humanities	0	2	1
Slavic Languages and Literatures	Humanities	0	1	1
European Studies	Humanities	0	0	0
Environmental Sciences	Natural Resources and Conservation	48	60	8
Natural Resources	Natural Resources and Conservation	38	49	7
Fisheries Science	Natural Resources and Conservation	28	34	5
Forest Resources/ Forestry	Natural Resources and Conservation	24	31	5
Wildlife Science	Natural Resources and Conservation	23	28	4
Biostatistics	Physical and Mathematical Sciences	149	168	14
Chemical Sciences, various	Physical and Mathematical Sciences	152	168	11
Astronomy and Astrophysics	Physical and Mathematical Sciences	141	157	11
Chemistry	Physical and Mathematical Sciences	125	147	12
Applied Physics	Physical and Mathematical Sciences	96	107	6
Physics, general	Physical and Mathematical Sciences	72	83	5

Continued

Table 2.4 Continued

Discipline	Broad Field	Citations per faculty member	Citations per author of a journal article	Citations per journal article
Oceanography, Physical Sciences	Physical and Mathematical Sciences	69	77	10
Atmospheric Sciences and Meteorology	Physical and Mathematical Sciences	64	71	8
Computational Sciences	Physical and Mathematical Sciences	55	65	6
Marine Sciences	Physical and Mathematical Sciences	54	62	9
Geology/Earth Science, general	Physical and Mathematical Sciences	52	61	8
Geophysics	Physical and Mathematical Sciences	43	50	7
Statistics	Physical and Mathematical Sciences	36	43	7
Applied Mathematics	Physical and Mathematical Sciences	33	40	5
Computer Science	Physical and Mathematical Sciences	28	33	4
Information Science/ Studies	Physical and Mathematical Sciences	21	29	4
Information Technology/ Information Systems	Physical and Mathematical Sciences	18	23	3
Computer and Information Sciences, various	Physical and Mathematical Sciences	16	22	3
Mathematics	Physical and Mathematical Sciences	12	17	4
Psychology, general	Social and Behavioral Sciences	42	54	9
Psychology, various	Social and Behavioral Sciences	22	31	7
Public Policy	Social and Behavioral Sciences	18	31	7
Social Sciences, various	Social and Behavioral Sciences	17	30	7

Continued

Table 2.4   Continued

Discipline	Broad Field	Citations per faculty member	Citations per author of a journal article	Citations per journal article
Geography	Social and Behavioral Sciences	22	30	6
Clinical Psychology	Social and Behavioral Sciences	19	29	7
Anthropology	Social and Behavioral Sciences	12	21	6
Public Administration	Social and Behavioral Sciences	9	17	5
International Affairs and Development	Social and Behavioral Sciences	7	16	6
Economics, general	Social and Behavioral Sciences	9	14	4
Sociology	Social and Behavioral Sciences	8	13	5
Counseling Psychology	Social and Behavioral Sciences	7	12	4
Social Work/Social Welfare	Social and Behavioral Sciences	6	11	4
Applied Economics	Social and Behavioral Sciences	7	11	3
School Psychology	Social and Behavioral Sciences	7	11	4
Criminal Justice and Criminology	Social and Behavioral Sciences	5	10	3
Educational Psychology	Social and Behavioral Sciences	5	8	3
Political Science	Social and Behavioral Sciences	4	7	4

standard deviation units (z-scores) for the programs or people in a discipline and comparisons across disciplines should use z-scores rather than raw data). The biggest differences among Broad Fields likely reflect disciplines where some scholars publish their work in books rather than in journal articles. This effect can be significantly reduced by replacing faculty number as the denominator with the number of authors of journal articles. When this is done, the Broad Field results appear somewhat more comparable because the results for the book and journal fields (business, education, humanities, and social sciences) are much more comparable with the range of values in the journal-dominated disciplines than is the case for articles per faculty-member counts. However, there remains a substantial discipline and Broad Field effect on this metric, which renders it useless to compare performance across disciplines except in a statistically standardized space.

There is a good deal of colinearity of data on counts of articles and counts of citations, so the FSP 2008 database also measures citations per paper, which is analogous to the citation impact factor for journals but applied to individual articles. This index should be less influenced by the number of scholars in a field or by the number of articles published in the field and might be expected to provide a better basis for comparison across fields (table 2.4). This index is clearly the one that has the least problems in comparing performance among the Broad Fields, but there is still a dramatic effect across disciplines that suggests comparisons of citations/paper also should only be made in statistically standardized space.

What these results mean is that *discipline-specific* metrics for scholarly performance must be used if faculty members are to be held accountable to appropriate standards for their field of scholarship. The use of generalized performance metrics will advantage some disciplines over others in a manner that could seriously damage the research and scholarly enterprise. Simply put, simple metrics are too simplistic to be useful. This means that the popular H-index has little value except for comparing the performance of scholars within a discipline and should certainly never be used to assess faculty more broadly in relation to hiring, promotion, and tenure cases.

The final analysis of citation data presented here is another return-on-investment approach that looks at the number of citations of journal articles that result from $1 million of federal research funding from the agencies included in this study. The rationale here is that the federal government funds research to produce knowledge that has value, and it seems appropriate to use the citations garnered as a proxy for the significance of the research that was funded. As was the case for the analysis of publications in relation to research funding, the results of this comparison are so intriguing that the discipline detail is presented in full (table 2.5).

It is puzzling that $1 million of research in Structural Biology results in 580 citations, while in neurobiology it produces 345, especially as there are so many more neurobiologists at work than structural biologists, and that the same amount results in 946 citations in astronomy, but only 190 in computer science.

Table 2.5 Citations of journal articles by national, discipline quintile of the faculty

Discipline	Broad Field	Citations per million dollars of federal research grants
Food Science	Agricultural Sciences	800
Soil Science	Agricultural Sciences	785
Animal Sciences	Agricultural Sciences	717
Agronomy and Crop Science	Agricultural Sciences	698
Agriculture, various	Agricultural Sciences	607
Agricultural Economics	Agricultural Sciences	591
Horticulture	Agricultural Sciences	578
Plant Sciences	Agricultural Sciences	469
Epidemiology	Biological and Biomedical Sciences	674
Structural Biology	Biological and Biomedical Sciences	580
Bioinformatics and Computational Biology	Biological and Biomedical Sciences	574
Human and Medical Genetics	Biological and Biomedical Sciences	571
Ecology	Biological and Biomedical Sciences	552
Plant Pathology	Biological and Biomedical Sciences	546
Pathology	Biological and Biomedical Sciences	542
Evolutionary Biology	Biological and Biomedical Sciences	539
Biological Sciences, various	Biological and Biomedical Sciences	539
Biology/Biological Sciences, general	Biological and Biomedical Sciences	525
Oncology and Cancer Biology	Biological and Biomedical Sciences	517
Biomedical Sciences, general	Biological and Biomedical Sciences	513
Entomology	Biological and Biomedical Sciences	499

Continued

Table 2.5 Continued

Discipline	Broad Field	Citations per million dollars of federal research grants
Immunology	Biological and Biomedical Sciences	478
Botany/Plant Biology	Biological and Biomedical Sciences	446
Biomedical Sciences, various	Biological and Biomedical Sciences	443
Zoology	Biological and Biomedical Sciences	442
Biophysics	Biological and Biomedical Sciences	434
Genetics	Biological and Biomedical Sciences	426
Pharmaceutical Sciences	Biological and Biomedical Sciences	424
Toxicology	Biological and Biomedical Sciences	423
Pharmacology	Biological and Biomedical Sciences	397
Molecular Pharmacology	Biological and Biomedical Sciences	389
Cell Biology	Biological and Biomedical Sciences	383
Biochemistry	Biological and Biomedical Sciences	382
Molecular Biology	Biological and Biomedical Sciences	380
Anatomy	Biological and Biomedical Sciences	367
Developmental Biology	Biological and Biomedical Sciences	365
Molecular Genetics	Biological and Biomedical Sciences	363
Oral Biology and Craniofacial Science	Biological and Biomedical Sciences	362
Microbiology	Biological and Biomedical Sciences	354

Continued

Table 2.5 Continued

Discipline	Broad Field	Citations per million dollars of federal research grants
Neurobiology/Neuroscience	Biological and Biomedical Sciences	345
Physiology, general	Biological and Biomedical Sciences	333
Cognitive Science	Biological and Biomedical Sciences	292
Engineering, general	Engineering	664
Materials Science and Engineering	Engineering	657
Chemical Engineering	Engineering	568
Aerospace Engineering	Engineering	535
Agricultural/Biological Engineering and Bioengineering	Engineering	491
Mechanical Engineering	Engineering	488
Engineering Mechanics	Engineering	473
Engineering, various	Engineering	470
Geological and Mining Engineering	Engineering	459
Materials Engineering	Engineering	459
Nuclear Engineering	Engineering	450
Electrical Engineering	Engineering	426
Environmental Engineering	Engineering	398
Civil Engineering	Engineering	370
Biomedical Engineering	Engineering	363
Computer Engineering	Engineering	347
Systems Engineering	Engineering	260
Operations Research	Engineering	230
Industrial Engineering	Engineering	227
Consumer and Human Sciences, various	Family, Consumer, and Human Sciences	913
Health, Physical Education, Recreation	Family, Consumer, and Human Sciences	598
Urban and Regional Planning	Family, Consumer, and Human Sciences	587

Continued

Table 2.5 Continued

Discipline	Broad Field	*Citations per million dollars of federal research grants*
Nutrition Sciences	Family, Consumer, and Human Sciences	526
Architecture	Family, Consumer, and Human Sciences	492
Family and Human Sciences, various	Family, Consumer, and Human Sciences	453
Health Promotion, Kinesiology, Exercise Science, and Rehab	Family, Consumer, and Human Sciences	397
Architecture, Design, Planning, various	Family, Consumer, and Human Sciences	377
Communication and Communication Studies	Family, Consumer, and Human Sciences	281
Mass Communications/Media Studies	Family, Consumer, and Human Sciences	231
Human Development and Family Studies, general	Family, Consumer, and Human Sciences	229
Health Professions, various	Health Professions Sciences	763
Environmental Health Sciences	Health Professions Sciences	652
Medical Sciences, various	Health Professions Sciences	645
Pharmacy	Health Professions Sciences	579
Public Health	Health Professions Sciences	548
Veterinary Medical Sciences	Health Professions Sciences	421
Nursing	Health Professions Sciences	189
Speech and Hearing Sciences	Health Professions Sciences	123
Communication Disorders and Sciences	Health Professions Sciences	102
Forest Resources/Forestry	Natural Resources and Conservation	1,051
Natural Resources	Natural Resources and Conservation	600
Environmental Sciences	Natural Resources and Conservation	524
Wildlife Science	Natural Resources and Conservation	466
Fisheries Science	Natural Resources and Conservation	341

Continued

Table 2.5 Continued

Discipline	Broad Field	*Citations per million dollars of federal research grants*
Biostatistics	Physical and Mathematical Sciences	1,475
Astronomy and Astrophysics	Physical and Mathematical Sciences	946
Applied Physics	Physical and Mathematical Sciences	626
Physics, general	Physical and Mathematical Sciences	570
Chemical Sciences, various	Physical and Mathematical Sciences	564
Chemistry	Physical and Mathematical Sciences	524
Statistics	Physical and Mathematical Sciences	503
Geology/Earth Science, general	Physical and Mathematical Sciences	410
Computational Sciences	Physical and Mathematical Sciences	382
Applied Mathematics	Physical and Mathematical Sciences	314
Atmospheric Sciences and Meteorology	Physical and Mathematical Sciences	282
Marine Sciences	Physical and Mathematical Sciences	244
Geophysics	Physical and Mathematical Sciences	234
Information Science/Studies	Physical and Mathematical Sciences	233
Oceanography, Physical Sciences	Physical and Mathematical Sciences	215
Mathematics	Physical and Mathematical Sciences	199
Computer Science	Physical and Mathematical Sciences	190
Computer and Information Sciences, various	Physical and Mathematical Sciences	182

Continued

Table 2.5   Continued

Discipline	Broad Field	Citations per million dollars of federal research grants
Information Technology/ Information Systems	Physical and Mathematical Sciences	181
Criminal Justice and Criminology	Social and Behavioral Sciences	462
Public Policy	Social and Behavioral Sciences	441
International Affairs and Development	Social and Behavioral Sciences	384
Geography	Social and Behavioral Sciences	379
Economics, general	Social and Behavioral Sciences	361
Social Sciences, various	Social and Behavioral Sciences	357
Psychology, general	Social and Behavioral Sciences	323
Anthropology	Social and Behavioral Sciences	317
Clinical Psychology	Social and Behavioral Sciences	287
Public Administration	Social and Behavioral Sciences	275
Counseling Psychology	Social and Behavioral Sciences	262
Political Science	Social and Behavioral Sciences	261
Applied Economics	Social and Behavioral Sciences	250
Social Work/Social Welfare	Social and Behavioral Sciences	232
Psychology, various	Social and Behavioral Sciences	202
Sociology	Social and Behavioral Sciences	166
School Psychology	Social and Behavioral Sciences	79
Educational Psychology	Social and Behavioral Sciences	51

Federal Grants in Support of Research

Many universities pay close attention to the volume of federally sponsored research grants at their campus and these figures are often seen as
a measure of the quality of the scholarly endeavor. While that is almost
certainly the case when making comparisons among funding levels
within a discipline, the results in table 2.6 suggest that great caution
should be applied in making comparisons across disciplines (or departments) within a university.

This is especially the case when comparing grant dollars per faculty
member, which is the most commonly employed metric. While these
differences have long been appreciated in recognizing that it is unwise to

Table 2.6 Awards by national, discipline quintile of the faculty

Discipline	Broad Field	Grant dollars per grant ($)	Grant dollars per faculty member ($)	No. of grants held per 1,000 faculty	No. of grants held per 1,000 authors of journal articles
Plant Sciences	Agricultural Sciences	189,895	96,454	508	653
Horticulture	Agricultural Sciences	200,209	66,288	331	416
Agriculture, various	Agricultural Sciences	181,191	57,725	319	419
Soil Science	Agricultural Sciences	141,341	53,930	382	490
Agronomy and Crop Science	Agricultural Sciences	202,605	49,592	245	301
Food Science	Agricultural Sciences	164,957	43,364	263	331
Animal Sciences	Agricultural Sciences	159,135	42,415	267	351
Agricultural Economics	Agricultural Sciences	143,458	15,001	105	155
Molecular Genetics	Biological and Biomedical Sciences	283,615	420,825	1,484	1,653
Molecular Pharmacology	Biological and Biomedical Sciences	277,143	380,198	1,372	1,608
Immunology	Biological and Biomedical Sciences	303,683	377,740	1,244	1,354
Biophysics	Biological and Biomedical Sciences	272,447	376,097	1,380	1,526
Structural Biology	Biological and Biomedical Sciences	285,674	365,376	1,279	1,378
Developmental Biology	Biological and Biomedical Sciences	275,443	361,675	1,313	1,501
Oncology and Cancer Biology	Biological and Biomedical Sciences	286,796	361,253	1,260	1,433

Continued

Table 2.6 Continued

Discipline	Broad Field	Grant dollars per grant ($)	Grant dollars per faculty member ($)	No. of grants held per 1,000 faculty	No. of grants held per 1,000 authors of journal articles
Cell Biology	Biological and Biomedical Sciences	273,779	355,875	1,300	1,478
Human and Medical Genetics	Biological and Biomedical Sciences	294,819	350,445	1,189	1,273
Molecular Biology	Biological and Biomedical Sciences	270,360	348,340	1,288	1,463
Biomedical Sciences, various	Biological and Biomedical Sciences	304,894	343,634	1,127	1,297
Neurobiology/ Neuroscience	Biological and Biomedical Sciences	279,390	330,745	1,184	1,334
Genetics	Biological and Biomedical Sciences	255,666	330,567	1,293	1,421
Biochemistry	Biological and Biomedical Sciences	254,445	317,514	1,248	1,448
Microbiology	Biological and Biomedical Sciences	270,415	311,454	1,152	1,325
Pharmacology	Biological and Biomedical Sciences	286,824	299,483	1,044	1,202
Biological Sciences, various	Biological and Biomedical Sciences	281,227	294,264	1,046	1,246
Bioinformatics and Computational Biology	Biological and Biomedical Sciences	225,113	289,856	1,288	1,406
Physiology, general	Biological and Biomedical Sciences	285,278	281,669	987	1,145

Continued

Table 2.6 Continued

Discipline	Broad Field	Grant dollars per grant ($)	Grant dollars per faculty member ($)	No. of grants held per 1,000 faculty	No. of grants held per 1,000 authors of journal articles
Biomedical Sciences, general	Biological and Biomedical Sciences	286,919	274,434	956	1,130
Epidemiology	Biological and Biomedical Sciences	397,571	250,807	631	728
Oral Biology and Craniofacial Science	Biological and Biomedical Sciences	293,584	250,791	854	1,000
Pathology	Biological and Biomedical Sciences	297,249	246,440	829	963
Toxicology	Biological and Biomedical Sciences	257,224	220,687	858	982
Biology/Biological Sciences, general	Biological and Biomedical Sciences	222,888	220,036	987	1,169
Botany/Plant Biology	Biological and Biomedical Sciences	163,870	173,395	1,058	1,226
Cognitive Science	Biological and Biomedical Sciences	200,241	161,027	804	962
Evolutionary Biology	Biological and Biomedical Sciences	121,762	156,564	1,286	1,448
Pharmaceutical Sciences	Biological and Biomedical Sciences	244,567	153,170	626	820
Ecology	Biological and Biomedical Sciences	129,521	149,902	1,157	1,302
Anatomy	Biological and Biomedical Sciences	249,625	148,398	594	785

Continued

Table 2.6 Continued

Discipline	Broad Field	Grant dollars per grant ($)	Grant dollars per faculty member ($)	No. of grants held per 1,000 faculty	No. of grants held per 1,000 authors of journal articles
Zoology	Biological and Biomedical Sciences	129,693	113,074	872	1,008
Plant Pathology	Biological and Biomedical Sciences	197,296	102,385	519	634
Entomology	Biological and Biomedical Sciences	150,108	76,935	513	658
Biomedical Engineering	Engineering	251,337	239,139	951	1,083
Agricultural/ Biological Engineering and Bioengineering	Engineering	215,047	182,078	847	977
Chemical Engineering	Engineering	134,933	151,895	1,126	1,272
Materials Science and Engineering	Engineering	132,243	142,560	1,078	1,194
Computer Engineering	Engineering	114,963	119,005	1,035	1,191
Electrical Engineering	Engineering	114,643	106,544	929	1,077
Environmental Engineering	Engineering	138,367	97,340	703	841
Engineering Mechanics	Engineering	100,409	90,022	897	1,032
Systems Engineering	Engineering	99,079	87,830	886	1,055
Materials Engineering	Engineering	111,187	76,441	688	802
Mechanical Engineering	Engineering	105,756	73,664	697	824
Operations Research	Engineering	96,454	70,187	728	910

Continued

Table 2.6 Continued

Discipline	Broad Field	Grant dollars per grant ($)	Grant dollars per faculty member ($)	No. of grants held per 1,000 faculty	No. of grants held per 1,000 authors of journal articles
Engineering, various	Engineering	122,919	66,647	542	730
Civil Engineering	Engineering	110,414	64,821	587	715
Industrial Engineering	Engineering	93,574	62,604	669	831
Nuclear Engineering	Engineering	177,672	62,127	350	405
Aerospace Engineering	Engineering	95,792	56,353	588	688
Engineering, general	Engineering	110,622	54,447	492	645
Geological and Mining Engineering	Engineering	77,207	32,764	424	549
Nutrition Sciences	Family, Consumer, and Human Sciences	266,880	156,341	586	689
Health Promotion, Kinesiology, Exercise Science, and Rehab	Family, Consumer, and Human Sciences	256,740	78,127	304	448
Family and Human Sciences, various	Family, Consumer, and Human Sciences	275,458	67,642	246	342
Human Development and Family Studies, general	Family, Consumer, and Human Sciences	292,202	61,069	209	357
Health, Physical Education, and Recreation	Family, Consumer, and Human Sciences	298,725	25,467	85	141
Communication and Communication Studies	Family, Consumer, and Human Sciences	192,823	18,246	95	212
Consumer and Human Sciences, various	Family, Consumer, and Human Sciences	172,305	17,571	102	161

Continued

Table 2.6 Continued

Discipline	Broad Field	Grant dollars per grant ($)	Grant dollars per faculty member ($)	No. of grants held per 1,000 faculty	No. of grants held per 1,000 authors of journal articles
Urban and Regional Planning	Family, Consumer, and Human Sciences	116,154	16,593	143	249
Architecture, Design, Planning, various	Family, Consumer, and Human Sciences	97,034	16,241	167	357
Mass Communications/ Media Studies	Family, Consumer, and Human Sciences	138,133	15,217	110	334
Architecture	Family, Consumer, and Human Sciences	152,154	11,627	76	236
Public Health	Health Professions Sciences	351,054	202,235	576	704
Communication Disorders and Sciences	Health Professions Sciences	349,373	149,483	428	652
Pharmacy	Health Professions Sciences	289,781	139,216	480	650
Environmental Health Sciences	Health Professions Sciences	285,827	126,645	443	526
Medical Sciences, various	Health Professions Sciences	295,464	126,047	427	745
Speech and Hearing Sciences	Health Professions Sciences	306,550	117,571	384	529
Veterinary Medical Sciences	Health Professions Sciences	236,731	86,816	367	442
Health Professions, various	Health Professions Sciences	280,907	66,801	238	318

Continued

Table 2.6 Continued

Discipline	Broad Field	Grant dollars per grant ($)	Grant dollars per faculty member ($)	No. of grants held per 1,000 faculty	No. of grants held per 1,000 authors of journal articles
Nursing	Health Professions Sciences	292,998	52,273	178	313
Environmental Sciences	Natural Resources and Conservation	122,834	92,263	751	939
Fisheries Science	Natural Resources and Conservation	167,762	82,477	492	601
Natural Resources	Natural Resources and Conservation	119,510	62,516	523	679
Wildlife Science	Natural Resources and Conservation	135,975	49,336	363	443
Forest Resources/ Forestry	Natural Resources and Conservation	104,429	23,049	221	278
Oceanography, Physical Sciences	Physical and Mathematical Sciences	159,909	322,457	2,016	2,249
Chemical Sciences, various	Physical and Mathematical Sciences	188,355	269,652	1,432	1,579
Chemistry	Physical and Mathematical Sciences	192,408	238,168	1,238	1,462
Atmospheric Sciences and Meteorology	Physical and Mathematical Sciences	141,461	226,825	1,603	1,778
Marine Sciences	Physical and Mathematical Sciences	144,620	221,058	1,529	1,768
Geophysics	Physical and Mathematical Sciences	114,054	184,855	1,621	1,860

Continued

Table 2.6 Continued

Discipline	Broad Field	Grant dollars per grant ($)	Grant dollars per faculty member ($)	No. of grants held per 1,000 faculty	No. of grants held per 1,000 authors of journal articles
Applied Physics	Physical and Mathematical Sciences	155,806	153,252	984	1,098
Astronomy and Astrophysics	Physical and Mathematical Sciences	126,887	149,082	1,175	1,311
Computer Science	Physical and Mathematical Sciences	120,503	145,620	1,208	1,467
Computational Sciences	Physical and Mathematical Sciences	132,543	142,908	1,078	1,278
Geology/Earth Science, general	Physical and Mathematical Sciences	86,569	127,267	1,470	1,724
Physics, general	Physical and Mathematical Sciences	149,990	126,543	844	968
Applied Mathematics	Physical and Mathematical Sciences	99,694	105,287	1,056	1,280
Biostatistics	Physical and Mathematical Sciences	229,392	100,772	439	496
Information Technology/ Information Systems	Physical and Mathematical Sciences	137,612	98,192	714	916
Information Science/Studies	Physical and Mathematical Sciences	124,294	91,274	734	1,012
Computer and Information Sciences, various	Physical and Mathematical Sciences	108,273	87,472	808	1,116
Statistics	Physical and Mathematical Sciences	109,578	71,423	652	788

Continued

Table 2.6 Continued

Discipline	Broad Field	Grant dollars per grant ($)	Grant dollars per faculty member ($)	No. of grants held per 1,000 faculty	No. of grants held per 1,000 authors of journal articles
Mathematics	Physical and Mathematical Sciences	71,682	60,919	850	1,182
Psychology, general	Social and Behavioral Sciences	240,309	131,240	546	693
Psychology, various	Social and Behavioral Sciences	304,659	109,128	358	506
Educational Psychology	Social and Behavioral Sciences	405,941	95,697	236	385
School Psychology	Social and Behavioral Sciences	347,507	82,792	238	384
Clinical Psychology	Social and Behavioral Sciences	328,147	66,798	204	309
Geography	Social and Behavioral Sciences	96,319	58,933	612	814
Social Sciences, various	Social and Behavioral Sciences	121,196	47,936	396	688
Sociology	Social and Behavioral Sciences	143,203	47,660	333	551
Public Policy	Social and Behavioral Sciences	183,184	40,013	218	379
Anthropology	Social and Behavioral Sciences	64,654	36,298	561	1,028
Public Administration	Social and Behavioral Sciences	211,487	32,280	153	299

Continued

Table 2.6   Continued

Discipline	Broad Field	Grant dollars per grant ($)	Grant dollars per faculty member ($)	No. of grants held per 1,000 faculty	No. of grants held per 1,000 authors of journal articles
Applied Economics	Social and Behavioral Sciences	265,494	27,896	105	165
Social Work/Social Welfare	Social and Behavioral Sciences	304,127	27,573	91	155
Economics, general	Social and Behavioral Sciences	122,932	25,694	209	314
Counseling Psychology	Social and Behavioral Sciences	229,107	25,074	109	195
International Affairs and Development	Social and Behavioral Sciences	112,044	18,521	165	366
Political Science	Social and Behavioral Sciences	76,850	13,532	176	361
Criminal Justice and Criminology	Social and Behavioral Sciences	101,043	11,631	115	212

compare funding levels between physical and social sciences, less attention has been paid to the very real differences in funding availability within broadly similar disciplines. These render comparisons of expenditure data among faculty members or departments almost meaningless unless they are adjusted to reflect disciplinary norms. On most campuses, administrators and faculty fail to make such adjustments when discussing success in obtaining external support for research.

Some of the factors underlying the differences in funding per faculty member among closely allied disciplines will now be considered, further based on empirical observations. The data in table 2.6 show that the average size of a grant varies significantly among disciplines, which further reinforces the fact that comparisons of performance need to be adjusted to discipline level norms. However, the total amount of sponsored research reflects not only the *average size* of a grant but also the *number* of grants held by faculty. It would be useful to measure the availability of grant funding, and this has been done by looking at the number of grants awarded per thousand faculty members in PhD programs in each discipline. These data show that not only are grants in some fields much larger but that grants are also more plentiful. Comparison of the range of values for the Broad Fields (table 2.6) shows huge differences among these areas of scholarly endeavor (including among fields such as biomedical science, engineering, and physical science that are all expected to succeed in obtaining external funding for research).

Once more, the inescapable conclusion to be drawn is that performance standards must be defined at the level of the discipline and that comparisons of performance among faculty in different disciplines can only reasonably be made in standardized statistical space.

Scholarship Published as a Book

For this discussion, the data on books have been limited to the Broad Fields: business; education; family, consumer, and human sciences; health professions sciences; humanities; and social and behavioral sciences where most of book publishing occurs. The results for the number of faculty who authored or edited a book, the number of books produced, the percentage of faculty in the discipline who produced a book, and the average number of books produced by those who authored a book are presented in table 2.7.

The same ten disciplines top the lists of the number of authors of books (history, English, political science, sociology, psychology, anthropology, philosophy, economics, business administration, and religion/religious Studies, in rank order) and the numbers of volumes produced (history, English, political science, sociology, psychology, philosophy, economics, anthropology, business administration, and religion/religious studies, in rank order).

Although discussions of scholarship in the humanities have long focused on the importance of books, it is striking that five (or six depending how one views history) of the top disciplines for book publishing are social and behavioral science fields. This reinforces the importance of including data on scholarly books in any assessment of productivity or quality. Results for the percentage of faculty to whom a book was attributed range from a high of 53 percent in religion/religious studies to a low of 9 percent in nutrition sciences. These results suggest that a six-year window for book publishing captures a large portion of the scholarly activity and that a ten-year

Table 2.7 Distribution of faculty performance by national, discipline-quintile-top private university

Discipline	Broad Field	No. of faculty in the discipline who authored or edited a book, 2003–2008	Total no. of books authored or edited	Percentage of faculty in the discipline who authored or edited a book	Average no. of books authored or edited by each author
History	Humanities	2,266	5,126	44.4	2.3
English Language and Literature	Humanities	1,972	4,089	40.2	2.1
Political Science	Social and Behavioral Sciences	1,297	2,851	40.3	2.2
Sociology	Social and Behavioral Sciences	856	1,796	33.3	2.1
Economics, general	Social and Behavioral Sciences	706	1,716	21.2	2.4
Philosophy	Humanities	724	1,709	37.2	2.4
Psychology, general	Social and Behavioral Sciences	760	1,539	18.8	2.0
Anthropology	Social and Behavioral Sciences	765	1,427	33.9	1.9
Religion/Religious Studies	Humanities	526	1,272	48.7	2.4
Comparative Literature	Humanities	457	1,008	40.7	2.2
Public Policy	Social and Behavioral Sciences	411	945	29.8	2.3
Theology/ Theological Studies	Humanities	404	918	38.0	2.3
Business Administration	Business	440	915	13.7	2.1
Curriculum and Instruction	Education	384	860	20.9	2.2
Art History and Criticism	Humanities	396	844	36.7	2.1
Management	Business	330	752	16.7	2.3
Communication and Communication Studies	Family, Consumer, and Human Sciences	345	713	26.1	2.1
American Studies	Humanities	282	662	42.0	2.3

Continued

Table 2.7 Continued

Discipline	Broad Field	No. of faculty in the discipline who authored or edited a book, 2003–2008	Total no. of books authored or edited	Percentage of faculty in the discipline who authored or edited a book	Average no. of books authored or edited by each author
Teacher-Education-Specific Subject Areas	Education	280	643	15.9	2.3
Educational Leadership and Administration	Education	270	641	20.1	2.4
Area and Ethnic Studies, various	Humanities	259	589	37.1	2.3
Criminal Justice and Criminology	Social and Behavioral Sciences	247	555	35.5	2.2
Public Administration	Social and Behavioral Sciences	215	540	28.3	2.5
Classics and Classical Languages	Humanities	254	487	41.4	1.9
Social Work/Social Welfare	Social and Behavioral Sciences	261	473	17.8	1.8
International Affairs and Development	Social and Behavioral Sciences	196	453	32.1	2.3
Education, general	Education	212	452	19.9	2.1
Linguistics	Humanities	251	441	29.0	1.8
Humanities/ Humanistic Studies, general	Humanities	243	437	30.6	1.8
Spanish Language and Literature	Humanities	224	403	26.6	1.8
Social Sciences, various	Social and Behavioral Sciences	190	402	28.4	2.1
Psychology, various	Social and Behavioral Sciences	208	401	14.6	1.9
Human Development and Family Studies, general	Family, Consumer, and Human Sciences	192	398	16.9	2.1
Nursing	Health Professions Sciences	233	397	8.2	1.7

Continued

Table 2.7 Continued

Discipline	Broad Field	No. of faculty in the discipline who authored or edited a book, 2003–2008	Total no. of books authored or edited	Percentage of faculty in the discipline who authored or edited a book	Average no. of books authored or edited by each author
Special Education	Education	154	370	21.4	2.4
French Language and Literature	Humanities	196	368	32.0	1.9
Geography	Social and Behavioral Sciences	207	363	19.8	1.8
Near and Middle Eastern Languages and Cultures	Humanities	183	361	46.3	2.0
Health Promotion, Kinesiology, Exercise Science, and Rehab	Family, Consumer, and Human Sciences	176	354	9.0	2.0
Asian Studies	Humanities	190	351	33.3	1.8
Clinical Psychology	Social and Behavioral Sciences	182	349	15.4	1.9
Educational Psychology	Social and Behavioral Sciences	151	345	19.1	2.3
Music, general	Humanities	178	308	19.6	1.7
Gender Studies	Humanities	165	289	34.6	1.8
Mass Communications/ Media Studies	Family, Consumer, and Human Sciences	164	278	17.5	1.7
Performing and Visual Arts, various	Humanities	134	274	23.4	2.0
Composition, Rhetoric, and Writing	Humanities	131	273	26.9	2.1
Germanic Languages and Literatures	Humanities	146	260	32.7	1.8
Business, various	Business	127	257	15.9	2.0
Ancient Studies	Humanities	114	243	38.0	2.1

Continued

Table 2.7 Continued

Discipline	Broad Field	No. of faculty in the discipline who authored or edited a book, 2003–2008	Total no. of books authored or edited	Percentage of faculty in the discipline who authored or edited a book	Average no. of books authored or edited by each author
Urban and Regional Planning	Family, Consumer, and Human Sciences	128	236	23.1	1.8
Public Health	Health Professions Sciences	126	227	10.3	1.8
Finance	Business	95	222	12.0	2.3
Accounting	Business	93	218	13.7	2.3
Asian Languages	Humanities	117	211	33.1	1.8
Foundations of Education	Education	84	188	28.3	2.2
Marketing	Business	86	186	11.9	2.2
Architecture	Family, Consumer, and Human Sciences	95	184	20.7	1.9
Languages, various	Humanities	95	177	21.9	1.9
Theatre Literature, History, and Criticism	Humanities	88	171	20.9	1.9
Health Professions, various	Health Professions Sciences	103	165	12.6	1.6
Counseling Psychology	Social and Behavioral Sciences	88	158	18.9	1.8
Counselor Education	Education	76	146	16.9	1.9
Nutrition Sciences	Family, Consumer, and Human Sciences	77	143	6.4	1.9
Medical Sciences, various	Health Professions Sciences	91	138	4.2	1.5
Teacher-Education-Specific Levels	Education	62	136	15.2	2.2
Architecture, Design, Planning, various	Family, Consumer, and Human Sciences	59	133	12.5	2.3

Continued

Table 2.7 Continued

Discipline	Broad Field	No. of faculty in the discipline who authored or edited a book, 2003–2008	Total no. of books authored or edited	Percentage of faculty in the discipline who authored or edited a book	Average no. of books authored or edited by each author
Music specialties	Humanities	81	133	19.9	1.6
Higher Education/ Higher Education Administration	Education	62	128	24.4	2.1
Management Information Systems	Business	65	128	10.9	2.0
School Psychology	Social and Behavioral Sciences	65	121	20.4	1.9
Veterinary Medical Sciences	Health Professions Sciences	58	111	5.5	1.9
Educational Evaluation and Research	Education	53	101	19.5	1.9
Science Education	Education	48	100	19.6	2.1
Slavic Languages and Literatures	Humanities	59	100	31.4	1.7
Italian Language and Literature	Humanities	44	87	37.6	2.0
Speech and Hearing Sciences	Health Professions Sciences	53	76	12.5	1.4
European Studies	Humanities	37	75	33.9	2.0
Family and Human Sciences, various	Family, Consumer, and Human Sciences	44	68	13.0	1.5
Health, Physical Education, Recreation	Family, Consumer, and Human Sciences	42	67	9.7	1.6
Applied Economics	Social and Behavioral Sciences	34	63	12.3	1.9
Consumer and Human Sciences, various	Family, Consumer, and Human Sciences	34	63	11.2	1.9
Mathematics Education	Education	23	59	10.3	2.6

Continued

Table 2.7   Continued

Discipline	Broad Field	No. of faculty in the discipline who authored or edited a book, 2003–2008	Total no. of books authored or edited	Percentage of faculty in the discipline who authored or edited a book	Average no. of books authored or edited by each author
Communication Disorders and Sciences	Health Professions Sciences	35	53	8.7	1.5
Environmental Health Sciences	Health Professions Sciences	32	46	5.6	1.4
Pharmacy	Health Professions Sciences	19	32	5.0	1.7

window, toward which the FSP database is heading, will likely provide a representative sample.

Productivity can also be measured as the number of books produced per person, and there are two reasonable denominators to use in such studies. First is the number of faculty; second, the number of authors. The second of these has the advantage that fields in which faculty may publish either books or articles are not disadvantaged. Based on books per book author, productivity levels are impressive, ranging from the highest average for a discipline of 2.55 books in accounting to a low of 1.47 books in environmental health sciences (table 2.7).

Honorific Awards in Recognition of Scholarly Performance

The 1995 NRC study included data on prestigious honors and awards and these data proved valuable to measure program quality in the lettered disciplines (for which data on books were not available). FSP 2008 includes a much wider range of honors and awards than were compiled for NRC 1995 and these are designed to be used within disciplines as the availability of awards is by no means uniform across disciplines (table 2.8).

For that reason, comparisons of success in gaining awards need to be made in standardized statistical space. Table 2.8 provides information on the number of awards held by the faculty in each discipline and the number of faculty members holding at least one award. Obviously these

Table 2.8 Distribution of faculty performance by national, discipline-quintile-top public university

Discipline	Broad Field	No. of faculty with honorific award	Total no. of honorific awards held	Percentage of faculty in the discipline holding an honorific award	Awards held per 1,000 faculty in the discipline
History	Humanities	1,545	2,545	30	499
English Language and Literature	Humanities	833	1,218	17	249
Chemistry	Physical and Mathematical Sciences	825	1,635	17	334
Physics, general	Physical and Mathematical Sciences	811	1,471	15	278
Neurobiology/ Neuroscience	Biological and Biomedical Sciences	744	1,230	11	184
Mathematics	Physical and Mathematical Sciences	664	1,123	12	211
Molecular Biology	Biological and Biomedical Sciences	633	1,129	10	185
Mechanical Engineering	Engineering	543	800	15	216
Political Science	Social and Behavioral Sciences	527	760	16	236
Biology/Biological Sciences, general	Biological and Biomedical Sciences	522	979	9	174
Cell Biology	Biological and Biomedical Sciences	510	915	10	179
Biochemistry	Biological and Biomedical Sciences	487	935	10	199
Anthropology	Social and Behavioral Sciences	484	727	21	322

Continued

Table 2.8 Continued

Discipline	Broad Field	No. of faculty with honorific award	Total no. of honorific awards held	Percentage of faculty in the discipline holding an honorific award	Awards held per 1,000 faculty in the discipline
Biophysics	Biological and Biomedical Sciences	425	890	19	399
Computer Science	Physical and Mathematical Sciences	408	606	9	137
Sociology	Social and Behavioral Sciences	381	545	15	212
Economics, general	Social and Behavioral Sciences	380	567	11	170
Psychology, general	Social and Behavioral Sciences	348	534	9	132
Electrical Engineering	Engineering	347	502	7	104
Civil Engineering	Engineering	344	497	13	186
Materials Science and Engineering	Engineering	335	496	15	221
Geology/Earth Science, general	Physical and Mathematical Sciences	332	535	12	193
Astronomy and Astrophysics	Physical and Mathematical Sciences	315	564	19	345
Chemical Engineering	Engineering	315	506	16	261
Philosophy	Humanities	315	433	16	223
Art History and Criticism	Humanities	297	466	28	432
Microbiology	Biological and Biomedical Sciences	291	502	9	151
Biomedical Sciences, general	Biological and Biomedical Sciences	286	495	8	136

Continued

Table 2.8 Continued

Discipline	Broad Field	No. of faculty with honorific award	Total no. of honorific awards held	Percentage of faculty in the discipline holding an honorific award	Awards held per 1,000 faculty in the discipline
Ecology	Biological and Biomedical Sciences	279	436	14	214
Statistics	Physical and Mathematical Sciences	273	397	20	286
Chemical Sciences, various	Physical and Mathematical Sciences	255	502	26	509
Comparative Literature	Humanities	247	364	22	324
Agricultural/ Biological Engineering and Bioengineering	Engineering	246	372	17	259
Genetics	Biological and Biomedical Sciences	245	430	10	183
Bioinformatics and Computational Biology	Biological and Biomedical Sciences	227	384	17	282
Evolutionary Biology	Biological and Biomedical Sciences	225	352	16	255
Animal Sciences	Agricultural Sciences	224	318	15	212
Computer Engineering	Engineering	222	310	7	101
Environmental Engineering	Engineering	212	334	13	212
Environmental Sciences	Natural Resources and Conservation	206	321	10	159
Applied Mathematics	Physical and Mathematical Sciences	204	354	15	265

Continued

Table 2.8 Continued

Discipline	Broad Field	No. of faculty with honorific award	Total no. of honorific awards held	Percentage of faculty in the discipline holding an honorific award	Awards held per 1,000 faculty in the discipline
Physiology, general	Biological and Biomedical Sciences	199	296	7	104
Religion/ Religious Studies	Humanities	195	307	18	284
Aerospace Engineering	Engineering	188	260	15	203
Humanities/ Humanistic Studies, general	Humanities	172	252	22	317
Industrial Engineering	Engineering	172	273	17	277
Biomedical Engineering	Engineering	171	228	9	115
Nutrition Sciences	Family, Consumer, and Human Sciences	166	229	14	189
Area and Ethnic Studies, various	Humanities	165	248	24	355
Classics and Classical Languages	Humanities	161	253	26	413
American Studies	Humanities	160	237	24	353
Natural Resources	Natural Resources and Conservation	152	241	9	143
Applied Physics	Physical and Mathematical Sciences	151	263	18	308
Public Policy	Social and Behavioral Sciences	149	220	11	160
Developmental Biology	Biological and Biomedical Sciences	146	261	10	182

Continued

Table 2.8 Continued

Discipline	Broad Field	No. of faculty with honorific award	Total no. of honorific awards held	Percentage of faculty in the discipline holding an honorific award	Awards held per 1,000 faculty in the discipline
Immunology	Biological and Biomedical Sciences	143	255	8	139
Asian Studies	Humanities	141	233	25	409
Business Administration	Business	141	194	4	60
Pharmacology	Biological and Biomedical Sciences	138	235	6	102
Geography	Social and Behavioral Sciences	137	196	13	187
Music, general	Humanities	137	215	15	236
Biostatistics	Physical and Mathematical Sciences	127	158	16	198
Computational Sciences	Physical and Mathematical Sciences	124	224	16	287
Engineering, various	Engineering	122	174	9	124
Food Science	Agricultural Sciences	121	186	16	246
Public Health	Health Professions Sciences	117	168	10	137
Communication and Communication Studies	Family, Consumer, and Human Sciences	116	161	9	122
Social Sciences, various	Social and Behavioral Sciences	115	185	17	276
Oceanography, Physical Sciences	Physical and Mathematical Sciences	109	215	10	197

Continued

Table 2.8 Continued

Discipline	Broad Field	No. of faculty with honorific award	Total no. of honorific awards held	Percentage of faculty in the discipline holding an honorific award	Awards held per 1,000 faculty in the discipline
Agricultural Economics	Agricultural Sciences	108	142	16	209
Curriculum and Instruction	Education	107	131	6	71
Teacher-Education-Specific Subject Areas	Education	106	126	6	71
Information Science/Studies	Physical and Mathematical Sciences	105	136	11	147
Botany/Plant Biology	Biological and Biomedical Sciences	104	147	10	145
Medical Sciences, various	Health Professions Sciences	103	162	5	74
Performing and Visual Arts, various	Humanities	102	136	18	238
Management	Business	100	143	5	72
Epidemiology	Biological and Biomedical Sciences	98	133	7	97
Pathology	Biological and Biomedical Sciences	97	155	5	79
Gender Studies	Humanities	94	139	20	291
Health Promotion, Kinesiology, Exercise Science, and Rehab	Family, Consumer, and Human Sciences	94	125	5	64
Operations Research	Engineering	94	145	20	316
French Language and Literature	Humanities	93	126	15	206

Continued

Table 2.8 Continued

Discipline	Broad Field	No. of faculty with honorific award	Total no. of honorific awards held	Percentage of faculty in the discipline holding an honorific award	Awards held per 1,000 faculty in the discipline
Marine Sciences	Physical and Mathematical Sciences	91	140	7	104
Entomology	Biological and Biomedical Sciences	90	135	10	154
Human Development and Family Studies, general	Family, Consumer, and Human Sciences	86	116	8	102
Ancient Studies	Humanities	85	132	28	440
Cognitive Science	Biological and Biomedical Sciences	84	130	12	181
Asian Languages	Humanities	83	131	24	371
Biological Sciences, various	Biological and Biomedical Sciences	82	135	11	179
Engineering Mechanics	Engineering	80	111	17	239
Public Administration	Social and Behavioral Sciences	80	117	11	154
Near and Middle Eastern Languages and Cultures	Humanities	79	122	20	309
Pharmaceutical Sciences	Biological and Biomedical Sciences	79	112	5	77
Nursing	Health Professions Sciences	76	88	3	31
Biomedical Sciences, various	Biological and Biomedical Sciences	75	112	7	109

Continued

Table 2.8 Continued

Discipline	Broad Field	No. of faculty with honorific award	Total no. of honorific awards held	Percentage of faculty in the discipline holding an honorific award	Awards held per 1,000 faculty in the discipline
Human and Medical Genetics	Biological and Biomedical Sciences	74	144	12	226
Oncology and Cancer Biology	Biological and Biomedical Sciences	74	163	8	174
Spanish Language and Literature	Humanities	74	89	9	106
International Affairs and Development	Social and Behavioral Sciences	73	89	12	146
Horticulture	Agricultural Sciences	72	86	12	145
Linguistics	Humanities	72	100	8	116
Toxicology	Biological and Biomedical Sciences	72	94	5	67
Germanic Languages and Literatures	Humanities	69	87	15	195
Criminal Justice and Criminology	Social and Behavioral Sciences	68	97	10	140
Agronomy and Crop Science	Agricultural Sciences	66	87	7	91
Atmospheric Sciences and Meteorology	Physical and Mathematical Sciences	63	111	8	147
Molecular Genetics	Biological and Biomedical Sciences	63	98	8	122
Educational Leadership and Administration	Education	62	80	5	60
Composition, Rhetoric, and Writing	Humanities	61	91	13	187

Continued

Table 2.8 Continued

Discipline	Broad Field	No. of faculty with honorific award	Total no. of honorific awards held	Percentage of faculty in the discipline holding an honorific award	Awards held per 1,000 faculty in the discipline
Music specialties	Humanities	61	94	15	231
Psychology, various	Social and Behavioral Sciences	60	77	4	54
Engineering, general	Engineering	59	100	12	195
Health Professions, various	Health Professions Sciences	58	77	7	94
Slavic Languages and Literatures	Humanities	58	99	31	527
Social Work/ Social Welfare	Social and Behavioral Sciences	58	66	4	45
Education, general	Education	56	65	5	61
Urban and Regional Planning	Family, Consumer, and Human Sciences	56	66	10	119
Systems Engineering	Engineering	55	87	12	190
Geophysics	Physical and Mathematical Sciences	54	95	12	214
Mass Communications/ Media Studies	Family, Consumer, and Human Sciences	54	70	6	75
Theology/ Theological Studies	Humanities	53	83	5	78
Architecture	Family, Consumer, and Human Sciences	49	74	11	162
Business, various	Business	48	65	6	81
Soil Science	Agricultural Sciences	46	63	7	100

Continued

Table 2.8 Continued

Discipline	Broad Field	No. of faculty with honorific award	Total no. of honorific awards held	Percentage of faculty in the discipline holding an honorific award	Awards held per 1,000 faculty in the discipline
Structural Biology	Biological and Biomedical Sciences	46	86	14	270
Forest Resources/ Forestry	Natural Resources and Conservation	45	53	6	65
Architecture, Design, Planning, various	Family, Consumer, and Human Sciences	40	52	8	110
Educational Psychology	Social and Behavioral Sciences	39	44	5	56
Languages, various	Humanities	39	51	9	118
Theatre Literature, History, and Criticism	Humanities	39	48	9	114
Foundations of Education	Education	38	58	13	195
Veterinary Medical Sciences	Health Professions Sciences	38	53	4	50
Plant Sciences	Agricultural Sciences	37	46	6	73
Nuclear Engineering	Engineering	36	57	12	186
Pharmacy	Health Professions Sciences	36	69	9	180
Plant Pathology	Biological and Biomedical Sciences	36	41	7	78
Finance	Business	33	51	4	64
Molecular Pharmacology	Biological and Biomedical Sciences	33	51	7	107

Continued

Table 2.8 Continued

Discipline	Broad Field	No. of faculty with honorific award	Total no. of honorific awards held	Percentage of faculty in the discipline holding an honorific award	Awards held per 1,000 faculty in the discipline
Anatomy	Biological and Biomedical Sciences	32	39	4	54
Management Information Systems	Business	32	42	5	70
Zoology	Biological and Biomedical Sciences	32	49	7	112
Environmental Health Sciences	Health Professions Sciences	30	48	5	84
Speech and Hearing Sciences	Health Professions Sciences	29	32	7	75
Wildlife Science	Natural Resources and Conservation	28	33	6	73
Educational Evaluation and Research	Education	27	32	10	118
Applied Economics	Social and Behavioral Sciences	26	40	9	145
Fisheries Science	Natural Resources and Conservation	26	30	5	63
Italian Language and Literature	Humanities	26	42	22	359
Computer and Information Sciences, various	Physical and Mathematical Sciences	25	36	6	89
Communication Disorders and Sciences	Health Professions Sciences	24	25	6	62
Special Education	Education	24	27	3	38

Continued

Table 2.8 Continued

Discipline	Broad Field	No. of faculty with honorific award	Total no. of honorific awards held	Percentage of faculty in the discipline holding an honorific award	Awards held per 1,000 faculty in the discipline
Consumer and Human Sciences, various	Family, Consumer, and Human Sciences	23	37	8	122
Agriculture, various	Agricultural Sciences	22	31	10	137
European Studies	Humanities	22	30	20	275
Geological and Mining Engineering	Engineering	22	32	9	134
Clinical Psychology	Social and Behavioral Sciences	21	23	2	20
Materials Engineering	Engineering	21	23	9	103
Science Education	Education	21	23	9	94
Marketing	Business	17	24	2	33
Teacher-Education-Specific Levels	Education	16	17	4	42
Information Technology/ Information Systems	Physical and Mathematical Sciences	14	22	4	57
Family and Human Sciences, various	Family, Consumer, and Human Sciences	13	14	4	41
Oral Biology and Craniofacial Science	Biological and Biomedical Sciences	10	16	3	54
Counseling Psychology	Social and Behavioral Sciences	8	9	2	19
Higher Education/ Higher Education Administration	Education	8	10	3	39
Mathematics Education	Education	8	12	4	54

Continued

Table 2.8   Continued

Discipline	Broad Field	No. of faculty with honorific award	Total no. of honorific awards held	Percentage of faculty in the discipline holding an honorific award	Awards held per 1,000 faculty in the discipline
School Psychology	Social and Behavioral Sciences	8	11	3	34
Health, Physical Education, Recreation	Family, Consumer, and Human Sciences	6	8	1	18
Accounting	Business	5	7	1	10
Counselor Education	Education	3	4	1	9

two metrics are strongly influenced by the scale of the discipline and the availability of awards. Table 2.8 also shows the number of awards held per thousand people in the discipline and the results show that there is tremendous variation in terms of the availability of awards among disciplines. This renders what has been the standard measure—percentage of faculty holding an award—useless to make comparisons across disciplines, though perhaps still of value for comparing program performance within a discipline. The dramatic differences in terms of the relative abundance of honorific awards by discipline in standard compilations (e.g., the NRC study or Academic Analytics' compilation) demonstrates, once again, that performance comparisons among disciplines based on raw data are at best problematic and probably misleading and ill advised.

Who Is Responsible for the Production of the Nation's Scholarship?

The final section of this chapter addresses the question of how much scholarly productivity varies among faculty. For these analyses the faculty members in each discipline were grouped into 20 percent bands (quintiles) with the first quintile being the faculty who are in the top 20 percent of productivity for their discipline, as measured by the faculty scholarly productivity index (FSPI). The first area to consider is the number of research grants held by faculty in each quintile (chart 2.1). Almost

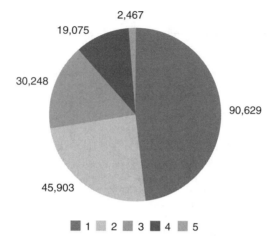

Chart 2.1 Grants by national, discipline quntile of the faculty.

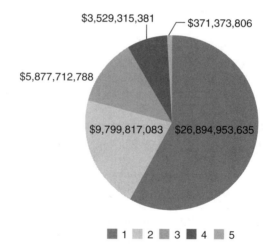

Chart 2.2 Grant dollars by national, discipline quintile of the faculty.

half of the research grants are held by faculty in the top 20 percent for scholarly productivity. Most striking is the fact that faculty in the fifth quintile hold only 2,467 grants while faculty in the first quintile hold 90,629 grants.

Another way to look at grant success is to look at federal research dollars held by faculty in each quintile (chart 2.2). The performance imbalance is even more striking in this comparison with faculty in the first quintile accounting for almost a hundred times the grant dollars as faculty in the fifth quintile.

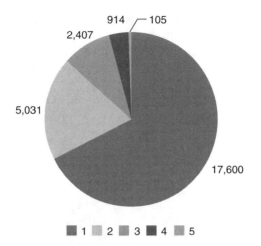

Chart 2.3   Books by national, discipline quntile of the faculty.

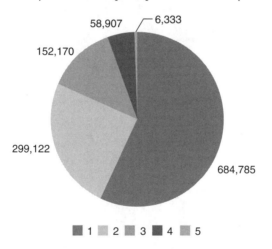

Chart 2.4   Journal articles by national, discipline quintile of the faculty.

An obvious concern is that the imbalance in performance reflects the highly competitive and perhaps skewed environment in which grant awards occur. Such factors should not influence the production of scholarly books as few scholars in the lettered disciplines are required to compete for funding to support their scholarly work. The results for the production of scholarly books (chart 2.3) are much more uneven than either the number of research grants held or the number of research grant dollars held. Faculty in the first quintile of their disciplines were matched to more than 17,000 books while faculty in the fifth quintile accounted for only 105 volumes!

Results for the publication of journal articles are shown in chart 2.4 with a remarkably similar pattern.

Faculty in the first quintile for their discipline account for more than a hundred times the number of articles compared to faculty in the fifth quintile.

The pattern is even stronger when looking at which faculty members publish articles that attract citations (chart 2.5). In this case, faculty

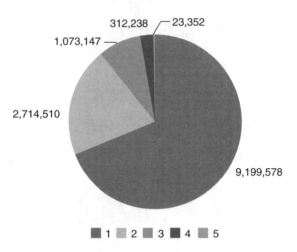

Chart 2.5   Citations of journal articles by national, discipline quintile of the faculty.

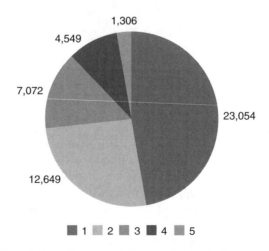

Chart 2.6   Awards by national, discipline quintile of the faculty.

members in the first quintile account for two thirds of all citations generated.

It would not be surprising to find that most honorific awards are held by faculty in the top performance category and these results are shown in chart 2.6. While it is the case that faculty members in the first quintile hold almost half of the honorific awards, this is the only metric for which the first quintile accounts for less than half of the productivity measure. The reason for this is likely that honors reflect on a career of scholarly achievement and may come later in a person's career when their productivity may have declined.

Where Are the Faculty Members Who Produce Most of the Nation's Scholarship?

The final issue considered is whether all of the most productive faculty reside at the most productive universities. Obviously these metrics are strongly linked as the top-ranked university is placed in that position by virtue of its faculty members' scholarly productivity. Nonetheless, it is striking that the most productive, private, large research university and the most productive, public, large research university, based on FSPI, have very similar profiles in terms of the distribution of performance among their faculty (charts 2.7 and 2.8). It was surprising to me to find that both top-ranked universities had so many faculty members whose scholarly performance placed them in the third, fourth, and fifth quintiles.

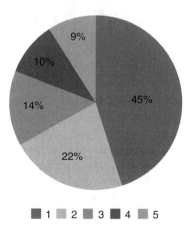

Chart 2.7 Distribution of faculty performance by national, discipline quintile—top private university.

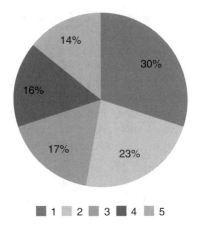

Chart 2.8   Distribution of faculty performance by national, discipline quintile—top private university.

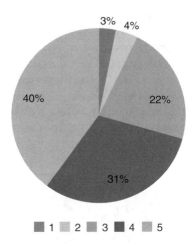

Chart 2.9   Distribution of faculty performance by national, discipline-quintile-lowest-ranked public university.

Charts 2.9 and 2.10 show a similar comparison of the make-up of the faculty members at the lowest-ranked, private, large research university and the lowest ranked public large research university.

It is perhaps to state the obvious that top-ranked universities are characterized by having a plurality of faculty who are highly productive scholars, while low-ranked universities are characterized by having

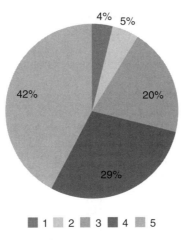

Chart 2.10 Distribution of faculty performance by national, discipline-quintile-lowest-ranked private university.

a plurality of faculty members who are not very productive. Perhaps less obvious is that all top-ranked universities have substantial numbers of PhD program faculty whose scholarly productivity is low and that all low-ranked universities have a modest number of faculty members whose scholarly productivity is as good as would be expected at the very best universities in the nation.

Conclusions

This chapter has examined data on faculty scholarly performance by discipline in terms of publication of scholarship (journal articles and books), citation data for journal articles, federal research funding, and the receipt of honors and awards. What is immediately clear is that few data elements lend themselves to performance comparison across discipline boundaries, as it is abundantly clear that the style of scholarship in a discipline dictates strongly how scholarship is packaged for publication (books, long articles, reports, etc.) so that raw counts mislead more than they inform. That being said, return-on-investment analyses reveal dramatic differences in the cost to produce publications of new knowledge and to achieve penetration into the field, as indicated by citation of the work by others, and these findings warrant further study.

As research productivity becomes part of the push for accountability, there are some important rules to follow:

1. Unless comparisons are being made among units with equal numbers of faculty (or narrowly constrained bands of department or program size) the metrics should be per capita.
2. The best metric to measure performance is the metric that answers the particular question that is most important to the stakeholder. This question must therefore be defined, which seems rarely to be done. I recommend the selection of one per-capita metric in each of the key areas of faculty scholarly performance: book publications, journal publications, citations, research grants, and honors and awards.
3. Performance comparisons among disciplines must be made in units standardized to reflect the varying availability of resources and different scholarly practices among disciplines. Means and standard deviations for national datasets should be used to generate z-scores that may then be used to compare relative success across disciplines (a gold medal is always better than a bronze whether won in swimming or in the marathon).

With these cautions in mind, data such as introduced in this chapter and contained in the FSP data set can be used to set appropriate performance standards for faculty recruitment and promotion to help a university to rise to a particular performance level. Standardized data on faculty scholarly performance can be used to compare programs within a university, using a measurement scale that is not discipline dependent and thus allows the identification of programs of different quality levels. Areas of performance strength for a program should help to define what the current faculty is capable of doing in other areas of scholarship. In other words, a program whose performance in journal publication exceeds the national mean for the discipline by one standard deviation might be expected to accomplish the same relative performance level in terms of winning research grants.

Finally, as a nation we are concerned about competitiveness in science and technology in the international arena, and there are frequent calls to increase our scholarly output. Until the writing of this chapter, I had not realized that more than half of the nation's scholarly output from PhD program faculty is produced by only 20 percent of the people, or that this most productive 20 percent may turn up at any of our nation's universities. If, as a nation, we wish to increase our scholarly output, it may be that we will do more by understanding what it takes to perform at the highest level and then to seek to empower faculty currently performing at the second quintile level to increase their output to match those currently in the first quintile. By that action, the nation would increase its scholarly output compared to current levels, and this burden could be carried by only 40 percent of the current PhD program faculty. The scholarly work of the remainder of the PhD program faculty in the nation would be a bonus.

Notes

1. Joan Lorden and Lawrence Martin, "Towards a Better Way to Rate Research Doctoral Programs: Executive Summary," position paper from NASULG's Council on Research Policy and Graduate Education.
2. Books, six years of data 2003–2008; journal articles, three years of data 2006–2008; citations of 2005–2008 articles in 2006–2008 articles; grants held or awarded 2006–2008; honorific awards five- to fifty- year duration.
3. College and University Professional Association for Human Resources, "Average Faculty Salaries by Field and Rank at 4-Year Colleges and Universities, 2009–10," *Chronicle of Higher Education* (March 8, 2010), http://chronicle.com/article/Chart-Average-Faculty-Sala/64500/
4. Jonathan Cole and Stephen Cole, "The Ortega Hypothesis: Citation Analysis Suggests that Only a Few Scientists Contribute to Scientific Progress," *Science* 178, no. 4059 (October 1972).
5. National Research Council, *Research-Doctorate Programs in the United States* (Washington DC: National Academy of Sciences, 1995).
6. Nancy Diamond and Hugh Graham, "How Should We Rate Research Universities?" *Change* magazine (July 2000).

3

Student-Unit Record Systems and Postsecondary Accountability: Exploiting Emerging Data Resources

Peter T. Ewell

The past decade has seen unprecedented growth in the quantity and scope of electronic student record data available to states and systems in higher education. All but eight of the fifty states have such records and collective experience is growing about how to harness them to yield information useful for building policy and exercising appropriate accountability.[1] This chapter reviews these developments by a) describing the characteristics and contents of extant systems, b) describing how they have been used to create indicators of institutional effectiveness, c) proposing a number of performance measures that can be calculated for accountability and consumer information purposes, d) exploring the promise of linking databases across educational sectors for multiple states and e) discussing some challenges associated with using such data effectively.

Background

A Student-Unit Record (SUR) database is a collection of electronic records about the enrollment behavior of every student enrolled in a given set of colleges and universities for each enrollment period. SUR databases date from the early 1980s when states needed a way to obtain student enrollment counts each term in order to drive enrollment-based resource allocation formulae. Whatever their origin, such systems have grown steadily in scope and complexity. At least twelve SURs now contain some information on independent and proprietary institutions—coverage made possible through the leverage induced by these institutions' participation in state scholarship programs—and more states indicate plans to do this. With regard to data contents, these databases all contain the data elements needed to generate institutional statistics on annual or term-to-term retention, degree completion, time to degree, and interinstitutional transfer (within the boundaries of a given state) on a consistent and comparative basis. About half contain additional data on individual course enrollments and performance for every student each term. This enables the development of performance measures on placement in developmental work, its completion, and performance in key "gate-keeper" courses such as English composition, college algebra, and calculus.

Postsecondary SURs are also being linked, enabling student tracking across a multistate region. At the same time, they are being matched with similar databases in K-12 education and with unemployment-insurance (UI) wage records. The first linkage allows K-12 systems and schools to evaluate their effectiveness in preparing graduates and former students for collegiate study by looking at whether these students need remediation when they enter college and how well they perform. Linking postsecondary SUR data to wage records, in turn, allows states and systems to construct additional performance measures such as the proportion of graduates and former students working in the field in which they took courses or earned degrees and documenting any gains in income.

One impetus for the development of linked systems is No Child Left Behind (NCLB) legislation. To help states comply with NCLB reporting requirements, the U.S. Department of Education has recently made substantial investments in developing the capabilities of SUR databases through State Longitudinal System Development grants. These grants will be supplemented with even larger investments in 2010, with preference given to systems that can link educational records in K-12 to postsecondary data systems and wage records.

Despite this progress, all has not gone smoothly. The National Center for Education Statistics (NCES) failed to get Congress to approve the establishment of a national unit record database for postsecondary education. Despite its potential benefits, the proposal was successfully resisted on privacy grounds by much of the higher-education community. Given the continued opposition, it is not likely to be revived any time soon. Fortunately, the linking of state databases through regional consortia, together with the data holdings of the National Student Clearinghouse (NSC), an organization that has compiled at least some data on enrollment and degree granting for over 90 percent of the nation's college students, are beginning to fill the gap, though they will never fill it completely.

SURs and Institutional Performance Reporting for Accountability

When states began developing performance indicators in the late 1980s, graduation rates, calculated using their SUR databases, were the most popular measures.[2] But each state was essentially operating on its own with respect to how these measures were constructed. Graduation rates were given definitional consistency in 1989, however, when Congress passed the Student Right-to-Know and Campus Security Act (SRK). This legislation required all institutions to report cohort-based graduation rates calculated on the basis of first-time, full-time starters, tracked out to six years for four-year institutions and three years for two-year institutions.[3] These statistics are disaggregated by gender and by race/ethnicity. Reporting also included year-to-year retention and allowed institutions to report successful transfers to other postsecondary institutions if they could be documented. SRK reporting was later incorporated into the Integrated Postsecondary Education Data System (IPEDS) in the form of an annual Graduation Rate Survey (GRS). The SRK/GRS definitions were quickly adopted by all states and helped rationalize completion-rate reporting on a national basis.

Student Right-to-Know, as its name implies, was also a milestone because it was explicitly structured as a "consumer protection" measure. Accordingly, institutions were required not only to calculate these statistics but also to display them prominently in catalog and recruitment materials. Federal officials subsequently moved increasingly toward an accountability approach centered on consumer information. This development reached its climax with the clamor for public reporting of student-learning outcomes that arose during the deliberations of the Secretary of Education's Commission on the Future of Higher Education (popularly known as the Spellings Commission) three years ago. Carl Perkins's accountability legislation also required vocational programs funded by this program to track student employment in the field in which they had received training, and the short-lived performance measures, established by the 1992 Reauthorization of the Higher Education Act (HEA), included a measure of income gain in relation to tuition charges for vocational-program graduates.[4]

The logic of this approach is simple: accurate information about collegiate outcomes, such as the probability of completing a program, will influence student and parent decisions about where to attend, and will consequently leverage institutions to improve. It remains unclear, though, if this logic is sound because the vast majority of students make decisions about where to attend college on the basis of location and price.[5] It is interesting to compare the interest of the states in following this federal logic. Forty-one of the forty-eight SUR databases surveyed by NCHEMS in 2006 used their SURs to calculate and report comparative graduation rates. But their applications were directed more toward direct accountability reporting than toward guiding consumer choice. For example, the Kentucky Council on Postsecondary Education maintains a highly visible aid-to-student-choice utility on its Web site, one click away from the agency's home page, through which students can access a range of information about program offerings and affordability across Kentucky's public and private institutions.[6] But it contains no information about performance. This is not because the agency has none. Detailed comparative data on retention, transfer, and completion rates are prominent in the agency's accountability reports—also available on the Council's Web site[7]—but casual student users would never know where to look for them. The Web site of the Minnesota State College and University System (MnSCU) has a similar utility for college choice that allows users to access a statistical "profile" for each institution. Once again, MnSCU has produced an eye-catching set of performance-measure displays that allow users to look at comparative persistence and completion rates, licensure examination pass rates, and in-field job placement rates by program and by institution. But this is located in a different place on the Web site and labeled "accountability," where prospective students are unlikely to go.[8] There is nothing inherently misguided in taking this approach. It merely recognizes that the leaders of state university systems believe that performance measures calculated from data contained in their SURs are more useful in steering institutional behavior directly through accountability than indirectly by informing the market.

There are many good examples of how states and systems have used SUR data resources for accountability purposes. One of the most effective is the so-called momentum-points performance funding scheme recently put into place by the State Board of Community and Technical Colleges (SBCTC) in Washington. This approach rewards institutions with additional funding to the extent that they move students through important intermediate outcomes or milestones on their way to a degree or certificate. Intermediate outcomes include successful completion of a General Education Diploma (GED) or literacy module, successfully completing developmental study, and the achievement of significant milestones in earning college credit. These intermediate outcomes are assigned particular point values that determine the amount of additional funding awarded to each college. This approach has the virtue of allowing colleges to demonstrate success at every point in the longitudinal enrollment pipeline, an important property for community colleges where, for a number of reasons, large proportions of newly enrolled students do not earn associate degrees.

Another good example of a performance funding application is provided by the Brain Gain initiative of the Oklahoma Board of Regents.[9] Under this approach, institutions are awarded additional funds for each student earning a degree beyond an established threshold, set on the basis of an analysis of existing retention and completion information about other colleges and universities. This analysis creates a regression model to estimate the "expected" performance level for the institution in question, based on such variables as average admissions test scores, gender and race/ethnicity, and a range of enrollment behavior factors such as full-time/part-time attendance. Institutions are awarded performance funding dollars in proportion to the amount that they outperform their statistically expected performance. Bonus dollars are provided for degrees earned by students drawn from at-risk backgrounds.

Both these examples contain best-practice features. First, they are transparent and simple. The benchmark statistics are not indirect estimates of an underlying property or performance (like test scores), but rather the actual output itself, and the calculations required are easy to understand. Second, the outcomes in question are linked demonstrably to the achievement of state policy objectives such as closing achievement gaps or addressing workforce needs. Third, both schemes only count a couple of things, so they send a straightforward message to institutions about what the state wants. The ill-fated performance-funding approach, adopted briefly by South Carolina about a decade ago, in contrast, rested upon thirty-seven separate performance measures, which made it difficult for institutions to determine state priorities. Finally, these outcome measures are easy for a state with comprehensive SUR resources to calculate consistently and fairly under circumstances in which it is in the institutions' interests to cheat. Tennessee's long-standing performance funding system, in contrast, is based on institution-reported measures, a feature that requires state authorities to invest considerable time checking the statistics reported.

Finally, there is a growing trend for SUR-based graduation and job-placement rate statistics to be tied directly to a statewide strategic plan or public agenda for higher education. For example, Indiana and Kentucky both have advanced statewide plans framed around citizen benefits provided by higher education, such as increased earnings or quality of life.

Web sites at the higher education agencies in both states allow users to click on each goal comprising the public agenda to access graphic displays of the relevant performance indicators.

Linking Databases across Sectors and States

Most of the examples of accountability measures using SUR data described in the previous section involve a single sector (postsecondary) in a single state. But more analytical power can be generated if data about multiple sectors in a multistate region can be linked. Florida, for example, has pooled data drawn from K-12 education, higher education, private and federal employment, military enlistments, tax and public service support, and corrections to produce a powerful picture of such topics as the impact of education on social mobility, or the importance for college success of taking the right kinds of courses in high school.[10] NCHEMS, moreover, recently completed a pilot project involving four states to examine patterns of student migration across state lines.[11] All of these require a reliable mechanism for linking large datasets using common record identifiers.

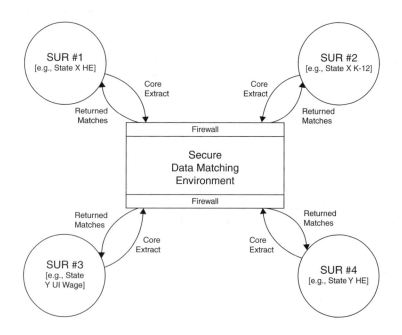

Figure 3.1   Basic Concept for Linking Databases.

Experience suggests that a multisector, multistate, data-exchange capability is best conceptualized as a single database containing data extracted from multiple "source" databases.[12] But implementation should be undertaken incrementally and be advanced under the rubric of "data exchange" rather than "building a centralized database."

The basic concept for accomplishing such an exchange is portrayed by figure 3.1. Its elements are as follows:

- Multiple SURs Maintained Independently for Different Sectors by State Agencies: These will necessarily differ with respect to data contents, data structures, and operating environments.
- One or More Unique Identifiers That Enable Records Corresponding to the Same Individual in Two or More Databases to Be Identified: The most common data element used for these purposes is the Social Security Number (SSN), which is the only way to match UI wage-record data. Most state postsecondary SURs continue to use the SSN, although they are moving away from this practice because of privacy concerns. State education departments are all developing unique identifiers for K-12 student records and these are increasingly being incorporated into postsecondary SURs as well.
- *A Secure Data Environment within Which Records Can Be Matched*: Selected unit record data supplied by individual participating agencies enters this environment through a secure access portal and matching takes place behind a firewall.
- *A Set of Core Data Elements Defined and Coded in a Standard Format*: Most accountability measures can be constructed using only a few key pieces of data. These describe the dependent variable of interest: whether and how a given student is enrolled in or has completed a degree at an institution covered by another SUR database, became employed in a particular industry at a given wage rate, and so on. Independent variables will be much more extensive but will already be in the SURs of participating states. Examples include demographic descriptors, receipt of state scholarship funds, and participants in particular programs. After matched records are returned to participating states, they can be linked with any desired combination of these independent variables with no need for linkages or common data structures across states.
- *An Input Protocol to Submit Core Data Elements*: Under full-scale implementation, all participating state agencies submit records for all students with active records. Under more limited forms of implementation, states might only submit records for the particular set of students they want to match.

- *An Output File That Returns the Results of the Matching Process to Participating States*: Ideally, this takes the form of a unique unit record that contains the core data elements, generated for each student-enrollment event at each institution outside the original source agency.
- One or More Memoranda of Understanding (MOU) That Formally Spells Out the Rules Under Which Data Can Be Accessed and Used: Some matches are governed by a single MOU. If more than one state is involved in the exchange, however, it is usually best to craft a series of bilateral arrangements between pairs of participating state agencies or between each agency and the third-party data manager because of differing legal environments in different states.

Adopting this approach to data linking has the advantage of keeping the amount of data actually exchanged to a minimum and of allowing each participating state to construct its own performance measures. But whatever approach is used, state agencies can benefit substantially with respect to the range of institutional performance that can be examined if the data contents of several SURs are tapped.

Statistics for Accountability

SUR databases can be used to produce many performance measures. With the exception of the graduation-rate measure established by SRK, however, states and systems currently lack common definitions for these measures. This section describes a common set of benchmark statistics that all states and systems should be able to produce by tapping and linking their SURs.[13] These recommended performance measures are defined longitudinally in terms of the relationship between two or more events in a given student's enrollment history. For example, the SRK two-year associate's-degree completion rate relates a given student's achievement of an associate degree with his or her first credit enrollment within a specified time period. An illustrative chart of milestone events of this kind is presented in figure 3.2.

These performance measures recognize the fact that that such milestone events may occur in a different order for different students. For example, students may enroll for their first college-level credit at a point either before or after their enrollment in a developmental course. Given that they will be calculated directly from statewide databases, these measures also recognize the fact that these events may take place at different institutions.

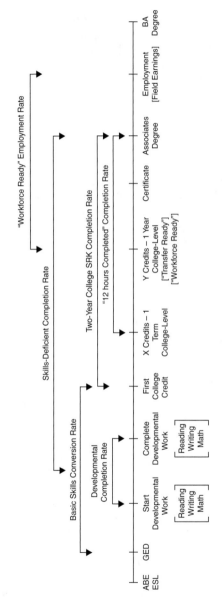

Figure 3.2 Milestone Events in a Student Enrollment Pathway.

These measures can be presented in two groups depending upon the complexity of the data needed to construct them. Measures in the first set depend only upon the presence of basic enrollment and completions data in state or system SUR databases. Exceptions are proposed measures on developmental education, which may require some states to produce flags for enrollment and completion of developmental education. For institutions that have the requisite data, these flags can be constructed by tapping transcript-level detail for developmental courses; otherwise, they must be reported directly to the state agency by each institution. None of the measures in the first set address noncredit instruction and none of them require linkages to other databases.

- *Completion Rate:* The proportion of students in a cohort who earn a credential or degree, tracked from the point at which they enroll for the first time in instruction that will count toward a credential, calculated at annual intervals out to six years.[14] Credentials include degrees, certificates, diplomas, or any other formal award. Students placed in developmental work are considered to have reached this start point if they are enrolled in a course of study that leads to a credential. Breakdowns include the attainment of various degree levels.
- *Annual Persistence Rate:* The proportion of students in a cohort who remain enrolled in a program leading to a credential or a degree at successive one-year intervals after first enrolling in instruction that will count toward a degree or credential, tracked annually out to six years.
- *Developmental Success Rate I:* The proportion of students who successfully complete developmental work, tracked from the point they begin developmental work and reported annually out to five years. Reporting should distinguish a) beginning developmental work in *any* field to the completion of *all* required developmental work, and b) be broken down separately to reflect reading, writing, and mathematics.
- *Developmental Success Rate II:* The proportion of students who successfully complete developmental work and enroll for credit at the college level, tracked from the point they begin developmental work and reported annually out to five years. Basic reporting should reflect *any* college-level enrollment after the successful completion of developmental work.
- *Transfer Rate:* The proportion of students in a cohort who are tracked from the point they first entered a degree program and who subsequently enroll in a degree program at another degree-granting

institution,[15] tracked annually out to ten years. A refinement of this measure would distinguish those who transferred to a higher level of study at a four-year institution.

Performance measures in the second set depend on the ability to access course-level information and to link postsecondary enrollment records to the UI wage record. Only a few states or systems are now able to generate all of these measures, either because of current limitations in the available data or because generating them would require considerable programming or analytical effort.

- *Twelve-Hours Earned Rate:* The proportion of students in a cohort who complete one term (that is, twelve student-credit hours [SCH] or equivalent) of college-level work, tracked from the point at which they enroll for the first time in instruction that leads to a credential, calculated at annual intervals out to six years.
- *Developmental Success Rate III:* The proportion of students who successfully complete developmental work and complete one term (that is, 12 SCH) of college-level work, tracked from the point they begin developmental work and reported annually out to five years.
- *Developmental Success Rate IV:* The proportion of students who successfully complete the college-level course in English composition (or equivalent), tracked from the point they begin developmental work in writing , and the proportion that begins developmental work in mathematics and successfully completes a college-level mathematics course, reported annually out to five years.
- *Transfer-Ready-Status Achievement Rate:* The proportion of students in a cohort who achieve transfer-ready status, tracked from the point at which they enroll for the first time in instruction that leads to a credential, calculated at annual intervals out to ten years. Transfer-ready status is achieved when the student has (a) completed one year (i.e., thirty SCH or equivalent) of college-level work, (b) passed or placed out of all developmental work, and (c) completed English composition, a college-level math course, and one college-level course in each basic discipline cluster (science, social science, and humanities).
- *Workforce-Ready-Status Achievement Rate:* The proportion of students in a cohort who achieve workforce-ready status, tracked from the point at which they enroll for the first time in instruction that leads to a credential, calculated at annual intervals out to ten years. Workforce-ready status is achieved when the student

has completed one year (as above) of college-level work at least half of which consists of vocational courses related to a particular occupational field.

- *Noncredit Conversion Rate:* The proportion of students who entered the cohort as noncredit students who subsequently enroll in instruction that will count toward a credential, reported annually out to five years. Reporting should distinguish between different noncredit tracks including GED, Adult Basic Education (ABE), and English as a Second Language (ESL).
- *Employment Rate:* The proportion of students in a cohort who are employed in the third UI-wage record reporting quarter after having a) completed a credential, or b) their last enrollment in the program, tracked from the point they first enrolled in instruction leading to a credential. Reporting should distinguish students who completed a credential from those who did not. A subset of these rates is the in-field employment rate, which means that the former student is employed in the field for which he or she received training.
- *Postenrollment Earnings:* The annualized earnings of a student in the third UI-Wage reporting quarter after having completed a credential or their last enrollment in the program.
- *Return on Investment:* The ratio between the total cost to the student to complete a given degree program and the average annual income earned by graduates of that program.

Midpoint measures such as developmental success rates, achievement of credit-earned milestones, and the achievement of transfer-ready or workplace-ready status should be priorities for future development because of their importance in providing indicators of success short of attaining a formal credential.

Measures of both kinds can at minimum be calculated for each institution in the state or system as a whole. But performance benchmarking will be considerably more informative if these measures are broken down by a set of agreed-upon subpopulations. The following subpopulations are among the most important:

1. *Gender*: IPEDS.
2. *Race/Ethnicity*: IPEDS.
3. *Age*: The following breakdown is typical:
   i. Traditional Age (under 22 years old)
   ii. Younger Working Age Adult (22–35)
   iii. Older Working Age Adult (36–64)
   iv. Older Adult (65 and above)
4. *Part-Time Status*: IPEDS for the first term of enrollment.

5. *Financial Status*: This is an increasingly important policy variable for disaggregation, but many states do not have the required data. The best proxy measure is whether or not the student is receiving a Pell grant.
6. *Transfer Status*: Entering as a first-time-in-college student or as a transfer student. (Further breakdowns of entering transfer students are recommended at term-length intervals of credits transferred.)

Statistics such as these can be used for many research and policy purposes, but it is useful to briefly review how states have used them specifically for accountability. Three main approaches have typically been used:

1. *Accountability Reporting*: Virtually all states with SURs use them to generate basic institution-level statistics on retention and degree completion, generally using the SRK method.[16]
2. *Performance Funding*: As already described for Oklahoma and the Washington SBCTC, some states have allocated additional funds to institutions that perform well on various outcome measures. A straightforward approach here, so far not adopted by any state, would be to base some proportion of the allocation—now based only on credits registered for at an early census date—on the basis of credits completed instead.
3. *Consumer Information*: Most state systems have a utility on their Web sites, designed to help prospective students look at public institutions to aid them in making a choice, but none of these provide any information about performance. A simple link to it in the student-choice utility could remedy this situation.

Challenges Associated with Developing and Using Such Measures

Growing state and system experience using SUR data in accountability reporting has uncovered a number of common challenges. These occur with sufficient frequency that they ought to be discussed. For each of these challenges, the nature of the problem must first be explained, followed by some suggestions for addressing it.

Defining the Base Population

Virtually all the performance measures discussed in the previous section are based on a population ratio of some kind. The trick in constructing such statistics is to set the denominator fairly. For example, community-college leaders have long complained that the GRS graduation rate under-reports their success because a large (and unknown) share of entering students do not intend to complete a degree. They therefore argue that these students should be removed from the denominator before the completion percentage is calculated. Similarly, higher-education officials in Utah successfully modified the originally proposed SRK calculation procedures to enable them to remove students who delayed completing their programs because they undertook a religious mission. A similar rationale was used for excluding students called up for active military service, as well as those who die.

The justification for making such adjustments rests on the principle that a good accountability statistic ought not to hold institutions responsible for things that are not under their control. The difficulty lies in determining just how far to go because each such adjustment distorts the true picture of performance. For example, NCES currently reports a three-year graduation rate for community-college starters of just under 22 percent. But an NCHEMS study, using data drawn from the National Student Clearinghouse (NSC), yielded only about half this proportion of degree earners in this time period. The difference lies in the fact that the denominator used in the NCHEMS study was almost twice as big as that used for the GRS calculation because no assumptions were made about who was a degree-seeking student. Which rate is more appropriate? On the one hand, backing out supposed nondegree students is fair because they are unlikely to complete. On the other hand, the excluded students were enrolled at least half-time in credit-bearing courses that count toward a degree, and there is no assurance that they might not later decide to earn a degree. The latter, moreover, although it admittedly holds the institution responsible for something beyond its control, is the actual performance level attained.

One way to address this difficulty is to report more than one number. The Florida Community College System uses an accountability measure based on the associate-degree completion rates of only those students who earned eighteen or more hours of credit.[17] But it also uses the standard first-time, full-time rate. For the 2001 entering cohort, tracked over four years, the first measure yields a rate of just over 50 percent, while the comparable rate for the standard measure is only about half this level.

Apples and Oranges

A related challenge associated with graduation rates and similar performance statistics is that most of the variation across institutions can be accounted for by differences in institutional characteristics that have nothing to do with performance. The most telling example is admissions selectivity, which accounts for by far the largest share of explained variation in graduation rates across institutions. Highly selective institutions routinely graduate more than 90 percent of an entering class, while open admissions institutions can fall to below 20 percent. Clearly it is not appropriate to directly compare these measures. Indeed, holding the latter institutions more accountable for their low performance may induce them to become more selective, contrary to the policy interests of the state.

To address this problem, states and systems have adopted a range of measures to adjust for factors like these. One of them, illustrated by the Oklahoma Board of Regents performance funding scheme described earlier, is to make statistical adjustments that remove the unrelated variation from the outcome measure. Another way to address this issue is to disaggregate outcomes for different student populations if student characteristics are known to be related to graduation. For example, Texas reports graduation rates for public institutions broken down by gender and race/ethnicity. The primary reason for doing this is the fact that reducing performance gaps across population groups is a prominent state goal for higher education. But because blacks and Hispanics typically have lower graduation rates than whites, it also helps sort out the fact that institutional graduation rates can be markedly influenced by their racial/ethnic mix. A final approach is to set individually tailored "stretch goals" for each institution on the basis of its operating environment. For example, one of the indicators used in the Washington SBCTC's original performance funding scheme was in-field job-placement rates for program completers. Because job markets vary across different regions of the state, SBCTC adjusted benchmark rates on a case-by-case basis to take away any advantages an institution might enjoy by being located in a region in which it was relatively easy to get an in-field job.

Student Mobility

A significant limitation on the use of SUR data for accountability is the fact that such data only cover students enrolled at institutions within a given state. If a student transfers to an institution in another state, it is not possible to identify the transfer using in-state SUR data alone. And this is far from an infrequent occurrence. Federal studies have indicated for years that of the 70 percent of bachelor-degree earners who attended more than one institution, more than 40 percent of them crossed state borders at some point in their enrollment histories.[18] This is why data sharing across states in a larger geographic region can be so important. Because most border crossing is local, a lot of the missing data can be captured in the postsecondary SURs of neighboring states.[19] But there are other ways to capture this missing information as well, using the data resources of the National Student Clearinghouse (NSC).

To demonstrate the potential of NSC data, NCHEMS recently completed a pilot project in partnership with the National Center for Public Policy in Higher Education.[20] The intent of the demonstration was to create and assess the quality of state-level graduation-rate statistics using NSC data alone. To do this, NCHEMS researchers defined starting cohorts within the NSC database using SRK/GRS definitions and tracked these students through the six subsequent years. Completion-rate statistics were then calculated for four-year and two-year starters, including the proportions earning a degree from a) the institution at which the student first enrolled, b) an institution located in the same state, and c) an institution located anywhere else.

Findings revealed that on a national basis, six-year graduation rates for four-year starters are boosted just over six percentage points if all institutions in a state are included, and an additional four percentage points if institutions anywhere are included. These patterns vary substantially by state. For example, states such as Arkansas and Texas show relatively low out-of-state graduation rates, while states such as North and South Dakota show relatively high rates. These variations are expected because of differences in general geographic mobility and differential tuition policies. Substantial variations are also apparent with respect to additional in-state completions. States such as Georgia and Wisconsin show relatively high rates of in-state transfer completion, while states such as Delaware and Vermont are comparatively low. These variations are due to a combination of geographic location and the structure of a state's public higher-education system.

Using a similar approach, growing numbers of states and systems are tapping NSC data to locate missing transfer students, thereby improving the quality of their longitudinal SUR-based accountability measures. The NSC is also under contract to the American Association of State Colleges and Universities (AASCU) and the Association of Public and Land-grant Universities (APLU) to complete the graduation-rate reporting portion of the Voluntary System of Accountability (VSA) recently launched by these two organizations.

Points of Comparison

Statistics acquire meaning only when they are placed alongside meaningful benchmarks. Three such benchmarks are typically used in performance statistics such as graduation rates. The use of fixed criteria implies that there is a recognized standard that can be applied to everyone indiscriminately. This is rarely used by states and systems in reporting longitudinal performance measures because no such standards currently exist. The closest approximations are the cut values used to define performance zones (red, yellow, and green) for student success and job placement on the MnSCU Accountability Dashboard.

Using normed or relative statistics implies a competitive situation in which absolute performance is valued less than how well one is doing compared to others. This is the most common approach to establishing points of comparison for performance indicators among states and systems. Usually the arithmetic mean across all institutions in the state or system is used, but some agencies report quartiles, or whether or not a given institution's performance is above or below one standard deviation of the mean. For example, the performance Web site for the North Carolina Community College System arrays progression measures in tables so that users can compare the performance of any given college against others individually, or against the state mean.[21]

Finally, measuring change over time implies a world free of both standards and competition, where "success" simply means steady improvement. The current Washington SBCTC momentum-points performance funding scheme described earlier incorporates this feature in that each time an institution exceeds its past best performance, the target is recalibrated so that it needs to achieve more in order to get rewarded.

Random Variation

Performance indicators such as graduation rates, like any real-world statistic, always vary slightly from year to year. These variations are for the most part independent of actual performance, but they may be mistaken by readers for changes that have substantive meaning. To achieve greater stability, some states or systems (for example, the MnSCU Accountability Dashboard and the North Carolina Community College System) use a three-year rolling average. Others, like the Indiana Commission on Higher Education, find ways to show the limits of variation through box plots or whisker charts. Very few go to the length of actually testing differences for statistical significance, but good practice does suggest reporting the numbers of cases associated with any reported statistic so that readers can roughly assess significant difference. This is done in the great majority of cases.

Analytical Capacity

A final challenge faced by growing numbers of states and systems under today's economic circumstances is retaining the staff capable of constructing longitudinal databases from base SUR records and creating performance measures. Keeping these staff members is generally considered less important during bad-budget times than retaining staff assigned to core functions such as resource allocation and payroll. In fact, the NCHEMS survey of state SUR databases in higher education revealed diminished analytical-staff capacity to be one of the top concerns of database administrators. There is little point in going to the trouble to collect these data if all that will happen is they remain in the agency's archives.

One promising way to address this condition is to recruit university scholars to undertake the necessary analytical work. Economic and educational researchers from Columbia, Harvard, the University of Pennsylvania, and Princeton have worked on SURs in Ohio, Florida, and Washington at the invitation of state and system administrators. In another instance, researchers at the Community College Research Center at Teachers College, Columbia University helped the Washington SBCTC construct the momentum-points performance funding scheme described earlier. The researchers gain access to a powerful dataset that they can use to answer scholarly questions. In return, state database administrators can ask the researchers to undertake work on behalf of the state. This can be done effectively only if the requisite data-access agreements are in place with clear understanding of the details of the quid pro quo between the researchers and the agency.[22]

Conclusion

The federal funds currently being made available to states to build K-12 longitudinal student-tracking capacity and to enhance existing capacity in postsecondary education will undoubtedly yield significant progress in our capacity to produce powerful, accountability-reporting statistics. Reinforced by the increasing availability of additional data from the National Student Clearinghouse, together with the expansion of NSC data holdings into K-12 education now underway, the nation is rapidly developing a seamless longitudinal data resource. This means that whatever the fate of any future NCES proposal for a national, student-unit record system in higher education, those responsible for running state college and university systems will be able to produce increasingly powerful and useful accountability measures. The result, hopefully, will be increases in levels of postsecondary attainment and more effective student learning.

Notes

1. Peter T. Ewell and Marianne Boeke, *Critical Connections: Linking States' Unit Record Systems to Track Student Progress* (Indianapolis, IN: Lumina Foundation for Education, 2007). This comprehensive fifty-state survey of state SURs is the basis for the descriptions of the characteristics and capacities of these systems made in the three following paragraphs.

2. Joseph C. Burke and Henrik Minnassians, *Performance Reporting: "Real" Accountability or Accountability "Lite"?* (Albany, NY: State University of New York, Rockefeller Institute of Government, 2003).

3. These tracking periods were established to represent 150 percent of the advertised catalog length of the degree program.

4. The latter statistic was also included in the measures proposed for "triggered" institutions under the short-lived State Postsecondary Review Entity (SPRE) programs in many states. See State Higher Education Executive Officers, *Developing Quantitative Performance Standards for SPRE Reviews: A Technical Assistance Primer* (Denver CO: State Higher Education Executive Officers [SHEEO], 1995).

5. Robert Zemsky, "The Dog that Doesn't Bark: Why Markets neither Limit Prices nor Promote Educational Quality," in *Achieving Accountability in Higher Education*, ed. J.C. Burke and Associates (New York: Jossey-Bass, 2005), 275–295.

6. Kentucky Council on Postsecondary Education, *KnowHow2GoKY*, http://cpe.ky.gov/forstudents/.

7. Kentucky Council on Postsecondary Education, *2007–2008 Accountability Report: Annual Progress Toward Meeting Kentucky's Postsecondary Education Goals*, http://apps.cpe.ky.gov/reports/AccountabilityReport0708final.pdf.

8. Minnesota State Colleges and Universities, *Accountability Dashboard*, http://www.mnscu.edu/board/accountability/index.html.

9. Oklahoma State Regents for Higher Education, *Brain Gain*, http://www.okhighered.org/studies-reports/brain-gain/braingain2008-update-screen.pdf.

10. Florida Department of Education, *Postsecondary Success Begins with High School Preparation*, http://www.fldoe.org/cc/OSAS/DataTrendsResearch/DT33.pdf.

11. See National Center for Higher Education Management Systems, "Tracking Postsecondary Students Across State Lines: Results of a Multi-State Data Exchange Initiative," http://www.nchems.org/c2sp/documents/ResultsofMulti-StateDataExchange.pdf.

12. National Center for Higher Education Management Systems, *Linking Student Enrollment Records Across State Lines: Extending the Concept*, http://www.nchems.org/c2sp/documents/Multi-StateDataExchangeConceptPaper.pdf.

13. These measures were initially developed through a state data initiative undertaken in 2005 under the auspices of the Achieving the Dream (AtD)

project funded by the Lumina Foundation for Education and the Community College Bridges to Opportunity project funded by the Ford Foundation. See Community College Research Center, *Community College Data and Performance Measurement Toolkit* (New York: Teachers College, Columbia University, 2008).

14. Because of system conversions or similar limitations in historical data, some states or systems will not be able to track students to the originally proposed ten-year mark, but all who can should be encouraged to do so.

15. Only aggregate information on transfers is available in many states. This may limit the subpopulation breakdowns that can be provided for this measure, although all participating states should be able to generate the basic statistic for the state as a whole. Also, even with states that have unit-record data on transfers, only transfers to public institutions are typically included. Finally, many states can supplement their transfer records with data obtained from the National Student Clearinghouse.

16. Ewell and Boeke, *Critical Connections*.

17. The Florida College System, *Lower Division Accountability, 2008*, http://www.fldoe.org/cc/OSAS/FastFacts/pdf/2009–03.pdf.

18. Clifford Adelman, *The Toolbox Revisited: Paths to Degree Completion from High School Through College* (Washington, DC: U.S. Department of Education, Office of Vocational and Adult Education, 2006).

19. NCHEMS found that increases in cross-state completions were significantly higher for institutions located near state borders than at other institutions. See National Center for Higher Education Management Systems, "Tracking Postsecondary Students Across State Lines: Results of a Multi-State Data Exchange Initiative," http://www.nchems.org/c2sp/documents/ResultsofMulti-StateDataExchange.pdf.

20. National Center for Public Policy in Higher Education, *State Level completion and Transfer Rates: Harnessing a New National Resource* (San Jose, CA: National Center for Public Policy in Higher Education, 2009).

21. North Carolina Community College System Research and Performance Management, *2009 Critical Success Factors*, http://www.nccommunitycolleges.edu/Publications/docs/Publications/csf2009.pdf.

22. National Center for Higher Education Management Systems, "Harnessing the Potential for Research of Existing Student Records Databases: An Action Agenda," http://www.nchems.org/c2sp/Promoting%20Researcher%20Access%20to%20State%20SUR%20Data%20Resources.pdf.

4

Higher-Education Finance and Accountability

Bridget Terry Long

Introduction

The finances of colleges and universities are increasingly under the scrutiny of policymakers, researchers, and families. Much of the attention focused on money has been in reaction to skyrocketing tuition costs. From 1980–81 to 2008–09, the average list price of a public, four-year institution rose twice as fast as inflation.[1] Questions about whether the escalation of college costs has been justified have translated into calls for greater accountability in postsecondary finance. The focus on college prices reached a fever pitch with a 2003 proposal by Rep. Howard P. (Buck) McKeon to penalize colleges that raise their prices too high by denying them eligibility to participate in federal student-aid programs. While the measure was hotly debated, the ensuing debate highlighted the view that colleges are doing little to keep costs in check.[2]

Rising college prices, however, are not the only concerns voiced by proponents of accountability. As more information has become available about the outcomes of college enrollees, there are questions about whether college expenditures are being used effectively to help students. Less than 60 percent of students at four-year colleges graduate within six years, and at some colleges, the graduation rate is less than ten percent.[3] Such high rates of attrition call into question whether colleges are working to maximize students' likelihood of success.[4] Certainly, there are reasons to question whether college expenditures are being devoted to student needs, given that the proportion of institutional spending on educational services has declined over time across higher education while expenditures on non-instructional activities, such as administrative services, have increased.[5] Perhaps it is not surprising that even college graduates have begun to question the return to higher education.[6]

Many postsecondary institutions have also become concerned about their own finances as additional external forces have made it more difficult for schools to balance their expenditures with their revenues. With increasing competition from other public services, state appropriations to public institutions have steadily declined as a proportion of revenue.[7] As other sources of revenue vary with economic conditions, many colleges and universities have been forced to consider cost models in which they make do with less.

While there is increasing scrutiny and pressure to monitor higher-education finances and ensure that funds are being used efficiently, little is understood about how to fold this within an accountability system. Many state attempts at performance funding and other forms of financial accountability have been discarded within a few years. With such a blemished history, is accountability really possible in higher-education finance?

This chapter considers the role of higher-education finance in accountability systems by discussing how an effective financing system, tied to improving productivity and learning outcomes, might be designed. The chapter begins by reviewing how we currently measure funding streams and the degree to which it is possible to determine how colleges and universities spend their resources. Then, I outline other key elements and considerations of accountability systems based on higher-education finance. The following section gives an overview of past experiences with performance funding in several states and summarizes some of the lessons learned. Finally, I lay out the key questions and criteria for designing financing systems that could be tied to improve both institutional productivity and student outcomes.

The Difficulty in Measuring College Spending

A first step in the implementation of any accountability system based on higher-education funding is to adequately measure the finance side of institutions. Such measures provide the necessary baseline and follow up information to judge the behavior of colleges. However, the real focus of higher-education finance accountability must be on the expenditure side of higher-education finance: how much and in what ways the institution uses its resources.

Problems Inherent in Measuring Higher-Education Costs

Before going deeper into the specifics of how college expenditures are measured, it is first worth noting several features of higher education that make a full and complete accounting of costs especially difficult. The first is the problem of joint products. Institutions have multiple missions (e.g., education, research, public service), and these missions overlap and may even be reinforcing. For example, a professor's research may contribute to his or her teaching. To address each of these multiple missions, there are fixed costs, such as administration and operations, which are shared. While the primary focus of accountability evaluations is often to isolate the costs of one particular function, this can be difficult because of the joint nature of the missions. The goals are not easily separable from each other, and therefore parsing out which costs go with each mission can be impossible. This is partly a problem of aggregation, but more importantly, given the overlap between those missions, it would be difficult to determine the relative cost of each even with a more detailed data collection. In the case of the professor whose research is used in his or her teaching, how should the costs between the research function and the teaching function be divided?

Further, higher education does not fit the traditional economic model in which a firm uses a combination of inputs in a production process to make its outputs. Typically, inputs are entirely separate entities from the outputs, and with regard to accountability efforts, one would focus on the costs of the inputs as well as how an institution chooses to use those inputs in the production process. However, in education, students complicate this basic framework. Students are not only the outputs of the process (i.e., an educated college graduate) but also important inputs. Peers have been shown to influence each other's academic and social outcomes.[8] Unfortunately, there is no good, systematic way to measure the value added by one student to another. Institutions implicitly compensate some students for their positive peer effects by giving them merit-based financial aid, but this is an imperfect measure, given that there are multiple motivations for giving merit aid (e.g., attracting students with high test scores with the hope of rising in the college rankings), and measures of institutional financial aid are also flawed.[9] To summarize, there is no convention on the best way to incorporate students' costs or benefits into finance models.

Concerns about How to Define Certain Costs

While there are inherent difficulties in accurately and completely measuring college costs, efforts continue. Still, expenditure studies are only as good as the underlying data. As summarized by Dennis Jones of the National Center for Higher Education Management Systems, full cost analyses "start with accounting data and rely on adjustments to, and allocations of, these financial data to yield final answers. As a consequence, the results are influenced heavily by the purposes, conventions, and limitations of such data."[10] Before even starting the process, one must first determine how to define certain costs using the available data. In studies of college finances, researchers have developed a variety of cost models and approximations of expenditures on educational activities, but the analysis is never straightforward because of the assumptions that must be made and the availability of data.

One issue that must be resolved when measuring institutional expenditures concerns is how one should deal with direct versus indirect costs. Early cost models suffered from the fact that the calculations of one institution might include a battery of indirect cost formulas while another institution might use an entirely different set of formulas. The Delta Project on Postsecondary Costs, Productivity, and Accountability focuses on what it calls education and related spending per full-time equivalent (FTE) student rather than the previous convention to highlight "instructional costs."

Another complication in cost accounting involves not a definitional issue but, instead, how measurements are reported because of the limits of data. College expenditures are often reported per student or credit hour to standardize across institutions of different sizes. These estimates, in essence, give the average cost within the system, and so they mask differences in the resources one student might receive versus another.

National Information on Expenditures

The primary source of information on college finances nationally is the Integrated Postsecondary Education Data System (IPEDS). Institutions that participate in any federal student-aid program are required to complete the IPEDS survey annually, and the finance data collection includes institutional revenues by source, expenditures by category, and assets and liabilities. The information is reported in aggregate terms, and so it is difficult to isolate the costs of particular activities to get a true sense of costs, spending efficiency, and funding streams. Still, because the coverage of IPEDS is extensive, it has been the foundation of multiple large-scale efforts to understand college expenditures. For example, as part of the 1998 Amendments to the Higher Education Act of 1965, Congress required that the National Center for Education Statistics (NCES) conduct studies on expenditures in higher education.[11]

More recently, the Delta Project examined college spending for nearly two thousand public and private colleges from 2002 to 2006. In its report, *Trends in College Spending* (January 2009), the Delta Project researchers found substantial variation in the resources available to institutions.[12] Most students attend colleges that have very limited budgets, while the richest institutions appear to be getting richer. Second, much of the new money to higher education outside tuition increases is restricted, meaning that it can only be used for special functions. Meanwhile, tuition increases are only partially making up for reductions in state appropriations at public institutions. Finally, efforts to investigate changes in productivity were hampered by a lack of outcomes and quality measures. However, they did find that the relationship between spending and the number of certificates and degrees produced has changed little in recent years. For several types of institutions, there is some evidence of a lower cost per credential, but this analysis is not definitive.

There are limits to cost accounting using the national IPEDS data. Even the researchers of the Delta Project recognize that "aggregate data are not a substitute for the more granular analysis that institutions and states need to perform regularly to examine their own spending patterns."[13] Some of the limitations of IPEDS include the fact that it does not distinguish between expenditures by discipline or level (remedial versus undergraduate versus graduate education). Institutional financial aid and tuition discounting are also not reported as spending in IPEDS. Instead, IPEDS uses a measure of "scholarships and fellowships," which is only a fraction of institutional aid. Still, as one of the only sources for national-level studies of higher-education spending, IPEDS is the foundation of much of what is known about college expenditures.

Other Studies of College Spending

The Delaware Study of Instructional Costs and Productivity was also developed in response to the 1998 mandate by Congress to study college costs and prices. The report focuses on direct instructional expenditures at four-year colleges and universities using data from multiple cycles of the Delaware Study of Instructional Costs and Productivity, which was begun in 1992 by the Office of Institutional Research and Planning at the University of Delaware.[14] The data contain information on teaching loads by faculty category, instructional costs, and externally funded scholarly activity, all at the level of the academic discipline, for over three hundred four-year institutions. Therefore, compared to IPEDS, much more detailed analysis is possible, taking into account teaching and differences across disciplines. However, because participation was voluntary, the data do not give a national picture of college instructional expenditures. This also raises the issues of nonresponse bias, and the authors of the study acknowledge that institutions that participated in the study were more likely to have at least five thousand students and be organizationally complex.

The focal measure in the Delaware study is the direct instructional cost per student credit hour taught. This was defined as total direct instructional expenditures divided by total student credit hours taught for 1998 to 2001. While the Delaware study provides an example of how costs can be measured, the true aim of the study was to explain why there are cost differences across institutions. The researchers conclude that multiple factors are related to cost differences, and importantly, relative to the accountability debate is the fact that they identify factors that have nothing to do with the effective or efficient use of resources. For example, the authors conclude that most of the variance in cost is due to differences in the mix of disciplines across institutions. Carnegie classification, which captures some of the differences in institutional missions, was another important factor in differences in costs. The authors surmise that the Carnegie classifications are associated with different faculty responsibilities; for example, faculty at research universities are expected to teach fewer student-credit hours so that they can be more engaged in research activities.

Documenting the important role of disciplinary mix, Carnegie classification and other factors suggests the need for nuance in comparisons across colleges and universities. Differences in mission, student body characteristics, and environment are important, but so too is the academic mix of departments, the number of credit hours taught, faculty characteristics, as well as the role of research. It is also worth noting that researchers found "no apparent relationship between the level of instructional expenditures at an institution and the tuition rate charged by that institution."[15] This is counter to the issues that were originally raised by Congress to motivate the need for such a cost study. They caution not to use price (i.e., tuition) and cost (i.e., institutional expenditures) as interchangeable constructs because price appears to be much more related to revenues than expenditures. As the Delaware study points out, "it is not practical for an institution to charge engineering majors a tuition rate three times that charged to sociology majors" just because of the differences in instructional costs.[16]

Other Key Considerations for Higher-Education Finance Accountability

After collecting the appropriate data, which as noted above is neither straightforward nor easy, one must make a series of additional decisions, including judging what are good and bad uses of funds and how to use cost information in an incentive structure with rewards and/or penalties. Underlying any accountability system, though, is the assumption that money is somehow related to postsecondary results. The goals of accountability include the improved use of funds with the hope that this will relate positively to student outcomes or the more efficient use of limited resources. In short, in higher education it is important to consider not only the amount of money spent but also how it is spent.

How Should One Judge College Spending?

The National Commission on the Cost of Higher Education called for more detailed data to enable better cost-measurement analysis, and better data would certainly help. However, such measures still require some interpretation and judgment about what are good versus bad uses for resources. As noted by Dennis Jones, accounting efforts naturally result in additional questions: "Even if the total level of resources is the same, the way institutions choose to utilize these resources will vary for reasons of both choice and circumstance... one is inevitably drawn to the next set of 'whys.'"[17] There are multiple ways resources could be used due to the situation and preferences of the institution. However, what is not clear is if the way in which the funds are allocated in one scenario versus another is better or worse.

The true difficulty in higher-education finance accountability is judging what is an "effective" (in terms of bringing about positive student outcomes) and "efficient" use of resources, as the focus of many of the calls for accountability have been in response to feeling that colleges are wasteful and/or fail to focus on producing good results. Because there is no clear standard for what these two key criteria mean in absolute terms, they can only be measured relative to other institutions or changes within an institution over time. For example, in comparison to other schools, if two institutions have the same outcomes but one spends more, all else equal, then one might conclude that the school with higher expenditures is not using resources as efficiently or effectively. Likewise, over time one would expect to see better outcomes as institutions spend more money. However, these comparisons across institutions and over time are still unsatisfying as measures of efficiency and effectiveness. For instance, these types of comparisons do not give one a sense of how close institutions are to using resources in the *most* effective way possible. Moreover, accountability systems have to deal with the added difficulty of being applied to institutions with differing missions, student bodies, and goals. This further clouds our understanding of spending patterns and standards for what might be effective or efficient.

Sticks versus Carrots: What Kinds of Incentives Should Be Used?

Accountability systems are based on some combination of sticks (i.e., penalties) and carrots (i.e., rewards). Central to this balance is the question of why there is a problem in the first place. In other words, *why is there a need for some kind of higher-education accountability based on finance?* The answer has implications for what types of incentives might be most appropriate.

One possible response is that accountability is needed because colleges and universities are not using their funds effectively due to laziness, intentionally wasteful behavior, and/or the lack of consequences for spending resources in an irresponsible way. For example, as Vedder opines, "The only thing missing so far is a will to change... American universities have made our nation a better place. But their inefficiency and indifference to costs could in the end bring them down."[18] If true, the implication is that an accountability system should focus on closely monitoring college finances and creating a set of penalties that punish colleges for being wasteful. The key to this view is that colleges and universities are capable of doing a better job, but they fail to act because of a lack of urgency or negative consequences.

Another possibility is that the lack of strong performance is because colleges do not have sufficient funds to meet the standards demanded by stakeholders. There is clearly a great deal of variation in the expenditure patterns and amount of resources available to different kinds of institutions. In particular, colleges that focus on serving students with the most financial and academic needs have much less to spend relative to their more selective counterparts. Therefore, there is a case to be made that the problem for some parts of higher education is that institutions need additional resources. The implication is that rewards might be the best type of incentive to use in an accountability system. If an institution demonstrates that it is using its limited funds in effective and efficient ways, then it could be given additional resources to help meet its needs.

Yet a third viewpoint on the key problem is that colleges and universities do not perform better because they lack a clear sense of best practices in terms of spending, and so the failure of schools to work more efficiently is because of ignorance. Certainly, research on this issue is scant, and there is little information about the educational process of colleges. In general, the production of higher education is largely considered a "black box," in which a number of inputs hopefully mix together to produce high-quality outputs. As Key points out, much more needs to be understood about the "science of higher learning," meaning how students learn, which teaching tools are the most effective, and how institutions can help even those with lower academic performance succeed.[19] Without such information, it is difficult to know how to improve teaching and student outcomes in higher education even with an influx of additional resources. If one believes the lack of professional guidance is the true problem, then one might consider creating incentives and opportunities for the constant evaluation of funding practices linked to outcomes and then compare these across institutions to establish a set of best practices. Another option would be to provide grants to help institutions develop and evaluate new and innovative practices.

In all likelihood, the true problem in higher education is a combination of all three scenarios. There are examples of institutional wastefulness, cases in which institutions have too few resources, and challenges that lack a clear set of solutions. When considering the design of any accountability system, one must consider which of the views is best supported by the available data and seems to apply to the target set of institutions.

State Efforts to Link Finance with Accountability

While the previous section highlighted several research studies that focused on college costs nationally, there are limits with any type of national comparison. In contrast, states have more specific budget information to understand the costs of their public institutions, and with a better understanding of the particular context, they may be better able to measure and interpret cost estimates. States have experimented with various forms of finance accountability for many years. The examples below showcase the range of decisions states have made regarding their policies, from the criteria used to how they have evaluated college performance, to the type, size, and timing of incentives. Table 4.1 summarizes some of the key decisions states have made. Although not an exhaustive list, the cases highlight the diverse actions and experiences of systems across the country.

Judging the Performance of Colleges and Universities

Performance funding or other types of finance accountability are usually not the first attempt by a state to engage with postsecondary institutions about their activities. When choosing indicators with which to judge the performance of colleges and universities, some states have based the criteria of their accountability systems on previous goals and priorities. For example, Missouri had long discussions about the importance of assessment, and the 1991 creation of the Missouri Assessment Consortium served as a precursor to the state's later approach to performance funding. The criteria used in the accountability system were marked by their direct links to previous planning priorities, and as noted by Burke, using these familiar measures helped the state avoid extreme reactions from colleges and universities.

Even if the idea of assessment is not new, when it is time to link performance indicators to finances, states must make concrete decisions about exactly what will be evaluated. Beyond the types of criteria, they must decide how these measures will be applied. Table 4.1 highlights some of the options and the decisions several states have made regarding the criteria used. Some have chosen to apply similar criteria to all college and universities, regardless of level or mission. For example, from 1994 to 1997 Arkansas judged colleges, using six major sets of criteria. As shown in table 4.1, retention measures received the most weight (39 percent),

Table 4.1   Examples of Criteria Used in State Performance Funding Systems

Type	State Example	
Same criteria for all institutions	ARKANSAS (with weights listed for each category) Retention (39%), including overall, minority, and transfer Quality (29.625%), including rising Junior exam and licensure/exit exams by discipline Efficiencies (17.25%), including program productivity Workforce Development (6.75%) Diversity of Faculty/Staff (4.875%) Graduation Rates (2.5%)	
Different criteria by college level	FLORIDA	
	Two-year colleges	Four-year colleges
	Number of degree completers Completers who fit special categories (e.g., required remediation, qualified as economically disadvantaged, were disabled, were placed in a job identified as critical for the state's workforce needs, etc.) Time to degree Placements, transfers, and partial completers	Six-year graduation rate for first-time students Four-year graduation rate for AA transfer students Percentage of students graduating with total credits less than or equal to 115% of the degree requirement Percentage who enroll in graduate schools in the state Ratio of externally sponsored research and training grant funds to state research funds

Continued

Table 4.1   Continued

Type	State Example
Some shared criteria; some developed by localities or institutions	ILLINOIS (applied to the public two-year colleges) Statewide Goals Student Satisfaction Student advancement (number who earned a degree or certificate, etc.) Student success in employment/continued pursuit of education Proportion of population served Academically disadvantaged students' success District-wide Goal Choose one of the following: Workforce preparation; technology; or responsiveness to local need KENTUCKY Twenty-six common indicators (mandatory), including the quality of educational outcomes, student advancement, the use of technology in student learning, the preparation of PK-12 teachers, and educated workforce development. Institution-specific (including mission-specific) indicators: effective use of resources, global perspectives in academic programs; review of gender issues; cooperative academic degree programs; alternative educational delivery; level of gifts, grants, and contracts funding; EEO plan implementation.
Criteria includes setting goals	KANSAS Institutions instructed to draft "stretch" goals linked to new funding. Institutions can only earn increases in year-to-year funding if they meet certain percentages of goals.

followed by quality indicators (e.g., exam passage rates), program efficiencies, workforce development, diversity of the faculty and staff, and graduation rates. Because the indicators were applied to two- and four-year colleges alike, they were widely criticized.[20]

Other states have, instead, developed criteria that differ by institutional level. In Florida, for instance, two- and four-year colleges were judged using a different set of indicators. Table 4.1 details the criteria for each level. The community colleges were evaluated based on degree awards, graduates from particular backgrounds (e.g., required remediation, economically disadvantaged, or disabled), the time to degree completion, and numbers on placements and transfers. In contrast, the four-year colleges were judged on their graduation rates (six-year rate for first-time students and four-year rate for transfer students), the percentage that graduated with credits close to the degree requirement, the percentage that went on to graduate school in Florida, and the ratio of external research funds to state research funds.

While the criteria chosen by Florida acknowledge differences between community colleges and four-year colleges or universities, other states have allowed the criteria to vary at a finer level. There are several examples in which states have used a combination of common indicators with other criteria chosen by the institutions or their local stakeholders. In Illinois, for instance, the community colleges all had to address five state-wide goals related to student satisfaction, educational advancement, success in employment or graduate school, the proportion of the population served, and the success of academically disadvantaged students. In addition, each community college was also subject to a goal that could be related to its local district. Each institution had to select one of the following areas on which to focus: workforce preparation, technology, or responsiveness to a local need. Virginia allowed even greater institutional autonomy. Although the state requires public institutions to gauge and report their own performance in a range of areas, it left it up to the individual institutions to decide which measures to use.

Allowing institutions to choose their criteria can sometimes backfire. For example, in Kentucky, the Higher Education Review Commission chose twenty-six criteria that all campuses had to have, but the campuses were allowed to select the weights applied to each indicator. Some institutions set such low standards that their targets were below then-current levels of performance. What resulted were several years of negotiation between the commission and university presidents, but by the time there was some agreement, politicians no longer believed the policy would be successful in bringing about meaningful change.[21]

Kansas is an example of a state that has asked colleges and universities to think not only of how to showcase their past performance but also set goals for the future. The state instructed institutions to draft goals that were then linked to new funding. "Each institution proposes its own performance contract, complete with proposed goals, proposed performance measures, and proposed performance targets. The Board requires that the goals included in the proposed agreements be 'stretch' goals that truly challenge the institutions to step up from business as usual."[22] Institutions earn increases in year-to-year funding only if they meet certain percentages of the goals.[23]

After choosing criteria for an accountability system, states have also had to decide how to apply those indicators and make judgments about the performance of institutions. Some have done this by comparing how an institution has done in a given year relative to its own prior performance. This appears to be the preferred method by institutions as other designs pit one institution versus another. For example, in Arkansas, because the funds not claimed by low-performing schools went instead to high-performing institutions, the campuses felt it created an unhealthy atmosphere of competition.[24] The community colleges in Florida also criticized a plan that measured a college's performance improvement against that of other colleges.[25]

The Role of Incentives in Finance Accountability Policies

In an accountability system focused on higher-education finance, the role of incentives is particularly important. The type, size, and timing of the incentives created by the policy are major factors in the determination of whether the system can spur better performance by institutions. Table 4.2 provides examples of the various decisions states have made regarding the incentives they have put as part of their policies. First, states

Table 4.2   Dimensions of Accountability Efforts—State Examples

Issue	State Example
THE TYPES OF INCENTIVES	
Reward	Tennessee: Institutions are capable of earning up to 5.45% of their state operating appropriations.
Maintenance plus inflation	Missouri: To receive inflationary increases in state funds, schools needed to abide by the "Funding for Results" (FFR) recommendation by the Missouri Coordinating Board for Higher Education
Penalty	Kansas: Schools that do not meet performance goals lose money. In 2006 all but three schools received full funding. The three schools that lost funds were at these levels: Highland Community College lost $80,374 (lost 2/3rd of funding); Independence Community College lost $17,306 (no funding); Salina Area Technical School lost $383,319 (no funding)
THE TIMING OF INCENTIVES	
Timing	Florida: The community colleges criticized WDEH for the way it left colleges uncertain about their funding because of its holdback feature
THE AMOUNT OF INCENTIVES	
Too little at stake	Arkansas: The reward was only a modest sum of total state appropriations.
	Florida: Performance Based Budgeting (PBB) encompassed around 1% of state appropriations to community colleges ($8.3 million in 2000). The state also had the Workforce Development Education Fund, which was much larger (see note below).
	Illinois: Funds equaled 0.4% of state appropriations to community colleges in 2000–2001 and were in addition to the main enrollment-based state funding.
	Minnesota: Up to a 1% increase in the noninstructional budgets of systems that met the performance indicators and standards established by their governing boards

Continued

Table 4.2   Continued

Issue	State Example
Large enough	Florida: WDEF ranged up to 5.6% of state appropriations. WDEF did not provide additional incentive funding. Instead the state withheld 15% of the prior year's workforce appropriations, and community colleges/tech institutes were then required to earn that money back based on their performances on certain indicators. Missouri: In 1993, the state supported performance funding with $3 million (less than 0.5% of appropriations to higher education), but from FY 1994 to FY 2001, "Funding for Results" (FFR) had an increase to $66 million in funding to institutional core budgets.
Increases over time	Florida: The community colleges criticized the lack of increases in state funding despite improvements in performance.

must determine whether the policy will incorporate rewards for meeting standards, just maintain funding levels for doing so, or enact penalties for failing to perform adequately. Then, the timing of when the reward or penalty is executed can be important to how institutions respond. Finally, the size of the incentives must be enough to encourage the intended behavior among colleges and universities.

Tennessee is an example of a state that uses rewards as incentives in its accountability program. As noted in table 4.2, institutions can earn up to 5.45 percent of their state operating appropriations. Quoting the state's performance-funding Web site, "This program is a rare incentive opportunity for institutions to earn resources above and beyond formula-based appropriations."[26] Instead of introducing new resources, Missouri designed its accountability system to reward institutions with an inflationary increase in their funding. Put another way, institutions that met standards had their funding maintained with an adjustment for inflation. The policy was meant to be a change in philosophy: inflationary increases were no longer automatic.[27] Starting in 2005 in Kansas, colleges and universities that did not meet performance goals lost money from the pot of new state funds. In 2006 all but three schools received full funding. As shown in table 4.2, one lost two-thirds of the funding, while two institutions lost all their funding. In making these decisions, the state board takes into account the school's level of compliance with its performance agreement and the funds available for distribution.[28]

Regardless of whether the incentives are in the form of rewards or penalties, the timing of the incentive also matters. The experience of Florida emphasizes the importance of providing the incentives in a timely fashion. In that state, the community colleges criticized one accountability program, the Workforce Development Education Fund (WDEF) because of the way it left schools uncertain about their funding.[29] Given the importance of planning in the administration of colleges, uncertainty could undermine the incentive created by a policy.

If incentives are not large enough to elicit a response, the policy will fail. There are many examples. As summarized in table 4.2, in Arkansas the reward for performance was only a modest share of total state appropriations. In Florida, performance-based budgeting (PBB) encompassed only about 1 percent of state appropriations to community colleges, or $8.3 million in 2000.[30] Likewise in Illinois, the accountability system only put at stake 0.4 percent of state appropriations to community colleges in 2000–2001. These funds were in addition to the funding schools received, based on an enrollment-based formula. Minnesota serves as a fourth example: schools that met their performance indicators and standards could only get up to a 1 percent increase in their noninstructional budgets. One reason for the lack of strong incentives has been that most systems have avoided putting base funding at risk. Instead, funding in accountability efforts such as performance funding has most often been confined to new sources of money.[31]

There are also state models with large incentives. As noted above, Florida had WDEF for several years. Its incentive ranged up to 5.6 percent of state appropriations, and the state could withhold up to 15 percent of the prior year's workforce appropriations. In Missouri, over time, the FFR program resulted in an increase of $66 million in funding to the core budgets of postsecondary institutions.[32]

Over time, the size of the incentive may grow in importance. If institutions continually do better and better, they may expect that their reward will also grow over time. Funding for the accountability system in Florida did not grow, thereby drawing criticism from the community colleges who wanted additional rewards for their improvements.[33]

The Sustainability of State Accountability Efforts

Although there have been many state experiments with accountability linked to higher-education finance, programs are often cut after several years, and few are around longer than a decade. There are a number of reasons for this. In Ohio during the mid-1990s, the state legislature adopted performance funding for the community colleges. However, it ended due to a myriad of problems. As noted by Burke: "It suffered from too little funding, vague objectives, and uneven implementation."[34] For other states, there is a key problem that caused the termination of an accountability policy. Table 4.3 summarizes some of the main explanations and gives examples of states for each issue.

Table 4.3   Issues with the Sustainability of Accountability Systems—State Examples

Issue	State Examples
Budget Cuts	Florida: When there were cuts, the colleges preferred to cut incentive funding rather than enrollment-based funding. Illinois: Program cut due to the state's fiscal crisis in 2002. Missouri: In 2002, due to fiscal stresses, the governor did not fund either inflationary or "Funding for Results" (FFR) dollars.
Incentives become small relative to appropriations	Minnesota: When appropriations to higher education increased because of improvement in the economy, the interest in performance funding declined. It was replaced with performance reporting.
Disappearing political support	Florida: The legislators who had championed WDEF were no longer around. Illinois: Loss of key champions in the state community-college board; new governor lacked interest in performance accountability in higher education; lack of significant support from other key constituents such as legislature and business.
The relative power of colleges	Kentucky: When it was passed that governors would be limited to one term, campus presidents and local boards of trustees gained greater influence on educational policy, and this helped to kill the policy.
Impatience	Kentucky: While the higher-education commission and university presidents debated appropriate criteria for their accountability system, the governor lost confidence that the policy could bring about meaningful change.

Foremost, budget cuts have been the blame for the dissolution of many state accountability systems. When there are budget cuts, colleges often prefer to cut incentive funding rather than core, formula-based funding. Such was the case in Florida. Illinois and Missouri also cut their programs during the recession of the early millennium. While fiscal crises explain the demolition of several accountability policies, economic booms can also be a culprit. In Minnesota, when the economy improved and state appropriations to higher education increased, there was less interest in performance funding, and the incentives were dwarfed relative to the main pot of money. Performance funding was then replaced by performance reporting.[35]

Declining political support has also been the reason why some finance accountability policies have been eliminated. In Florida, after a few years, the legislators who had originally championed WDEF were no longer around, and so support for the program disappeared. Likewise in Illinois the key champions of the accountability effort on the state community college board were no longer there after a while. Because the new governor was not interested in performance accountability, the policy ended. Other key constituents, such as the legislature and business, also had little interest in the topic.[36] Instead of a lack of political support, sometimes the relative power of college presidents can derail accountability efforts. In Kentucky, for instance, campus presidents and local boards of trustees were able to garner greater influence on education policy after a new law limited governors to one term. As noted by Burke, this shift in power helped to kill the accountability program.[37]

Impatience can also have a negative effect on the sustainability of a policy. It is not clear how quickly colleges can and should respond to incentives with improvements in performance, but the political time frame is short. As discussed in a previous section, the Higher Education Review Commission and university presidents in Kentucky spent several years negotiating appropriate criteria for the performance plan. In the meantime, however, the governor created the Task Force on Postsecondary Education and resolved that "efforts to implement a meaningful system of performance funding have been ineffective, and efforts to improve the formula for funding higher education have not resulted in meaningful change."[38]

Lessons Learned from the States

While research has not shown definitively that finance accountability can have positive effects, and the low rate of success among states remains disconcerting, there are, nonetheless, lessons that can be learned. First, the size of the incentive matters a great deal. If it is not large enough, it will not have an effect. For example, if the size of the incentive is dwarfed by other sources of state funding, then the accountability program will not have much of an effect. Second, to ensure sustainability, the funding for accountability systems must be maintained and from a source not susceptible to easy reductions. There are several examples of states that cut their programs during fiscal crises. Sustainability is also threatened by changes in political power. Over time, policies often lose their original champions or become the victim of growing power among the colleges and universities. The above examples also highlight criticisms about how colleges are evaluated, whether they all face the same criteria or are pitted against each other. Uncertainty about funding also can wreak havoc on the reactions of postsecondary institutions.

The literature highlights other lessons from the experiences of states. The first focuses on a major problem many systems have faced: the lack of good information. Without informative basic indicators and a system that helps to interpret that information, it is difficult to believe that an accountability initiative would have much success.

The measures chosen can also be problematic. Ultimately, states hope that their investments in higher education yield public and private benefits such as the production of degrees (i.e., human capital) along with the new information that might be beneficial to society and the local economy (i.e., innovation). However, in their approaches, states have tended to focus on aggregated measures, such as the total number of degrees awarded or the average credits taught by faculty. As emphasized by Carey, very little attention has been paid to what one hopes underscores these measures: student learning.[39] On the other hand, the positive side of the accountability movement of the 1990s is the fact that nearly every state now has institutions publicly report information on some aspects of its activities. However, more information has not necessarily translated into greater understanding of institutional performance or how that ties to higher-education finance.

Higher-Education Finance and Accountability: What Is Possible?

Is it possible to design a strong accountability system focused on higher education? Stated another way, to what degree could postsecondary finance systems be aligned with an accountability policy? As shown in this chapter, there are many challenges that would make one pessimistic about the chance for true higher-education finance accountability. States that have tried to accomplish this have most often met with failure, and even the "successful" cases have little proof of the beneficial effects of their policies.

Moving forward it is essential that states and systems are thoughtful about the particular obstacles they face along with acknowledging the lessons from the past. To be successful, accountability systems must consider the following:

1. Foremost, good information systems need to be created. Recent research such as that undertaken by the Delta Project underscores the holes in current finance data systems. A finer level of detail is necessary to better gauge how money is being spent and to what end. Aggregating instructional expenditures to the school level tells us little; instead, one might want to learn about the multiple forms

and types of instruction, by whom, for whom, and in what subject. Standard methods of categorizing the educational enterprise are needed to start such a data collection with some understanding of the diversity of missions of postsecondary institutions. Because significant costs are also spent on other functions, such as administration, operations, and research, methods of categorizing these expenditures at a finer level is also necessary.

2. With more information, institutions must do a better job explaining how these resources relate to specific goals, populations, and outcomes. Mississippi is a state that changed the conversation about budgeting from the typical set of requests to the more fundamental issue of how all resources are being used. The Board of Trustees of State Institutions of Higher Learning discusses with institutions how spending in major functional areas does or does not match with priorities. If spending appears to be out of line with a stated goal in comparison to other Mississippi colleges or national peers, then there is a discussion about changes that should be made. The board has also used information on spending to review expenditures for administrative and support functions, and as a result, they have made reductions in energy and purchasing.[40] As shown in Mississippi, even the simple exercise of checking to make sure that institutional priorities are reflected in spending levels can be informative and helpful. Core to such discussion is examining what spending practices are based on old assumptions or decisions no longer applicable. It is no longer sufficient to justify spending patterns based on the adage that what was done last year is appropriate for this year.

3. There must be real commitment from the state in the form of adequate incentives. While accountability efforts will certainly require the involvement of institutions, state governments must also be committed to the goal. The incentives must be large enough to justify colleges and universities working toward better outcomes but not create unduly destabilizing uncertainty in college finances. As such, the sponsoring organization must be prepared to put at stake sufficient funds in the accountability system. The appropriate benchmark will differ, depending on the state, current funding sources, and levels of support, but examining such patterns should yield good estimates of adequate incentives that can be adjusted over time.

4. The commitment to making accountability work must be held by multiple stakeholders and sustained. The goal of improving

higher-education efficiency and effectiveness must also be held by multiple stakeholders so support for the initiative does not decline over time with changing leaders or economic conditions. The experience of the University System of Maryland is an example of this principle. In 2000 the chancellor began an "effectiveness and efficiency" initiative with the goal of attacking the perception that the campuses did not pay enough attention to fiscal stewardship. Multiple stakeholders worked together to develop a set of system-wide goals, including optimizing the use of resources. Wellman writes that the system has increased teaching loads and limited funding to 120 credits for baccalaureate programs. The system estimates that it has saved $40 million during the last three years, and as a result, tuition increases have been mitigated and political leaders have been willing to fund additional enrollments. According to Wellman, "Maryland is an example of a place where transparency about spending has directly paid off in increased public credibility for higher education and a growth in state support when other states were reducing funding or raising tuitions."[41]

While there are certainly great challenges ahead, the accountability movement is not without examples of practices that might hold promise for future, better-designed accountability policies. The need and desire to find a way to improve postsecondary efficiency and effectiveness continues to be strong, and success is possible. Given the past history, it is worth noting that the expectations for success are low among many, and initially it may be better for states to go after the "low-hanging fruit." What inefficiencies are evident in even the incomplete data that we are currently limited to analyzing? Like Maryland, Wisconsin has also targeted credit accumulation above what is necessary for a bachelor's degree with positive effects.[42] Still, with the vast amounts spent on higher education and the substantial and continual growth rate of costs, widespread change may be necessary. While the answers are not clear, higher education is a business in which researchers work for years to uncover what once seemed inconceivable or impossible. That may also be the case in terms of accountability. Each year, each discussion, and each new dataset refines what is understood about higher-education finance and college performance.

Notes

1. Sandy Baum and Jennifer Ma with Kathleen Payea, *Trends in College Pricing* (Washington, DC: College Board, 2008).

2. Other criticisms focused on the argument that such price controls would lead to the deterioration of college quality. McKeon later revised his proposal by exempting many low-priced colleges from being penalized and delaying when colleges would be penalized for raising prices too much. Stephen Burd, "Republican Introduces Bill to Penalize Colleges for Tuition Increases," *Chronicle of Higher Education*, October 24, 2003.

3. Frederick M. Hess et al., *Diplomas and Dropouts: Which Colleges Actually Graduate Their Students (and Which Don't)* (Washington, DC: American Enterprise Institute, 2009).

4. Bridget Terry Long and Dana Ansel, "As Student Debt Increases, Colleges Owe More in Performance," *Connection: The Journal of the New England Board of Higher Education* 21, no. 4 (Winter 2007): 23–24.

5. Jane V. Wellman, "The Higher Education Funding Disconnect: Spending More, Getting Less," *Change* (November–December 2008).

6. One recent alumna sued her college for her inability to obtain postcollege employment. Peter F. Lake, "Will Your College Be Sued for Educational Malpractice?" *Chronicle of Higher Education*, Commentary, August 11, 2009.

7. Thomas Kane and Peter Orszag, *Higher Education Spending: The Role of Medicaid and the Business Cycle*, Policy Brief 124 (Washington, DC: Brookings Institution, 2003); Michael Rizzo, *A (Less Than) Zero Sum Game? State Funding for Public Higher Education: How Public Higher Education Institutions Have Lost* (Working Paper 42, Cornell Higher Education Research Institute, Cornell University, Ithaca, NY, 2003).

8. For example, see Gordon Winston and David Zimmerman, "Peer Effects in Higher Education," in *College Choices: The Economics of Where to Go, When to Go, and How to Pay for It*, ed. Caroline M. Hoxby (Chicago: University of Chicago Press, 2004), 394–421; Michael Kremer and Dan M. Levy, *Peer Effects and Alcohol Use among College Students* (Working Paper 9876, National Bureau of Economic Research, Cambridge, MA, 2003).

9. Most data only gives institutional aggregates in terms of financial aid. Even when aid figures are divided into types (e.g., need-based versus merit-based aid), it is clear that aid is often awarded due to a combination of need and merit criteria, and so the categorizations may not be that helpful. Only in rare instances is data available on student-level aid awards.

10. Dennis P. Jones, "An Alternative Look at the Cost Question," in *Higher Education Cost Measurement: Public Policy Issues, Options, and Strategies* (Washington, DC: Institute for Higher Education Policy, 2000).

11. Alisa F. Cunningham et al., *Study of College Costs and Prices, 1988–89 to 1997–98* (Washington, DC: National Center for Education Statistics, 2001). It was highly influenced by the National Commission on the Cost of Higher Education's report *Straight Talk about College Costs and Prices* (Phoenix: Oryx Press, 1998).

12. Delta Project, *Trends in College Spending: Where does the money come from? Where does it go? What does it buy?* (Washington, DC: Delta Project on Postsecondary Education Costs, Productivity, and Accountability, 2009).

13. Ibid., 6.

14. Michael F. Middaugh et al., *A Study of Higher Education Instructional Expenditures* (Washington, DC: National Center for Education Statistics, U.S. Department of Education, Institute of Education Sciences, 2003).
15. Delta Project, *Trends in College Spending*, xi.
16. Ibid.
17. Jones, "An Alternative Look at the Cost Question," 50–51.
18. Richard Vedder, "Colleges Have Little Incentive to Hold Down Costs," *Los Angeles Times*, July 18, 2004.
19. Lake, "Will Your College Be Sued for Educational Malpractice?"
20. Joseph C. Burke et al., *Funding Public Colleges and Universities for Performance: Popularity, Problems, and Prospects* (Albany, NY: Rockefeller Institute Press, 2002), 225.
21. Ibid.
22. Ernest G. Bogue and Kimberley B. Hall, *Quality and Accountability in Higher Education: Improving Policy, Enhancing Performance* (Westport, CT: Greenwood, 2003).
23. According to the Kansas Board of Regents' *Performance Agreements Guidelines and Procedures* (2006): "Commencing on July 1, 2005, each postsecondary educational institution's receipt of new state funds shall be contingent on achieving compliance with its performance agreement...The state board shall determine the amount of new state funds to be received by each postsecondary institution, taking into account the postsecondary educational institution's level of compliance with its performance agreement and the funds available for distribution."
24. Bogue and Hall, *Quality and Accountability in Higher Education.*
25. Kevin J. Dougherty and Rebecca S. Natow, "The Demise of Higher Education Performance Funding Systems in Three States" (Working Paper no. 17, Community College Research Center, Teacher's College, Columbia University), http://ccrc.tc.columbia.edu/Publication.asp?UID=693.
26. Tennessee Academic Affairs, *Performance Funding*, http://www.tn.gov/moa/strGrp_prefFund.shtml.
27. Burke, *Funding Public Colleges and Universities for Performance*, 118.
28. Kansas Board of Regents, *Performance Agreements: Guidelines and Procedures* (2006).
29. Dougherty and Natow, "The Demise of Higher Education Performance Funding Systems in Three States."
30. For some time, Florida also had WDEF, which was much larger.
31. Burke, *Funding Public Colleges and Universities for Performance.*
32. Ibid.
33. Dougherty and Natow, "The Demise of Higher Education Performance Funding Systems in Three States."
34. Burke, *Funding Public Colleges and Universities for Performance*, 176.
35. Ibid., 241.
36. Dougherty and Natow, "The Demise of Higher Education Performance Funding Systems in Three States."

37. Burke, *Funding Public Colleges and Universities for Performance*, 230.
38. Ibid., 235.
39. Kevin Carey, "Measuring What Matters," *Washington Monthly*, June 2007.
40. Wellman discusses several examples of promising practices in "The Higher Education Funding Disconnect: Spending More, Getting Less."
41. Ibid.
42. Ibid.

5

Death of a University

Kevin Carey

Southeastern University had the saddest bookstore you'll ever see. It was more of a walk-in closet, really, a tiny space off the lobby of the university's one and only building. When I walked through the bookstore doorway in May 2009, the shelves were half bare, haphazardly stocked with Kleenex and sundries, introductory business textbooks, and, inexplicably, two brand-new copies of William T. Vollmann's sprawling 2005 novel, *Europe Central*.

I left without buying anything and wandered down a nearby hallway, which was filled with the kind of notices and advertisements ("Roommate needed—no smokers or pets!") found on college walls everywhere. But on closer inspection, some of the notices seemed strange. "Listing of Classes Without an Instructor," one said, followed by a lengthy roster of courses such as Principles of Accounting and Health Services Information Systems. Oddly, it didn't suggest that the classes had been *cancelled* due to the lack of someone to teach them. It was more, "Hey, FYI."

After further wandering, I was drawn back to the closet-cum-bookstore. There was a small stack of T-shirts in one corner, along with hats, bags, and paperweights, all bearing the university's official seal. "Chartered by the Congress of the United States," the seal proclaimed, in circumnavigational text, along with a bid for aged-based gravitas: "1879." I bought a paperweight—$1.99, on sale—and dropped it in my bag before walking across the lobby to a kiosk under a sign that read Admissions.

"I'm interested in university course offerings," I said to the woman behind the counter. "Do you have a catalog?"

"I'm not allowed to give out that information," she replied.

"But the sign says Admissions."

"I know. But we're not allowed to give it out. Everything's on hold right now because of the—you know—the situation."

There was an aura of gloom in the squat, deteriorating building on the fenced-in corner lot that comprised the beginning and the end of the Southeastern campus in Washington, DC. And for good reason: the university was about to be shut down. Two months earlier, the Middle States Association of Colleges and Schools had decided to revoke the school's accreditation. Because only accredited schools can accept federal financial aid, upon which the large majority of Southeastern students depended, the decision amounted to a death sentence for the beleaguered college.

But the fact that this had happened was less surprising than the fact that it hadn't happened sooner. Southeastern had lived for many years on the most distant margins of higher education, mired in obscurity, mediocrity, cronyism, and intermittent corruption. Students routinely dropped out and defaulted on their student loans while the small, nonselective school lurched from one financial crisis to another. Yet during all that time, Southeastern enjoyed the most gold of gold, approval seals: "regional" accreditation, the very same mark of quality granted to Ivy League universities including Princeton, Columbia, Penn, and Cornell along with world-famous research institutions such as Georgetown University, which sits in wealth and splendor above the Potomac River just a few miles away.

The decades-long saga of Southeastern's perpetual dysfunction and ultimate demise exposes a gaping hole in America's system of consumer protection for higher education. The government exercises remarkably little oversight over the colleges and universities into which hundreds of billions of taxpayer dollars are poured every year, relying instead on a tissue-thin layer of regulation at the hands of accreditors that are funded and operated by the colleges themselves. The result is chronic failure at hundreds of colleges nationwide, obscure and nonselective institutions where low-income and minority students are more likely to end up with back-breaking student-loan debt than a college degree. The accreditation system is most egregiously failing the students who most need a watchdog looking out for their interests. The case of Southeastern shows how.

History

The Middle States Association of Colleges and Schools was founded in 1887 by a small band of Pennsylvania college officials to "seek at the hands of the present Legislature the passage of a new act ... to render impossible the further taxation of any property of institutions of learning."[1] This attitude toward paying taxes—and government in general—is among the many aspects of American higher education that have changed little throughout the centuries.

The following decades were a time of expansion and confusion in higher education. More students were enrolling in college and new, sometimes dubious, institutions were springing up. Standards for admission and credit transfer were chaotic. Worried that the government might step in to impose order, the Middle States Association of Colleges and Schools and its peers decided to do the job themselves by defining what, exactly, it meant to be an institution of higher learning. In 1917 the association formed a Committee on Standardization of Colleges. After due deliberation, the committee came back in 1919 to recommend the creation of a Commission on Higher Education. The commission would create standards defining what a college should be (e.g., "an institution must have at least eight professors," a half-million dollar endowment, and certain required courses in the liberal arts). Teachers' colleges, junior colleges, and technical institutions would not be considered.

Colleges immediately understood the importance of the designation. As Ewald B. Nyquist, chairman of the Middle States Commission on Higher Education in the 1950s, later wrote, "the most turgid, emotional and often irrelevant prayers for relief were made by presidents of institutions scheduled to be left off the initial accredited list."[2] After much debate, the original roster of fifty-nine institutions was released in 1921. The Middle States Commission on Higher Education would go on to become one of the six powerful accreditors that eventually carved up the United States into geographically defined territories or regions, giving them the deceptively modest designation of regional accreditor.[3] In most things (including other aspects of higher education), regional is synonymous with provincial and second-rate. In accreditation the regionals reign. Today, the Middle States Commission on Higher Education has jurisdiction over Delaware, Maryland, New Jersey, New York, Pennsylvania, and the District of Columbia.

From the beginning, Middle States adjusted its approach to accreditation to accommodate the demands of the times. The growing diversity of higher-education institutions quickly became an issue. While the Ivy League has not grown since 1921, many other types of institutions have come into being since then or have evolved radically from earlier forms. The higher-education system as a whole has exploded in size to accommodate a vastly larger and more varied population of college students. In 1926 Middle States agreed to accredit engineering schools. The first junior colleges were accredited in 1932, and teachers' colleges were added in 1937. To make room for these very different institutions, Middle States gradually generalized its criteria, moving from fixed quantitative measures such as "at least eight professors" to qualitative evaluations of standards broad enough to accommodate Columbia University, the technical college up the street, and everything in between.

Middle States also quickly ran up against the limits of its authority as a voluntary, nongovernmental organization that relied on the members it regulated for financial support. Due to various scandals and outrages associated with intercollegiate athletics, the commission resolved in 1933 to ban members from offering athletic scholarships. Two years later, it mailed out a questionnaire asking members if they were in compliance. They all dutifully replied in the affirmative. "Upon reflection," wrote Nyquist, "it seems probable that several institutions were not in harmony with the Commission's action and their uniform replies indicated a canting simulation of goodness."[4] Powerless in the face of widespread noncompliance, the commission abandoned the standard. Chairman Wilson H. Farrand concluded the matter by saying:

> Although in the face of manifest opposition we are unable to enforce the rule, the Commission takes this opportunity to reiterate its firm conviction that no college that grants athletic scholarships is worthy of a place on our accredited list.[5]

Today, athletic scholarships and related outrages remain widespread in the middle states, as elsewhere.

The commission was a creature of the institutions that formed it and thus adopted a fundamentally collegial approach to quality control. The association was a club, a guild, and difficult conversations would remain safely within shared walls. "To divulge the name of an institution which is just not quite good enough or which is in trouble," wrote Nyquist, "is a form of pitiless publicity probably never intended in 1921 and never practiced since."[6]

Middle State began with an inspectorate model of accreditation, sending staff to visit campuses and ensure that everything was up to snuff. Institutions chafed at the intrusion. One such dean noted "the well-known principle that an expert is an ordinary person who is away from home. These outsiders are brought in because of their objectivity, objectivity being the capacity for discovering faults abroad which you cannot recognize at home. To be a good educational surveyor...you must have a sharp eye for foreign motes, but a dull one for domestic beams."[7] By the 1950s, Middle States had switched to a process of institutional self-study. Combined with the abandonment of quantitative standards in the face of institutional diversity, this meant that institutions were being asked to evaluate themselves against standards of their own choosing.

As time wore on, state and federal governments grew steadily more involved in higher education. This presented a major challenge for accreditors: the associations were in many ways specifically constituted to prevent such encroachment. As one of the original Middle States commissioners said, "Fear of government in educational affairs and yet a realization that there must be some means of educational control and guidance produced the accrediting agency."[8] The accreditors would likely have preferred to maintain the collegial, guild-like atmosphere of accreditation indefinitely. But they were powerless in the face of tectonic historical trends.

In the 1950s and 1960s federal funds began pouring into higher education to fund various enterprises, including the education of veterans and the scientific research needed to wage the Cold War. In 1952 Congress passed the Veteran's Readjustment Assistance Act, a new version of the iconic G.I. Bill. It required the U.S. Commissioner of Education to produce a roster of officially recognized accreditors. The federal Higher Education Act of 1965 expanded these responsibilities. That same year, the National Vocational Student Loan Act opened up a whole new class of institutions to federal funds, including trade schools, technical institutes, and community colleges.

By the 1970s federal lawmakers had established the system of student-centered, grant- and loan-based financial aid that remains in place today. Rather than create a new system of federal evaluation and oversight, Congress tied Pell grants and other forms of aid to accreditation. Students could give their federal dollars to accredited colleges and no others. For institutions, accreditation was now more than just an issue of status: large amounts of money were at stake.

Meanwhile, college-going among high-school graduates went from being the exception to the rule. Advances in transportation and communication created national (and then international) higher-education markets. An abundance of media and growing societal wealth produced a thriving consumer culture and helped make the most famous colleges objects of striving middle-class aspiration. Both consumers and governments thirsted for information about higher education.

All of these changes produced a series of tensions and outright contradictions for accreditors such as Middle States. The association may have been founded on antagonism toward paying money into the public treasury, but its members had few qualms about taking public money *out*. So organizations created to repel government interference became increasingly enmeshed with the federal bureaucracy, becoming de facto public agents subject to ongoing oversight and review.

Public officials wanted accreditors to enforce rigorous standards of quality and judge colleges at arm's length. But the accreditors existed at the pleasure of their members, and—as the disastrous foray into intercollegiate athletics showed—could only push the people who paid the bills so far. Those people also did not want the bills to get very large. The massive increase in the number of institutions seeking accreditation created a commensurate need for more staff at the regional accreditors. Rather than ask for more money to pay for more full-time, independent inspectors, the accreditors began relying heavily on a force of volunteers from other colleges to conduct site visits and help render judgment. It was an inexpensive approach, but it opened the door for log rolling (you give my institution a pass, and I will return the favor) as well as the inevitable dull edges of collegiality.

The public demand for consumer information was a challenge in any case; colleges and universities, particularly in the modern age, are inordinately complex, multidimensional institutions. And whatever ability accreditors might have had to meet that demand was stymied by the inherent secrecy of the guild, an aversion to "pitiless publicity" in all its forms.

Before the advent of federal financial aid, schools that did things such as teach night classes for adults in business and accounting had no need for accreditation; they had no aspirations of joining the tony college club. But by the mid-1970s, accreditation had come to mean evaluating yourself against standards of your own choosing in order to indirectly receive large amounts of free government money. Unsurprisingly, a lot of the unaccredited colleges decided to take that deal. One of them was Southeastern, which was granted accreditation by Middle States in 1977. It was a decision the accreditor soon had cause to regret.

Difficulty from the Beginning

Signs of trouble were not long in coming: in 1981, the university fired its comptroller after an audit found she had inappropriately directed over $100,000 in university funds to a local culinary school, of which the president of Southeastern was a trustee.[9]

Founded by the YMCA in 1879 and chartered by the United States Congress in 1937, Southeastern had for most of it history been an unaccredited trade school. As a private institution, it had to charge higher tuition than nearby public colleges. Because most of the university's students come from modest socioeconomic backgrounds, many had to borrow to pay their tuition bills. For a significant number of students, repaying those loans was a struggle. In 1982 the U.S. Department of Education put Southeastern on a list of sanctioned institutions, due to loan default rates exceeding 25 percent.

Southeastern's business manager was the next to go, fired in 1983 after he and his wife were accused, as the *Washington Post* described, of "defraud[ing] the university of more than $500,000 through several local companies in which they were secretly involved."[10] The business manager's lawyer loudly proclaimed his client a scapegoat for "monumental management and accounting problems" inherited from previous university leaders. The manager pled guilty two years later, detailing how he had paid students $4,000 a month for janitorial services, charged the university $13,300 a month, and pocketed the difference.

Meanwhile, instead of fixing its student-loan problems, the university let them get worse: by 1987, the default rate had ballooned to 42 percent. In 1989 the U.S. Department of Education again cut the university off from federal loan funds. Southeastern continued to decline throughout the early 1990s with enrollment dropping from 1,800 to barely 500. The U.S. Department of Education threatened it with a $3.6 million fine for failing to properly account for federal financial-aid dollars.

Then, in 1996 the university hired DC city councilwoman Charlene Drew Jarvis as president. A PhD neuropsychologist, Jarvis was the daughter of Dr. Charles Drew, the famed African American doctor and blood-bank pioneer. The presidency eventually became a political liability for Jarvis: critics noted that her $110,000 presidential salary came on top of her $80,605 council salary, and questioned how she could adequately perform both jobs at once. In 2000 she lost her council seat to a twenty-nine-year-old political upstart named Adrian Fenty, now the mayor of Washington, DC. But Jarvis's leadership brought Southeastern temporarily back from the brink. She negotiated the government fine down to $500,000 and aggressively recruited new students. For a few years the university seemed to be on track.

Throughout all of these travails, Southeastern remained a regionally accredited institution, eligible to grant credits and degrees and accept public funds. Middle States was not, however, indifferent to the university's many troubles. Almost as soon as it granted Southeastern accreditation, it began threatening to take it away. In fact, the university enjoyed unqualified accreditation for only fourteen of the thirty-two years from 1977 to 2009. The other eighteen were spent in various states of probation, sanction, conditionality, and general opprobrium, including a near-death experience in the early 1990s.

The first years of Jarvis's presidency were fairly positive, and in June 2001, Middle States voted to reaffirm accreditation, albeit with a request for an unusually swift (for accreditation) follow-up report in 2003. Then, Washington, DC was hit by the terrorist attacks of September 11. The federal government responded with an immediate clamp-down on foreign student visas. Students from overseas (particularly Asia) had long been an important part of Southeastern's student body. It had also enjoyed steady enrollment in computer-science courses. The one-two punch of 9/11 and the Dot-com bust put a serious dent in enrollment, and the university had little financial cushion to spare.

In response, Southeastern began to aggressively move people into online courses, which, if implemented properly, can be a valuable option for the adult working students who comprise most of the university's enrollees. But soon the *majority* of all enrollments were online. This was illegal (the so-called 50-percent rule has since been repealed), and the U.S. Department of Education levied another multimillion dollar fine.

Southeastern's board did little to prevent these problems or help the university to firmer ground. "They were her friends," one university employee told me, referring to President Jarvis. "They were there to give or get money. There was little governing involved."

After receiving the 2003 follow-up report, Middle States demanded evidence that Southeastern had a plan to address its declining enrollment and deteriorating balance sheet. In 2005 the accreditor issued an official warning that Southeastern's accreditation was in jeopardy, one of the methods accreditors have developed to signal displeasure without officially revoking accreditation and thus administering the "death penalty" of removing access to federal funds. Middle States demanded more enrollment and financial data along with more information about student dropout and loan-default rates and "clarification of the institution's mission." In March 2006 it issued another official warning. Southeastern seemed headed for oblivion.

Then on June 22, 2006, Middle States took the warning away and "reaffirmed accreditation." What changed in the intervening months isn't clear, particularly since Middle States continued to require frequent data reports and plans. Four months later the accreditor approved an *expansion* of the university's scope: four new certificate programs in allied health that would be offered in southeast DC.

The respite did not last long. In June 2007 the commission sent another long list of demands for information and plans. In November of that year it put Southeastern back on "warning" status. Unsatisfied with the response, it moved two months later to put the university on "probation," which is worse than "warning," because of:

"lack of evidence that the institution is currently in compliance with Standard 1 (Mission and Goals), Standard 2 (Planning, Resource Allocation, and Institutional Renewal), Standard 6 (Integrity), Standard 7 (Institutional Assessment), and Standard 13 (Related Educational

Offerings) as well as Standard 3 (Institutional Resources) and Standard 8 (Student Admissions and Retention)."

It also had deep concerns about:

"Standard 4 (Leadership and Governance)...Standard 5 (Administration)...Standard 10 (Faculty)...Standard 11 (Academic Rigor)...and Standard 14 (Assessment of Student Learning)."

In other words, Southeastern was broke, depopulated, unorganized, and dishonest, with students who were unlikely to graduate or learn much along the way. Of the fourteen Middle States standards, Southeastern was failing twelve.

In March 2008 the commission reaffirmed that Standards 1, 2, 3, 6, 7, 8, and 13 were deficient. Three months later, in June, it sent a letter requiring Southeastern to "show cause, by November 1, 2008, as to why its accreditation should not be removed"—"show cause" being worse than "probation," which is worse than "warning."

Southeastern tried to put its best face on the situation. It continued to enroll students, and its Web site prominently featured a picture of President Jarvis in full academic regalia, clasping hands with then-Senator Barack Obama. "Is it business as usual at Southeastern?" the Web site asked rhetorically. "Absolutely," it replied. "*Southeastern University remains accredited by the Middle States Commission on Higher Education*" (italics and bold in original). In a public statement, Jarvis said "We are inspired by this exploration of our potential." The university filed a new report on February 25, 2009.

But by that point the hole was too deep to escape. Barely a week later, on March 6, 2009, Middle States sent Jarvis a letter informing her that the commission had voted to remove Southeastern's accreditation, effective August 31, 2009. Most publicly available accreditation-related documents are maddeningly vague or steeped in impenetrable jargon. This letter featured the kind of candor and clarity that one uses in discussing a broken relationship that is unlikely to be repaired. In justifying its decision, the commission described a litany of findings of and failures, including:

1. "The strategic plan has no timelines for implementation."
2. "Most of the various plans documented in the response might be characterized as wish lists rather than plans."
3. "The institution was spending more on fund-raising than it was receiving gifts and donations."

4. While Southeastern "pledged to establish a fund…to meet the immediate financial, operational, and human resources needs…no information was provided on what those needs are, how large the fund will be, or how or when it will be deployed."

5. "While the institution copied the Commission on its November 3, 2008 response to a U.S. Department of Education review, the institution's failure to include any mention of this review in its November 1, 2008 report demonstrates a lack of integrity."

6. "The team noticed seriously invalid student data presented with the institution's November 1, 2008 report."

7. "The most recent six-year graduation rate for all first-time (full-time and part-time) baccalaureate students was 14%, with another 11% returning."

8. "Southeastern University began the Fall 2008 quadmester with only six full-time faculty members for over 30 academic programs. Two of the full-time faculty members —the registrar and assessment coordinator—also had administrative responsibilities."

9. "The response documented pass rates on six assessment exams administered by the [recently created, with Middles State approval] Center for Allied Health Education. Pass rates were 0% on three of the exams, 16% on one exam, 33% on one exam, and 40% on one exam."

10. The team "found no evidence that students have knowledge, skills, and competencies consistent with institutional and appropriate higher-education goals."

11. "Adding to the uncertainties of Southeastern's present status and plans for the future is the complete absence in the February 25, 2009, report of any mention of Southeastern's incumbent president, Charlene Drew Jarvis, in the text or as a signatory."

The list of shortcomings and broken promises goes on for pages. It provides more than ample evidence for revoking accreditation. But it also raises the question of why such dismal performance was allowed to persist. Given the university's extended history of loan defaults, financial struggles, and scandal, it is fair to assume that a similar report could have been issued years or even decades before. Why wait so long to pull the plug? Surprisingly, Middle States provided an entirely plausible answer at the end of the document:

"Ever since Southeastern University's initial accreditation by the Middle States Commission on Higher Education in 1977, the Commission has recognized the University's mission of serving diverse and underserved student populations. It is largely as a consequence of this recognition that the Commission has been so forbearing in its actions to date regarding Southeastern University, spending significant time discussing the Commission's expectations, accepting an exceptional number of late and supplemental reports, and deferring accreditation decisions when institutional circumstances have changed. Despite these accommodations, Southeastern University's history with the Commission has been characterized by a pattern of Commission sanction and ineffective institutional response...The issues considered by the Commission at today's meeting have been cited as ongoing concerns in Commission actions over the past thirty years."

One might logically conclude that low-income, traditionally underserved students are *most* in need of a high-quality university education and the protections of external regulatory bodies. Such students live at the margins of economic opportunity, often receive substandard K-12 schooling, and are most likely to drop out of college, even when they attend a nonterrible institution. They are also less likely to have access to the social networks and personal experience needed to evaluate institutional quality on their own.

Yet Middle States lowered its standards for Southeastern to near-subterranean levels precisely *because* the institution served vulnerable students. Rather than act with unusual haste to protect Southeastern undergraduates, it allowed the university to flail about in mediocrity and failure for three decades, leaving thousands of loan defaults, nongraduates, and students without the "knowledge, skills, and competencies" they needed in its wake.

One could argue that Southeastern is not representative of the entire Middle States membership, which is entirely true. But regional accreditation is not a factor in the upper echelons of higher education, where institutions are far above minimum standards. Middle States may accredit half the Ivy League, but the only practical consequence of this is to give institutions such as Southeastern what Ewald Nyquist described as "gilt by association."[11] Accreditation only truly matters at the lowest margin. Southeastern exposed just how low those standards have sunk.

This outcome was not an aberration. It was the unavoidable consequence of the basic contradictions that have plagued the accreditation process for most of its history. If those contradictions are not resolved, more such failures will surely come. Indeed, de-accreditation happens so rarely that when I spoke with her in January 2010, Jarvis seemed surprised that Middle States had brought down the hammer on Southeastern at all. "The accreditors used to say, 'We're your colleagues, we're here to help you,'" she said. "They're becoming regulators now." Emilia Butu, a former professor of business management at Southeastern, told me, "I had a colleague who had worked at Southeastern for over thirty years and she told me there were times in the 1980s and 1990s when the university was actually in much worse shape than it was in 2009 when Middle States finally revoked accreditation. She liked to quote one of the former Southeastern presidents who said, 'Nobody can kill an institution of higher education.' "

Divergent Interests and Goals

Accreditation has been controversial for as long as it has existed. Some of the conflict has come from within the accreditation community itself, with regional accreditors vying for power with "specialized" accreditors that examine and approve specific schools or programs (e.g., law schools and departments of education). Colleges were already fed up with the cost, hassle, and overlap of competing accreditors by the late 1940s. In 1949 the biggest, national, higher-education groups formed the National Commission on Accreditation (NCA) in an attempt to bring order to the chaos of multiple accreditors and address, per Nyquist, "rising national concern over the abuses and evils of accrediting."[12] It largely failed. Regional accreditors valued their independence and didn't want to cooperate with university presidents driving the NCA agenda. The regionals went on to form their own association, which evolved into the Federation of Regional Accrediting Commissions of Higher Education (FRACHE).

Not long after the federal government gave regional accreditors the keys to the federal financial-aid kingdom in the 1960s, policymakers began having second thoughts. In 1969 the Secretary of the Department of Health, Education and Welfare tasked Stanford University official Frank Newman with leading a Task Force on Higher Education. With funding from the Ford Foundation, the group worked for two years before presenting the first of what became known as the Newman Reports in 1971. It was, as one historian later wrote:

> "a blistering attack on accreditation as it was then organized. The Newman Report proposed that the [U.S. Department of Health, Education and Welfare] set its own institutional standards, which would then be administered by a national commission. It particularly favored disclosure and a separation of [financial aid] eligibility from accreditation. The Newman Report attacked the accrediting process, and thus the regional accrediting associations and commissions, as 'self-interested, without due process, and educationally conservative.' "[13]

FRACHE itself had sponsored critiques of accreditation; the 1970 Puffer Report, led by Claude Puffer of the University of Buffalo, charged regional accreditors with being overly secretive and unconcerned with the public interest. It also called for a single national authority that would enforce uniform standards across regions, one that would resemble a "public utility commission with a responsibility for protecting the public [which] becomes less oriented toward the membership and more toward the public as a whole."[14]

Volleys from Washington, DC continued throughout the decade. As one Middle States historian wrote, "it was a rare Commission meeting in the seventies at which a major item on the agenda was not an extended discussion of how and in what ways the CHE should respond to some government action at the federal or state level."[15] In 1975 legislation was introduced in Congress that tracked Newman's recommendations. Feeling the heat, accreditors worked to bring more order and national coordination to accreditation. That year, NCA and FRACHE merged into the Council on Postsecondary Accreditation (COPA).

In 1979 President Carter created the U.S. Department of Education, elevating the secretary of education to cabinet rank and further strengthening the role of the federal government over education, including colleges and universities. The administration proposed severing the link between financial aid and accreditation and handing that responsibility over to state governments. States were becoming increasingly aggressive actors in higher education, a consequence of the massive build-out of state university systems over the previous three decades. Accreditors were able to fend off these ideas and maintain control.

The 1980s were calmer: President Reagan was more interested in abolishing the U.S. Department of Education than expanding its control. But by the early 1990s, accreditors were once again under attack. "Accreditation is now seen as part of the problem, not as part of the solution," said COPA President Kenneth Perrin.[16] In 1992 Congress reauthorized the federal Higher Education Act and included major reforms to accreditation. Power was transferred to fifty state-level State Postsecondary Review Entities (SPREs), which would be charged with investigating institutions identified by the U.S. Department of Education as deficient on criteria such as high student-loan default rates. Regional accreditors would lose authority while institutions could fall beneath the federal thumb.

The change was short-lived. The "Republican Revolution" of 1994 brought antigovernment conservatives to power. The higher-education establishment quickly made common cause with Newt Gingrich and abolished the SPREs.

Resistance to Change

By this time, COPA had been replaced by CHEA (the Council for Higher Education Accreditation), an organization created by higher-education institutions to self-regulate accreditors in much the same way that accreditors were created to self-regulate higher education institutions. But the underlying flaws and contradictions of accreditation remained. The system provided little useful information to the public and did not enforce high standards of learning or student success. It was just a matter of time before someone who was concerned about these problems and had the power to do something about it came along.

That time came in 2005 when U.S. Secretary of Education Spellings created a high-profile Commission on the Future of Higher Education to examine a range of issues including financial aid, student learning, and accountability. Accreditation quickly became a flash-point issue, particularly after Robert C. Dickeson, a former university president and senior advisor to several governors, wrote a white paper for the commission that included a stinging critique of the accreditation status quo.[17]

Accreditation is a "crazy-quilt of activities, processes, and structures," he wrote, one that is "fragmented, arcane, more historical than logical, and has outlived its usefulness." Standards for regional accreditation, Dickeson noted, are "based on an institution's self-study of the extent to which the institution feels it has met its own purposes...Accreditation settles for minimal standards," he said. "Nearly all institutions have it, very few lose it, and thus its meaning and legitimacy suffer."[18]

"Any serious analysis of accreditation as it is currently practiced," concluded Dickeson, "results in the unmistakable conclusions that institutional purposes, rather than public purposes, predominate...This is not to suggest that institutions are ignorant of or antagonistic toward the public purposes of accreditation. But a system that is created, maintained, paid for and governed by institutions is necessarily more likely to look out for institutional interests."[19] Dickeson called for the creation of a national accreditation foundation, built as a public–private operating partnership that would take over the job of determining financial-aid eligibility and provide more transparent results to the public at large.

The accreditation community objected strongly to these ideas. The proposed national accreditation foundation would "[attack] the unique combination of responsibility and freedom that has historically defined our colleges and universities,"[20] said Judith Eaton, president of CHEA. Early drafts of the commission's recommendations included a major overhaul of the accreditation system. But under pressure from the higher-education establishment, the final report was watered down to include a finding of "significant shortcomings," including excessive secrecy, inattention to student learning outcomes, and hostility to innovation.

Secretary Spellings was not through with accreditation, however. She was determined to bring more transparency and information to consumers. Accreditation offered one of the few federal policy levers to accomplish this because the U.S. Department of Education controlled the National Advisory Committee on Institutional Quality and Integrity (NACIQI), a body that essentially accredits accreditors in their role as gatekeepers to the federal financial aid system.

While NACIQI has occasionally taken a hard look at the lesser "national accreditors" that have sprung up in recent decades to approve for-profit colleges, its attitude toward regional accreditors such as Middle States has been distinctly hands-off. Then Spellings began appointing new members to NACIQI with a very different attitude. In December 2007 the New England Association of Schools and Colleges came before the panel. New England was the first regional accreditor, established in 1885, and ever since has enjoyed the elevated status of accrediting Harvard, Yale, and other august institutions that predate the founding of the nation.

In the past, NACIQI recognition had been a mere formality. This time, one of the newly appointed committee members took a different tack. Her name was Anne Neal, a former aide to National Endowment for the Humanities chair Lynne Cheney and now the president of the conservative American Council of Trustees and Alumni. Neal was no stranger to higher education in New England, having graduated magna cum laude from Harvard as an undergraduate before going to earn a JD from Harvard Law School. She was not, however, willing to take the New England Commission on Institutions of Higher Education's word that all its institutions were up to snuff. Reading the commission's published standards aloud, Neal noted that individual institutions essentially had carte blanche to decide whether they were doing a good job. "What," she asked the commission's director, "do you view as acceptable with regard to an institution's success with regard to institutional achievement?"[21]

The director responded that institutional diversity made it impossible to set minimum requirements, but that every accredited institution "aims high…None aims to offer an average or merely adequate education."[22] She did not assert that every accredited college actually *achieves* its lofty aims, which would have been a difficult statement to defend, given that the New England Commission on Institutions of Higher Education grants its mark of quality to institutions such as the University of Bridgeport, which charges students almost $40,000 per year, has a four-year graduation rate of approximately 28 percent, and has been identified on multiple occasions as "America's Worst College."[23]

Neal pressed on. "How do you know that graduates of the institutions you accredit have achieved the standards of literacy to become informed citizens?" she asked.

"There is no accepted minimum standard," the director replied.

That was the issue in a nutshell. Secretary Spellings wanted regional accreditors to enforce some kind of minimum standards of quality, defined in terms of student success in learning and earning credentials. They would not necessarily enforce the *same* standards for all institutions, just *some* standards. Accreditors and institutions objected, arguing, essentially, that if the U.S. Department of Education were to judge whether accreditors were enforcing standards, it could only do so by having its *own* standards lurking somewhere in the background, and that this in turn constituted a wholly unacceptable federal intrusion into the sacred autonomy of higher education. For organizations founded to ward off government control there could be no greater peril.

As a result, the accreditors and college lobbyists took their cause directly to the United States Congress, which in 2008 passed a law prohibiting the U.S. Department of Education from requiring colleges to measure how much students learn. It also abolished NACIQI and replaced it with a panel whose members would be primarily appointed by the United States Congress. The accreditors had once again lived to fight another day.

The More Things Change...

It is remarkable how constant the criticisms of accreditation have been. For decades, people have complained that the self-regulatory, guild-like process is ineffective when it comes to enforcing rigorous standards of quality and making hard decisions about low-performing institutions. They have observed that the combination of self-defined standards and self-directed evaluation allows institutions to be their own, inevitably forgiving, judges of success. They have decried the secrecy and opacity of the process, the reflexive aversion to "pitiless publicity," particularly in light of the growing need for public information. In 1970 Middle States President Taylor Jones laid out ten theses for accreditation. The ninth was, "The public has the right to know more than the accredited status of the institution. (In 2009 when I asked Middle States for a copy of Southeastern's self-evaluations—reports submitted in order to receive millions of taxpayer dollars—I was told that the defunct university's records were unavailable for "privacy" reasons.)

And for decades people have been proposing the same solutions: decoupling accreditation from federal financial aid and moving beyond the archaic regional system. The fact that these reforms have been repulsed should not be taken as evidence against them. Instead, the history of institutions such as Southeastern should be taken as evidence that the reformers were right all along.

The past half-century has been a time of great success for the upper-echelon colleges and universities for whom accreditation is all but irrelevant. They have become wealthy and famous beyond their considerable ambitions. The predominantly well-off students who attend them have gone on to fame and fortune.

But the lower-echelon institutions—the only colleges and universities for whom accreditation really matters—have been far less successful. They have struggled with inadequate resources and a tidal wave of new students who emerged from high schools without basic skills in literacy and math. They have reported shockingly high failure rates. Hundreds of accredited institutions have graduation rates below 50 percent, and scores are much lower: 40 percent, 30 percent, 20 percent and even, as with Southeastern, lower still. The most recent survey of college-student literacy found that less than half of all recent four-year *graduates*—that is, those among the 40, 30, and 20 percents—were proficient in prose literacy and the use of numbers.[24] Minority college graduates scored substantially worse than their white peers.

While the survey did not break down the numbers by institution, it is a safe bet that illiterate college graduates are not coming from Columbia, Johns Hopkins, or Georgetown. Many years ago, the nation decided—or, through lack of any centralized decision making, simply allowed—that the best way to achieve mass higher education was to replicate the existing university model and ensure quality through the existing accreditation system. Today's deeply inadequate graduation and literacy results suggest that this was a tremendous mistake.

Accrediting agencies themselves, it should be said, are by and large staffed with dedicated professionals who sincerely want the institutions they oversee to succeed and thrive. But accreditors are severely and deliberately underresourced. As Ralph A. Wolff, president of the Western Association, has noted, the regionals accredit "nearly three thousand institutions serving over fourteen million students, with a combined professional staff of only 46 full-time members and 57 support staff."[25]

The fact that de-accreditation is the equivalent of a financial "death penalty" creates tremendous pressure for accreditors to forestall meaningful action until the last possible minute. As a result, accreditors often end up doing little more than stand next to the financial abyss and give collapsing institutions a small additional nudge on their way over the cliff. Even then, it can be difficult. In August 2009 Paul Quinn College successfully sued to temporarily block de-accreditation by the Southern

Association, despite the Southern Association's finding of persistent deficiencies in financial stability, qualified staff, faculty credentials, governance, control of finances, and student achievement, among others.[26] A historically black institution, Paul Quinn has a 16-percent graduation rate for black students. For black men, the rate is 7 percent. After the judge's ruling, Paul Quinn's president issued a statement declaring that "it means that our diplomas and credit hours mean exactly the same as any other accredited institution in America."[27]

The nation and its college students deserve a better higher-education accountability system than this. We should start by distinguishing between public and institutional interests, and reforming accreditation accordingly.

What Can Be Done?

The public interest should be protected by a single regulatory body, a commission on higher education (CHE), created by Congress and governed by an independent, bipartisan group of commissioners. In an increasingly borderless world, it makes no sense to leave access to the huge and growing system of federal financial aid in the hands of six different regional organizations whose jurisdictions are a function of historical accident and who are financially and culturally beholden to the institutions they regulate.

Instead, the CHE would enforce a uniform set of standards. Financial viability would be an important factor and the commission's independent, professional staff would have the ability to audit and examine the financial status of institutions, much as the Securities and Exchange Commission can examine publicly traded corporations. The CHE would work aggressively with law-enforcement agencies to clamp down on diploma mills and other forms of higher-education fraud.

The CHE would be much more outcome focused than are regional accreditors. It would work with higher-education representatives to develop a suite of common student learning measures that institutions could voluntarily use to report their success. In making accreditation decisions, the CHE would put a premium on results, not process. It would provide a quicker path to accreditation for the most promising new higher-education providers. (Currently, new providers are caught in a catch-22: they have to successfully operate and enroll students for several years before receiving even provisional or "candidate" accreditation, but it can be very difficult to attract students to an unaccredited provider.) It would not limit accreditation, as the regionals currently do, to institutions that provide complete degree programs. Students are increasingly assembling credits and degrees from multiple sources. An organization that is able to successfully specialize in one of those areas—providing only math courses, for example—should not be discriminated against.

The CHE would also have a quicker process for *revoking* accreditation. Failure would not be tolerated for decades, as it was at Southeastern, and as it continues to be at other obscure and marginal institutions. The commission would be far more aggressive about fulfilling F. Taylor Jones's ninth thesis and communicating accreditation results. It would not provide public information grudgingly; doing so would be part of its core mission. Results would be published quickly and clearly on a Web site specifically designed for students and parents choosing which college to attend.

The CHE would serve as a national clearinghouse for students transferring credits from one higher-education provider to another. The present difficulty of credit transfer is a large and underappreciated problem and another failure of the current accreditation system. Despite the alleged quality assurance of regional accreditation, accredited institutions routinely reject credits granted by other accredited institutions for inscrutable and self-interested reasons. The CHE would provide a nexus of information for students, the majority of whom earn credits from multiple institutions. It would also establish a baseline assumption of credit transferability; accredited providers would be required to accept credits from all other accredited providers unless they specifically explain why certain credits are unacceptable.

The CHE would not eliminate the need for regional accreditors, or for the specialized accreditors that provide in-depth examination of discipline-specific programs. Advocates for regional accreditation have testified on many occasions to the crucial benefits of in-depth, confidential peer review. The need for such processes to be conducted in an atmosphere of trust and secrecy is often cited to rebuff critics calling for more transparency in accreditation. In this new regime regional accreditors could provide peer review unmolested. They could conduct meetings in sound-proof vaults and store reports behind steel doors if they prefer. If the process is really as valuable as both institutions and accreditors often claim, then regional accreditors should have no trouble convincing institutions to continue engaging in it and paying to support its expense.

Handing the keys to the public financial-aid system back to the public (where they belong) would also free regional accreditors to return to their original purpose: establishing true standards of quality in higher education. The Middle States Commission, along with the other regional accreditors, was founded on the idea that a liberal education means something and as such does not mean just anything.

"At least eight professors" probably does not work anymore as a standard. (Although it would have knocked out Southeastern.) But it would not be unreasonable for a voluntary association to enforce legitimate, ambitious standards for the knowledge, skills, and abilities that members impart to their students, not merely in terms of defined curricula, but in terms of what students actually, demonstrably learn. Such standards could be set high enough to make meaningful, public distinctions between excellence and mere adequacy.

Accreditors argue that institutional variance makes this impossible. Indeed, the centrality of the "diversity" concept to arguments defending the accreditation status quo cannot be overstated. Asked for thoughts on the newly reconstituted NACIQI, former North Central Association President Steve Crow said that commission members need to "understand the tremendous diversity in U.S. higher education and, consequently, the decentralized programs of quality assurance related to that diversity."[28] Bernard Fryshman of the New York Institute of Technology said, "Our independent and diverse system of higher education depends on accreditation serving as a barrier against the Department of Education's direct involvement in college and universities." Susan Hatten, consultant to private colleges, said that "accreditation continues to be the best means for promoting quality while respecting diversity." Judith Eaton said that the committee should "operate within a context of respect for responsible institutional independence and academic freedom, as well as investment in the diverse higher education enterprise that has served the nation so well."[29]

Diversity is thus the main justification for both the *structure* of accreditation, with authority fractured and dispersed among dozens of weak, idiosyncratically defined, often contradictory organizations, and the *ethic* of accreditation, which manages to finds glimmers of promise in the most marginal and abject institutions. But while the defenders of accreditation allege that the all-powerful diversity idea is rooted in differences of organizational philosophy and mission, this is untrue. Instead, the American system of accreditation has evolved over time to accommodate diversity in *quality* to an almost infinitely elastic degree.

There was, after all, nothing remotely innovative or divergent about Southeastern's approach to higher education. It offered associate's and bachelor's degrees in business, the most common academic major in the nation. It conducted classes in square rooms where students sat in chairs, listening to an instructor. It had departments and degree programs and gave its employees titles such as registrar and dean of faculty and academic affairs. The lock-step imitation of standard higher-education forms extended all the way to the simulacrum of a book store and the Harvard-alluding "Veritas" on the university seal.

The only thing that truly distinguished Southeastern—the only aspect of the university that might legitimately be labeled "diverse"—was the abnormal tendency of enrolled students to not graduate and/or default on their student loans. That, and a propensity for financial misadventures among employees and multimillion dollar U.S. Department of Education fines.

Accreditation in America has settled into a series of unacceptably low equilibria: accreditors without the resources to adequately monitor institutions, standards that hover just above total institutional dissolution, a process subject to constant criticism, and loss of legitimacy that always manages to live another day. This is not good enough, particularly in a time when more students than ever want and need higher education, when economically marginal students such as those enrolled at Southeastern suffer from declining income and increased economic instability, and when the consequences of higher-education failure are more dire than they have ever been before. The Enron accounting scandals and the role of rating agency-endorsed toxic financial instruments in bringing about the recent near-collapse of the global economy show the inevitable consequences of allowing vital institutions to be monitored by allegedly independent organizations that depend on those they oversee for funds.

Higher education is too important to allow similar crises to occur. Small and insular, borne of antagonism to government control, accreditation was established at precisely the wrong moment in history, just before the nation's higher-education system exploded in size and became irrevocably tied to government funds. Public and institutional interests have been confused and compromised by the accreditation process since the beginning. It is time to separate them, once and for all. Both will be better for it.

Epilogue

By the spring of 2009, Charlene Drew Jarvis had left the Southeastern building. Accreditors may do little to prevent colleges from crumbling to the ground, but they have at least developed some protocols for helping students emerge from the wreckage in an orderly fashion. Middle States helped appoint an interim president to manage the institution's last days. The university held a final summer session to help as many students as possible finish their degrees. The nearby University of the District of Columbia (which has had its own troubles graduating students over the years) announced that it would accept Southeastern credits in transfer. Trinity Washington University, a private college that serves many DC residents, also stepped in. Students attempting to bring their credits else-where were victimized by the accreditation system's inability to manage credit transfer and were frequently refused.

The final class of Southeastern students reacted to the shutdown with a mix of anger and resignation. "I lost $1,300 because one of the classes I took could not transfer," wrote a student who enrolled for the first time in January 2009, only to leave three months later when he learned of the accreditation problem.[30] Said another:

> All I have received to date regarding the accreditation debacle is a series of emails. Initially we were told that they were shutting down online courses due to issues with the accreditation. Based on what I was told at the time, it didn't seem like this would be a long term problem, just a short term issue. If I had known that this was coming I would have accelerated my studies to graduate before this mess took place. Now I find myself in a situation where I only need four courses to graduate but I may have to start all over someplace else. In addition, I am out thousands of dollars in loans that I have to repay for an education that, on paper, is worth nothing. Near the end, they were not even offering the classes that I needed.[31]

On August 31, 2009, Southeastern finally lost the accreditation it had clung to, barely, for thirty-two years. The students and faculty dispersed and the tiny campus sits empty today. In December 2009 the university's few remaining assets—the building, student records, and materials associated with the degree programs—were absorbed by the Graduate School, a thriving continuing-education program that was associated with the U.S. Department of Agriculture until 2008. Southeastern itself seems destined to fade into memory. The picture of President Obama has disappeared from the Web site, which now simply says "we are not accepting students at this time."

Notes

1. All accounts of the history of the Middle States Commission on Higher Education are from *History Revisited: Four Mirrors on the Foundations of Accreditation in the Middle States Region*, ed. Oswald M.T. Ratteray (New York: The Middle States Commission on Higher Education, 2008), including Ewald B. Nyquist, "Life Begins at Forty: A Brief History of the Commission," and Richard D. Challener, "The Middle States Association at Age One Hundred, The Last Twenty Five Years: Issues and Challenges 1887–1987."
2. Nyquist, "Life Begins at Forty," 4.

3. The other five are the New England, North Central, Northwest, Southern, and Western Associations/Commissions. Jurisdictions roughly track names, but there are exceptions: North Central's bailiwick extends all the way to Arizona, while Middle States oversees Puerto Rico and the Virgin Islands.

4. Nyquist, "Life Begins at Forty," 6.

5. Quoted in Nyquist, "Life Begins at Forty," 8.

6. Nyquist, "Life Begins at Forty," 5.

7. Ewald B. Nyquist, "The Princeton Conference and the Birth of the Self-Study Process: June 20–21 1957," in *History Revisited: Four Mirrors on the Foundations of Accreditation in the Middle States Region*, 51.

8. Nyquist, "Life Begins at Forty," 2.

9. Ed Bruske, "SEU Aide Awarded $600K," *Washington Post*, March 4, 1983.

10. Karlyn Barker, "Former Business Manager Claims He's a Scapegoat," *Washington Post*, September 10, 1983.

11. Nyquist, "Life Begins at Forty," 5

12. Ibid., 12.

13. Harland G. Blolan, *Creating the Council for Higher Education Accreditation* (Phoenix, AZ: The American Council on Education and The Oryx Press, 2001). Our independent and diverse system of higher education depends on accreditation serving as a barrier against the U.S. Department of Education's direct involvement in college and universities.

14. Quoted in Glen S. McGhee's comment on Doug Lederman, "Whither Accreditation?" *Inside Higher Ed*, January 28, 2009, http://www.inside-highered.com/news/2009/01/28/accredit (accessed April 9, 2010). Puffer Report 1, 261.

15. Richard D. Allener, "The Middle States Association at Age One Hundred: The Last Twenty-Five Years: Issues and Challenges, 1887–1987," in *History Revisited: Four Mirrors on the Foundations of Accreditation in the Middle States Region*, 26.

16. Blolan, *Creating the Council for Higher Education Accreditation*, 39.

17. Robert C. Dickeson, "The Need for Accreditation Reform," (Issue Paper 5, The Secretary of Education's Commission on the Future of Higher Education, U.S. Department of Education, 2006), http://www2.ed.gov/about/bdscomm/list/hiedfuture/reports/dickeson.pdf.

18. Ibid.

19. Ibid.

20. Judith S. Eaton, *Inside Accreditation* 3, no. 2 (2006), http://www.chea.org/ia/IA_041006.htm.

21. Doug Lederman, "Someone Didn't Get the Memo," *Inside Higher Ed*, December 19, 2007.

22. Ibid.

23. "The Worst Colleges in America," *Radar*, August 2008.

24. Justin D. Baer, Andrea L. Cook, and Stephane Baldi, *The Literacy of America's College Students* (American Institutes for Research, 2006).

25. Ralph A. Wolff, "Accountability and Accreditation: Can Reforms Match Increasing Demands?" in *Achieving Accountability in Higher Education: Balancing Public, Academic, and Market Demands*, ed. Joseph C. Burke (San Francisco: Jossey-Bass, 2004).

26. Southern Association of Colleges and Schools, "Disclosure Statement Regarding the Status of Paul Quinn College," http://www.sacscoc. org/2009%20June%20Actions%20and%20Disclosure%20Statements/ Updated%20PQC%20Disclosure%20Statement.pdf.

27. Paul Quinn College, www.pqc.edu.

28. As quoted in Doug Lederman, "Advice for U.S. on Accreditation," *Inside Higher Ed*, June 24, 2009, http://www.insidehighered.com/news/2009/06/24/ naciqi.

29. Ibid.

30. E-mail message to author, June 17, 2009.

31. E-mail message to author, June 16, 2009.

6

What's Governance Got to Do with It?

Anne D. Neal, Erin O'Connor, and Maurice Black

Just over a century ago, there was an outspoken economics professor named Edward Ross. Ross had some very particular views on the western railroads' use of Chinese immigrant labor and did not hesitate to make them known. As it happened, his employer was none other than Stanford University, which was founded in 1885 by the railroad magnate Leland Stanford and his wife, Jane. Mr. Stanford thought nothing about Ross's opinions, for he had passed away before Ross arrived in Palo Alto. But his wife, then the university's sole trustee, took exception to Ross's views and insisted that he be relieved of his professorship.

Mrs. Stanford's actions ignited a firestorm. Seven other professors—among them philosopher Arthur O. Lovejoy—resigned in protest. A national debate about free expression on campus ensued, fueled through the years by similar episodes at other universities.[1] By 1915, the nation's professors had decided to organize. Lovejoy and Columbia philosopher John Dewey founded the American Association of University Professors (AAUP) with the intention of establishing academic freedom—then a new concept in America—as a foundational professional principle.

The story of how American academics secured their autonomy through a steady and principled defense of academic freedom and tenure is both familiar and inspiring. It occupies a prime position in the AAUP's account of its origins and also figures prominently in histories of academic freedom and the university in the United States.[2] Mrs. Stanford's punitive pursuit of Professor Ross is a paradigmatic story, uniting academics (and often administrators) in a shared commitment to professionalism and in defending that professionalism against the inappropriate intrusions of lay trustees. As such, it is an event that cuts two ways: it provides American academics with a foundational narrative, but also tends to make them envision themselves as perpetually—even inevitably—under siege.

This chapter explores the evolution of this double-edged biography, tracing how clashes between academics and trustees have shaped their mutual perceptions (and misperceptions). Paying particular attention to how those perceptions have affected both groups' understanding of what academic governance is and ought to be, we suggest that much of higher education's dysfunctional governance traditions are the unfortunate result of a century spent attempting to limit the trustees' role to one of unquestioning deference and delegation. Examining how, over the last decade, policy changes, calls for reform, and rising public awareness have enabled trustees to reconfigure their roles, we conclude with a series of recommendations for how governors and policymakers can ensure that trustees meet their legal and fiduciary responsibilities toward the colleges and universities they oversee.

A Brief History of Trusteeship

Mrs. Stanford was not the first intrusive trustee, nor was she the last. At the turn of the last century, trustees and presidents took analogous action at the University of Wisconsin, the University of Chicago, Brown University, Indiana University, Northwestern University, and a host of other schools.[3] Indeed, the 1890s and the early years of the twentieth century saw a steady spate of clashes between outspoken professors and trustees along with an emerging consensus about trustees' nefarious intentions.

In 1901 for example, Ruskin College dean, Thomas Elmer Will, published an essay entitled "A Menace to Freedom: The College Trust." In it, he argued that conflict between "the industrial monarchy" and free inquiry was "inevitable." Since "free investigation is all that is necessary to expose the rottenness of the existing economic system," he wrote, "our plutocracy has issued its edict that the colleges and universities must fall into line."[4] Will's portrait of earnest, right-thinking professors being systematically and unfairly quashed by powerful vested interests—his stark contrasting of intellectual "freedom" against interested "menace"—set the tone for academic attitudes toward trustees despite, or perhaps because of, its overbroad and antagonistic strokes. Over the years, contemporary commentators adopted and developed his framework, as did the AAUP when it issued its founding document, the 1915 *Declaration of Principles on Academic Freedom and Academic Tenure.*[5]

The *Declaration* is an inspiring evocation of what academic freedom is and why it matters, and it is also a stinging indictment of the danger posed by intrusive governing boards. Echoing Will's influential "Menace to Freedom" essay, the *Declaration* outlines the "menace to academic freedom" posed by attempts to control or limit scholarly inquiry. It also adopts, in slightly diluted form, Will's caricature of trustees as wealthy conservatives who must be prevented from imposing their partisan will upon free-thinking and presumably liberal professors:

> As the governing body of a university is naturally made up of men who through their standing and ability are personally interested in great private enterprises, the points of possible conflict are numberless. When to this is added the consideration that benefactors, as well as most of the parents who send their children to privately endowed institutions, themselves belong to the more prosperous and therefore usually to the more conservative classes, it is apparent that, so long as effectual safeguards for academic freedom are not established, there is a real danger that pressure from vested interests may, sometimes deliberately and sometimes unconsciously, sometimes openly and sometimes subtly and in obscure ways, be brought to bear upon academic authorities.

Casting trustees as sources of "conflict," "danger," and "pressure," the *Declaration* places strict limits on trustees who are viewed as unreliable, antagonistic, and even uncivilized enemies. Boards that impose their will on professors are simply—here the *Declaration* quotes Harvard president Charles Elliott—"barbarous."[6]

In his 1951 classic *Academic Freedom in the Age of the University*, Walter P. Metzger calls Will's "thesis of conspiracy" "simplistic," noting that it prefers sweeping generalization to detailed contextualization and declaring that, "like all highly partisan theories, it falsely ascribed to one faction—in this case, to economic conservatives—a uniquely sinister role."[7] Metzger further observes that "virtue was not monopolized by 'liberals' and that guilt was very widely distributed."[8] It isn't hard to see why he felt that way. Between 1883 and 1913, the percentage of young adults attending college more than doubled and the size of the professoriate tripled; the curriculum expanded and diversified, placing greater classroom burdens on faculty even as standards of professionalism began to shift toward the research model still in place today. Concerns about defining and ensuring faculty quality led to debates about graduate school training, recruitment, hiring, promotion, and compensation.[9] Likewise, board composition changed dramatically; business magnates began making major, multimillion-dollar gifts to colleges and universities, and board membership naturally came to reflect this philanthropic infusion. Many trustees brought with them a businesslike orientation, and an expectation that matters such as management and faculty employment would follow corporate protocol.[10] Meanwhile, the concept of academic freedom was not something that was widely understood by trustees, or even by professors themselves.

All in all, the late nineteenth and early twentieth centuries were, for American academia, a time of rapid change accompanied by widespread uncertainty about what sort of entity an institution of higher learning was, about how colleges and universities differed in organization and purpose from businesses, and about what those differences meant, if anything, for how they ought to be run. The situation was ripe for precisely the kinds of clashes that took place, and the clashes themselves were often far more complex than history has made them out to be.

Edward Ross, for example, was not exactly an innocent, unsuspecting victim. As Ross recounted in his memoirs, he went to Stanford with the express intention of setting Mrs. Stanford up: "I would test this boasted 'academic freedom,'" he wrote of his arrival at Stanford. "If nothing happened to me, others would speak out...If I got cashiered, as I thought would be the case, the hollowness of our role of 'independent scholar' would be visible to all."[11] For years, Ross went out of his way to offend his employer's sensibilities, advocating for public ownership of utilities and free silver and articulating a socialism that was closely aligned with that of the controversial labor organizer Eugene V. Debs. Ross was also a committed eugenicist. Credited with the dubious historical distinction of having coined the phrase, "race suicide," he was so certain that "subhuman...Immigrant Blood" was polluting pure "American Blood" that he publicly advocated firing on ships carrying Asian immigrants into U.S. ports.[12] Ross's attacks were a direct strike against Mrs. Stanford's outlook; the Stanford railroad fortune, after all, was built on Chinese immigrant labor.

Mrs. Stanford, for her part, tolerated Ross's attempts to bait her for years before insisting that he be fired, and when she did, she expressed a not unreasonable concern that "however brilliant and talented he may be...a man cannot entertain such rabid ideas without inculcating them in the minds of the students under his charge."[13] If Mrs. Stanford got the practical points of governance wrong with Ross (it is now generally agreed that academics must have freedom of extramural utterance), she was at least aware that professors should not use the classroom to indoctrinate—something the AAUP took care to address in its 1915 *Declaration*.[14] Ross, for his part, skillfully parlayed his termination into a national scandal. Notifying the press the day after he was fired, he anointed himself as a *cause célèbre* for academic freedom.[15] He remains one today.[16]

As this brief history shows, debate about the nature of higher-education governance and the trustees' role within it has a long and complex lineage, one rooted at least as much in cultivated mistrust as in real experience. And small wonder. Unlike public corporations, universities do not generally pursue profit, or have shareholders to hold them accountable. Nor do universities typically face litigation for failure of fiduciary responsibility. As a result, higher-education governance has historically been defined by those with the greatest immediate interest—namely, the faculty. For the most part, the story of higher education governance has been told by faculty groups. And while these groups pay lip service to the fact that governing boards are ultimately responsible for their institutions, they have defined higher education governance in such a way as to suggest that trustees should not actually have full fiduciary power.

The concept of "shared governance," formalized by the AAUP's 1966 *Statement on Government of Colleges and Universities*, was motivated partly by continuing faculty concerns about inappropriate trustee intrusion. Issued in conjunction with the American Council on Education and the Association of Governing Boards of Universities and Colleges, the *Statement* announced that "the colleges and universities of the United States have reached a stage calling for appropriately shared responsibility and cooperative action among the components of the academic institution."[17] Pledging to foster "constructive joint thought and action, both within the institutional structure and in protection of its integrity against improper intrusions," the *Statement* insisted that faculty participate in institutional decision making from the setting of policy to long-range planning to budgeting to allocating resources and facilities to presidential searches.[18]

The faculty carried its point. As campus turmoil and faculty discontent escalated during the decade, trustees delegated ever more authority to the faculty.[19] Harvard's seven-member governing board began including faculty representatives, and the University of California Board of Regents delegated to the faculty all matters even minimally related to the classroom with scarcely a mention of oversight. Over the years, "shared governance" has largely come to mean that trustees should serve as fundraisers or boosters and should defer to faculty and other internal constituencies on everything else.

The facts surrounding academia's long struggle to establish and defend academic freedom as a recognized professional value should neither be diminished nor denied. As we have argued, however, part of the history of academic freedom in America is the history of how conceptions of and debates about academic freedom have traditionally been refracted through an often overwrought and divisive rhetorical lens. If trustees have deserved to be regarded with some wariness, their academic critics have done little to address a reflexive tendency to see boards as untrustworthy enemies.

So it is that, decades after the first AAUP statements, professional discussions of academic freedom are still oriented around the mistrust of governing boards that originally animated the struggle for academic freedom. It was back in 1914 that Princeton professor Charles Osgood argued that "[t]his power, which is properly that of the Faculty, declines in many institutions to almost nothing, and is, I believe, more gravely menaced every year."[20] But you would think it was only yesterday. In 1989 the AAUP highlighted Osgood's comment as a key moment in the association's founding. And in 2002, Princeton professor and former AAUP Committee A chair Joan Wallach Scott incorporated Osgood's comment into an AAUP lecture about the "major threat" (her words) that intrusive boards pose to American higher education. Osgood's words, Scott observed, "could have been written today."[21] Through such language, academics' original sense of professional "menace" is kept alive and well.

The result is intellectual impasse, an almost endemic inability on the part of reform-minded academics to imagine how necessary change could occur. Stanley Fish, for instance, acknowledges that too many professors have politicized the classroom. He has devoted an entire book to the premise that they should "save the world on their own time." But even though Fish knows faculty are misbehaving, he is unwilling to empower trustees to hold them accountable: If trustees had the power to do that, he contends, they would "simply take over the university and conform its operations to neoconservative imperatives."[22]

Calls for Trustee Accountability

Throughout the 1980s and 1990s, faculty and education leaders insisted on hands-off trustees. But higher education's rapidly changing landscape made this paradigm increasingly untenable. Broadly speaking, during these years higher education moved from a postwar boom to an era of comparatively limited resources; from decades of low tuition to tuition increases far beyond the rate of inflation; from a structured system that systematically exposed students to broad areas of knowledge to a lax one that left students to choose among hundreds of narrow and trendy course offerings. Political correctness grew commonplace and inflated grades became the norm. Student attrition and substance abuse rose. Teacher-education schools became cash cows that failed to prepare qualified teachers. Tenure began to disappear as colleges and universities relied increasingly on adjunct teachers; academic freedom hung in the balance.

In short, higher education experienced problems of accountability at all levels.[23]

More to the point: the reigning model of governance began to be seen as part of the problem. While shared governance was premised on faculty participation and self-policing, there was growing evidence—and growing concern—that many faculty were interested in neither. Recognizing that something had to be done, a few iconoclasts began calling for greater trustee involvement and accountability.

An early, stinging salvo came from former Columbia University professor Martin Anderson whose 1996 *Impostors in the Temple: A Blueprint for Improving Higher Education in America* attributed higher education's travails to a massive failure of governance. Acknowledging that "plenty of people...can be blamed for the decline of the American university," he concluded that one group bore "the chief responsibility for the current sorry state of affairs."[24] According to Anderson, this was the "group of men and women who constitute the governing boards of our universities and colleges—the trustees, the overseers, the regents":

> We should not blame those who play by the rules laid down or condoned by the trustees of the universities. We should blame those who make the rules, for they are the ultimate governing bodies, they are the ones who bear the guilt and the shame. These governing boards, not the presidents or the faculty, are primarily responsible for the scandals of recent decades. When Stanford was casting out of its curriculum some of the canons of Western Civilization and cheating the taxpayer with phony research charges, it was James Gaither who was chairing the board of trustees, not president Donald Kennedy. When Harvard was violating the nation's antitrust laws by price-rigging of tuition fees and financial aid, it was Samuel Butler, not president Derek Bok, who was overseeing the overseers. When Dartmouth was infringing on the academic freedom of a student newspaper, the *Dartmouth Review*, it was George Monroe, not president James Freedman, who headed the trustees. When the University of California was substituting students for professors to teach its freshmen and sophomores, it was Roy Brophy, not president David Gardner, who chaired the board of regents.[25]

Anderson's comments took root. In June 2002 former Yale general counsel and federal judge Jose Cabranes weighed in with a pointed speech before the National Association of College and University Attorneys. While conceding that higher education was not a business per se, Cabranes asserted that universities shared some "deep similarities with business corporations," and predicted dire consequences if these similarities were not reflected in their governance practices. "Failing to see the similarities," said Cabranes, may "obscure the need to impose on universities mechanisms of transparency and accountability similar to those we impose on business corporations." Cabranes argued that universities' increasing reliance on external funding obligated them to reassure the public that they would not abuse or squander its investment or trust: "A university board that cannot ensure transparency and accountability in allocating the investments of its co-owners will have trouble attracting such investments in comparison with an institution that does ensure transparency and accountability."[26]

In 2006 former Harvard dean Harry Lewis provided a further gloss on the problem. Noting the growing scrutiny on corporate boards, Lewis worried that nonprofit trustees were not being held to the same standard. Using Harvard as a prime example, he observed that the university's Board of Overseers

> has become carefully managed and quite docile. Its members learn of important changes at Harvard by reading about them in the papers. Remarkably, this shift has continued even as the regulation of corporate governance in other businesses has intensified as a result of the misdeeds of notoriously inattentive boards of directors... Changing direction requires candor about the forces that have caused the errant course. It also requires leadership that views the university idealistically, as something more than a business and something better than a slave to the logic of economic competition.[27]

Former Harvard president Derek Bok echoed Lewis's concerns in his 2007 *Our Underachieving Colleges*. Acknowledging that faculty and administrators did not typically care about educational quality, Bok called on trustees to make sure that their institutions fulfilled their academic responsibilities:

> Who else [but the trustee] is capable of altering the current system of incentives and rewards to hold deans and presidents accountable for the quality of their educational leadership? No faculty ever forced its leaders out for failing to act vigorously enough to improve the prevailing methods of education... If trustees ignore the subject, there may be no one to press academic leaders to attend to those aspects of the educational program that are in greatest need of reform.[28]

Bok's call to action built on his longstanding conviction that the trustees' function "is not merely to interpret and justify the university to the larger society but to convey the legitimate needs of that society to the institutions they serve and to inquire whether more imaginative, more effective responses should be forthcoming."[29]

As Anderson, Cabranes, Lewis, Bok, and others argued for greater trustee engagement and accountability, policymakers and elected officials followed suit. Governors, for example, began looking more closely at their appointing function. Former Virginia governor James Gilmore personally interviewed all public-university trustees, instructing them about the importance of active, thoughtful stewardship.[30] Former Massachusetts governor Mitt Romney tasked the Public Education Nominating Council with identifying the most able and dedicated citizens to serve. Ohio governor Ted Strickland gave regents authority to overhaul the state university system.[31] Alumni and donors began speaking up as well, persuading trustees to insist on high academic standards and strong core curricula.[32]

On the federal level, a high-profile scandal involving presidential compensation at American University prompted the Senate Finance Committee to recommend substantive changes to board structure and practices. Internal Revenue Service reporting requirements are now more extensive than ever before. Following the 2008 market crash and the widely felt fallout from the Bernie Madoff scandal, universities such as Harvard, Yale, and Stanford have been publicly questioned about how they manage their tremendous endowments; boards' potential liability for failure to fulfill their fiduciary responsibilities has figured prominently in these inquiries.[33]

Higher education's accountability shortfall formed the centerpiece of the 2006 report from the Spellings Commission on the Future of Higher Education. A watershed moment in higher education assessment, *A Test of Leadership: Charting the Future of U.S. Higher Education* focused on the interlocking issues of access, affordability, and educational quality, noting that our ability to improve our colleges and universities is marred by "a lack of clear, reliable information about the cost and quality of postsecondary institutions, along with a remarkable absence of accountability mechanisms to ensure that colleges succeed in educating students."[34] This absence, the report noted, "hinders policymakers and the public from making informed decisions and prevents higher education from demonstrating its contribution to the public good."[35] To resolve the problem, the report enjoined colleges and universities to "become more transparent about cost, price, and student success outcomes" and to ensure that this information is "available to students, and reported publicly in aggregate form to provide consumers and policymakers an accessible, understandable way to measure the relative effectiveness of different colleges and universities."[36]

Rather than assuming trustees were passive players, there only to ratify or confirm actions of faculty and administrators, the commission called explicitly on "higher education governing and coordinating boards, entrusted with the responsibility to ensure both internal and external accountability... [to] work with colleges to improve information about costs as well as prices for consumers, policymakers and institutional leaders."[37] Offering recommendations for collecting and disseminating data, as well as for establishing accountability mechanisms, the report bundled those recommendations with something closely resembling a plea: "We urge the creation of a robust culture of accountability and transparency throughout higher education. Every one of our goals, from improving access and affordability to enhancing quality and innovation, will be more easily achieved if higher education institutions embrace and implement serious accountability measures."[38] Implicit in this statement is an admission that higher education lacks those very things, that in its present state, academic culture is anything but a "robust culture of accountability and transparency."[39] The anthropomorphic suggestion that colleges and universities should "embrace" the ideal of accountability likewise suggested that it is time for professors, administrators, and trustees to kiss and make up.

That is easier said than done, as the history chronicled here reveals. If academic culture is not committed to accountability and transparency, it is because the tradition and practice of shared governance is actively estranged from those values. Over the past century, faculties, administrators, and trustees have formed a governance culture that is not only unaccustomed to the ideals of accountability and transparency, but may even be said to be actively opposed to them. Defining trustees as a "menace" to their "freedom," academics have, in too many cases, set a tone that presumes bad faith from trustees and presidents and that urges professors to focus foremost on protecting themselves from the depredations of others. Receptiveness to change and openness to evaluation do not follow logically from these premises.

It is for this reason that calls for academic accountability are so often described by professors as "attacks" on academic freedom. And it is for this reason, too, that when boards attempt to become more actively engaged in oversight, they often find themselves embroiled in controversy, accused (sometimes with justification) of overstepping their bounds. A century of mistrust has not prepared the ground for the new era of academic accountability; in fact, it has done quite the opposite, producing so many roadblocks and stalemates that we now have what Professor Neil Hamilton of the University of St. Thomas calls a "crisis of ethic proportion."[40]

This is not lost on a post-Enron public alive to the need for new standards of governance. As the accountability principles established by the Sarbanes-Oxley Act make their way into the nonprofit world, academe's governance issues are becoming all the more visible, acute, and anomalous. And, as the Spellings report shows, our national conversation about the future of American higher education is in many ways a conversation about how academic governance must change. That conversation, in turn, is quite new. Before the American Council of Trustees and Alumni was formed in 1995, only one national organization, the Association of Governing Boards (AGB), focused on the role of trustees. But, as one trustee has noted, "The overwhelming message of the AGB is to cheerlead for the campus administration"; too often the AGB adopts "the proposition that any disagreement with the administration is micromanaging or intolerable failure to support the president."[41] The AGB is quite strong on this point: in its 1997 annual report, the AGB castigated trustees who sought "sources of information independent from that provided by the chief executive," arguing that such behavior amounted to an "attack on the university's integrity."[42]

To counter such destructive messages, the American Council of Trustees and Alumni and others have issued recommendations for what trustees can and should be doing to fulfill their fiduciary responsibilities, challenging the ruling assumptions that faculty and administrators constitute the governance structure, and that trustees exist to serve the institution first and the public interest second.[43] These efforts mark the beginning of a long overdue debate about what higher-education governance is, where faculty prerogatives end and fiduciary responsibilities begin, and what kinds of practical changes our colleges and universities need to make if they are to be truly accountable to the public trust. But debate about proper procedure will be pointless and may even fuel the ongoing problem if it is not accompanied by a concerted effort to reform the dysfunctional institutional culture that makes that debate so necessary.

Rules of Engagement: Accountability in
Twenty-First Century Academe

How, then, should we approach reform? There are many answers, but it seems clear enough that we should begin with education. Trustees are the ultimate fiduciaries of their institutions. But they cannot perform their duties if they do not know what that means. And all indications are that trustees are not being properly trained or integrated into academic culture. A 2009 survey found that most board orientation sessions last less than half a day; only 20 percent of orientations are a day long.[44] Such superficial preparation is consonant with the assumption that boards should be kept at arm's length, and should not be fully empowered to exercise their fiduciary roles. As a 2007 study found, less than 15 percent of trustees felt "very well prepared," and 40 percent said they were either "slightly" or "not at all" prepared.[45] Lack of preparation was strongly correlated with trustees feeling undervalued, dissatisfied, and at odds with the president, their primary liaison with the institution in their care. These factors, in turn, were associated with lack of interest in continuing as a trustee.

It is not surprising, then, that boards often suffer from the fiduciary equivalent of a personality disorder. Some are hyperactive and controlling micromanagers, intruding where they do not belong. Confusing governance with micromanagement, they insert themselves into decisions that are far beyond their fiduciary purview.[46] Others take an entirely hands-off approach, believing that their job is to raise money, wield the rubber stamps, and then get out of the way. Still others descend into sociopathic behavior, using their positions to perform political favors or to pad their wallets.

Nor is it surprising that faculties, for their part, often adopt oppositional stances rather than cooperative and proactive ones. "Many of my colleagues understand the power they have to stonewall proposals, filibuster new ideas, and engage in general foot dragging that effectively kills the ability of their organizations to react to the changing needs of society," writes Professor Sam Minner of East Tennessee State University.[47] In their struggle to protect academic freedom, faculty may, indeed, have become their own worst enemies. As Minner notes, "If we in the academy do not change in this respect, then board members or some other group (e.g., administrators) should act, and they should not feel bad when the howls of faculty protest begin."[48] Similar comments have been made about professors' lackluster record with the self-policing work of peer review. "It is imperative that we in higher education take the initiative to examine ourselves," writes former University of Colorado president Hank Brown.[49] "There are many lawmakers at the state and federal level willing to intervene if we do not do so."[50] Senator Lamar Alexander recently echoed this refrain, bluntly observing that "If colleges and universities do not accept more responsibility for assessment and accountability, the federal government will do it for them."[51] Such statements speak to how faculties' systemic failure to ensure their own adherence to professional standards compromises their ability to justify both greater faculty involvement in governance and their independence from regulatory intrusion.

Neil Hamilton has eloquently described how the professoriate has become so fixated on blocking and preventing regulatory intrusion that it "has been failing for many years in its ethical duty to acculturate new entrants into the tradition and ethics of the profession."[52] This failure not only yields bad behavior, but also results in academics' self-defeating unwillingness—or inability—to explain and defend their interests to boards and to the public. "The boards at many colleges and universities have been renegotiating a sweeping change in the academic profession's social contract over many years to reduce the profession's autonomy and control over professional work," Hamilton observes.[53] But, he continues, that does not necessarily mean that trustees are deliberately attacking academic freedom and its associated professional prerogatives. Rather, it shows how academics have produced a perilous self-fulfilling prophecy: "The predictable result of an anemic defense of a profession's social contract," he argues, "is that the society and employers will restructure control of the profession's work toward the regulatory and employer control typical for other occupations—essentially the default employment arrangements in a market economy. This is what has been happening to the academic profession."[54] As with people, then, so with boards and faculties: ignorance, willfulness, and lack of training produce destructive behavior. Presidents, deans, and provosts whose job it is to bridge the gap between trustees and faculties are caught in the middle: regarded by the faculty as the managerial enemy, they are often either micromanaged or given far too much autonomy by boards.[55]

Trustees should be properly trained for their fiduciary roles, and that training should include nuts-and-bolts procedural information; background on the history, philosophy, ethics, and legalities of governance; and substantive guidance on central educational values. Faculty, likewise, need systematic preparation for the "duties correlative with rights" (these are the AAUP's words) that form academic freedom. Professors should understand that the privileges of relative professional independence require them to hold themselves to high ethical standards and ensure adherence to them.[56] Administrators, for their part, need the managerial skills to work effectively with both faculty and trustees: they should understand the interests of both, and serve as a solid and fair bridge between them. All should know the history and mission of their institution, and all should grasp how their governance roles complement those of other constituents. If academia is to create a "robust culture of accountability and transparency," this is the place to begin.

Governors and policymakers have a vital role to play in ensuring that public university board members are appropriately chosen, well trained and, crucially, prepared to accept the substantial responsibility vested in them. In most states, governors appoint public university trustees, a fact that allows them to set the standard for positive reform. We have seen what Governors Gilmore, Romney, and Strickland did to bolster trustee engagement and accountability in their states; their examples should energize governors across the country not only to insist on responsible, thoughtful stewardship from trustees but to set the agenda for change and to give trustees a mandate to carry that agenda out. Toward this end, governors can commission studies of their states' higher-education systems, using them to identify areas where costs, accessibility, and educational quality can be improved. Governors can draw attention to their reform agenda and encourage discussion and debate by hosting regular trustee training sessions and by holding statewide conferences on higher education. Such conferences should engage the media, which should be paying far more attention to higher-education governance than it does and should also include all publicly appointed trustees; they will connect the dots between what the state university system should be doing better and what trustees can do about it. ACTA has already helped facilitate such conferences in Florida, Colorado, Massachusetts, and Virginia; these have featured such sessions as "What Will Students Learn?" "The Challenge of Academic Standards," and "Getting the Biggest Bang for the Buck."[57]

State legislatures, for their part, can do much to build public support for genuine and meaningful higher-education reform. While it is inappropriate for legislators to intrude upon trustees' decision-making powers or professors' academic prerogatives, they can and should foster necessary information-gathering by sponsoring hearings on key issues such as core curricula, grade inflation, and intellectual diversity on campus. They should also consider adopting resolutions calling on trustees to insist on more rigorous educational standards designed to graduate more informed and engaged citizens. States should mandate trustee training for public university trustees and authorize funding to make this possible. They should also insist on separate funding for boards to secure their independence, and should seriously consider a legal shift—proposed by Judge Cabranes—to increase board-member liability and grantor standing.[58] Only after such changes are made will states be able to say with certainty that public university trustees are prepared for their fiduciary responsibilities and empowered to carry them out.

Private colleges and universities are necessarily exempt from the gubernatorial and legislative input outlined above, but that just means the responsibility for ensuring that boards are properly trained and accountable takes shape differently. At private institutions, trustees are often hand-picked by the president, and are chosen more for their fundraising abilities than their expertise and willingness to ask questions. That needs to change. Governance committees, taking advice from constituent groups, should recruit capable and committed board members with independent judgment and diverse professional experience. Private boards should have their own funding to ensure their independence, should mandate annual board reports, and should set aside funds each year for training and continuing education.[59]

Change and Hope: Accountability Gains

Higher education's new era of accountability offers trustees a clear path to enhanced transparency, productivity, and ultimately improved affordability and educational quality. Newly empowered to ensure that their institutions truly serve the public interest, trustees are doing just that. Some boards, for example, are leading the way in controlling costs. When Atlanta's Spelman College cut a community-outreach program for budget reasons, the president credited the board with helping the college deal with the backlash.[60] The trustees of the Minnesota state colleges and universities system made a concerted effort to increase efficiency and reduce costs by approving 191 new programs and closing 345 between January 2007 and December 2009 after assessing enrollment numbers, student retention and graduation rates and employment outcomes. They also cut their own budget.[61] And Tulane University aggressively restructured the university after Hurricane Katrina, making it both more student-centered and cost-effective. The president, working with his board, consolidated undergraduate colleges and promoted a common cohesive academic experience for undergraduates. Tulane also pledged to focus limited resources on its most outstanding programs, while suspending those that did not meet high academic standards. The changes have had their critics, but record numbers of applicants attest to how Tulane turned a crisis into an opportunity to improve.[62]

Some boards are tackling the concept of accountability head-on, devising systematic metrics for ensuring excellence, efficiency, and integrity. In 2006, for example, the curators of the University of Missouri responded to cuts in state appropriations by eliminating redundant programs, streamlining the administration, and creatively using technology. They saved $20 million while still ensuring that students complete core coursework in composition, mathematics, and science. In 2009 the board, working with the system head, unveiled a comprehensive list of "accountability measures" aimed "to provide transparency and accountability regarding the University's overall performance."[63] The metrics included head-count enrollments, applicant acceptance rates, yields, student diversity, retention rates, graduation rates, cost and financial aid, pass rates on licensing exams, and number of inventions received.[64] The City University of New York has put into place a strong accountability framework, available on-line and called the Performance Management System, which outlines overall system goals and objectives including strengthening priority programs, attracting and nurturing a strong faculty, ensuring a quality general education, increasing retention and graduation rates, and increasing revenues and decreasing expenses and then judges the system and its component institutions on progress at all levels.[65] And the MnSCU system recently rolled out its Accountability Dashboard to provide information to the public and to "open up conversations about the best practices that produced exemplary results and the underlying causes of unsatisfactory results." The dashboard, which is available on the board's Web site, presents key performance measures such as related employment, licensure exams pass rate, completion rates, and student engagement.

Accountability metrics necessitate self-study, a long-neglected practice, which is finally coming into its own. The University of Georgia board of trustees, for example, recently commissioned a major, system-wide self-study of the campus climate, publishing its results and promising to repeat the survey annually. Faced with evidence of a lack of intellectual diversity on campus, the Georgia trustees also acted to ensure that grievance policies at all campuses provided students with the means of voicing concerns about classroom bias, speech codes, and similar matters. The University of North Carolina conducted a similar self-study.[66] Such proactive board endeavors identify problems and strengths and they help trustees, administrators, and faculties understand what changes may be needed and how best to implement them.

Most dramatic of all has been trustees' work to guarantee consistently high educational quality. In 1999 the trustees of the State University of New York voted to require a system-wide core curriculum. Today SUNY can boast not only of its size—it is the largest public university in the country—but of the rigor and depth of its undergraduate academics. Since 2000 all SUNY baccalaureate degree candidates have completed a core curriculum centered on natural and social sciences, mathematics, foreign languages, Western and world civilizations, American history, humanities and the arts, information management, critical thinking, and communications. Rather than expecting eighteen-year-old freshmen to intuit what they need to know, the trustees identified critical areas for students to study. Since adopting the core, SUNY has seen rising enrollment and admissions standards, both clear signs of heightened academic quality and increased educational prestige.[67] The California State University trustees and the CUNY board have taken similar steps to increase educational accountability and raise academic standards.[68]

As these examples suggest, governing boards are gradually but decisively adjusting their historically defined roles, becoming more knowledgeable and assuming greater fiduciary responsibility. There has been grumbling and resistance as there always is when change is afoot. Still, the era of accountability is here to stay, and the boards, administrations, and faculties that embrace it are the ones most likely to be steering successful, sustainable institutions far into the future.

What's Governance Got to Do with It?

Studies show that most people believe a college degree is key to getting ahead. But Americans express growing concern that they are being priced out of the higher-education market, and many wonder whether the ever-rising cost of a college education is worth it. Meanwhile, there is mounting evidence that the public's legitimate concerns will not be addressed without more informed leadership from those vested with the financial and academic health of our colleges and universities—namely, trustees.[69]

Responsible decision making is key to reforming and preserving higher education. That means rejecting an entrenched campus culture that resists active trusteeship and tries to limit the flow of independent information. It also means radically reshaping a board culture that views membership as a perk rather than a responsibility. For too long, ignorance, misbehavior, and mistrust have shaped academic governance. We can and should expect more. It is time to replace dysfunction, factionalism, and irresponsibility with the awareness, understanding, and intelligent engagement that can only come from systematic preparation for trustees, faculty, and administrators alike. This will be empowering and enabling for all. It will help ensure a bright future for our colleges and universities and for the young men and women these institutions prepare for work, citizenship, and life.

Much of our current conversation about higher education focuses on symptoms rather than root causes. When faced with rising costs and declining quality, scandals, and loss of public confidence, people expect to see administrators trimming budgets and faculties doing a better job of teaching and staying out of trouble. In the midst of crisis, it's easy to forget about trustees. But the reform we need begins with them. The answer to the question, What's governance got to do with it? is, in the end, very simple indeed. The answer is: everything.

Notes

1. This story is recounted in detail in Walter P. Metzger, *Academic Freedom in the Age of the University* (New York: Columbia University Press, 1955), 139–93.
2. American Association of University Professors, "History of the AAUP," http://www.aaup.org/AAUP/about/history/.

3. Metzger, Academic Freedom in the Age of the University, 139–93.

4. Thomas Elmer Will, "A Menace to Freedom," *Arena* 26 (1901): 246–47.

5. Examples include James McKeen Cattell's 1913 collection *University Control* and Thorstein Veblen's 1918 *Higher Learning in America: A Memorandum on the Conduct of Universities by Business Men*, both of which Metzger sees as characterized by "Jacobinic" rhetoric and "splenetic" metaphors. See "Origins of the Association," *AAUP Bulletin* (Summer 1965): 230, 234.

6. American Association of University Professors, *1915 Declaration of Principles on Academic Freedom and Academic Tenure*, http://www.aaup.org/AAUP/pubsres/policydocs/contents/1915.htm.

7. Metzger, Academic Freedom in the Age of the University, 176.

8. Ibid.

9. Metzger, "Origins of the Association," 230–33.

10. Metzger, Academic Freedom in the Age of the University, 139–93.

11. Edward Alsworth Ross, *Seventy Years of It: An Autobiography* (New York: Arno Press, 1977): 64–65.

12. See Thomas Haskell, "Justifying the Rights of Academic Freedom in the Era of 'Power/Knowledge,'" in *The Future of Academic Freedom*, ed. Louis Menand (Chicago: University of Chicago Press, 1996), 50; and Edward Digby Baltzell, *The Protestant Establishment: Aristocracy and Caste in America* (New Haven, CT: Yale University Press, 1987), 105–106.

13. Orrin L. Elliott, *Stanford University: The First Twenty-five Years* (California: Stanford University Press, 1937), 339–40, 343–44.

14. The *Declaration* notes that "The teacher ought also to be especially on his guard against taking unfair advantage of the student's immaturity by indoctrinating him with the teacher's own opinions before the student has had an opportunity fairly to examine other opinions upon the matters in question, and before he has sufficient knowledge and ripeness of judgment to be entitled to form any definitive opinion of his own."

15. Metzger provides a detailed history of Ross' highly tactical tenure at Stanford in *Academic Freedom*, 163–66.

16. American Association of University Professors, "History of the AAUP," http://www.aaup.org/AAUP/about/history/default.htm.

17. American Association of University Professors, "Statement on Government of Colleges and Universities," http://www.aaup.org/AAUP/pubsres/policydocs/contents/governancestatement.htm.

18. Ibid.

19. "The Robert L. Levine Distinguished Lecture: Myth and Reality of University Trusteeship in the Post-Enron Era," Jose A. Cabranes, *Fordham Law Review* 76: 960: "Today, the faculty's authority is exercised separately from, and even in spite of, the board's formally prescribed authority. Regardless of the role of the trustees as legal representatives of the university in its dealings with external forces, it is still the faculty that actually governs."

20. Quoted in "75 Years: A Retrospective on the Occasion of the Seventy-Fifth Annual Meeting," *Academe* (May–June 1989): 5.

21. Joan Wallach Scott, "The Critical State of Shared Governance," *Academe* (July–August 2002), http://www.aaup.org/AAUP/pubsres/academe/2002/JA/Feat/Scot.htm.
22. Stanley Fish, *Save the World on Your Own Time* (New York: Oxford University Press 2008), 122–23.
23. Statement of Anne D. Neal, President, American Council of Trustees and Alumni before the Commission on the Future of Higher Education, April 7, 2006, Indianapolis, IN, www.goacta.org/publications.
24. Martin Anderson, Impostors in the Temple: A Blueprint for Improving Higher Education in America (New York: Simon and Schuster, 1992).
25. Ibid., 195–96.
26. José A. Cabranes, "University Trusteeship in the Enron Era," National Association of College and University Attorneys Annual Meeting (June 26, 2002), available at http://www.nacua.org/documents/enron_speech_07–23–02.pdf; see also Richard Posner, *The University as Business*, www.theatlantic.com/issues/2002/06/posner.htm.
27. Harry L. Lewis, *Excellence Without a Soul: How a Great University Forgot Education* (Cambridge, MA: Public Affairs, 2006),15, 18.
28. Derek Bok, Our Underachieving Colleges: A Candid Look at How Much Students Learn and Why They Should be Learning More (Princeton, NJ: Princeton University Press: 2006), 333–34.
29. Derek Bok, *Universities and the Future of America* (Durham, NC: Duke University Press 1990), 112.
30. Virginia boards thereafter maintained a relatively high level of engagement, provoking faculty pushback. The George Mason University board voted to implement a comprehensive core curriculum that included Western Civilization and American history and succeeded, despite a faculty vote of no confidence. The James Madison board similarly demanded, and received, assurance from the administration that American history would remain part of the college core. See Institute for Effective Governance, *Restoring a Core: How Trustees Can Ensure Meaningful General Education Requirements* (Washington, DC: American Council of Trustees and Alumni, 2009), http://www.goacta.org/.
31. Occasional trustee misconduct such as that recently exposed at the University of Illinois, where trustees were implicated in an admissions "clout scam," fuels university insiders' push to diminish governors' appointing authority, but these "solutions" only deepen existing problems. See Anne D. Neal, "Governor Should Appoint U of I Trustees," *Chicago Sun-Times*, August 1, 2009.
32. Karen Arenson, "Hearing Brings Out City University's Staunchest Defenders," *New York Times*, January 6, 1999; Ben Gose, "U. of Chicago President's Plan to Resign Doesn't Quiet Debate Over His Agenda," *Chronicle of Higher Education*, June 18, 1999, http://chronicle.com/article/U-of-Chicago-Presidents-Plan/16150/.
33. Carrie Coolidge, "Blumenthal May Investigate Charities Ripped Off by Madoff," *Forbes* magazine, December 22, 2008; Scott Carlson, "What

College Trustees Could Learn from the Madoff Scandal," *Chronicle of Higher Education*, December 18, 2008, available at http://chronicle.com/article/What-College-Trustees-Could/1416/.

34. U.S. Department of Education, *A Test of Leadership: Charting the Future of U.S. Higher Education* (Washington, D.C., 2006): x. 4, 21, http://www.ed.gov/about/bdscomm/list/hiedfuture/reports/final-report.pdf.

35. U.S. Department of Education, *A Test of Leadership.*

36. Ibid.

37. Ibid.

38. Ibid., x. 4, 21.

39. U.S. Department of Education, *A Test of Leadership.*

40. Neil W. Hamilton, "A Crisis of Ethic Proportion," *Inside Higher Ed*, June 12, 2009, http://www.insidehighered.com/views/2009/06/12/hamilton.

41. Drew Miller, "What Trustees Must Do, After A.U.," *Inside Higher Ed*, May 16, 2006, http://www.insidehighered.com/views/2006/05/16/miller.

42. Richard T. Ingram, "Are You an Activist Trustee?" Annual Report (Washington, DC: Association of Governing Boards, 1997).

43. ACTA's numerous trustee guides at https://www.goacta.org/publications/index.cfm?categoryid=7E8A88BF-C70B-972A-68008CC20E38AF8A. The Association of Governing Board's publications are available at http://www.agb.org/; Anne D. Neal, "The Potty Trained Trustee," *Inside Higher Ed*, July 23, 2009; see also José A. Cabranes, "How to Make Trustees Worthy of Their Constituents' Trust," *Chronicle of Higher Education*, October 18, 2002, http://chronicle.com/article/How-to-Make-Trustees-Worthy/6459/; and Derek Bok, "The Critical Role of Trustees in Enhancing Student Learning," *Chronicle of Higher Education*, December 16, 2005, http://chronicle.com/article/The-Critical-Role-of-Truste/26139/.

44. Paul Fain, "Trustees Are More Engaged but Still Need Improvement, Survey Finds," *Chronicle of Higher Education*, July 15, 2009, http://chronicle.com/article/Trustees-Are-More-Engaged-but/47378/.

45. Jeffrey Selingo, "Trustees More Willing Than Ready," *Chronicle of Higher Education*, May 11, 2007, http://chronicle.com/article/Trustees-More-Willing-Than/15883/.

46. Richard P. Chait, "How to Keep Trustees from Being Micromanagers," *The Chronicle of Higher Education*, May 6, 2005, http://chronicle.com/article/How-to-Keep-Trustees-From/5821/. See also Chait's "When Trustees Blunder," *Chronicle of Higher Education*, February 17, 2006, http://chronicle.com/article/When-Trustees-Blunder/3038/.

47. Sam Minner, "Improving Shared Governance," *Chronicle of Higher Education*, September 25, 1998, http://chronicle.com/article/Improving-Shared-Governance/10246/.

48. Ibid.

49. Ibid.

50. Hank Brown, "Tenure Reform: The Time Has Come," *Inside Higher Ed*, March 26, 2007, http://www.insidehighered.com/views/2007/03/26/brown.

51. David C. Paris, "The Clock Is Ticking," *Inside Higher Ed*, November 6, 2009, http://www.insidehighered.com/views/2009/11/06/paris.

52. Hamilton, "A Crisis of Ethic Proportion."

53. Ibid.

54. Ibid.

55. Chait, "How to Keep Trustees from Being Micromanagers" and "When Trustees Blunder."

56. American Association of University Professors, *1940 Statement of Principles on Academic Freedom and Tenure*, http://www.aaup.org/AAUP/pubsres/policydocs/contents/1940statement.htm.

57. Trustees and policymakers interested in further guidance on these issues should consult ACTA's online trustee guide library and policy publications at https://www.goacta.org/publications/index.cfm?categoryid=7E8A88BF-C70B-972A-68008CC20E38AF8A.

58. José A. Cabranes, "University Trusteeship in the Enron Era," National Association of College and University Attorneys Annual Meeting (June 26, 2002), available at http://www.nacua.org/documents/enron_speech_07–23–02.pdf;

59. See statements of Anne D. Neal and Phyllis Palmiero before the Senate Finance Committee Roundtable, March 3, 2006, https://www.goacta.org/publications/downloads/NealSenateFinance3-3-06.pdf, https://www.goacta.org/publications/downloads/PamieroSenateFinance3-3-06.pdf. The American Legislative Exchange Council, working with ACTA, has also adopted model resolutions calling for regular training of college and university trustees and for trustees to ensure academic quality.

60. Paul Fain, "Tight Times Call for Trustees Who Push Back, Presidents Say," *Chronicle of Higher Education*, April 21, 2009, http://chronicle.com/article/Tight-Times-Call-for-Truste/47198/.

61. American Council of Trustees and Alumni, *At a Crossroads: A Report Card on Public higher Education in Minnesota* (Washington, DC 2010).

62. Suzanne Johnson, "Renewal: Academic Reorganization," January 18, 2006, http://tulane.edu/news/tulanian/renewal_academic_reorganization.cfm.

63. University of Missouri Board of Curators, Review of System Accountability Measures, Resources and Planning Committee (2009).

64. Ibid. See also ACTA, *Show Me: A Report Card on Public Higher Education in Missouri* (Washington, DC, 2008).

65. The City University of New York, "Performance Management Process," http:// web.cuny.edu/administration/chancellor/performance-goals.html.

66. American Council of Trustees and Alumni, *Shining the Light: A Report Card on Georgia's System of Public Higher Education* (Washington, DC: 2008); and *Protecting the Free Exchange of Ideas: How Trustees Can Advance Intellectual Diversity on Campus* (Washington, DC, 2009).

67. Anne D. Neal, "The SUNY Core Curriculum in Context," delivered at the SUNY 60th Anniversary Conference (Albany, NY), April 3–4, 2009.

68. Jeffrey Selingo, "Plans to Reshape California State U. Disturb Many Faculty Members," *Chronicle of Higher Education*, February 5, 1999; Jeffrey Selingo,

"Cal State Approves Controversial Academic Plan," *Chronicle of Higher Education*, March 26, 1999. See also "Advisors to Regents Back CUNY's Remedial Plan," *New York Times*, October 1, 1999, http://www.nytimes.com/1999/10/01/nyregion/advisers-to-regents-back-cuny-s-remedial-plan.html.

69. John Immerwahr and Jean Johnson, *Squeeze Play 2009: The Public's Views on College Costs Today* (New York: Public Agenda, 2009), http://www.publicagenda.org/pages/squeeze-play-2009.

7

How College Rankings Are Going Global (and Why Their Spread Will Be Good for Higher Education)

Ben Wildavsky

It would be hard to overstate just how contentious rankings of U.S. colleges and universities have become in recent years. As editor of the *U.S. News & World Report* college guides in the mid-2000s, I became accustomed to a steady stream of college presidents and admissions officials visiting the magazine's Washington, DC offices to complain about the magazine's influential college rankings. Some thought outsiders—especially journalists—should not be ranking colleges at all. Some took exception to one or more aspects of the methodology used to calculate each college's standing. Others insisted that if only their own data had been properly tabulated by the magazine, their ranking would be higher. Outside the magazine's offices, of course, those that fared well in the rankings often trumpeted the results on their Web sites.

Several years later, the rankings debate had spread far beyond United States. In the fall of 2007 I listened intently—from the sidelines, mercifully—as the elegantly dressed director of the École Normale Supérieure, Monique Canto-Sperber, addressed an international conference hosted by Shanghai Jiao Tong University. An expert in Greek philosophy, she delivered a meticulous demolition of the university's closely watched global college rankings, explaining why they could not possibly do justice to the strengths of her celebrated institution. The only difference from the debate in the United States was that U.S. universities at the very top of the pecking order tend to publicly ignore the rankings, whereas in Shanghai the president of an elite institution made clear that, for her university, the global rankings were a serious business indeed.

The colloquy that took place in Shanghai is by no means an isolated one. In recent years college rankings have experienced explosive growth around the globe, as the same calls for accountability and objective evaluation seen in American higher education have become ubiquitous. Rankings now exist in more than forty nations,[1] whether established by journalists, government agencies, nonprofit organizations, or universities themselves. There are global rankings too, of course. All are closely watched and are also a source of great controversy, in part because of the serious consequences that sometimes result for universities that are deemed not to measure up. All this should come as no surprise. Students everywhere increasingly behave like consumers. At the same time, governments closely follow the extent to which the universities they fund are contributing to innovation and national economic growth. As students become more mobile, universities move across borders, and competition for world-class status becomes ever more intense, little wonder, then, that college rankings have gone global. They are an unmistakable reflection of global academic competition. Many would say they fan that competition as well. Rankings seem destined to be a fixture on the global education scene for years to come. Detractors notwithstanding, as they are refined and improved, they can and should play an important role in helping universities get better.

Birth of the Rankings

In the United States, whose college rankings have been uniquely influential, a number of efforts at evaluating colleges long predate those inaugurated by *U.S. News* in 1983. Some, intended earnestly, look rather whimsical in retrospect. In the 1895 *Illustrated History of the University of California* a detailed chart[2] offers a "before" and "after" snapshot of the fitness level of the men of the then-young university, comparing the physical prowess of its undergraduates to those at three of the university's well-established East Coast rivals: Yale, Amherst, and Cornell. Upon entering the university, the illustrated chart demonstrates, the average UC man had biceps, chest, thigh, calf, and arm measurements, plus strength in various body parts, well below the average of a sample of fifteen thousand of his blue-blood competitors. But following two years of calisthenics in the healthy California air, the chart shows, brawny Berkeley students had surpassed their effete East Coast counterparts. Perhaps this early cross-college comparison is more analogous to today's intercollegiate sports ratings than to any academic ranking. Still, its focus on how much students improve while in college is striking for the way it foreshadows the value-added analysis that is much sought after in today's higher-education world.

That outcomes-oriented approach was only hinted at in the earliest truly academic college rankings in the United States, which date back to the turn of the twentieth century.[3] They focused simply on which universities produced the most distinguished graduates, following the example of an Englishman named Alick Maclean. In 1900 Maclean published a study called *Where We Get Our Best Men*, which looked at the characteristics of the eminent men of the day, including nationality, family, birthplace, and university attended. In the back of the book he published a list of universities ranked by the number of their prominent alumni. The first U.S. ranking in 1910 took a similar "reverse-engineering" approach, examining successful individuals and crediting their alma maters for their eventual success. A number of different rankings were attempted over subsequent decades, most looking at graduate-level education and almost all continuing the emphasis on either some version of the "great man" theory of educational quality, or, in one case, of how well a college's graduates performed in graduate school.

By the early 1960s, however, survey-based reputational methodology began to supplant the rankings' earlier focus on outcomes. Soon, almost every published ranking was based on an institution's reputation among its peers rather than the accomplishments of its graduates. Interest in examining undergraduate education reemerged during that time, too. And with the emergence of commercially successful rankings such Allan Cartter's discipline-by-discipline *Assessment of Quality in Graduate Education*, which sold 26,000 copies and received great critical acclaim, reputation-based college rankings began to come into their own.

Nevertheless, rankings were still scrutinized mostly within the guild of academe rather than in the wider world of college-bound students and their families. That would soon change. By the late twentieth century, attending college had become a mass phenomenon. By 1972, nearly half of all high-school graduates continued directly to either a two- or a four-year institution.[4] And while most U.S. undergraduates have always attended public institutions near their homes, the growth of meritocratic admissions at the nation's elite universities led to growing competition for admissions slots. Where selective colleges were once fed largely by a small number of Eastern prep schools, the opening of those colleges to a broader swath of society—beginning in the 1960s and continuing at a faster pace during the 1970s—led to wider interest in how to make a sound college choice, and, in an increasingly competitive admissions climate, how to get in.

Into this void stepped a number of different efforts to inform students and parents about their college choices. One, *The Gourman Report*, was published from 1967 to 1997, ranking colleges to within two decimal places despite having a methodology that was shrouded in mystery.[5] A far more credible effort was launched in 1981 by Edward B. Fiske, then education editor of the *New York Times*, under the title *The New York Times Selective Guide to Colleges* (a name that was later changed, when the guidebook became too controversial for the *Times*, to *The Selective Guide to Colleges*, and then *The Fiske Guide to Colleges*). Like its main competitor, the *Yale Daily News's Insider's Guide to the Colleges*, Fiske's guide was compiled with the help of a network of student reporters at campuses around the nation. It profiled several hundred colleges, using a narrative feature-article style to paint a picture of academics and student life at each university. The guide, which remains popular today, uses a version of the Michelin star system to rate the social life, academic rigor, and "quality of life" at each campus, with a maximum of five points available in each category. Perhaps because it is a rating rather than a ranking—there is no ordinal numbering of top, middle, and bottom colleges, and many colleges can earn a four- or five-star rating in a given category—it has never been as controversial as other efforts to see how colleges stack up against one another. "I originally got a lot of flack, since colleges were used to doing the judging of students, not being judged," Fiske says. "But *U.S. News*, bless its heart, took the pressure off me. People love rankings, which is not really what I do, and the way people use the rankings really irks colleges and, for that matter, college counselors."[6]

Indeed, the *U.S. News* rankings were contentious from the very start. Launched in 1983, the rankings began simply enough as an outgrowth of another journalistic project for which the newsmagazine had received significant attention: a survey asking U.S. leaders to identify the most influential Americans. In a detailed account, Alvin Sanoff, the longtime managing editor of the rankings project,[7] writes that the magazine's editors at the time were hoping to gain similar notice—and, to be sure, sell some magazines—with an effort to identify the best colleges in the United States. Although today's *U.S. News* rankings are often criticized for focusing too heavily on reputation rather than actual accomplishments, the magazine's first rankings were exclusively based on reputation. *U.S. News* surveyed college presidents around the country, asking them to identify the nation's best universities. It published the results in a regular issue of the magazine, first in 1983 and again in 1985. It was only in 1987 that the magazine published a separate guidebook entitled *America's Best Colleges*, extending its reach to include not only undergraduate education but also law, business, medical, and engineering schools.

The debut of the rankings was well timed, coming at the height of the U.S. consumer movement. "A generation of parents who were college-educated brought both pragmatism and status-seeking to the college search process," writes Sanoff. "While many members of earlier generations were simply pleased that their children were going to college, members of the Baby Boom generation cast a more critical eye toward higher education. They wanted value for their money." The first generation of *U.S. News* rankings catered to that appetite in a fairly simple way. The presidents surveyed were asked to pick the ten colleges that provided the best undergraduate education in the academic category to which their university belonged. These nine categories, based loosely on the so-called Carnegie Classifications established by the Carnegie Foundation for the Advancement of Teaching, included National Universities, National Liberal Arts Colleges, Southern Comprehensives Institutions, Eastern Liberal Arts Colleges, and so forth. In the first two most closely watched categories the magazine published a ranking of the top twenty-five institutions. In the remaining categories it ranked the top ten. This straightforward early effort—a fairly standard journalistic approach to a consumer-advice story—had within a few years become more complex, more popular, and more contentious. "No one imagined that the rankings would become what some consider the eight-hundred-pound gorilla of American higher education," writes Sanoff, "important enough to be the subject of doctoral dissertations, academic papers and conferences, and endless debate."

When the first full-fledged *U.S. News* guidebook was published in 1987, a delegation of college presidents and senior administrators met with the magazine's editors and asked that the rankings enterprise be stopped. Purely numerical indicators are an inappropriate way to measure the varied institutions and missions of U.S. higher education, they argued (as would umpteen critics in years to come). Moreover, the reputational survey of college presidents amounted to nothing more than a beauty contest. The *U.S. News* editors listened, but rather than do away with their already flourishing enterprise, they made significant changes to the rankings instead. As Sanoff recounts, they consulted with outside experts and decided to divide the rankings into two components. The reputational survey was revamped to include not only college presidents but also provosts and deans of admission who would bring a broader base of expertise to the task. At the same time, a range of quantitative measures was introduced, each requiring data collection followed by the application of a weighting determined by the magazine's editors. The objective data included several components: (a) student selectivity measures, such as a college's acceptance rate and the average SAT or ACT scores of the entering class; (b) student retention data, notably the graduation rate and the percentage of first-year students who returned for their second year; (c) institutional resources, mostly consisting of research spending; and (d) faculty quality, including average faculty salaries and the percentage of faculty with PhDs.

In one form or another the basic structure of the rankings has remained roughly similar ever since, notwithstanding the addition of a few supplementary factors, changes in data sources (the quality of the magazine's data is widely regarded to have improved), and the weighting of each category. *U.S. News* has also made a concerted effort to be more transparent with its methodology and to take suggestions from critics. The magazine invites a group of admissions deans to its offices every year to serve as an informal advisory board. And despite bouts of defensiveness, it does make changes that it believes improve the rankings. One example came in 1997. Detractors had argued for years that the rankings focused excessively on "inputs" rather than "outputs" by giving colleges credit for admitting well-qualified students rather than for how well they actually educated those students. In response, the magazine expanded a so-called value-added measure (now referred to as graduation-rate performance), accounting for 5 percent of the total ranking in the National University and National Liberal Arts College categories, which assesses graduation rates on a curve, taking into account students' incoming qualifications and socioeconomic backgrounds. This measure of persistence controlling for social and academic backgrounds doesn't really capture how much students learn—an elusive question that is in many ways the Holy Grail of college rankings—but it does reflect an effort to fine-tune the rankings where possible.

Still, criticisms of the rankings have continued unabated. Colleges eager to present their numbers in the most flattering possible light have frequently been accused—sometimes with good reason—of gamesmanship or outright fraud. In one recent instance the former director of Clemson University's Office of Institutional Research declared at a June 2009 conference that senior administrators at the school had deliberately given low "reputational" scores to rival universities in their zeal to help Clemson rise in the rankings. (The officials denied the charge.) Fierce battles have also been waged over methodology. Detractors note, among other things, that because of the inclusion of research spending and average class size (which is expensive for colleges to achieve), the rankings invariably reward well-endowed private institutions and punish public universities, many of which, ironically, were ranked far higher when *U.S. News* considered only reputation rather than including quantitative variables. More generally, the argument goes, the factors used in the rankings provide colleges with perverse incentives to focus on the factors that are measured rather than taking on the more elusive task of providing the best possible education for their students. "The *U.S. News* methods are really indefensible," says

Fiske. "They ask the wrong question. The issue is what is the best college for any particular student, not what is the best college in some abstract sense...You cannot quantify the really important questions like matters of fit."[8]

In a sense the *U.S. News* editors who designed the rankings became paradoxical victims of their own earnest efforts to make the rankings more rigorous. What began as a fairly conventional journalistic parlor game—a simple survey seeking the views of college presidents had morphed into an exercise that took on many of the trappings of social science, with nationwide data collection, a detailed methodology, regression analysis, and so forth. But at heart, the rankings remained a journalistic rather than an academic exercise. Thus, it was not much of a surprise when the Chicago-based National Opinion Research Center, an outside consulting firm hired by *U.S. News* in 1997 to evaluate the ranking methodology, reached a conclusion that gave further fuel to critics. "The principal weakness of the current approach is that the weight used to combine the various measures into an overall rating lacks any defensible empirical or theoretical basis," it said. To be sure, the report also noted that the weights might not be off-base. But it said they could not be defended "on any grounds other than the *U.S. News* staff's best judgment on how to combine the measures."[9]

As such criticisms mounted, a large academic literature sprung up making the case that the *U.S. News* rankings create deeply perverse incentives for universities. Broadly speaking, these analysts say rankings push universities to engage in activities that are likely to improve their standings but are unrelated to academic quality. Detractors maintain, for example, that colleges place undue emphasis on standardized tests in the admissions process, sometimes offering merit scholarships to high-scoring applicants, and downplaying more "holistic" qualities such as leadership abilities. They note too that some colleges solicit applications from students with little prospect of being admitted in an effort to improve their performance on the selectivity measure used by *U.S. News*.[10] As universities strive to climb the rankings ladder, the argument goes, they focus excessively on reputation rather than what should be their core activities: teaching and learning.

U.S. News editors have continued to defend the rankings vigorously, challenging the magazine's role as stock villain in the competitive world of college admissions. They argue that the characteristics measured—from research spending to class size to graduation rates to alumni satisfaction to qualifications of incoming students—are all factors that prospective college students and their families might reasonably want to know about. And they point out that the rankings always come with a cautionary note and accompanying articles that stress the importance of finding the right "fit" in a campus, and tell students they should use the rankings only as a starting point. Whatever ranking decisions the magazine makes, it is left in a no-win situation: When it changes the methodology, it is accused of seeking to sell more magazines by shaking up the previous year's pecking order. When the formula goes unchanged from the previous year, the magazine remains vulnerable to the charge that it has done nothing to correct the rankings' many imperfections.

Moreover, while the rankings certainly have many flaws, some popular critiques have proved to be urban legends. For years college officials alleged that *U.S. News,* by including "yield" as a factor in its selectivity measure, was stoking the surge in binding "early decision" admissions programs. Early decision requires students to attend a college to which they have applied early. Yield refers to the percentage of students offered admissions who decide to attend. Early decision is controversial because it has often been blamed for adding stress to an already frenzied admissions process and for disadvantaging low-income students who lose the ability to compare financial-aid packages from multiple schools in the spring when they are required to say yes to an early admissions offer in December. Because binding early decision by definition results in 100 percent yield, the use of yield by *U.S. News* was said to give colleges an incentive to boost their yield stats by relying more heavily than ever on early decision. This argument had one flaw, however: first, yield counted for only 1.5 percent in the ranking methodology. More important, when the magazine decided to remove itself from the controversy by removing yield from the ranking equation, early decision continued unabated. Rarely did critics acknowledge that universities have many self-interested reasons for maintaining a practice that, in an age when "enrollment management" is extremely important, permits them to predict more accurately the size and composition of incoming freshman classes.

As the debate continues, one thing is certain: more than twenty-five years after they were inaugurated, the rankings are routinely cited as having transformed the world of U.S. college admissions. In 2009, for instance, the University of Chicago announced the retirement of Theodore "Ted" O'Neill, the university's longtime dean of admissions, who is best known for introducing Chicago's quirky "uncommon application," which asks applicants to write essays on offbeat topics. (A sample question: "Chicago professor W.J.T. Mitchell entitled his 2005 book *What Do Pictures Want?* Describe a picture and explore what it wants.")[11] O'Neill presided over a huge increase in applications as Chicago, notorious for its demanding academics, worked hard to expand its recruiting net to a broader range of students. But he bemoaned the increased pressure on universities, citing *U.S. News* in the process. "At some point, we were put on this nationally observed competition for numbers," O'Neill said. "*U.S. News* did that, or we did it to ourselves. There's this grander competition that is about numbers and ratings. Some of us resist that, some go along with it, but it affects us all."

The *U.S. News* college rankings were preceded by, or in some cases joined by, a vast array of other college guides and rankings, including the silly (the *Princeton Review*'s annual "top party schools"); the cut-and-dried (the phonebook-sized Barron's, Peterson's, and Lovejoy's guides); the niche-oriented (guides identifying the best colleges for African Americans, Christians, and conservatives, for instance); and the serious-minded (assorted efforts to measure the student experience and academic strengths of campuses around the United States without sorting the results into ranked order, as with the National Survey of Student Engagement [NSSE] and Web-based report cards developed by groups such as the Association of Public and Land-grant Universities (APLU) and the National Association of Independent Colleges and Universities).

With the exception of NSSE, which is aimed primarily at universities that wish to improve their own efforts to educate students, all these efforts cater, in one way or another, to the huge hunger of educational consumers for more and better information about educational quality and value for money. But whatever their strengths and credibility within academic circles, it is probably fair to say that none has had the sheer influence and popularity of the *U.S. News* rankings, their faults notwithstanding.

Ranking the World

That influence goes well beyond U.S. shores, which should perhaps be no surprise, given that some of the same factors that made rankings ubiquitous in the United States have led to their rapid spread elsewhere. Often called league tables, the same term used in Europe for sports rankings, university rankings at the national level became common in the 1990s.[12] The forty-plus national rankings that now exist around the world[13] can be found from Eastern Europe and the Middle East to Latin America and sub-Saharan Africa. By 2007, according to the region-by-region tally of Jamil Salmi, the World Bank's tertiary education coordinator,[14] countries with rankings included Argentina, Australia, Brazil, Canada, Chile, China, Germany, Hong Kong, India, Italy, Japan, Kazakhstan, Korea, Malaysia, Mexico, the Netherlands, New Zealand, Nigeria, Pakistan, Peru, Poland, Portugal, Romania, Russia, Slovakia, Spain, Sweden, Switzerland, Thailand, Tunisia, Ukraine, the United Kingdom, and the United States.

The groups that prepare the rankings are as varied as the nations where they have emerged. Rankers include newspapers or magazines, accreditation organizations, universities themselves, and, increasingly, government agencies such as higher-education ministries. Thus, country-level rankings in Britain, Germany, Canada, Italy, and Mexico are published by the *Financial Times* and the *Sunday Times, Der Spiegel, Macleans, La Repubblica,* and *Reforma,* respectively. Government and higher education organizations that rank institutions include Germany's CHE (Center for Higher Education Development), India's NAAC (National Assessment and Accreditation Council) and NBA (National Board of Accreditation), Turkey's Council of Higher Education (YOK) and TÜBİTAK (The Scientific and Technological Research Council of Turkey), and the Philippines' PAASCU (Philippine Accrediting Association of Schools, Colleges and Universities). There are also many commercial guides, including Australia's *Good Universities Guide,* Germany's Bertelsmann Stiftung, and Canada's Re$earch Infosource, Inc.[15]

The factors included in these rankings vary, of course, as do the weightings, but they typically include indicators that should be familiar to any student of the *U.S. News* rankings. Institutions are usually ranked from highest to lowest based on a combination of quantitative and qualitative measures, including core statistics from universities about their research and teaching outcomes, along with surveys of students, peers, or outside analysts. Ellen Hazelkorn, director of the Higher Education Policy Research Unit at the Dublin Institute of Technology, notes that these national rankings, like those pioneered by *U.S. News,* began as a consumer information tool to provide students and parents with information that was comparable across institutions and often not easily obtainable from universities themselves.

Over time, however, more evidence has accumulated, suggesting that rankings are being used by a much wider variety of users, including government policymakers and industry officials. "Undoubtedly, part of the increasing credibility of league tables and rankings," Hazelkorn writes, "derives from their simplicity and the fact that they are perceived as independent of the higher-education sector or individual universities."[16] Despite profound worries over methodological shortcomings and misuse of rankings—just as in the United States—analysts such as Boston College's Philip Altbach acknowledge that the assorted forms of rankings and league tables found around the world "serve a useful role" because of the spotlight they shine on "key aspects of academic achievement."[17]

At the same Shanghai meeting of ranking experts where Canto-Sperber voiced her dismay at the way the École Normale Supérieure fared in global rankings, a number of other education officials detailed their own nations' efforts to develop indicators of excellence, some quite different from others. In Taiwan, for instance, Tamkang University published the country's first national college ranking in 1993 with a twofold aim: understanding the overall academic performance of Taiwan's 139 varied institutions and creating a useful self-improvement tool for Tamkang University itself. The creator of those rankings, Angela Yung-chi Hou, a professor at the university's Graduate Institute of Higher Education, notes that they were explicitly modeled after those created by *U.S. News*, with multiple criteria established—both quantitative and survey-based—and then weighted in order to rank each institution in one of eight categories. College rankings remain controversial in Taiwan, she concedes. But, she maintains, "it is expected that the quality of Taiwanese higher education could be improved through rankings."[18]

In Romania too, where no fewer than three rankings have been inaugurated, a group of researchers who have studied the classifications concludes that "ranking makes universities aware of their very weak and strong points and prepares them to measure up to competition under the circumstances of liberalizing the education and labor markets, once Romania accedes to the European Union."[19] Similarly, in the Republic of Kazakhstan, the Ministry of Education and Science directed its National Accreditation Center to conduct rankings of the nation's universities beginning in 2006. The goals of the initiative, as in other nations, are to help provide decision-making tools to students and parents, government workers, employers, and international organizations; to promote competition between universities; and to encourage quality assurance within universities.[20]

Even in places where rankings have not yet penetrated, it seems, there is a hunger for them—at least among some. In Greece, two other researchers explained, rankings are strongly discouraged. Indeed, researchers are typically restricted from classifying and evaluating public universities, thanks in part to opposition from student groups and unions representing academic staff. Nevertheless, they suggested a number of possible approaches to ranking Greek universities, arguing that such measures could be useful to a number of groups: students seeking reliable information about campuses, universities seeking a diagnostic tool and measure of quality, the government, and society more generally.

While national-level university rankings have continued their seemingly relentless march around the world, probably the most influential comparisons between postsecondary research institutions are the global rankings that have emerged and become popular in the past fifteen years. The first international ranking was conducted in 1997 by *Asiaweek* magazine, but it was limited to universities in Asian nations.[21] Five years later, in 2002, the Swiss Centre for Science and Technology Studies released its

Champions League, which ranked universities and other research institutions on the basis of their research journal publications.[22] However, the first closely watched worldwide ranking to appear on the global scene came the following year with publication of the *Academic Ranking of World Universities*, produced by Shanghai Jiao Tong University's Institute of Higher Education and widely viewed as the most influential international ranking. First released in June 2003, the Shanghai rankings had their origins several years earlier in 1999. Shanghai Jiao Tong administrators, worried about the university's decline from its once-exalted position in prerevolutionary days, began a series of planning meetings aimed at assessing where the university stood compared to others, particularly in the key area of research productivity.[23] One particularly active participant, a professor of chemistry and chemical engineering named Nian Cai Liu, was drafted as the university's first-ever director of strategic planning. His first task? Compiling a report comparing his university's performance to that of others in China and elsewhere.

Liu's timing was good. The rankings prototype, initially circulated privately to administrators and campus officials, came as China was embarking on a broad, ambitious, and expensive initiative to create a much-larger group of high-level research universities. Even well-known institutions had set ambitious targets to reach the much-coveted "world-class" status quickly: Peking University set its sights on 2016, for instance, while its cross-town rival, Tsinghua University, aimed for 2020. But without benchmarking against universities at home and abroad, determining just what was meant by world-class would have been difficult. That was where Liu's work came in, and it was quickly expanded to include a much larger number of institutions around the world. That broader scope permitted the entire nation, not just Shanghai Jiao Tong, to figure out where it stood vis-à-vis universities around the world, and just how far it would have to go to close the gap.

Although the early rankings were aimed at a small audience, after Liu posted them online, the demand—and controversy—soon became enormous. By his count, four million people have visited the Shanghai rankings Web site since 2003—an average of two thousand per day.[24] Liu and his research team pride themselves on having developed a transparent methodology, clearly explained on their Web site, which requires no complicated (or costly) survey research and instead relies on a range of publicly accessible indicators. His rationale for the Shanghai approach rests on several premises. First, while universities' impact on economic development has become well established, "it is impossible to obtain internationally comparable indicators and data" of that contribution. Furthermore, while education is certainly "the basic function of any university," differences across national systems make qualitative comparisons unworkable. The best approach, Liu concludes, is to look objectively at the research performance of universities, which he argues can be standardized and compared globally, providing a good indication of the relative standing of different institutions.

The Shanghai rankings begin by examining any university in the world whose faculty includes Nobel laureates; winners of the Fields Medal, granted every four years to a handful of elite mathematicians age forty and younger; and researchers who have published papers in *Nature* or *Science*, or whose work is frequently cited by others. It also looks at the overall number of academic papers at universities around the world indexed in the Science Citation Index Expanded (SCIE), the Social Science Citation Index (SSCI), and the Arts and Humanities Indices (ACHI). The World University Rankings researchers examined more than two thousand universities and ranked more than one thousand, posting the top five hundred on their Web site.

The methodology itself bears some surface resemblance to the *U.S. News* ranking system in that it assigns varying weights to each of the factors measured. That said, unlike *U.S. News*, its research-intensive approach pays no attention to undergraduate-oriented measures such as student qualifications, class size, student retention, and graduation rate, nor to peer reputation. It assigns a weight of 10 percent for the number of an institution's alumni who have won Nobel Prizes and Fields Medals since 1901; 20 percent for university staff winning those honors (with higher weights assigned to more recent winners); 20 percent for the number of highly cited researchers in a range of fields, including life sciences, physical sciences, medicine, engineering, and social sciences; 20 percent for articles published in *Nature* and *Science* within the past five years; 20 percent for the total number of articles by university faculty indexed in the SCIE, the SSCI, and the ACHI within the past year; and 10 percent for a size-adjustment measure that attempts to gauge per capita research performance by dividing each subtotal indicator by the number of full-time faculty and academic staff at each university.

Liu exhibits a refreshing lack of defensiveness when discussing his rankings, making the case for their strengths while cheerfully acknowledging their weaknesses. In some cases he and his team have attempted to improve their methodology in response to critics; a case in point: many detractors have complained about the Shanghai rankings' bias toward science. After confirming that academics in the humanities typically have lower rates of publication than scientists, Liu doubled the weighting of articles that appear in the SSCI. The rankings are still viewed as heavily tilted toward science ("the easiest way to boost rankings is to kill the humanities," one university rector told Hazelkorn). Still, Liu says he is glad to receive more suggestions for improvement. "We love those ideas," he told the *Chronicle of Higher Education*. "We may not be able to implement all of them, but they're great."[25]

The institutions at the very top of the Shanghai rankings come as no great surprise; the global pecking order closely resembles the one that exists within the United States. Thus, the top ten universities in 2008 were Harvard, Stanford, Berkeley, Cambridge, MIT, Caltech, Columbia, Princeton, Chicago, and Oxford. That all but two of the top ten institutions are U.S. universities reflects the massive dominance of the American research model on the world stage—all the more so, of course, when the scientific and technological accomplishments most closely associated with that model are so richly rewarded by a ranking methodology such as Shanghai's. At the same time, the rankings can provide bragging rights for those well beyond the inner circle; the University of Maastricht, for instance, is categorized in the band of universities between 300 and 400 (there are no numbered rankings beyond the top one hundred), along with institutions such as the University of Oregon and the University of Stuttgart.

One year after the debut of the Shanghai rankings, a second global effort to compare university systems was launched by a British publication, the *Times Higher Education Supplement* (THES). The World University Rankings quickly began vying with their Chinese rivals for influence on the world education scene. Views are mixed as to which ranking has garnered more attention from students, universities, and government policymakers, but it is broadly accepted that the THES assessment has far surpassed the Shanghai rankings in generating controversy.

The THES rankings were launched by John O'Leary, the onetime education editor of the London *Times*, who had previously overseen the national league tables produced by the *Times*, as well as a spinoff publication called the *Times Good University Guide*. In 2008, just before the magazine released its fifth annual rankings, O'Leary published an article that declared the ever-increasing importance of such global measures. "Particularly where research is concerned, Oxford and Cambridge are as likely to compare themselves with Harvard and Princeton as with other U.K. [institutions]," he wrote. "And governments all around the world have expressed an ambition to have at least one university among the international elite." The league-table exercise was conducted during its formative years in conjunction with the research firm Quacquarelli and Symonds (QS) and thus formally called the *THE-QS World University Rankings* (after a change of ownership the THES was renamed Times Higher Education [THE]). Its goal was to give a "rounded assessment" of top universities "at a time of unprecedented international mobility both by students and by academics."[26]

O'Leary's reference to a "rounded assessment" is an unmistakable allusion to one of the key features differentiating the THE rankings from their Chinese counterpart. In contrast to the almost exclusive focus on research in the Shanghai rankings, the *Times Higher Education* methodology counts a much wider range of factors. Academic peer review is at the heart of the THE approach. It is based on about 9,400 responses over three years to an online survey distributed to academics worldwide with the results weighted at 40 percent of the total,[27] by far the largest factor (and considerably larger than the 25 percent that *U.S. News* devotes to its peer survey, a weighting that itself is often criticized for its disproportionate influence on the magazine's college rankings).

The magazine's rationale for such heavy use of a subjective reputational measure is that it avoids penalizing universities with nonscience strengths. Unlike the citations-per-professor score, the World University Rankings Web site explains, "the peer review component offers an even-handed perspective on the various broad subject areas with institutional strengths in Arts & Humanities and Social Sciences able to contribute significantly to the overall view of an institution." Somewhat undermining this defense, however, is the magazine's acknowledgment in the very next sentence of its "frequently asked questions" that if it could identify "additional reliable measures of institutional quality," it would likely reduce the weighting of peer review.[28] Still, it does make good on its promise of scrutinizing universities' strengths in a variety of disciplines: in addition to its master rankings of universities worldwide, it also publishes tables each year based on the peer review survey that assesses the best institutions for arts and humanities, social sciences, life sciences and biomedicine, natural sciences, and technology.

The second component of the THE methodology is "employer review," weighted at 10 percent, which was introduced in 2005 and is based on a survey distributed to public- and private-sector employers around the world. In 2009 this score was based on about 3,300 responses over three years. An additional 20 percent is devoted to student-faculty ratio, based on the assumption that this measure serves as the best available proxy for an institution's commitment to teaching. Next, THE uses citations per faculty member, weighted at 20 percent, to assess each university's research prowess. Relying on Scopus, the largest database of abstracts and citations in the world, it draws on the most recent five years of citation data. The use of a per-professor measure is intended to control for institutional size. The measure doesn't carry greater weight, the magazine explains, because it tends to be weighted toward research in scientific and technical fields.

Finally, the magazine measures the percentage of international students and faculty at a university, on the grounds that this serves as a market test of an institution's ability to attract brainpower in an ever-more globalized world. International students and faculty are each weighted at 5 percent for a total international measure of 10 percent.[29]

Like the designers of the Shanghai rankings, the journalists and researchers behind the THE rankings say that they try hard to make the factors behind their evaluations easily accessible to the public. "It's important that we get it right and that it is utterly transparent," says Ann Mroz, the current editor of the THE, over lunch at a London restaurant.[30] She is also, like Shanghai Jiao Tong University's Liu, quite happy to discuss misgivings about her publication's rankings and entertain criticisms or suggestions for improvement. "I'm very keen for there to be a debate about it," she says. "Any criticisms I'm quite happy to print. I would prefer that people came to us and there was some sort of debate about it and see whether maybe we have got a few things wrong. Until we discuss it, we're never going to know." Mroz herself says that she is "uncomfortable" with the faculty-student ratio, for instance. "It's so crude. Does it tell you how good the teaching is?" She would like to use a better measure, she says—if one can be found.

Even as she acknowledges shortcomings in the rankings, however, Mroz firmly defends their usefulness. "If you're talking about the students, what else do they have to go by?" she says. "There's very little information, especially for foreign students. How are you going to try to compare a university of one country against another if you want to go abroad and study? I don't think you should probably base your entire decision on the rankings because that would be daft. You have to do a lot more research, but this is a good place to start." Universities too rely on the ranking, she notes, whether as grist for marketing efforts when their standing rises or as a gauge of whether a prospective international partner has comparable worldwide standing.

While the THE is proud of its aspiration to create a more "holistic" assessment of universities than the Shanghai ranking, critics such as Simon Marginson of the Centre for the Study of Higher Education at the University of Melbourne view its methodology as more problematic on a variety of grounds. They often fault the THE's index for its high volatility, particularly vis-à-vis its relatively stable Shanghai counterpart. This was particularly true in 2007 when changes in data and methodology contributed to Stanford University's drop from number 6 to 19, the National University of Mexico's plunge from 74 to 192, and the National University of Singapore's decline from 19 to 33. "Think 'yo-yo' and you've about got it," Marginson writes.[31]

In some sense, of course, the charge of volatility punishes rankers for attempting to remedy their past sins. Large changes in an institution's ranking typically come when the ranking organization—whether *U.S. News* or *Times Higher Education*—makes methodological changes in response to previous criticisms. In 2007, for example, THE prevented reviewers from assessing their own universities, changed its citation database to reduce what it called a "pronounced bias" toward U.S. institutions, and began using statistical normalization to control for outlier scores.[32] Still, to Marginson, the frequent changes in the *Times Higher* rankings are highly suspect, as is the survey's dismayingly low response rate (as little as 1 percent, he states).

Marginson also objects to what he terms a regional bias in which the survey's "pool of responses was heavily weighted in favor of academic 'peers' from nations where the *Times* is well known, such as the U.K., Australia, New England, and Malaysia." Because of the survey's "composition bias," he argues, British institutions are vastly overrepresented. In 2007 "an amazing nineteen" U.K. universities placed in the top one hundred, compared to thirty-eight U.S. universities, a relatively modest showing given that fifty-four American universities placed in the top one hundred of the Shanghai rankings in the same year.[33]

In 2008 the very top of the THE and Shanghai lists overlapped significantly; seven of the ten universities were the same. But four British institutions placed in the THE top ten, while just two made it to the top of the Shanghai rankings. The *Times Higher's* top ten in 2008 were Harvard; Yale; Cambridge; Oxford; Caltech; Imperial College, London; University College, London; Chicago; MIT; and Columbia. British institutions inched up still further in 2009 when they occupied four of the *Times Higher's* top six slots. Meantime, U.S. superiority dwindled considerably: the number of North American universities in the *Times Higher* top one hundred dropped to thirty-six from forty-two the previous year.[34] But the pecking order could well be shaken up even further in the future: several weeks after releasing its 2009 rankings, THE announced that it would end its partnership with QS. It said it would develop a brand-new ranking methodology in consultation with Thomson Reuters, a prominent data research firm, together with its academic advisory board and readers. "We acknowledge the criticism and now want to work with the sector to produce a legitimate and robust research tool for academics and university administrators," Mroz said.[35] For its part, QS said it would continue to publish and circulate its own rankings, an indication that rankings proliferation shows no signs of letting up.[36]

Even as the comparative strengths of each major global ranking continue to be debated—or as each is emphatically rejected by some university officials and students of higher education—their influence seems to be ever greater. In addition to consumer uses of the world rankings, they are increasingly an object of anxiety for universities and a significant factor in their decision making. In a study commissioned by the OECD, the Dublin Institute of Technology's Ellen Hazelkorn surveyed university leaders from 202 higher-education institutions in 41 countries, both new and old, teaching- and research-intensive. Rankings, she found, had become a hugely important factor in self-perception and decision making. "Despite the existence of 17,000 higher education institutions worldwide, there is now a near-obsession with the status and trajectory of the top 100," she wrote in a summary of her findings.[37] Across a wide range of institutions, she told *University World News*, "there is enormous attention given to every league table that is published as well as its quality ranking. And they are taken seriously by students, government, and especially by the media. Because of this, they have a huge influence on university reputations and thus they promote competition and influence policy-making."[38] One manifestation of this intense interest in rankings is the controversial efforts to "incentivize" administrators with cold hard cash to boost their institutions' standing. For example, in Australia a number of vice-chancellors have received salary bonuses predicated on their success in nudging their campuses up in the rankings.[39]

Hazelkorn's multination study found that 58 percent of respondents were unhappy with their current ranking, that 70 percent wanted to be in the top 10 percent of their national league table, that 71 percent wanted to be in the top 25 percent internationally, that 57 percent had a formal mechanism to review where they stood in the rankings, and that 57 percent thought that the willingness of other universities to form partnerships with them was influenced by their position in league tables and rankings. These perceptions are not just idle musings. Hazelkorn found that universities have often backed them up with concrete actions. Some go out of their way to hire more Nobel laureates, for example, given that this is a metric in the Shanghai rankings. More broadly, entire nations have paid special attention to revamping their university systems in the hope of achieving higher stature in the rankings. "Excellence initiatives in Germany, Russia, China, and France are policy responses to rankings," Hazelkorn writes. "The pace of higher-education reform is likely to quicken in the belief that more elite, competitive, and better institutions are equivalent to being higher ranked."

Beyond survey data, it is not hard to find ways in which the siren call of rankings is heard far and wide. In India both the THE and Shanghai rankings are scrutinized at the highest levels of government, according to Montek Singh Ahluwalia, who heads the nation's Planning Commission.

"We know about these lists. We look at them," says Ahluwalia in an inter-view in his New Delhi office.[40] The Oxford graduate, whose formal title is deputy chairman of the commission, says the rankings serve in part to confirm India's sense that some of its elite institutions—the Indian Institutes of Technology, the Indian Institute of Science, the Indian Institutes of Management, Jawaharlal Nehru University, and Delhi University—have earned a legitimate place among the world's best. "If tomorrow they were to drop all of them, we would say it's all biased and useless," he quips.

At the same time, the rankings provide a gauge whereby a nation that urgently wants to increase both the quantity and quality of its institutions can measure its progress. "Assuming we have about four or something like that [among the several hundred top institutions in the global rankings], everybody in India thinks that in ten years we should have at least ten and hopefully twenty," he says. "That's not easy to do, because you don't create a good university in ten years. But maybe you can upgrade some of the existing ones and so on." Improvement at the elite levels is even more daunting than improving mass access to higher education, he says. "Taking the number from four to ten will require some of the brightest brains in government to do some very innovative thinking on reforms for universities."

In addition to serving as a broad measure of quality for nations intent on improving their international standing, rankings can also act as a great leveler. In the best-case scenario they allow individual institutions or pro-grams to prove their worth against better-established competitors. This can be seen particularly clearly in the case of business schools, which were early adapters to globalization.

As goods, services, and people started to move evermore freely across borders, a far-reaching market for globally literate MBAs soon emerged. Business schools began to market themselves aggressively to foreign students, to start branch campuses, and to forge alliances with their counterparts in other nations. The results of all this internationalization were striking. To take a few examples: Between 2004 and 2008, the num-ber of U.S. MBA applicants sending scores on the Graduate Management Admissions Test to non-U.S. programs increased by 35 percent. At INSEAD in Fontainebleau, no more than one in ten faculty members comes from any single country. Madrid's IE Business School has recruitment offices in Berlin, Dubai, Lisbon, and Singapore. And Alpina, a dairy and beverage manufacturer in Colombia, extended fifteen job offers to MBA grads from IE in 2008 and planned to begin recruiting at INSEAD and the London Business School.[41]

This rapid globalization was accompanied, and perhaps hastened, by a slew of business-school rankings. Like comprehensive university rankings, these began at the national level before expanding globally. *BusinessWeek*, for example, pioneered U.S. MBA rankings in 1988 and was later joined by *Forbes* and the *Wall Street Journal*. Now *BusinessWeek* has added to its offerings an annual list of "Best International B-Schools," while the *Economist* and the *Financial Times* have developed their own high-profile, global, business-school rankings. The methodology of each ranking differs, but all include some measurement of alumni salaries, postgraduation career success, or both. One analysis found a fairly high correlation between almost all the MBA rankings.[42]

Like other rankings, the business school league tables have attracted critics and controversy. However, by providing a neutral yardstick that measures schools' effectiveness on key measures that matter to students and employers, the rankings have the power to confer instant legitimacy on relatively new players on the global B-school scene. China's CEIBS (China Europe International Business School), for instance, is only fifteen years old. But it has thrived in a short time and now touts its high rankings on its Web site: number eight worldwide in the 2009 *Financial Times* global MBA rankings, number four in the *Forbes* 2009 list of top non-U.S. business schools, number one in *BusinessWeek/China*'s ranking, and so on.[43] By offering an external measure of CEIBS's success, these international business school rankings illustrate a point that economics columnist Robert Samuelson has made in the context of U.S. college rankings:[44] there is a strong case to be made that rankings have the potential to radically democratize the entrenched academic pecking order on the global as well as on the national scene.

Rankings are also being used more generally by students or national governments as the equivalent of the Good Housekeeping Seal of Approval. They can give educational consumers a sense of which overseas institutions are likely to offer value for money. Similarly, they can inform governments about whether their own policies are well considered or their scholarship funds well spent. The Mongolian government has weighed a policy that would give study-abroad funding only to students admitted to a university that appears in one of the global rankings.[45] In the Netherlands an immigration-reform proposal aimed at attracting more skilled migrants would restrict visas to all but graduates of universities ranked in the two top tiers of global league tables.

But if government quality-assurance efforts, consumer advice, and performance incentives for campus officials represent a largely benign aspect of global rankings, another is the ignominy—and real-life consequences— that can fall upon individuals and institutions that are viewed as not measuring up. The most oft-cited case of this phenomenon came in 2005 at the University of Malaya (UM). One year earlier the Malaysian university drew accolades when it was ranked eighty-ninth in the world in the inaugural *Times Higher Education Supplement* rankings. So important an accomplishment was this for the university, and for a nation bent on creating a knowledge economy, that the vice-chancellor ordered banners reading "UM a World's Top 100 University" and had them hung around that city and, Marginson notes, "on the edge of the campus facing the main freeway to the airport where every foreign visitor to Malaysia would see it."[46]

The next year, however, the results of the *Times'* two reputational surveys were less favorable to the university. Compounding matters was the discovery and correction of an error in the classification of foreign students at UM, which served to further lower the university's rating. The result? A drop from 89 to 169 in the THE survey and widespread calls for a royal commission of inquiry into the unfortunate episode. "A Shocking Global Slide," read one headline.[47] "Crisis in Malaysia's Public Universities?"[48] inquired another. Within a few months, the vice-chancellor, who had been vilified in the media, was effectively fired. "Though apparently extreme, this reaction is not uncommon in university systems around the world," writes World Bank higher-education expert Jamil Salmi.[49] It has certainly remained common in Malaysia. Just a few years later, when none of the country's universities placed in the THE top two hundred in 2008, Lim Kit Siang, leader of the opposition Democratic Action Party, gave a speech to party supporters, declaring that Malaysia "is losing out in the unrelenting battle for international competitiveness," not only worldwide but vis-à-vis regional competitors such as Thailand, Indonesia, and the Philippines. He complained bitterly about the showing of the Universiti Sains Malaysia, which the government had singled out for cultivation as a world-class institution, calling its 313th showing "sad and pathetic." The rankings, the opposition leader concluded, "should be a wake-up call to the Higher Education Minister and the cabinet of the advanced crisis of higher education in Malaysia."[50]

In Britain too analysts reacted with similar alarm, albeit in less heated language, when the 2008 THE rankings showed a drop for many U.K. universities. Both Oxford and Cambridge slipped slightly in the top-ten pecking order, and overall twenty-two of the twenty-nine British universities in the top two hundred fell in the rankings. While Britain still had more highly ranked universities than in any nation outside the United States (which held thirty-seven of the top one hundred slots), the *Daily Telegraph* noted that universities from thirty-three different countries made it into the top two hundred, an increase from twenty-eight in 2007.[51] Though relatively modest, these shifts were enough to prompt a follow-up article headlined "Without Investment Our Top Universities Will Fall Behind Global Competition."[52]

Its author, Wendy Piatt, head of the Russell Group, a consortium of twenty elite research universities, noted that the United States invests more than twice what Great Britain does in higher education as a proportion of gross domestic product. What's more, she said, Chinese universities "have been steadily climbing up international league tables" and are on the verge of overtaking their British counterparts in faculty publication of research papers. Adding to the competitive environment, "closer to home, France and Germany are both pumping millions into their leading research universities," Piatt wrote. Her conclusion, predictably, was that notwithstanding concerns about the rankings' accuracy, their message should nevertheless be heeded as a sign that increased investment in U.K. universities is imperative.

While the range of responses to the global rankings from universities and policymakers shows their unmistakable influence, many detractors believe the rankings are unworthy of any kind of response. To begin with, there are the familiar and highly specific criticisms. These include, on the one hand, the frequently denounced bias toward science in the Shanghai rankings, coupled with the incentives the Shanghai approach gives universities to engage in questionable chasing of Nobel-winning professors whose work may or may not be of sufficiently recent vintage to add meaningfully to the institution's intellectual firepower. They comprise on the other hand, of course, the excessive reliance on peer reputation, low sample size, volatility, and English-speaking bias of the THE rankings.

But to some, the very notion of attempting to determine how an entire university stacks up against others is an exercise that has little meaning as an instrument of national policy. Ross Williams and Nina Van Dyke of the Melbourne Institute at the University of Melbourne argue that evaluating individual disciplines across universities makes more sense. After all, for many students and researchers making decisions about where to apply and study or work, and for government agencies seeking to fund excellent research, the quality of specific departments and disciplines is more important than the university's overall standing. Broad institutional rankings can make universities look worse or better than they really are. Their survey of a range of disciplines at thirty-nine Australian universities—arts and humanities, business and economics, education, engineering, law, medicine, and science—found that in twenty-three cases, a discipline at a particular institution was rated among the top one hundred in the world.

With universities in Australia and beyond under considerable pressure to place ever higher in the world rankings, Williams and Van Dyke argue that a focus on disciplines would, instead, encourage more specialization in fields in which a university may have a particular strength or comparative advantage. "At whole-of-institution level," they write, "it is not reasonable to expect, under current resourcing levels, more than three or four Australian universities to be in the top one hundred in the world, but it is feasible for many more Australian universities to be in the top one hundred in individual disciplines...A system in which each Australian university was recognized internationally for some activity, including teaching, would be preferable to the current situation."[53] Indeed, beginning in February 2007, the designers of the Shanghai rankings began ranking universities by broad subject fields in addition to overall quality. Still, in many places, the obsession with making it to the top remains, however unrealistic the goal may be. Another Australian university official, Tony Sheil of Griffith University's Office for Research, argues that it would be prohibitively expensive for Australia and other small nations to make the kind of investments necessary to catapult a university into the top ten or twenty of the global research rankings, notwithstanding the expressed desire of several recent Australian federal education ministers to reach that goal. (The current minister has moved in a different direction, focusing on creating a world-class university system nationwide rather than on rising to the top of the rankings.)[54]

More broadly, just as many critics of the *U.S. News* rankings question the premise that institutions with widely varying missions can be meaningfully evaluated by outsiders, some academics protest the notion that global league tables capture the essence of institutional quality. While the aspiration to be world-class seems to be at the top of every university's to-do list, this argument goes, worldwide rankings are unavoidably a zero-sum game that implies excellence is found only at the heights of the league tables. As Franz Van Vught of the European Center for Strategic Management of Universities argued at an OECD conference on measuring quality in higher education, if just 3 percent of the world's 17,000 universities are world-class as measured by rankings, surely the rest cannot have utterly failed.[55]

France has been a particular hotbed of rankings discontent. Even as Prime Minister Nicolas Sarkozy has pushed to shake up the nation's moribund university system and create a lavishly funded group of world-class research universities, academics and some government officials have simultaneously expressed vocal discontent with global rankings. They complain among other things that the Shanghai rankings favor universities in English-speaking countries, do not take institutional size into account, and fail to measure the quality of teaching.[56] Moreover, some fear that student qualifications have been lost in the global rankings frenzy. Canto-Sperber of the École Normale Supérieure (ENS) argued before her Shanghai audience that ultraselective colleges such as France's *grandes écoles* don't get rightful credit for the rigors students must undergo before they even begin their studies.

After graduation from *lycée*, she explained, the most brilliant students in France enroll in rigorous *classes préparatoires* before they can attempt entry to ENS. In these courses "the competition between students is such that one who succeeds by the end of *classes préparatoires* would have typically studied for twelve to sixteen hours a day without holiday for two or three years." Among the graduates of these courses, she noted, "only the top few are allowed to enter the École Normale Supérieure," which stands as the most selective educational institution in France. Notwithstanding this intense selection process, ENS took the seventy-third slot in the Shanghai ratings in 2008. Institutions such as the University of Paris VI or the University of Paris XI were ranked higher despite, Canto-Sperber observed pointedly, having "completely nonexistent selection procedures (i.e., everyone who applies is admitted)." Ironically, other rankings that take student qualifications into account, notably those produced by *U.S. News*, are frequently denounced for focusing excessively on inputs rather than outputs. Still, Cantor-Sperber insisted, "the quality of a university is based on its own procedures of student selection. Therefore, the criterion of student selection has to be considered for the evaluation of universities."

Given all this discontent, it is probably unsurprising that some of those deeply dismayed by the shortcomings of existing rankings have begun to develop what are essentially counterrankings. In India, where relatively few universities have merited inclusion in the global rankings, the University Grants Commission in 2009 proposed its own ranking system, to be called the India Education Index, which would grade Indian institutions with respect to their international peers.[57] In France another prestigious *grande école*, Mines Paris Tech, released its second Professional Rankings of World Universities in October 2008, leading to a memorably tautological headline in the online publication *University World News*: "French Do Well in French World Rankings." Perhaps inevitably, however, this alternative ranking itself has been criticized for being one-dimensional: its sole criterion for sorting the 350 institutions surveyed is the number of graduates serving as CEO or the equivalent in companies listed in *Fortune* magazine's Fortune Global 500. Using this measure, five French universities placed in the top twenty alone, including two in the top ten. By contrast, just three French universities appeared in the entire top one hundred Shanghai slots, and only two were included in the top one hundred of the *Times Higher Education* league table.[58]

Despite Sarkozy's determination to place some French universities in the world's top tier by 2012, France's disdain for the current rankings

(Valérie Pécresse, the nation's higher-education minister, once said that the problem with rankings was that they existed) has extended to efforts to create a Europe-wide alternative. As France took over the presidency of the EU, it convened a Paris conference in late 2008 to explore a range of international comparative measures that participants hoped might do better justice to the strengths in, say, teaching and innovation, which tend to be underrecognized by existing measures. By the summer of 2009 the European Union announced that it would begin developing a new "multidimensional global university ranking." Mostly focused on Europe, the goal of the new assessment, still in the exploratory stage, is to move beyond research in hard sciences to include humanities and social sciences, as well as teaching quality and "community outreach."

Better Information

Is there really a better way to rank universities? In addition to nationalist efforts such as those of India and France, which invariably generate suspicions of chauvinistic intent, other attempts have been made to zero in on specialized aspects of the higher-education enterprise that are overlooked by conventional rankings. In Spain, for instance, the "Webometrics Ranking of World Universities" was launched in 2004 to measure universities' Web-based activities—specifically the "volume, visibility, and impact of the Web pages published by universities."[59] Developed by the Laboratoria de Cybermetrics, a division of the National Research Council, Spain's largest public research body, these rankings place special emphasis on Web-based publication of scientific output, including refereed papers, conference contributions, theses, and reports, as well as courseware, digital libraries, databases, personal Web pages, and more.

The goal of the effort, which was first launched in 2004 and is now updated every six months, is to promote electronic publication by universities, and in particular to encourage university administrators to do more Web-based dissemination if their institution ranks poorly. While students should not use these rankings as the sole criteria for choosing a university, the Webometrics creators say, a top position among the 17,000 higher education institutions worldwide[60] that are listed in the survey tells candidates that "the institution has a policy that encourages new technologies and has resources for their adoption." Despite this disclaimer, analysts such as Richard Holmes of the MARA Institute of Technology in Malaysia note that important aspects of a university's quality—teaching excellence or book publication, for instance—are not captured by this Webcentric indicator.

Another alternative measure that has attracted considerable attention in the past few years as a kinder, gentler form of evaluation comes from the Center for Higher Education Development (CHE), a German higher-education-reform think tank. In collaboration with a media organization (once *Stern*, later *Die Zeit*) the organization surveys 200,000 students and 15,000 professors at more than 250 universities,[61] mostly in Germany but also in Austria, Switzerland, the Netherlands, and recently Italy. The rankings include a range of quantitative measures, including student-professor ratio, average length of studies, failure rates, number of PhDs, and research productivity and funding; however, about two-thirds of its indicators are based on the survey questions. Students are asked about their experiences and overall satisfaction on their campus. Faculty are asked about their "insider's pick": which three institutions in their own field they would recommend to their own son or daughter.

After all these data are collected, they are not weighted or in any way used to create an ordinal ranking of participating universities. That would be far too simplistic, say the survey founders. "There simply is no 'best higher education institution,' not in one subject and certainly not in all subjects," the organization's Web site declares. "For example, a university may indeed be a leader in the field of research, but the equipment it offers its students may be miserable, or it may be strong in German Studies, but poor in Economics and Business Administration. Instead of crowning some presumed overall winner, we offer a multidimensional ranking."[62] Along with avoiding comparisons between entire institutions, even within disciplines CHE stays away from numerical rankings and simply categorizes a given department as either in the top third, middle third, or bottom third compared to its peers. It also gives its rankings a strong element of consumer empowerment by permitting individual users to create their own combinations of the indicators they consider most important, and then order institutions accordingly.[63]

Still, while the CHE approach to rankings may appeal to certain constituencies, by design it sidesteps what may be a natural desire by policymakers and consumers alike to make judgments about which institutions are most effective overall, which ones are the *best*. Nor does CHE address the increasing interest in value-added assessment in higher education, which aims to assess how good a job universities do, not just in garnering research laurels—and Nobel laureates—but in passing on knowledge to their students.

One of the most closely watched experiments in ranking and assessment is attempting to do just that. This new initiative is known as AHELO, the Assessment of Higher Education Learning Outcomes. Its origins trace back to June 2006, when a group of OECD education ministers met in

Athens and concluded that as higher education expanded massively, it was important to do more to measure quality as well as quantity. The resulting project is premised on the notion that students and employers are seeking better information with which to make choices about either attending universities or hiring their graduates, that universities and professors need to know more about the strengths and weaknesses of different institutions, and that policymakers need a better sense of the impact of their decisions on university quality. The OECD's response has been to create an instrument intended to be valid "for all cultures and languages."[64] It is explicitly intended not to be a ranking in the Shanghai or *Times Higher Education* vein, but instead to focus on teaching and learning—not on inputs, but on outputs and value added.

The initial design of the test focuses on four "strands" intended to reflect some of the crucial aspects of higher education. The first "generic skills" component attempts to measure students' abilities in such areas as analytical reasoning, written communication, ideas generation, and application of theory to practice. Such abilities are not explicitly linked to a particular course of study but are nevertheless vital characteristics of what students should be learning on campus. "The point is that the simple acquisition of knowledge is not enough to count as an education," as the OECD puts it.[65]

The model for this part of the OECD's new outcomes project is a test known as the Collegiate Learning Assessment, or CLA, which was developed in the United States by the Council for Aid to Education, an offshoot of RAND, the social-science research organization. Since 2000 it has been used in hundreds of American colleges and universities to measure the kinds of skills all undergraduates should acquire, regardless of major. Researchers administer a computer-based exam, including essay questions, to a sample of students, typically a group of freshmen and a group of seniors. By controlling for the qualification of incoming students (as measured by their scores on the SAT or ACT), the CLA staff arrives at a value-added measure that attempts to show just how much students at a given university tend to improve their writing and analytical skills during their time on campus. Their research methodology has been controversial among some of their higher-education colleagues, but the CLA's designers are highly regarded social scientists, and the question they attempt to answer—what do students really learn on campus?—has rarely been addressed in such a systematic way. For the AHELO project, the College Learning Assessment will be adapted to fit an international range of universities. As in the United States, the notion is to ask nonspecialized questions that undergraduates in any field of study can answer. The inaugural participants in this part of the new test will certainly test its cross-national aspirations; they are Finland, Korea, Mexico, and Norway.

The second component of the OECD's exam is designed to acknowledge that universities most often define their missions in terms of subject-specific knowledge, not generic skills. "Students and faculty would be astonished if an assessment left out the very reason they are in higher education," the OECD says. Thus, this strand tests what students have learned within their own disciplines. At the feasibility-study stage, the two areas tested will be engineering and economics, with the expectation that more disciplines will be added if the project goes to scale. AHELO's designers are quick to note that subject knowledge is not just about understanding facts but about putting that content knowledge to use, "often in novel circumstances." Australia, Japan, and Sweden will take part in the inaugural round of engineering testing, while the economics tests will be administered in Italy, the Netherlands, and Mexico, and the Flemish-speaking parts of Belgium. As OECD officials prepare to begin testing during the 2010–11 academic year, they continue trying to recruit more participants, including the United States.

The third of AHELO's four sections rests on the notion that student-learning outcomes have to be understood in context, from students' backgrounds to the characteristics of the universities they attend to what employers expect of them. To better understand such variables, this "context" section examines campus characteristics, such as total enrollment and male-female ratio; educational practices and quality, including student-faculty interaction, emphasis on hands-on learning, and level of academic rigor; what the OECD terms "psycho-social and cultural attributes," from what society expects of postsecondary institutions to students' career expectations; and various outcomes, both in behavior and attitudes, from degree completion and progress into the job market or graduate school to student satisfaction, self-confidence, and self-reported learning gains. Researchers will gather data for all these measures by examining public statistics, reviewing earlier research, and surveying students, professors, and university administrators. Eventually, they hope to develop alumni and employer surveys if and when a full-blown AHELO assessment is developed.

The fourth and final strand is intended to zero in on the value-added component of higher education, one that is increasingly scrutinized in the era of measurement and accountability. AHELO researchers pose an important question: When a top student enters a university and exits with similar levels of accomplishment, how much has the institution really done with the "raw material" that walked through its doors? By contrast, when a student enters with a B average and leaves campus with an A average, a case can be made that the university has performed a more valuable pedagogical role. "What a student brings to a degree programme and what he or she leaves with are a powerful indicator of teaching quality, availability of resources, and the capacity of students to learn." OECD researchers acknowledge that consumers of league tables care a lot about absolute measures of quality, not just relative growth. Nevertheless, they say, a comprehensive assessment such as AHELO should offer both "bottom line" as well as "value-added" measures to provide a full picture of how well universities are educating their students. Unlike the other three strands, however, the value-added measure is not yet being carried out even in an experimental way. Given the complexity of the task, researchers say, there is not enough time to develop an appropriate measurement tool during the initial AHELO study. Instead, they are considering possible methodologies, drawing on similar work being done by the OECD at the secondary-school level.

Indeed, the implicit model for the OECD's new international effort is a respected assessment known as PISA, the Program for International Student Assessment, which was developed by the organization in 2000 and is administered to fifteen-year-olds in most OECD countries (and in some nonmember nations) to gauge the academic progress of students in one country vis-à-vis their peers in other industrialized nations. While it is not without critics, PISA provides an easily understandable gauge of global student achievement at the secondary school level. Indeed, as the AHELO project was getting under way, an OECD paper describing the new effort was titled "PISA for Higher Education." Despite the attention received by existing national and international university rankings, they may distort resource allocation and thus give short shrift to teaching and learning, the October 2006 background memo observed. Instead, it declared, "a direct assessment of the learning outcomes of higher education could provide governments with a powerful instrument to judge the effectiveness and international competitiveness of their higher-education institutions, systems and policies in the light of other countries' performance, in ways that better reflect the multiple aims and contributions of tertiary education to society."[66]

However, drawing a direct parallel to PISA has proven contentious. Given the controversy surrounding rankings, it is perhaps unsurprising that within a couple of years, OECD officials were insisting that the word not be applied to their still-in-gestation postsecondary effort. "AHELO is *not* PISA for higher education," declared Barbara Ischinger, director of OECD's education division, at the opening of a major OECD conference on assessing quality in higher education. In a similar vein OECD officials maintain that their current efforts to test out the new measure in a range of nations (they will assess students at some ten postsecondary institutions in three or four countries for each of the four strands) should not be considered a pilot but merely a "feasibility" study. Any next steps, they say, will be determined only on the basis of the outcomes of their exploratory work. Still, OECD representatives acknowledge that the project is being conducted "with an eye to the possible creation of a full-scale AHELO upon its completion,"[67] and some of those involved in the process say it is a virtual certainty that it will go forward.

Together with the contentious PISA analogy, however, a related concern quickly surfaced. Influential American higher-education officials expressed deep misgivings about the OECD's initial efforts, arguing that efforts to create a global postsecondary measurement and accountability system were inherently problematic, given the difficulty of finding a measurement instrument suitable for the wide variety of institutions involved in the effort. After all, huge controversy had already surrounded the Secretary of Education's Commission on the Future of Higher Education, which endorsed the use of outcome-measurement tools such as the Collegiate Learning Assessment, opposed by some university officials as overly simplistic. "The conversations in the last year have underscored for many folks both the importance of addressing issues of student learning outcomes and the difficulty of finding a common instrument for measuring them in the United States," Terry Hartle, a senior official at the American Council on Education, the umbrella lobbying group for U.S. colleges and universities, told *Inside Higher Ed.* "If we haven't been able to figure out how to do this in the United States, it's impossible for me to imagine a method or standard that would work equally well for Holyoke Community College, MIT, and the Sorbonne."[68]

But defenders of the new approach argue that while international comparisons may be challenging, there is nothing particularly new or objectionable about them. For instance, rankings expert Alex Usher, who heads the Canada office of the Educational Policy Institute, points to the example of the International Adult Literacy Survey, which is administered around the world, including in the United States, without incident. What's more, reiterates Andreas Schleicher, head of education research for the OECD and a key designer of the PISA testing regime, the key breakthrough of AHELO is that it will shift the rankings conversation in a crucial new direction. "Rather than assuming that because a university spends more it must be better, or using other proxy measures of quality, we will look at learning outcomes," he says.[69] Initially, of course, the small number of universities taking part in the test in each country means that only national-level results are likely to be available. Ultimately, however, with sufficiently widespread participation, the OECD would be able to publish its own cross-national league tables with the important difference, champions of the new approach say, that they would be based on results rather than on reputation. "We will not be reflecting a university's history, but asking: what is a global employer looking for?" Schleicher says. More important still, such measures have the potential to help students, governments, and universities themselves focus on more meaningful measures of quality when making educational decisions.

In a relatively short period of time a remarkably wide variety of rankings has spread and evolved around the world, from the national to the global, from reputation based to research based, from subject specific to university-wide, from Web oriented to multidimensional and unweighted, from the *Princeton Review*'s annual list of "top party schools" to the OECD's sophisticated amalgam of value-added approaches. The interest such efforts has attracted in far-flung locales is reflected in the meeting places periodically chosen by a geographically diverse group of global ranking experts who have roamed from Washington DC to Berlin to Shanghai and then, in 2009, to Kazakhstan.

This cacophony of assessments, while likely at times to be hard to compare and contrast, is surely something to be embraced. For many years, relatively few external measures of university performance were available, particularly measures easily understood by consumers and policymakers. Rankings have emerged to fill that void. They are no doubt going to multiply and become more sophisticated as they mature. And they are no doubt going to remain a fixture on the higher-education scene, emblematic of a world in which apples-to-apples, cross-border comparisons of educational quality are evermore necessary.

Still, rankings remain highly contentious nearly everywhere, from the United States to Europe to Asia and beyond. For some critics the very enterprise of sorting colleges in rank order is suspect. Uwe Brandenburg, project manager at Germany's Center for Higher Education Development, quotes Einstein to make the point: "Not everything that can be counted, counts, and not everything that counts can be counted."[70]

Nevertheless, Brandenburg acknowledges that rankings can provide useful transparency so long as they are used in combination with other factors. A recent study of rankings in four countries, conducted by the Institute for Higher Education Policy, found that despite some potentially negative effects, such as encouraging a focus on elite research institutions at the expense of those that tend to serve less-advantaged students, rankings had a useful impact on how universities make decisions, including more data-based assessment of success.

It is easy to see why, in a global market, students, universities, and governments have a growing need for better information about the comparative effectiveness of postsecondary institutions. But they need the right kind of information. And there are numerous barriers to providing it: many rankings are imperfect, to say the least, and refinements both large and small are badly needed. Even some of the most promising efforts, such as the OECD's AHELO project, may prove hard to implement and also have the central flaw of paying zero attention to research. While human capital is an important output of universities, so is the research on which so much innovation and economic growth is dependent. Striking the right balance in assessing universities will be very important: one could imagine a ranking that takes three parts Shanghai, adds five parts AHELO, then throws in two parts *Times Higher Education*, to create a mixture that is useful to students and policymakers alike.

As more sophisticated rankings are developed, what are the chances that they will be widely implemented? The United States is a good proving ground for this question: it is the nation where college rankings were pioneered and remain hugely influential and, at the same time, a country where rankings routinely encounter withering criticism and steep resistance from academics and university leaders. Even as better measures of student-learning outcomes are developed, barriers to their introduction at American colleges and universities will likely remain high. What should state and federal policymakers do to help develop better rankings or to ensure that universities cooperate?

At the federal level, probably nothing. In some nations—Kazakhstan, perhaps—universities would likely have little choice but to participate in rankings sponsored and mandated by the government. But in the United States, with no tradition of centralized federal control of education, top-down efforts to mandate participation in either international or domestic assessments are unlikely to be successful. To be sure, for twenty-five years, the U.S. Higher Education Act—the standard-setter for accreditation rules, and thus the ultimate gatekeeper for billions in federal financial aid—has required colleges to report evidence of student academic achievement. However, efforts to satisfy this mandate through the accreditation system have taken what one analyst calls "a kaleidoscopic" variety of forms, and despite recent improvements, many have been ineffectual as instruments of accountability either within or outside universities.[71] Even rather tame suggestions that colleges should use uniform measures of student learning outcomes have met with alarm. The Spellings Commission's support for the CLA and NSSE was quickly, and perhaps mischievously, said to mean that it was advocating a federal No Child Left Behind Act for higher education, anathema to the academy and likely to be a political nonstarter.

States might have better luck introducing standardized measures of learning outcomes, and even using them for accountability purposes. After all, while U.S. higher education is remarkably diverse, high percentages of students are enrolled in state colleges and universities that are subject to the scrutiny, sometimes intense, of state lawmakers. Texas probably offers the best example of a successful state-mandated accountability system, which in many ways can be viewed as an extension of its widely followed elementary and secondary accountability framework. Beginning with an executive order from Governor Rick Perry in 2004, the state has developed a comprehensive accountability system that requires state universities, among other things, to participate in the CLA and NSSE and to make the results public. Early results are positive, and if any state is likely to jump on the AHELO bandwagon, it would surely be Texas. Elsewhere, however, it is by no means clear that enough states share Texas's results-oriented education culture to allow for the meaningful national comparisons that are crucial to assessing universities' relative educational effectiveness.

It may well be that the best route toward widespread participation in the new generation of national and global rankings and assessments is the *Consumer Reports* model. No federal regulations or state laws require dishwasher manufacturers or automakers to submit their wares for testing and inspection by the widely consulted magazine. They do so anyway, knowing that the results will be pored over and referenced for years by potential customers because the only thing worse than such comparative scrutiny would be no scrutiny at all. Indeed, in most of the nations where rankings have become increasingly pervasive and influential, universities face no government mandates to participate; they comply voluntarily with journalistic efforts such as those of Japan's *Asahi Shimbun* or Canada's *Maclean's*. Similarly, most American universities do respond, albeit reluctantly, to the *U.S. News* survey.

But it will be more challenging to persuade them to participate widely in more sophisticated and publicly available measures of their educational effectiveness, either nationally or internationally. So far, U.S. universities have shown a greater appetite for self-assessment than for transparency. Most of the colleges that participate in the CLA and NSSE prefer to keep their results private, using them for "self-study" rather than to inform potential students, parents, taxpayers, and lawmakers about how much students are actually learning.

One promising effort that moves colleges toward increased openness is the Voluntary System of Accountability, or VSA, which grew out of the increased pressure the Spellings Commission put on the higher-education world to assess student outcomes. A joint effort of the American Association of State Colleges and Universities and the Association of Public and Land-grant Universities (APLU), which together grant 70 percent of the bachelor's degrees awarded in the United States,[72] the VSA requires participating schools to choose one of several learning assessment tests. Following a period of experimentation, the results must be published, along with other data, such as graduation, in a College Portrait that is uniform across institutions. It remains to be seen how effective this initiative will be, and whether a critical mass of universities will sign up for a voluntary endeavor that risks highlighting their weaknesses in public. But it certainly moves universities in the right direction.

Indeed, a strong case can be made that highlighting weaknesses could actually have a salutary effect on many American universities. When the OECD's secondary school PISA test debuted in 2001, it showed that U.S. high-school students were far behind many of their global counterparts. Finding out that America's K–12 education was lagging behind the rest of the developed world did not hurt U.S. primary and secondary schools; it pushed them to make needed reforms. So far, U.S. colleges have little to fear from the currently available international rankings, which focus heavily on the research and reputation measures at which the long-established and top tier of American schools excel. But new rankings that shine a spotlight on student learning as well as research could deliver far less pleasant results, both for American universities and for others around the world that have never put much focus on classroom learning.

That does not mean U.S. institutions should follow the advice of many in American higher education and try to steer clear of assessments such as AHELO. Such a move would only preserve U.S. schools' international reputations in the short term; if the rest of the world cooperates with the OECD assessments, claims of American exceptionalism will look absurd. Furthermore, if the news AHELO brings about American higher education is worse than expected, the United States will be better off knowing it sooner rather than later. AHELO could be an instrument of much-needed change in the teaching side of American higher education, a useful way to get around the recalcitrance of those educational institutions that resist attempts at bringing some accountability to their multibillion-dollar enterprise. Even more broadly, Jamie Merisotis, president of the Lumina Foundation for Education, argues that improved rankings can help universities innovate and thus maintain their standing in the face of intensified competition from upstart institutions. In undergraduate education, for instance, he suggests that a university that did away with the conventional credit system based on "seat time" in classrooms, moving instead toward measuring learning outcomes—the kind of content knowledge emphasized in the OECD's nascent AHELO assessment system—could quickly establish itself as an entrepreneurial front-runner in the global brain race.

Ultimately, it is unrealistic to imagine that complaining about rankings and lamenting their popularity will do anything to slow their growth and appeal. Moreover, despite their shortcomings, their proliferation is a healthy indicator of a well-functioning and burgeoning global education marketplace. That universities so often oppose rankings reflects, says Kevin Carey of the think tank Education Sector, "an aversion to competition and accountability that ill serves students and the public at large."[73] The real challenge will be how to improve rankings in order to give better guidance to students about university quality, and to provide more quality-driven incentives to universities that are eager to improve their national or international standing in the global academic race. If rankings ultimately spur universities to improve the quality of the research they produce, as well as the education their students receive, then the much-disparaged metrics will have succeeded, naysayers to the contrary, in providing their very own version of added educational value.

Notes

This chapter is adapted from Ben Wildavsky, *The Great Brain Race: How Global Universities Are Reshaping the World* (Princeton, NJ: Princeton University Press, May 2010). The author thanks Mindee Forman and Indira Dammu for their invaluable research assistance.

1. Tia T. Gordon, "Global Ranking Systems May Drive New Decision Making at U.S. Higher Education Institutions," *Institute for Higher Education Policy* (May 21, 2009). http://www.ihep.org/press-room/news_release-detail.cfm?id=166.

2. William Carey Jones, *Illustrated History of the University of California* (San Francisco: F. H. Dukesmith, 1895), 217.

3. The historical information in the two paragraphs that follow is drawn from Luke Myers and Jonathan Robe, *College Rankings: History, Criticism and Reform* (Washington DC: Center for College Affordability and Productivity, March 2009), 7–13. http://www.centerforcollegeaffordability.org/uploads/College_Rankings_History.pdf.

4. Michael Planty et al., *The Condition of Education 2009* (Washington DC: U.S. Department of Education, National Center for Education Statistics, Institute of Education Sciences, June 2009), http://nces.ed.gov/pubs2009/2009081.pdf.

5. Myers and Robe, *College Rankings*, 15.

6. Edward B. Fiske, message to author, March 5, 2009.

7. Alvin B. Sanoff, "The *U.S. News* College Rankings: A View from the Inside," in *College and University Ranking Systems: Global Perspectives and American Challenges* (Washington DC: Institute for Higher Education Policy, April 2007). Much of the discussion here of the history of the rankings is drawn from Sanoff's account.

8. Fiske, message to author, March 5, 2009.
9. National Opinion Research Center (NORC) report quoted in Sanoff, "*U.S. News* College Rankings."
10. Marc Meredith, "Why Do Universities Compete in the Rankings Game? An Empirical Analysis of the Effects of the *U.S. News and World Report* College Rankings," in *Research in Higher Education* 45, no. 5 (August 2004): 445.
11. Eric Hoover, "U. of Chicago's 'Uncommon' Admissions Dean to Step Down," *Chronicle of Higher Education*, March 4, 2009.
12. John Walshe, "OECD: Worldwide 'Obsession' with League Tables," *University World News*, November 11, 2007.
13. Gordon, "Global Ranking Systems."
14. Jamil Salmi, "Recent Developments in Rankings: Implications for Developing Countries?" (presentation at Third Meeting of the International Ranking Expert Group, Shanghai Jiao Tong University, October, 2007).
15. Ellen Hazelkorn, "Learning to Live with League Tables and Rankings: The Experience of Institutional Leaders" (presentation at Third Meeting of the International Ranking Expert Group, Shanghai Jiao Tong University, October, 2007).
16. Ibid.
17. Quoted in Hazelkorn, "Learning to Live with League Tables."
18. Angela Yung-Chi Hou, "A Study of College Rankings in Taiwan" (presentation at Third Meeting of the International Ranking Expert Group, Shanghai Jiao Tong University, October, 2007).
19. P. Agachi et al., "What Is New in Ranking the Universities in Romania? Ranking the Universities from the Scientific Research Contribution Perspective" (presentation at Third Meeting of the International Ranking Expert Group, Shanghai Jiao Tong University, October, 2007).
20. Sholpan Kalanova, "The Methodology of Higher Education Institutions Ranking in Kazakhstan" (presentation at Third Meeting of the International Ranking Expert Group, Shanghai Jiao Tong University, October, 2007).
21. Alex Usher and Massimo Savino, "A Global Survey of Rankings and League Tables," *College and University Ranking Systems: Global Perspectives and American Challenges* (Washington, DC: Institute for Higher Education Policy, April 2007).
22. Griffith University, "University Ranks," "World Rankings of Universities," http://www.griffith.edu.au/vc/ate/content_uni_rankings.html
23. Mara Hvistendahl, "The Man Behind the World's Most-Watched College Rankings," *Chronicle of Higher Education*, October 17, 2008.
24. Nian Cai Liu, "Academic Ranking of World Universities Methodologies and Problems" (presentation at Shanghai Jiao Tong University, February 8, 2007). Details of ranking methodology and rationale drawn from this presentation; http://www.authorstream.com/presentation/Heather-19518-Nian-Cai-Liu-presentation-Outline-Dream-Chinese-WCU-Goals-Top-Universities-Questions-Academic-Ranking-World-Featu-as-Entertainment-ppt-powerpoint/.

25. Hvistendahl, "The Man behind the World's Most-Watched College Rankings."

26. John O'Leary, "THE-QS World University Rankings Preview," QS Top Universities, http://www.topuniversities.com.dev.quaqs.com/world universityrankings/university_rankings_news/article/2008_ the_qs_world_university_rankings_preview/

27. QS Top Universities, "Methodology: A Simple Overview," www.topuniversities.com/worlduniversityrankings/methodology/simple_overview.

28. QS Top Universities, "University Rankings FAQs," http://www.topuniversities.com.dev.quaqs.com/worlduniversityrankings/faqs/.

29. QS Top Universities, "World University Rankings: Methodology," http://www.topuniversities.com/university-rankings/world-university-rankings/methodology/simple-overview.

30. Ann Mroz, interview by author, London, November 13, 2008.

31. Simon Marginson, "Global University Rankings" (presentation version, Thirty-second Annual Conference of the Association for the Study of Higher Education, Louisville, KY, November 10, 2007), http://www.cshe.unimelb.edu.au/people/staff_pages/Marginson/ASHE%202007%20PRESENT%20global%20university%20rankings.pdf.

32. QS Top Universities, "Methodology: Weightings and Normalization," http://www.topuniversities.com/worlduniversityrankings/methodology/normalization/.

33. Marginson, "Global University Rankings."

34. John Gerritsen, "Global: US Dominance in Rankings Erodes," *University World News*, October 11, 2009.

35. Phil Baty, "New Data Partner for World University Rankings," *Times Higher Education*, October 30, 2009.

36. David Jobbins, "Break-Up Means New Global Rankings," *University World News*, November 8, 2009.

37. Ellen Hazelkorn, "OECD: Consumer Concept Becomes a Policy Instrument," *University World News*, November 11, 2007.

38. Walshe, "Worldwide 'Obsession' with League Tables."

39. Aisha Labi, "Obsession with Rankings Goes Global," *Chronicle of Higher Education*, October 17, 2008.

40. Singh Ahluwalia Montek, interview with author, New Delhi, February 4, 2008.

41. Jane Porter, "How to Stand Out in the Global Crowd," *BusinessWeek*, November 24, 2008.

42. Myers and Robe, *College Rankings*.

43. China Europe International Business School, "Top-Tier Global Rankings," http://www.ceibs.edu/today/rankings/.

44. Robert J. Samuelson, "In Praise of Rankings," *Newsweek*, August 1, 2004.

45. Marguerite Clarke, "The Impact of Higher Education Rankings on Student Access, Choice, and Opportunity" (background paper prepared for the Institute for Higher Education Policy and the Lumina Foundation for Education, September 2006).

46. Marginson, "Global University Rankings."
47. *Little Speck*, "A Shocking Global Slide," http://www.littlespeck.com/region/CForeign-My-051031.htm.
48. Francis Loh, "Crisis in Malaysia's Public Universities? Balancing the Pursuit of Academic Excellence and the Massification of Tertiary Education," *Aliran Monthly* 25 (2005), http://www.aliran.com.
49. Jamil Salmi, *The Challenge of Establishing World-Class Universities* (Washington, DC: World Bank, 2009), 1.
50. John Gill, "Malaysian Rankings Flop 'Shames' the Nation," *Times Higher Education*, December 4, 2008.
51. Graeme Paton, "British Universities Slip in Global League," Telegraph.co.uk, October 8, 2008.
52. Wendy Piatt, "Without Investment Our Top Universities Will Fall Behind Global Competition," Telegraph.co.uk, October 10, 2008.
53. Ross Williams and Nina Van Dyke, "Measuring University Performance at the Discipline/Departmental Level" (paper presented at the Symposium on International Trends in University Rankings and Classifications, Griffith University, February 12, 2007).
54. Tony Sheil, e-mail message to author, October 20, 2009.
55. "Breaking Ranks," *OECD Observer*, no. 269 (October 2008), http://www.oecdobserver.org.
56. André Siganos, "Rankings, Governance, and Attractiveness: The New French Context" (paper presented at the Second International Conference on World-Class Universities, Shanghai Jiao Tong University, October 31–November 3, 2007).
57. Anubhuti Vishnoi, "No Indian Universities in Global Toplist so UGC Has a Solution: Let's Prepare Our Own List," *Indian Express*, March 10, 2009, htt://www.indianexpress.com.
58. Jane Marshall, "France: French Do Well in French World Rankings," *University World News*, October 26, 2008.
59. "Methodology," *Ranking Web of World Universities*, http://www.webometrics.info/methodology.html.
60. Ranking Web of World Universities, http://www.webometrics.info/.
61. "Rankings," *Zeit Online*, http://ranking.zeit.de/che9/CHE_en?module=Show&tmpl=p511_methodik.
62. Ibid.
63. Alex Usher and Massimo Savino, "A Global Survey of Rankings and League Tables," in *College and University Ranking Systems: Global Perspectives and American Challenges* (Washington, DC: Institute for Higher Education Policy, April 2007), 32.
64. Organisation for Economic Co-operation and Development (OECD), Directorate for Education, "OECD Feasibility Study for the International Assessment of Higher Education Learning Outcomes (AHELO)," http://www.oecd.org/document/22/0,3343,en_2649_35961291_40624662_1_1_1_1,00.html.

65. OECD, Directorate for Education, "AHELO: The Four Strands," http://www.oecd.org/document/41/0,3343,en_2649_35961291_42295209_1_1_1_1,00.html.

66. OECD, Directorate for Education, "PISA for Higher Education," http://www.paddyhealy.com/PISA_HigherEduc_OECD.pdf.

67. OECD, "OECD Feasibility Study."

68. Doug Lederman, "A Worldwide Test for Higher Education?" *Inside Higher Ed*, September 19, 2007.

69. "Measuring Mortarboards," *The Economist*, November 15, 2007.

70. Susan Robertson and Uwe Brandenburg, "Ranking—in a Different (CHE) Way?" *GlobalHigherEd*, January 18, 2009.

71. Geri H. Malandra, "Creating a Higher Education Accountability System: The Texas Experience" (speech delivered at the OECD conference Outcomes of Higher Education: Quality, Relevance, and Impact, Paris, September 8–10, 2008), http://www.oecd.org/dataoecd/3/31/41218025.pdf.

72. Voluntary System of Accountability Program, http://www.voluntarysystem.org/index.cfm?page=about_vsa.

73. Kevin Carey, "Rankings Go Global," *Inside Higher Ed*, May 6, 2008.

8

The Politics of Higher Education

Mark Schneider

For most of my career I was an academic political scientist teaching courses on the public-policy process. In 2004 I came to Washington on a year's sabbatical to finish a book on charter schools. Four years later, having succumbed to Potomac fever and serving as the commissioner of the National Center for Education Statistics, I told my home university, the State University of New York at Stony Brook, that I was not returning. On a trip back to Stony Brook to clean out my office, my colleagues asked me to give a talk to the political-science faculty and graduate students about my time as an official in the U.S. government.

At first I demurred, saying that I no longer considered myself an academic and therefore did not have much to say to an academic department. After some back and forth, I finally agreed.

I opened my talk along the following lines: "After thirty years of teaching public policy, I should be sued by my former students for wasting their time, maybe even malpractice. Little I taught in all those years would prepare anybody for even a mid-level job in the policy branches of government."

The discomfort in the room was palpable, but since academics are trained to ask questions, the tenor of the questions that followed was along the lines: "Well, something you taught must have some relevance." Finally I admitted that James Q. Wilson's work, especially his 1989 volume *Bureaucracy*, was important (although even Wilson's insightful work did not encompass the craziness of modern government bureaucracy where, for example, in less than one year I fired the same person twice—once for a clear constitutional violation—and neither termination stuck).

I then suggested that my experience with various aspects of higher education while at the U.S. Department of Education suggested that some classic political-science works on the power of interest groups were close but were still wrong, not because they overestimated the power of interest groups, but because they *underestimated* it.

In the following pages, I look at the politics of student loans and then the politics of information systems to illustrate how powerful interest groups can be in driving higher education policy, and these politics impose limits on how far and how fast we can go toward accountability in higher education.

The Power of Interest Groups

Political scientists have long used the term *iron triangle* to describe the relationship that builds up over time among interest groups, Congress (especially congressional committees) and the bureaucracy as they interact to create and maintain public policies and government rules and regulations.

Built into this concept is the assumption that bureaucratic agencies seek to build their own power base often at the expense of the citizens the agency was established to serve. This comes about because an agency's resources are determined by members of Congress who are more strongly influenced by well-organized (and comparatively well-endowed) interest groups than by the citizens who are the consumers of the services most agencies were presumably established to serve.

As the term *triangle* implies, there are three focal points in the system. At one point sits interest groups, often representing an industry or a set of producer groups with overlapping goals in shaping public policies, rules, and regulations. These groups often share tightly focused goals and their greater resources (both financial and personnel) give these groups a natural organizing advantage over citizen/consumer groups.

At the second point in the triangle sit members of Congress (especially those on committees or subcommittees with direct responsibility for writing the laws that affect the specific interests of those groups and overseeing the relevant agencies). From the iron-triangle perspective, members of Congress actively support the goals of interest groups in exchange for resources and political support.

Bureaucrats occupy the third point in the triangle. Rather than being an independent force to support the interests of citizen/consumers, they are pressured by the other actors in the triangle to skew their actions in favor of the interest groups. The relationships between these three sets of actors are cemented by repeated interactions, by the flow of resources (for example, information and campaign contributions), and by the "revolving door" in which personnel move between industry, Congress, and government.

Notably missing from the iron triangle are consumers, the intended beneficiaries of the services provided by government agencies. Compared to the concentrated power of organized interest groups, most consumer groups face challenges in mobilizing to protect their interests. Often, citizens who are the potential members of a consumer group are geographically scattered, find it hard to identify and mobilize members of the group, and often lack the time, money and other resources needed to lobby or otherwise affect policies and the delivery of services.

Faced with this imbalance in power, it is easy for an agency to switch its focus away from the citizens it was designed to serve in favor of the interest groups that can make its life more pleasant and more rewarding.[1]

The *iron* in iron triangle carries with it the implication of a highly stable and enduring set of relationships. Indeed, because of this durability, iron triangles were often described as constituting *subgovernments*, implying a power to determine policy without oversight or input from broader public interests.

Recent research has transformed the concept of iron triangles. Policy studies now tend to employ the term *policy subsystem* as the lens for viewing public policy. Embedded in the idea of subsystems is a more dynamic view of public policy than the stability implied by iron triangles.

In contemporary theories of policy subsystems, competing coalitions with varying levels of power are viewed as contesting for dominance and recent studies see change as more common than assumed from the iron-triangle perspective. The theory of "punctuated equilibrium" has now become the lens by which political scientists view the policy process. From this perspective, winners and losers can change surprisingly quickly. Much of the research in this vein has sought to identify the factors that disrupt relationships within a policy subsystem.[2]

I begin by exploring some of the core characteristics evident in the politics of higher education by looking at student aid and higher-education information systems. In the case of student aid, changes in external conditions (what political scientist Bryan Jones would term an "exogenous shock") resulting from the credit crisis of 2008 may have disrupted the entrenched politics of what looked like a highly stable subgovernment. In the case of information systems, change is more slowly creeping up on those who have fought to keep information out of the hands of consumers.

The Escalating Cost of Higher Education

We need to begin with a basic fact: higher education is costly and getting ever more so. For example, between 2004 and 2007, while the Consumer Price Index increased by about 10 percent, the price of attending a college or university increased by around 17 percent.[3] This recent growth in higher education costs in excess of inflation is not an aberration. According to the 2008 "Measuring Up" report issued by the National Center for Public Policy and Higher Education, since the early 1980s the growth in college tuition and fees have outstripped the changes in the Consumer Price Index by a factor of four and, according to their calculations, outstripped even growth in the cost of medical care.[4] Many argue that federal student aid has played a role in enabling colleges and universities to increase their tuition at such a pace.

Federal Student Aid and College Finances

The current federal system of financial aid traces back largely to 1972 when Congress decided to provide federal aid to students rather than to institutions, creating "basic" (now Pell) grants instead of expanding the existing campus-based student-grant program. This focus on student aid has characterized federal postsecondary education policy ever since.[5] Pell grants are the largest source of federal higher-education grants and were funded at about $18 billion in the 2008–2009 academic year. New legislation passed in early 2010 provides for large increases: as much as $32 billion is expected to be spent in the 2010–2011 academic year. Pell grants are focused on low-income students and funded 100 percent from the federal treasury, with no matching or maintenance-of-effort requirements placed on institutions.

In addition to these grant programs, student loans constitute another component of federal student aid. There are two paths through which the federal government has provided loans to students. First, there are student loans issued through the William D. Ford Federal Direct Loan Program (FDLP), often referred to as Direct Loans. This is a U.S. Department of Education program in which the department acts as a lender. The Direct Loan program was signed into law by President Clinton in 1993; historically, funding for the Direct Loan Program has been dwarfed by the Federal Family Education Loan Program (FFEL). FFEL was created by the Higher Education Act of 1965, and in 2007–08, FFEL served 6.5 million students and parents, generating around $55 billion in new loans (or 80 percent of all new federal student loans).

In the FFEL Program, private lenders make federally guaranteed loans to parents and students. Students are steered to the government's direct program or to outside lenders, depending on their school's preference. Many believe that the Direct Loan Program costs the federal government less money and better treats students who are having difficulty in repaying their loan; nonetheless, about 75 percent of postsecondary institutions participate in FFEL. Some suspect that this choice is driven by "deals" that colleges and universities have negotiated with the private lenders who participate in FFEL.

Under the subsidized loan program, loans are made by Citigroup, Bank of America, Nelnet, Sallie Mae, and other private firms. Congress sets both the subsidy and the maximum interest rate for borrowers and lenders face little risk because the government pays a lender 96 to 98 percent of the interest and principal it is owed in case of a student default. Under FFEL, others entities—guaranty agencies—are paid to provide default insurance for lenders, work with delinquent borrowers to help them avoid default, and collect or rehabilitate defaulted student loans. This arrangement created a powerful set of interests, populated by big banks and other organizations such as Sallie Mae, which have considerable resources, money, personnel, and incentives to keep this system alive.

Many analysts believe federal student aid has fueled the growth of higher-education expenditures. In 1987 William Bennett, then secretary of education under Ronald Reagan, put forward this link in a *New York Times* op-ed piece. Never shy, Bennett called his piece "Our Greedy Colleges" and wrote that:

> If anything, increases in financial aid in recent years have enabled colleges and universities blithely to raise their tuitions, confident that Federal loan subsidies would help cushion the increase. In 1978 subsidies became available to a greatly expanded number of students. In 1980 college tuitions began rising year after year at a rate that exceeded inflation. Federal student aid policies do not cause college price inflation, but there is little doubt that they help make it possible.[6]

Others have followed up on what is often called the Bennett hypothesis. For example, Arthur Hauptman has endorsed the idea that student loans have driven up tuition and other college costs over time. From Hauptman's perspective, a key factor is that traditional student-loan policies use total costs of attendance as calculated by the institution to determine eligibility to borrow. However, this "cost of attendance" is determined by the sticker price for tuition and room and board, even though most students aren't paying it. And the cost of attendance is also laden with what Hauptmann calls "consumer choice," including fancy dorms, great gym facilities, and upscale food plans. Because the cost of attendance is key in determining the amount of aid needed and the amount borrowed, Hauptman argues that "it is hard to believe that this arrangement has not been a factor in the level at which colleges set their tuition and fees."[7]

According to Jon Oberg, a former state budget administrator and federal researcher in education finance, the higher-aid–higher-tuition financing model has many advantages for colleges and universities: because the federal government does not tie Pell grants to any performance criteria, such as graduation rates, institutions are more than happy to tap this added source of revenue to free up their own resources for expanding services in which they are interested.[8]

Such a controversial hypothesis has not gone unchallenged. The major problem is that evidence linking increasing federal aid and increasing tuition is correlational, making it difficult to determine a direct causal relationship. Economist Bridget Terry Long has argued that there is no "smoking gun" linking the two.[9]

However, Long does identify a host of other factors that she believes are driving up tuition, and some deserve comment. First is the growing cost of staff and the fact that colleges and universities are increasing their spending on administrative functions more rapidly than on instruction-related ones.[10]

Another factor pushing up tuition is the growing amount of money institutions use to recruit students (institutional aid). However, institutional aid benefits more affluent students. Simply put, as the federal government has increased Pell grants to pay for access for low-income students, many institutions directed more of their own money to middle-class students. According to Kevin Carey and Erin Dillon, institutional aid in both public and in private not-for-profit schools *increases* with income, a trend that has grown over time.[11]

In short, Congress provides Pell grants, which may have little effect on student well-being but likely benefit colleges and universities.[12] Part of the problem is that Congress has not included any performance monitoring or accountability mechanisms in return for federal aid; as in other cases of the iron triangle, the consumer gets the short end of the stick while the producers get the long end.

The Student Loan Industry—A Strong Point in the Iron Triangle

As Lord Acton famously observed, "Power tends to corrupt, and absolute power corrupts absolutely." This observation can be rewritten to apply to the student-loan industry: "Money tends to corrupt and lots of money corrupts lots more." Unfortunately, the amount of money generated by the student-loan industry provided much temptation to the members inside the iron triangle of student aid.

The development of powerful financial interests coalescing around federal student aid traces back to the creation of Sallie Mae as a government-sponsored enterprise (GSE) in 1972. Built on the model of Fannie Mae and Ginnie Mae in the housing market, Sallie Mae was charged with maintaining a secondary market for student loans to ensure the liquidity of the FFEL Program by buying student loans from lenders.[13] Such a secondary market provides education lenders with fresh capital to make new student loans. In the early 1990s, as part of the Clinton administration's National Partnership for Reinventing Government initiative, Sallie Mae became a model of how to convert GSEs into private, for-profit entities.

Even as it shed its government status, Sallie Mae was allowed to keep its name for purposes of "branding." This lead to confusion among borrowers, many of whom probably did not realize that the organization was no longer government connected and that its profit motive had changed dramatically.[14]

Right next to Sallie Mae at this point in the iron triangle is Nelnet, which was arguably the main beneficiary of Senator Edward Kennedy's effort to help a different company, the Massachusetts-based Nellie Mae, which wanted to convert from nonprofit to for-profit status. As described by The Institute for College Access and Success (TICAS) in a 2005 briefing paper:

> Before 1996, it was difficult for non-profit secondary markets to convert to for-profit, because some of their assets and debt instruments could not legally be held by a for-profit entity. Then, late one night in Washington, D.C., at the urging of executives of non-profit student loan charities, a Senator quietly inserted an amendment into a tax bill, opening the door to conversion.[15]

Nellie Mae, the intended beneficiary, took advantage of the Kennedy amendment, but was ultimately bought out by Sallie Mae in 1999. Other nonprofits, including Nelnet, also seized the opportunity presented by the law and converted to for-profit status. Many of the executives who arranged to convert from nonprofit to for-profit status made fortunes.[16] Sallie Mae and Nelnet became large, multifunction student-loan companies, originating loans, servicing them, and collecting them.

In 1997 Nelnet told the Securities and Exchange Commission (SEC) that it was going to diversify out of the student-loan business. To ease the diversification, Nelnet asked the SEC to allow it to retain the existing tax-exempt student-loan bonds in an affiliated entity rather than selling them. The SEC approved.[17] However, by 2004 Nelnet had used its tax-exempt bonds with special subsidies guaranteeing a 9.5 percent return to extract hundreds of millions of dollars in subsidies from the U.S Department of Education.[18] Nelnet was not alone in collecting these payments, and much of them were, in fact, overpayments, perhaps as much as $1.2 billion.[19]

The U.S. Department of Education's inspector general released an audit report in 2006 describing the illegality of Nelnet's actions. While Secretary Spellings cut off future payments, she rejected the IG's recommendation that Nelnet be forced to return $278 million in overpayments. Spellings justified this action by citing the confused actions and advice issued by the department, which she claimed left the department open to lawsuits by Nelnet.

This was only a prelude to 2007, which was truly an *annus horribilis* for the student-loan industry and began to signal some serious challenges to existing practices. In May 2007 Secretary Spellings testified to Congress that, "Federal student aid is crying out for reform. The system is redundant, it's Byzantine, and it's broken. In fact, it's often more difficult for students to get aid than it is for bad actors to game the system. For example, throughout the 1990s, millions of dollars, meant to help families foot the bill for college, were subject to waste, fraud, and abuse."[20]

No doubt driving the secretary's description of a broken system were the various student-aid scandals that made the headlines, almost day after day, as an endless array of kickbacks, conflicts of interest, illegal claims, payoffs, and investigations captured the nation's attention. For example, the New America Foundation showed that financial-aid officials at Columbia, Southern California, the University of Texas, and Johns Hopkins held stock or took undisclosed payoffs from lenders, while others had invested in these companies.

In March 2007 Eugene W. Hickok, a former deputy secretary of education under President Bush, agreed to pay $50,000 for breaking conflict-of-interest rules by failing to sell off hundreds of shares of Bank of America stock during his tenure despite an earlier departmental ethics ruling.

Also in 2007, investigations by Andrew Cuomo, New York's attorney general, into the relationship between colleges and student loan agencies resulted in multimillion-dollar settlements with lenders and over a dozen schools for inflated loan prices created by revenue-sharing agreements. Cuomo described an "unholy alliance" between lenders and universities and threatened legal action in order to convince them to mend their ways. As a result, six universities reimbursed students over $3 million and ten major lenders paid between $500,000 and $2 million into a national education fund established by Cuomo. Spurred on by Cuomo's findings, a Senate investigation found many of the practices Cuomo documented were common throughout the nation.

Given the money involved, financial interests and university practices coalesced to grow a system that has long been marked by fraud and abuse. At the same time, the flow of money from interest groups to powerful members of Congress was unabated.

In 2006 according to *Fortune* magazine,[21] three of the top six individual contributors to the National Republican Congressional Committee were Nelnet's president and its co-CEOs. Nelnet itself was the committee's largest corporate donor. Mike Enzi, the Wyoming Republican who was the chairman of the Senate Committee on Health, Education, Labor, and Pensions, has a political-action committee called Making Business Excel. In 2006 top contributors were Sallie Mae employees who gave $20,000, Corinthian Colleges employees who gave $15,348, and Nelnet employees who gave $10,000.

In 2008, according to the Center for Responsive Politics (OpenSecrets. org), Sallie Mae spent $3.4 million in lobbying. In the same year, Sallie Mae employees gave over $900,000 to candidates, leadership PACs, and party committees, divided nearly equally between the parties.[22] That's more than American Express, Visa, and MasterCard gave. Nelnet gave out $142,000 in political donations, also split fairly evenly between the two parties.[23]

Well lubricated, this system survived repeated scandals and investigations and is only now dissolving in large part because of the magnitude of the credit crisis of 2008–9, a crisis from which the student-loan market was not exempt. In May 2008 Congress enacted the Ensuring Continued Access to Student Loans Act to keep money flowing to students by buying loans from lenders in the federal guaranteed-loan program who were unable to meet demand, thereby pumping liquidity into the market for student loans. The spiraling Wall Street crisis in the fall of 2008 made it even tougher for college students to borrow to cover tuition. Using the authority given to her in May, Secretary Spellings increased the amount of federal support for the FFEL, buying back billions of dollars of these loans.

Many critics of FFEL had always viewed private lenders as unnecessary middlemen in the business, driving up costs.[24] As the U.S. Department of Education increased its purchases, the number of people who saw these lenders as unnecessary grew, and the distinction between the Direct Loan Program and the FFEL seemed to be dissolving.

While scandals and high costs were long part of student loan policy, the relationship between Congress, the financial industry, and parts of the U.S. Department of Education seemed remarkably durable—a sturdy iron triangle. However, the credit crisis seems to have been so fundamental a challenge to this subgovernment that change became the order of the day.

Indeed, in the spring of 2009, President Obama called for an end to FFEL, fully replacing it with direct loans and promising savings of $87 billion. Ending the subsidy to private lenders became a key part of the Student Aid and Fiscal Responsibility Act (SAFRA), which cleared the House in the fall of 2009 but was not passed until March of 2010 as part of the reconciliation bill that overhauled the nation's health-insurance industry. Because SAFRA was part of the reconciliation bill, only a simple majority was needed for passage, not the sixty votes that major legislation in the Senate requires nowadays. Indeed, the vote on the reconciliation bill was fifty-six to forty-three, and it's not clear if SAFRA standing alone would have gotten the sixty votes needed as part of the normal legislative process.[25]

Given the amount of money involved, it was not surprising that the private loan industry and its allies in Congress fought these changes. For example, after the House voted to support direct lending over FFEL, Sallie Mae began a grass-roots campaign opposed to the legislation, focusing on towns where its largest facilities are located. Over 186,000 people nationwide signed a petition in favor of FFEL. Sallie Mae targeted some moderate Democrats, trying to secure their vote against the bill. Not coincidentally, one of their key targets was Senator Evan Bayh of Indiana where two of Sallie Mae's largest processing facilities are located. Bayh eventually voted for the reconciliation act.[26] (Perhaps not surprisingly, Ben Nelson, the Democratic Senator from Nelnet's home state of Nebraska, was one of only three Democrats to vote against the reconciliation bill).

During the fight over subsidies to private lenders, Sallie Mae also turned to another traditional route: it hired well-connected lobbyists. Among them Tony Podesta (his brother, John, was White House chief of staff under President Bill Clinton and led the Obama transition) and Jamie S. Gorelick, a former deputy attorney general in the Clinton administration.[27] Sallie Mae also tapped other Washington lobbying firms, including Clark & Weinstock, Global USA, ML Strategies, and Von Scoyoc Associates, and according to the *Chronicle of Higher Education* "spent millions of dollars lobbying Congress and contributing to lawmakers' campaigns."[28]

According to an analysis by Danielle Knight at the *Huffington Post*, this was just the opening gambit in Sallie Mae's attempt to "leverage its lobbying muscle and years of showering money on lawmakers to push an alternative plan that would position itself not only as a survivor, but as a clear winner with an even larger share of the market."[29] Key to this strategy is

Sallie Mae's argument that if lenders are still allowed to originate and service the loans that the government holds, they could produce similar savings that could also go toward Pell grants. Knight points out an essential part of the strategy: Sallie Mae proposed that companies that don't already service loans wouldn't be able to participate in the new system. This, of course, could leave Sallie Mae a more open field with the possibility of winning an even bigger market share. Sallie Mae started implementing this strategy in June 2009. As major changes in the FFEL were becoming increasingly likely, the U.S. Department of Education announced that four lenders had won contracts to service the existing portfolio of federal student loans. Two of the lenders that won the competition were Nelnet and Sallie Mae.[30]

According to *Inside Higher Ed*, the competition was "controversial" because the department limited it to lenders of a certain size, freezing out smaller nonprofit and other lenders, thus biasing the outcome in favor of Sallie Mae and Nelnet.[31] The more things change...

The Revolving Door

One aspect of policy subsystems is a revolving door through which personnel move between the private sector and public service. The revolving door is problematic to the extent that public officials may be inclined to use their authority to shape policies that benefit the industry from which they came, but which they are now supposed to regulate in the public's interest. The flow between government and industry can go either way, with many government officials moving to the private sector, which benefits from the official's contacts and experience.[32] Also common is the flow from industry to government in which government should benefit from the expertise these individuals have acquired, but many fear these individuals may use their power and authority to benefit the industry from which they came (and to which they are likely to return after a stint in government).

In the Bush administration there was a revolving door between the financial-aid industry and the U.S. Department of Education that became part of the problem in federal student-aid policies. Top officials in the department's Federal Student Aid Office—including Theresa Shaw, its head; Matteo Fontana; Stanley Dore; and Mariana O'Brien—all worked at Sallie Mae, the nation's largest student lender. The U.S. Department of Education's Office of Inspector General audited the offices responsible for the federal student-assistance system and in 2006 found that appointed personnel felt their mission was that of "partnership" with the loan industry rather than protecting the interests of students and taxpayers.[33] In 2009 the inspector general (IG) wrote a more pointed report recommending an assessment of the damage done and calling for corrective action where conflicts of interest existed.[34]

Other doors revolved. In June 2008 documents revealed that Sallie Mae had a contractual relationship with USA Funds, the nation's largest guarantor, which gave Sallie Mae extensive control over the very agency that was supposed to supervise its work. In 2000 the U.S. Department of Education's IG had recommended that the department forbid this relationship as a conflict of interest. However, in December 2004 the IG's recommendation was overruled by Matteo Fontana, as noted above, a former Sallie Mae employee who was then acting as head of the department's office that oversees lenders and guarantee agencies. Fontana was placed on paid leave in April 2007, following reports that he owned stock in Student Loan Xpress, another student-loan company, clearly a conflict of interest because he was serving as a government official in charge of regulating those companies.

When Enough Is Enough

Even iron can snap when put under enough stress, and even though triangles are among the most durable forms in nature, they too can fail when subject to enough stress. Whether or not the accumulating scandals and investigations would have been sufficient to break this iron triangle is unknown, but what we do know is that the most recent fiscal crisis seems finally to have produced a "stress test" that this iron triangle will not survive—at least in its present form.

While the political system of student loans seem to be on the edge of radical transformation, next we turn to much more glacial change that is emerging around information about higher education. Many believe that any system of accountability requires reliable information that is widely disseminated and readily available. Unfortunately, that's not what we have—an absence rooted in strong opposition from entrenched interest groups.

Why You Don't Know What You Should Know: The Politics of Higher-Education Information Systems

While I was on the periphery of the student-loan debacle, as commissioner of NCES, I was intensely involved in the conflicts over the flow of information about higher education to the public. Indeed, in the space of three years I was called on the carpet several times because of impolitic remarks I made regarding the need to get more information into the hands of consumers.

In an interview to *Inside Higher Ed* a few months after I took office, I was depicted as favoring "IPEDS on Steroids."[35] (IPEDS is the Integrated Postsecondary Education Data System, the nation's most comprehensive higher-education data system; more on this below.) My (perhaps naïve) belief was that taxpayers, who put so much money into higher education, and parents and students, who are literally betting thousands upon thousands of dollars in tuition and potentially years of their life pursuing a degree, should know more about how well colleges and universities were doing. Sounds reasonable, but the uproar from the higher-education "community" was deafening, including calls from members of Congress demanding that the "privacy" of students be protected from the intrusive behavior of federal bureaucrats.

An even louder uproar ensued when, under my direction, NCES proposed to collect data on higher-education accountability practices through IPEDS. The proposed changes in IPEDS asked institutions to answer three questions: Did they participate in any accountability tests? If so, which ones? And, if they published these results, where?

The proposal did not endorse any particular accountability strategy; it did not ask schools to take any assessment, and it did not ask schools to give NCES the results so that we could publish them. This (again naively) seemed to be a straight-forward collection and dissemination of information already in the public domain. Again, the uproar was deafening and the proposed data collection was killed.

My own experiences are part of a much larger problem. The Commission on the Future of Higher Education noted many problems facing America's system of postsecondary education. According to the commission, compounding these problems is a lack of "clear, reliable information about the cost and quality of postsecondary institutions."[36] Without good information, parents, consumers, taxpayers, and government officials are left with no way of judging which colleges are doing their jobs better and cheaper than others.

A Creaky Federal Information System

Underlying much of the lack of information is an outdated and inadequate federal data system, IPEDS, which, for all its problems, is supported by the higher-education industry, in part because it is so flawed.

All institutions of higher education that accept federal student aid (such as Pell grants) must provide information to IPEDS on an annual basis, and around 6,700 institutions do so, including research universities, state colleges and universities, private religious and liberal arts colleges, for-profit institutions, community and technical colleges, and nondegree-granting institutions such as beauty colleges. This makes IPEDS the only national system for collecting institutional level data from such a wide range of schools.

As noted above, the Spellings commission singled out the lack of data on the real price students pay for attending schools and on graduation rates as key limits on accountability. IPEDS collects data about the characteristics of higher-education institutions, so, theoretically, IPEDS should have this information. However, the design of IPEDS is flawed.

Much of IPEDS data focuses on first-time, full-time, degree- or certificate-seeking, undergraduate students. For example, its price data is based on the "sticker" tuition and fee data and its student financial-aid data includes the percentage of full-time, first degree- or certificate-seeking students who receive different types of grants and loans, as well as the *average* dollar amount of aid these students receive at each institution. The *average* aid package doesn't help a student figure out what she might expect, given what other students like her have received (and keeps the institution's control over institutional-aid data paramount).

IPEDS is also the only national source for graduation-rate data across the range of institutions in the country. IPEDS collects what's known as the student-right-to-know (SRK) graduation rates, which are based on first-time, full-time, degree- or certificate-seeking, undergraduate students. Under the SRK, graduation rates are calculated as the percent of an entering cohort of these types of students that graduates from that college or university within three years (for a two-year college) or six years (for a four-year institution). Under government rules, students who transfer from their first institution and graduate elsewhere are counted as noncompleters by the first institution.

While this all sounds technical, the effects are profound because less than half of postsecondary students in the United States fit into the category of students IPEDS tracks. IPEDS might be an adequate information system if the United States hadn't changed since the 1950s or if all institutions were Harvard, which graduates almost all of its freshman class within six years and from which almost no students transfer. But because the world has changed and most schools are not Harvard, IPEDS does not capture the experience of the majority of American students.

As a result, a parent or student trying to estimate what a more typical student attending a more typical institution of higher education might pay or how likely that student is to graduate is out of luck.

We know the solution: IPEDS should be abandoned in favor of a student-level database (often referred to as a student-unit record system, or SUR). Indeed, in 2005, NCES issued a report that investigated the feasibility of such a system.[37] The report succinctly notes the problem:

> The current IPEDS framework cannot accurately capture changing enrollment and completions patterns in the postsecondary education sector, especially given increasing numbers of nontraditional students, and cannot describe the prices various types of students face after financial aid is taken into account. To do so, it would be necessary to collect accurate student-level information on persistence system-wide...It would also be necessary to collect student-level information on prices and financial aid, in order to calculate net prices that take into account the individual circumstances of each student. By its very nature, a UR system would enable the collection of data that would lead to more accurate estimates of these variables.

The report notes that technical problems are solvable and that privacy issues could be addressed so that moving IPEDS to a modern information system is not a "could" question; rather, it is a "should" question that asks:

> Whether the federal government should develop a system that is based upon individually identifiable information about enrollment, financial aid, and attainment. This system would, for the first time, give policymakers and consumers much more accurate and comprehensive information about postsecondary education in this country. Some of the benefits of a UR system include the collection of new data that would measure the success rates of students at institutions to which family and federal student aid monies flow, provide more accurate consumer guidance, and improve federal programs that support those families and students.

The "should" question answers itself, and Peter Ewell's chapter in this book outlines steps that states have taken to improve the quality of the data in their own student-unit record systems. There is a reasonable debate about the balance that should be struck between state systems and a federal system of student-unit records, but the outcome of that debate has been decided, at least for now, by the 2008 reauthorization of the Higher Education Opportunity Act, which specifically bans the U.S. Department of Education from collecting such individual student level data.[38]

By now the readers should guess where the political pressure for that ban came from: much of the higher-education lobby (especially the National Association of Independent Colleges and Universities, known by its acronym NAICU) pushed to keep the flawed IPEDS intact to preserve the information asymmetry that allows them to continue their practices with limited scrutiny.

The current higher-education opposition strategy emphasizes the importance of privacy (a combination of technical concerns and an emphasis on distrusting government from holding data) and emphasizes voluntary efforts by higher-education institutions to provide information that the industry lobbies to prevent NCES from presenting.[39]

It should be noted that much of the data that are presented on these voluntary sites comes from IPEDS (and hence shares the same fundamental problems of IPEDS). Moreover, because the sponsoring organizations do not want to encourage competition between institutions that are voluntarily participating, these Web sites are not designed to allow the "kitchen table," side-by-side comparison of schools, which consumers want.[40]

Finally, many institutions provide much of the same information contained in the NCES student-unit record proposal to the National Student Clearinghouse. But the clearinghouse is a private organization supported by individual colleges and universities and has neither obligations nor incentives to make data widely available. While NCES is committed to have a reasonable balance between data in and information out, the clearinghouse faces a different calculation.

Absent any crisis of the size that is threatening the student-loan industry, improvements in the national system of information will only slowly emerge, and if, as the saying goes, "the past is prologue to the future," those changes will be fought by the higher-education lobby.

Conclusions

Political scientists seek to understand the factors that preserve subsystems and those that lead to change. Among the factors analysts have identified that preserve the status quo and make change difficult are the high status of the interest groups involved in the policy subsystem (doctors and the American Medical Association are the clearest examples) and the aura of success (for example, the American pharmaceutical industry).

Both of these factors have benefited higher education. The argument that the United States has the best system of higher education in the world populated by Nobel Prize winners producing world-class science has benefited the industry and preserved it from careful scrutiny and reform. Yet we spend more on higher education than any other nation and many now argue that we are not getting sufficient return on this huge investment. Moreover, given our mediocre college graduation rates, students and their families are accumulating large debt in pursuit of degrees they will never receive.

No wonder that, as documented by the 2009 report by Public Agenda and The National Center for Public Policy and Higher Education, public support for colleges and universities is low. That study found that over half of its respondents believed that higher education is run like most businesses with less concern for educational mission than profit.[41] Throughout this chapter, we have seen events and practices that may support those attitudes and may be creating the opportunities for large-scale change.

The seemingly never-ending scandals of the student-loan industry began prying open a window for policy change, but it took an event the size of the fiscal crises of 2008–2009 to finally swamp the existing system of student financial aid.

In the pursuit of better information about outcomes and costs, the conditions for reform are accumulating more slowly, but at some point more accurate information about the costs and outcomes of colleges and universities will be made more widely available and more usable.

As we achieve these changes, we can imagine the creation of a viable system of accountability for a higher education system delivering a world class education at a reasonable price.

Notes

1. Mancur Olson, *The Logic of Collective Action: Public Goods and the Theory of Groups* (Cambridge, MA: Harvard University Press, 1971), and Theodore Lowi, *The End of Liberalism* (New York: Norton, 1979) provide the classic analyses.
2. Tracy Sulkin, Bryan Jones, and Heather Larsen, "Policy Punctuations in American Political Institutions," *American Political Science Review* 97, no. 1 (2003); Christian Breunig and Chris Koski, "Punctuated Equilibria and Budgets in the American States," *Policy Studies Journal* 34, no. 3 (2006); Michael Howlett and Benjamin Cashore, "Re-Visiting the New Orthodoxy of Policy Dynamics: The Dependent Variable and Re-Aggregation Problems in the Study of Policy Change," *Canadian Political Science Review* 1, no. 2 (December 2007); B. Dan Wood and Alesha Doan, "The Politics of Problem Definition: Applying and Testing Threshold Models," *American Journal of Political Science* 47, no. 4 (October 2003).

3. Author's calculations based on the "cost of attendance" measure from the U.S. Department of Education's Integrated Postsecondary Education Data System.

4. National Center for Public Policy and Higher Education, *Measuring Up 2008: The National Report Card on Higher Education* (San Jose, CA: 2008), http://measuringup2008.highereducation.org/.

5. Student aid makes up the bulk of the activities of the U.S. Department of Education, employing about one-third of its employees, consuming about one-quarter of its discretionary appropriations, and accounting for the bulk of its entitlement spending. Most Federal aid is governed by Title IV, first included in the Higher Education Act (HEA) of 1965, and which now occupies most of the over one thousand pages of the Higher Education Opportunities Act of 2008, the latest reauthorization of the HEA.

6. William Bennett, "Our Greedy Colleges," *New York Times*, February 18, 1987, http://www.nytimes.com/1987/02/18/opinion/our-greedy-colleges.html?pagewanted=1.

7. Interview with author, July 17, 2008.

8. John Oberg, "Testing Federal Student-Aid Fungibility in Two Competing Versions of Federalism," *Publius* 27 (1997).

9. Bridget Terry Long, "What Is Known about the Impact of Financial Aid? Implications for Policy" (working paper, National Center for Postsecondary Research, Teachers College, Columbia University, New York, April 2008), http://www.postsecondaryresearch.org/i/a/document/6963_Long-FinAid.pdf.

10. See for example, Jane V. Wellman et al, *Trends in College Spending* (Washington, DC: Delta Project on Postsecondary Education Costs, Productivity, and Accountability, 2009), www.deltacostproject.org/resources/pdf/trends_in_spending-report.pdf; Mark Schneider, "Where Does All That Tuition Go?" *AEI Education Outlook* 12 (December 2009), http://www.aei.org/outlook/100924.

11. For an extended analysis of this see Kevin Carey and Erin Dillon, "Drowning in Debt: The Emerging Student Loan Crisis," EducationSector, July 9, 2009, http://www.educationsector.org/analysis/analysis_show.htm?doc_id=964333.

12. Indeed, some have even pointed out that there is little evidence showing that Pell grants have increased access to higher education. For example, see W. Lee Hansen, "Impact of Student Financial Aid on Access," in *The Crisis in Higher Education*, ed. Joseph Froomkin (New York: Academy of Political Science, 1983), 84–96; Donald Heller, "Student Price Response in Higher Education: An Update to Leslie and Brinkman," *Journal of Higher Education* 68 (1997); Thomas Kane, "College Attendance By Blacks Since 1970: The Role of College Cost, Family Background and the Returns to Education," *Journal of Political Economy 102*, no. 5 (1994); and Michael McPherson and Owen Schapiro Morton, *The Student Aid Game: Meeting Need and Rewarding Talent in American Higher Education* (Princeton, NJ: Princeton University Press, 1998). In 2002, the U.S. Government Accountability Office concluded

that "Little information is available to Congress on the relative effectiveness of Title IV grants and loans...in promoting postsecondary attendance, choice, and completion" (U.S. Government Accountability Office, *Student Aid and Tax Benefits: Better Research and Guidance Will Facilitate Comparison of Effectiveness and Student Use,* report to Congressional Committees (Washington, DC, September 2002), http://www.ed.gov/about/bdscomm/list/acsfa/gao02751.pdf.

13. Another major initial function of Sallie Mae was to warehouse loans—lending to banks using student loan paper as collateral—but this function has sharply declined over time.

14. See, for example, Alan Michael Collinge, *The Student Loan Scam: The Most Oppressive Debt in U.S. History—and How We Can Fight Back* (Boston: Beacon, 2009).

15. The Institute for College Access and Success, *How Non-Profit Student Loan Officials Get Rich,* briefing paper, May 26, 2005 (Berkeley, CA: Institute for College Access and Success) http://www.ticas.org/ticas_d/2005_05_25_Briefing.pdf

16. Ibid.

17. This approval was contained in a letter from the SEC's Division of Enforcement Management on February 10, 1998 in response to the request from Nebraska Higher Education Loan Program, Inc. (SEC Ref. No. 97–471-CC).

18. The "9.5 percent program" forms yet another part of the sorry spectacle of money going from the taxpayers to the financial industry. The Higher Education Act guaranteed lenders a 9.5 percent return on loans funded through nonprofit bonds floated before 1993. This was a time of high interest rates and this guarantee was needed to keep loans flowing. This was supposed to be a short-term fix and the loans were supposed to be canceled as market conditions changed. However, when interest rates declined, many lenders actually expanded this loan program through a variety of accounting mechanisms, which produced the large profits for Nelnet and others.

19. In early September 2009 a law suit filed by Jon Oberg was unsealed, in which he is asking ten loan companies to reimburse the federal government $1 billion in these improper payments. Also see Paul Basken, "Government Losses on 9.5-Percent Loan Loophole May Exceed $1-Billion," *The Chronicle of Higher Education,* September 18, 2008. http://chronicle.com/article/Government-Losses-on-Loan-L/1169/.

20. House Committee on Education and Labor, *Hearing on College Student Aid and Reading First,* 110th Cong., 1st sess., 2007, http://www.ed.gov/news/pressreleases/2007/05/05102007.html.

21. Bethany McLean, "Dems: make student loans student friendly," *Fortune* magazine, November 13, 2006, http://money.cnn.com/2006/11/13/magazines/fortune/democrats_student_loans.fortune/?postversion=2006111313.

22. Aaron Kiersh, "Direct or Indirect Loans? Either Way, It's Win-Win Deal for Major Political Contributor Sallie Mae," Center for Responsive Politics

(Opensecrets.org), July 23, 2009, http://www.opensecrets.org/news/2009/07/direct-or-indirect-loans-eithe.html.

23. Walter Alarkton, "Beneficiaries of Sallie Mae, Nelnet fight Obama's student-aid proposal," *The Hill*, March 9, 2009, http://thehill.com/homenews/news/18654-beneficiaries-of-sallie-mae-nelnet-fight-obamas-student-aid-proposal.

24. U.S. Department of Education, "Continuing the Commitment to Students and their Families to Ensure Access to Student Loans," press release, November 2008, http://www.ed.gov/students/college/aid/ffelp-facts.html.

25. As part of the legislative process, much of what the administration wanted in SAFRA was eliminated. The growth of Pell grants was scaled back and the president's programs to support community colleges and increase college completion rates were also gutted.

26. Note that in February 2010 Bayh announced his retirement from the Senate. Whether or not that freed him up to vote this way is of course an interesting but unanswerable question.

27. For more on Sallie Mae's lobbying efforts see Danielle Knight, "Lobbying Showdown Over The Future Of Student Loans," *The Huffington Post*, July 29, 2009, http://www.huffingtonpost.com/2009/07/29/lobbying-showdown-over-th_n_247506.html.

28. See Paul Baskin, "Historic Victory for Student Aid is Tinged by Lost Possibilities," *Chronicle of Higher Education*, March 25, 2010, http://chronicle.com/article/Historic-Victory-for-Student/64844/.

29. Danielle Knight, "Lobbying Showdown Over The Future Of Student Loans," *Huffington Post*, July 29, 2009, http://www.huffingtonpost.com/2009/07/29/lobbying-showdown-over-th_n_247506.html.

30. The other two were AES/PHEAA, and Great Lakes Education Loan Services, Inc.

31. "U.S. Chooses 4 to Service Student Loans," *Inside Higher Ed*, Quick Takes, June 18, 2009, http://www.insidehighered.com/news/2009/06/18/qt#201449.

32. Truth in advertising: after serving as the commissioner of Education Statistics, I moved to the American Institutes for Research (AIR) as a vice president.

33. Office of Inspector General, "Review of Financial Partners' Monitoring and Oversight of Guaranty Agencies, Lenders, and Servicers," (Washington, DC: U.S. Department of Education, September 2006), http://www.ed.gov/about/offices/list/oig/auditreports/a04e0009.pdf.

34. Office of Inspector General, "Special Allowance Payments to Nelnet for Loans Funded by Tax-Exempt Obligations," (Washington, DC: U.S. Department of Education, September 2006), http://www.ed.gov/about/offices/list/oig/auditreports/a07f0017.pdf.

35. Doug Lederman, "IPEDS on Steroids," *Inside Higher Ed*, December 1, 2006, http://www.insidehighered.com/news/2006/12/01/ipeds.

36. U.S. Department of Education, *A Test of Leadership: Charting the Future of U.S. Higher Education*, a report of the commission appointed by Secretary

Spellings (Washington, DC, 2006), x, http://www.ed.gov/about/bdscomm/list/hiedfuture/reports/final-report.pdf.

37. Alisa F. Cunningham, John Milam, and Cathy Statham, "Feasibility of a Student Unit Record System Within the Integrated Postsecondary Education Data System," (Washington, DC: National Center for Education Statistics, March 2005), http://nces.ed.gov/pubs2005/2005160.pdf.

38. The act allows states to collect these data (and over forty do), though the quality of these data systems vary widely and the degree to which they "talk" to each other ("inoperability" to use the jargon) is still a serious question.

39. An example: in 2005, NCES undertook a concerted effort to allow consumers to more easily access the data in IPEDS through a Web site called College Navigator; http://nces.ed.gov/COLLEGENAVIGATOR/ NAICU objected to this. At about the same time, it started its UCAN (University and College Accountability Network), http://www.ucan-network.org/, claiming that this effort made government efforts to improve consumer information unnecessary. Launched in 2007, UCAN now has 728 schools providing 47 elements. Other types of institutions have followed suit; for example, see College Portraits, http://www.collegeportraits.org/, which is part of the Voluntary System of Accountability developed by the National Association of State Universities and Land-grant Colleges and the American Association of State Colleges and Universities, or Transparency by Design, http://www.collegechoicesforadults.org/, focusing on adult learners who are interested in online and distance-education programs offered by for-profit institutions.

40. Perhaps not surprisingly, NCES's College Navigator has this function. On nongovernmental efforts, see Doug Lederman, "The Challenge of Comparability," *Inside Higher Ed*, August 4, 2009, http://www.insidehighered.com/news/2009/08/04/transparency; Doug Lederman, "The Competition to Be Transparent," *Inside Higher Ed*, September 29, 2008, http://www.insidehighered.com/news/2008/09/29/vsa.

41. John Immerwahr and Jean Johnson, "Squeeze Play 2009: The Public's Views on College Costs Today," (Washington, DC: Public Agenda and the National Center for Public Policy and Higher Education, 2009), http://www.highereducation.org/reports/squeeze_play_09/index.shtml.

9

Accountability for Community Colleges: Moving Forward

Sara Goldrick-Rab

R ecent calls for increased investments in postsecondary education have been accompanied by demands for greater accountability from colleges and universities. It is politically difficult in a time of scarce resources to allocate new funds without requiring measurable outcomes in return. At the same time, effective accountability systems in education are rare. Therefore, in this chapter I consider the potential for successfully framing and enacting accountability frameworks for community colleges. I argue that the usual approach to accountability requires substantial reform if it stands any chance of succeeding in this sector, but that success is possible and likely.

Accountability systems only work if they are given significant legitimacy by those being held accountable. Actors need to feel part of the process and believe that their performance is assessed in meaningful, worthwhile ways.[1] My research indicates that community-college leaders are prepared, given the right circumstances, to enter into new accountability arrangements with not just acquiescence but enthusiasm. This could create a great deal of positive change in an institution often simultaneously applauded for its very existence and derided for its current levels of performance. In fact, robust accountability arrangements implemented with the consent and participation of community colleges could be a way to solve decades-old, seemingly intractable problems such as underfunding and lack of social prestige.

Next, I provide a brief overview of the work of community colleges and the attention they have recently received, particularly from policymakers.

I also describe the contours of their current outcomes. Then, I address a key problem of many accountability systems—their inability to gain the consent and willful participation of their subjects—and explain why I believe this may not be a significant problem in the case of community colleges. My assessment is informed by numerous conversations with community-college leaders over the last five years and a recent survey of forty-one community-college presidents. Together, these shed light on the ways a new accountability regime might effectively develop. Finally, I end by outlining a process through which accountability for community colleges could progress during the next five years.

Community Colleges: Then and Now

Practically since Joliet Junior College was established in 1901, the very existence of community colleges has been the subject of critique and debate. For decades they have been described as places that enforce "continued dependency, unrealistic aspirations, and wasted 'general education.'"[2] At the same time, the public two-year sector effectively facilitated the nation's desires for a massive expansion of higher education that brought more than two-thirds of all high-school graduates into some form of postsecondary coursework. Most Latino and low-income students who will ever attend college will enroll in a community college, the most affordable and accessible entryway.[3]

Critics of community colleges tend to focus on their rates of degree production: specifically, the percentage of students transferring to four-year colleges and/or earning credentials. Relative to their sizable population of entrants, the percentage of degree recipients is small; more than one in two beginning community-college students leave empty-handed. This leads many to call community colleges places of access but not success, leading some educational observers to charge that their students are being "cooled out" and "diverted" when channeled into their doors.[4] Notably, their completion rates also make many policymakers hesitant to contribute the additional resources that may be necessary to improve outcomes.[5]

But the last year has seen significant changes to these trends. In a recent speech at Macomb Community College, President Barack Obama called community colleges an "undervalued asset" to the nation, recognizing that they are often treated like a "stepchild" and an "afterthought." He summoned the "can-do American spirit" of community colleges everywhere to help transform the American economy.[6] His American Graduation Initiative (as of the time of this writing, passed by the House of Representatives in

HR 3221 and pending in the Senate) calls for a substantial investment in the public two-year sector (approximately $9 billion), coupled with performance targets intended to innovate and transform community colleges into efficient, degree-producing institutions.

Would it work? In particular, are community-college leaders receptive to greater accountability and will they respond to the new forms of federal investment by changing policies and practices in sustainable ways? Some say no. For example, Frederick Hess of the American Enterprise Institute contends that President Obama's initiative will effectively slow efforts to reform community colleges, perpetuating the "subpar community-college status quo" since the colleges and their leaders are not "up to the challenges they face."[7] Accountability (and increased funding), Hess implies, are merely nudges, and likely ineffective nudges at that.

My research leads me to doubt the accuracy of Hess's assertions. Community-college leaders are generally a reform-minded group eager to gain the support needed to change practices, and that serves as motivation to embrace accountability. While I dispute his assessment that the colleges themselves are inherently "subpar," I think that the longstanding treatment of the community-college sector as inferior and not "up to the challenge" spurs its leaders to embrace new ways to attract respect and resources to their colleges. As noted earlier, one reason that accountability often fails is that it is not embraced by those it relies on; it is an external third party often unwelcomed by the main players. If the will of community-college leaders is widespread and reasonably established, the path to progress is illuminated and potentially promising.

The perspectives I present in this chapter draw on two types of data. My primary source of information is an online survey of community-college presidents and other leaders that I conducted between August and November 2009. In that survey I solicited information on presidents' perceptions and attitudes toward accountability with a focus on identifying areas of agreement and disagreement on the measurement of community-college success. I circulated an invitation to participate through multiple channels, asking respondents to draw on their own social networks to gather additional recruits (often called "snowball sampling"). I sent this request to presidents at institutions large and small, urban and rural, and asked the national associations to assist as well. In total, forty-one community-college presidents participated. Since I promised anonymity in exchange for participation, and the survey was intentionally kept short to increase participation, I did not collect demographic information on individuals or institutions.[8] Therefore, I do not claim the survey has demonstrable generalizability; it does not use a nationally representative sample; I cannot calculate rates of participation, nor is it safe to assume that the broadest array of potential perspectives is represented. Instead, the information gleaned from these results is most appropriately interpreted in conjunction with other surveys and research on the attitudes and actions of community colleges toward accountability. Therefore, whenever possible I note points of convergence or divergence with the results of a 2009 survey of community-college leaders in ten states, conducted by the Community College Research Center, as well as a national interview-based study of college presidents conducted by Public Agenda in 2008.[9] In addition I draw on lessons from the numerous formal and informal conversations with community-college presidents I experienced over the last five years as part of other studies.[10]

The Status Quo and the Future

There is widespread dissatisfaction with the current production rates of community colleges and their leaders know this. Even among students with stated degree intentions, dropout is common.[11] In terms of national averages, after three years just 16 percent of first-time community-college students who began college in 2003 had attained a credential of any kind (certificate, associate's degree, and/or bachelor's degree), and another 40 percent were still enrolled. Given six years to complete instead of three, completion rates improve somewhat; for example, 36 percent of students entering community colleges in 1995 attained a credential by 2001. Another 17.5 percent were still enrolled.[12] While this indicates that completion rates need to account for the pace of progress toward completion, the noncompletion rate (no degree; not enrolled) hovers very close to 50 percent, even given longer time horizons. Of course, this number decreases when degree completion is measured over a longer period of time, but in the aggregate it represents a substantial loss of human capital and resources.[13]

At the same time, many also acknowledge that inputs driving the system contribute to current rates of completion. Community colleges serve more disadvantaged students but receive far fewer per-student resources from state and federal governments when compared to public four-year institutions. Their resources tend to decline during recessions just as enrollments are at their peak.[14] They are often overcrowded and have too few faculty and counselors to serve students.[15] A significant portion of the community-college population is comprised of older adults from disadvantaged backgrounds who often enter higher education with low levels of literacy. Nationally, 57 percent of two-year institutions rank the academic preparation of their entering students as fair or poor.[16] The faculty workforce is disproportionately comprised of part-time adjuncts receiving little professional development and having scarce time to spend with students.[17] For all of these reasons, while observers tend to find completion rates of community colleges unacceptable, they also find them unsurprising.[18]

Where should community colleges aim in terms of achieving greater levels of success? Even attaching a descriptor to current levels of performance (e.g., labeling them mediocre or subpar) depends on first establishing some kind of benchmark for comparison, or an absolute target. Since open-access institutions are, by definition, nonselective, students enter with a wide range of goals and expectations, making assessment of their outcomes complicated. For example, if we define "success" based on the outcomes of all entrants, performance will be depressed unless success is very broadly defined. By the same token, if we measure success only for a select group (e.g., those who indicate degree intentions or achieve credit thresholds), we risk producing a falsely positive appearance of success while also encouraging access to diminish (e.g., through creaming). Clearly, results vary depending on how broadly the pool of potential completers is defined and how success is measured.[19] Community-college leaders are highly cognizant of this fact and actively resist performance measures that would seem to have the potential to narrow their focus to a single group of students. Said a community-college president interviewed by Public Agenda: "We are constantly balancing access with quality. Here we are with maybe half of the high school graduates coming to us who are not college ready, and we are being held accountable for producing high-quality graduates. It is a balancing act." The clear implication, according to a president in my survey, is that "those developing, implementing and measuring accountability in community colleges [must] understand the institutions and their variety of students."

A related concern is the community college's long history of having multiple missions. While resources for the workforce development mission are most abundant, the twin emphases on promoting college access generally and access to the baccalaureate in particular (via the transfer function) dominate public perception. In keeping with those emphases, it is common to compare the success of community-college students to the success of two different groups: high-school graduates who do not attend college at all, and students who began at (usually nonselective) four-year institutions. These comparisons facilitate the calculation of a "positive" democratizing effect of bringing students into higher education who otherwise wouldn't attend college, and a "negative" diversion effect of lowering rates of bachelor's degree completion among students who otherwise would have attended a four-year college. The most rigorous studies tend to find relatively small negative differences in the outcomes of students who start at community colleges compared to nonselective, public four-year institutions, but many times those differences are offset by the positive increases in college attainment of those attending community college rather than no college at all.[20] Of course, when the latter part of the "community college" effect is not taken into account, the "penalty" of starting at a community college appears larger.

As more and different kinds of postsecondary institutions emerge, and the number of missions of community colleges expands, various additional comparisons also become possible. For example, the outcomes of community colleges have recently been compared (negatively) to those of the for-profit, two-year sector.[21] Instead of focusing on credential completion, others argue for measuring incremental milestones marking progress toward a degree. Crediting colleges for helping students make the transition from remedial to credit-bearing coursework is one example.[22] Furthermore, many community-college leaders contend that completion of noncredit courses and/or workforce training ought to also count toward measures of success.[23]

But a key question is whether any types of comparisons (even across-state or within-state comparisons *among* community colleges) are fair and effective at motivating agents to change. State community college systems vary in their missions (and their demographics) and also have different outcomes.[24] Therefore, some critics of accountability argue that it is not appropriate to compare community colleges across states. For example, one might have a strong articulation system (said to reflect a stronger transfer mission) with a neighboring state lacking such a system.[25] But that presents a problem in terms of making comparisons only if we believe that differences in policies or missions drive outcomes (in other words, that outcomes might reflect policy choices). Instead, it is also possible that outcomes are driving community-college policies or definitions of mission (in other words, that policy choices reflect past or current levels of performance). It is far from clear that accountability systems should combat "mission restriction" by including measures related to *all* missions. Instead, we should strike a balance by providing additional resources to support certain missions, while avoiding taking explicit actions to compromise others.

In addition to identifying a benchmark against which to compare the *relative* performance of community colleges, we might also consider setting some *absolute* standards. For example, are there any conditions under which a completion rate of less than 10 percent would be deemed acceptable? Right now, according to the federal calculations (in IPEDs), the community college performing at the fiftieth percentile graduates just over 21 percent of its students within three years (this includes certificates and degrees, not counting those earned at another institution), and helps another 19 percent transfer. Compared to that average rate of 40 percent "success," the worst-performing community colleges (those at the tenth percentile) achieve success in less than one-fifth of cases (18 percent), while those at the ninetieth percentile see over 80 percent succeed.[26] While using relative criteria serves to emphasize continuous improvement and encourages competition among schools,[27] setting absolute targets might help to improve the colleges' public standing—images are easily tarnished when one can locate a community college with a dropout rate greater than 85 percent.[28]

The good news is that there is general agreement among both community-college "insiders" and "outsiders" about the need to improve. The majority of presidents in my survey indicated that a clearer focus on "success" and "what matters most" would be a benefit of increased accountability. These results are also broadly consistent with the opinions of community-college presidents who participated in interviews with Public Agenda in 2008.[29] The many caveats about inadequate student preparation and multiple missions do not ameliorate the need to assess success, particularly given a climate of scarce fiscal resources and a push to increase the nation's stock of human capital.[30] Moving the bar (no matter how far) requires establishing a range of acceptable outcomes and setting some goals. This effort must be a precursor to any new accountability regime because knowing what the regime is meant to achieve will be the only way to assess its success.

In Search of Respect

Given the potential that focusing on a set of outcomes might narrow their work or compromise valued missions, what accounts for the willingness of community-college leaders to embrace accountability? I put the question to community-college presidents, and their responses indicate a strong belief that the opportunities provided by accountability will outweigh its potential costs. Faced with declining resources, relative invisibility in the eyes of the media and the public, and yet growing expectations for performance, they seek new solutions.

In particular, many community-college presidents spoke of an interest in having the chance to *demonstrate institutional value* in a visible way. This is a sector often frustrated by the lack of attention and knowledge of their work exhibited by the general public. As one community-college president put it, "Accountability provides an opportunity for policy makers and the public to better understand the mission of community colleges and the students they serve." Another said, "Accountability can defuse the argument that community colleges are 'failing.' " Given that a recent report confirmed that community colleges are largely invisible in terms of media coverage, this is an important concern.[31]

Community-college presidents are also interested in leveraging accountability to strengthen the claims of that sector on *public resources*. Competition for resources is stiffer than ever, and community colleges often feel they lose out to universities, K-12 schools, health care, prisons, and more. A president interviewed for the Public Agenda study said, "This is a kind of a bias from a community-college person, but I think that the state has always been willing to provide more funds for four-year colleges and universities than they have for community colleges. I feel that community college has kind of gotten left out."[32] He is correct; a recent analysis colleagues and I conducted for the Brookings Institution revealed that significant funding disparities between the two- and four-year public sectors exist at the federal level as well (even after netting out disparities in student financial aid and resource funding).[33]

Two-year college leaders also embrace the potential for accountability in order to help *organize the work* of their colleges and motivate their staffs. For example, one president told me that he hopes accountability will "lead to honest discussion of issues and the ability to manage organizational change." Another added that by facilitating the discovery of "what works" and what does not, the use of data can help leaders "to direct time and funding away from initiatives we cannot show that work and toward new ventures." Such an approach to establishing the effectiveness, and particularly the cost-effectiveness, of programs and practices in higher education is long overdue.[34] Moreover, it is the explicit focus of the Lumina Foundation's Making Opportunity Affordable initiative.

Admittedly, these are high expectations for any set of policies—perhaps too high. For when data is collected and shared, it does not always match with projections. But hope reigns eternal, as clearly evident in the words of the president who told me that accountability provides "a chance to demonstrate that community colleges far exceed every other educational entity in return on the dollar, and that the "delta" (that is, the magnitude of change) in educational outcomes is tremendous."

It is also worth noting that, in one sense, faith among leaders that accountability will bring status and recognition to the sector is paradoxical. As many presidents noted, accountability for community college is not new (though it may come to take new forms at a new scale) but it has not done much thus far to enhance status and recognition. One said:

> Community colleges have always been held accountable by our students and the communities we serve to fulfill our stated missions. For example, we have always been accountable to grant funders, financial aid

providers, state agencies, foundations, donors, and more for being responsible stewards of our resources. We have always been accountable to local employers and transfer institutions for the quality and preparation levels of our graduates. We have always been accountable to our students, first and foremost, to ensure that they have every opportunity to achieve their educational goals whether they are to successfully complete a single class, a degree or something in between. So accountability is not coming to community colleges; it has always been here.

Despite the presence of accountability in the past, community colleges have sunk even lower on the higher-education totem pole as evidenced, for example, by growing disparities in their funding relative to other sectors. This is true even though community college administrators feel they are already operating in an environment in which their information and outcomes are very public and already perceive that they are held responsible by local communities and boards. They "believe in the story" they have to tell, yet their outcomes have not improved, and their position in higher education has not grown stronger.

Of course, presidents may only appear to embrace "accountability"; the term itself is vague and therefore easily interpreted in different ways. This was difficult to get a sense of using the online survey, but the results suggest that to some community-college presidents accountability means little more than "reporting information." To others, who speak in more concrete terms about specific standards for achievement, it implies both reporting and responsiveness to demands for improvement. Friendliness toward accountability could vary, then, by how it is defined.

It is also important to note that most leaders express the idea that accountability *alone* will not work; it is simply insufficient. The financial constraints under which community colleges currently operate both contribute to and reflect their status. Their meager levels of funding complicate how and under what conditions they respond to demands for improvement. They watch their enrollment and graduation rates carefully, but struggle with how to make the investments needed to improve. And in some cases, when money is not available to make improvements, it is probably easier to ignore the numbers entirely.

The Opportunity and the Challenges

At the time of this writing, there is mounting evidence that the political will to move an accountability movement forward in the two-year sector is present. The number of states tying at least some community college funding to outcomes has grown. For example, South Florida Community College uses sixteen core indicators of effectiveness that are used in tandem with the state-level accountability measures.[35] The Washington State Board of Community and Technical Colleges has implemented a performance incentive funding system based on key momentum points that evidence student success.[36]

The Achieving the Dream initiative, which promotes the use of data and benchmarking as part of regular community-college practice, is now widely respected and community colleges actively seek to join in. Its focus on effective use of data to improve student success, common measurement of core achievement indicators, and disaggregation of data to pinpoint gaps in student achievement are good examples of community colleges willingly embracing accountability. This may be attributable to the approach of the initiative, in particular its emphasis on using outcomes to promote learning. This is critically important to leaders; as one president told Public Agenda, "Accountability needs to be used to help us improve and learn from one another and get better. It doesn't need to be used as a club, or a stick, or an excuse not to fund schools."

Another positive sign is that nearly all community colleges are participating in the Community College Survey of Student Engagement, and they allow institutional-level survey results to be released to the public. This stands in sharp contrast to the unwillingness of four-year colleges in the National Survey of Student Engagement to make their institution-level data widely available.[37] Recently, the Bill and Melinda Gates Foundation and the Lumina Foundation announced a $1 million effort to support a new voluntary accountability system being developed by the American Association of Community Colleges, the Association of Community College Trustees, and the College Board. Eight community colleges in eight states (AZ, CA, IN, LA, OH, OK, SC, and TX) have agreed to participate in a pilot test of the system with the intention to next ramp up to include twenty colleges in the next two years.

If we accept that interest among educational leaders is alive and well, what are the main tasks which need to be dealt with in creating new accountability frameworks for community colleges? My sense is that there are at least three: (a) reaching agreement on appropriate measurable outcomes, (b) developing (or reinforcing) systems capable of producing data on those measures, and (c) determining the extent to which accountability will be tied to funding, governance, and strategic planning.

Defining the Measures

The first, defining the accountability measures, is the most critical. As Jamie Merisotis, president of the Lumina Foundation, recently stated, "The first step will be to get everyone speaking the same language."[38] The measures used must reflect on long-standing debates over institutional missions, and student and faculty goals. For example, if the measures place disproportionate weight on the transfer function of community colleges, those who value and work on the workforce side will object and vice versa. If the measures do not capture outcomes that college administrators can use (and ideally that faculty and students can use too), they will not last. And finally, the process through which definitions are constructed will serve to define how community colleges relate to the accountability system. This is a sector accustomed to being told what to do, rather than being given the tools and rights with which to set their own terms. Great surprises could result if that typical approach were upended.

To be clear, this *does not mean* allowing each college to develop their own accountability measures using their own data. Such an approach will greatly diminish any potential for establishing standards and setting goals that go beyond a single institution. Instead, there are several potential ways to identify appropriate accountability measures, including (a) drawing on performance outcomes used in other settings or systems, (b) considering the use measures already in place in state accountability systems for community colleges, and/or (c) identifying measures community college leaders prefer.

In the first case the likely result would involve importing measures used for four-year colleges. The greatest fear of community-college leaders appears to be that policymakers will simply seek to transform them into four-year colleges. Their unique functions, particularly their ability to enroll students who otherwise would not attend college, and their relationships to business leaders and local citizens, are very important to them. When they speak of inappropriate measures, then, they refer to those "based upon an outmoded understanding of our colleges and their students" or those that employ "metrics calibrated to four-year colleges, and metrics that do not assess impact on community." To be more specific, one community-college president told me that "our community colleges are too often judged by measures that are more appropriate to liberal arts colleges with residence halls and homogeneous student bodies." Similar fears were expressed by community-college leaders in interviews conducted by the Institute for Higher Education Policy in 2006.[39]

In a recent study assessing performance measures already used in ten states to calculate outcomes for community colleges, researchers at the Community College Research Center identified 140 specific indicators already used, including those related to inputs, process, and outputs. Notably missing from existing indicators, those researchers pointed out, are measures of student learning.[40]

The current measures of institutional success used in IPEDs, known as the student-right-to-know graduation rates, are good examples of what most community-college presidents would deem inappropriate. These calculations are done only for first-time, full-time, degree- or certificate-seeking students. Clearly, as analysts at the Community Colleges Research Center have put it, the SRK isn't "all you need to know" to measure community-college student success.[41]

A failure to involve community-college leaders in the process of grappling with the problem of crafting appropriate measures could lead to several additional problems, some quite unintentional. One president was quite blunt when he said, "without the freedom to choose the measures and targets that are appropriate for their students and programs, community colleges may feel forced to resort to other ways to meet inappropriate targets, such as limiting access for students who are least likely to succeed. Obviously that would be counter to the overarching goal of improving college graduation and reducing inequities at the national level." Several leaders also expressed concern that the fear of negative press may inhibit colleges from trying new programs that might result in inadequate outcomes.[42] This is consistent with the responses of community-college presidents (and often four-year college presidents as well) in interviews about accountability conducted by Public Agenda. In that study, researchers found that "the presidents were nearly unanimous in saying that their institutions should be accountable; at the same time, however, they felt that many of the current approaches to accountability are more harmful than helpful."[43]

In an effort to assess what community-college presidents would embrace, I asked survey participants to name five outcome measures they would be comfortable with using in an accountability system to which their colleges should be subjected. The most common responses from community-college presidents were indicators of attainment, employment, and access (see figure 9.1). They are broadly consistent with those identified by CCRC's survey, though they focus more heavily on outputs and less on process. This is important since the process indicators could include measures of the relative resources colleges have to achieve outcomes such as tuition and fees, and funding per full-time employee. Yet, even though assessments of performance without consideration of these measures are more likely to feel "unfair" to presidents, they were notably absent from the presidents' suggestions. This suggests a need to carefully explain their purpose and then include them.

The measures suggested by presidents also somewhat overlap with the measures proposed in the American Graduation initiative as well as those

Question: If funding for your college was going to be tied to 5 measures of outcomes, what would those measures be?

<u>Educational Outcomes</u>

  1. Continued Enrollment (fall to spring, fall-fall, and growth over time)
  2. Course completion rates (% attempted and passed)
  3. Transfer rates
  4. Degree or certificate completion rates

<u>Workforce Outcomes (1, 3, and 5 years after graduation)</u>

  5. Job placement
  6. Earnings after enrollment (not merely after completion of credential)

<u>Promoting Access</u>

  7. Unduplicated headcount
  8. Enrollment of low-income students (e.g. percent receiving Pell grants)
  9. Completion of developmental coursework

<u>Serving the Community</u>

  10. Satisfaction rates (as measured by survey of employers and students)

Figure 9.1 Acceptable Accountability Measures (as reported in a survey of forty-one community-college presidents).

developed in the Achieving the Dream initiative. Some are "milestone" measures; those that occur prior to final outcomes. There is controversy in the community-college community over whether employing such measures in an accountability framework will be productive (e.g., by rewarding colleges for their incremental achievements) or instead serve to narrow the ways in which colleges attempt to achieve the same outcomes. Since innovation is usually worth encouraging, it might be unwise to dictate the ways in which colleges should increase graduation rates (e.g., by increasing rates of full-time enrollment versus increasing the financial-aid budget).

While presidents might be strategic to include milestone or other nontraditional measures in their lists as a way to garner credit for every aspect of their work, only a handful did so. For example, despite widespread recognition that colleges do not receive "credit" for noncredit courses—by definition, it is near impossible to measure outcomes of those unless credit is granted—using rates of noncredit course completion as an accountability measure was mentioned by only two survey respondents.

It is also notable that presidents in my survey did not mention two of the key modifications to the current federal method of assessing community-college performance proposed by the Achieving the Dream initiative. These include tracking outcomes over six rather than three years, and measuring success among part-time students.[44] However, this may reflect concerns that the latter change would likely reduce performance rates. And as noted earlier, the presidents do want a measure of transfer included (consistent with Achieving the Dream). Overall, most agreed with the sentiments of one president who said, just "tie accountability to what we most want for our students and bring it on!"

Collecting Data

The second obstacle, developing the data systems needed for measuring outcomes, is widely recognized and efforts are already underway to make improvements. The federal government has made a substantial investment via the State Longitudinal Data Systems Grant program administered by the U.S. Department of Education's Institute for Education Sciences. This grant program awarded over $52 million in FY06 to fourteen state educational agencies (SEAs); in FY07, thirteen SEAs were awarded over $62 million; and in FY09, twenty-seven SEAs were awarded over $150 million. Additionally, for a FY09 American Recovery and Reinvestment Act (ARRA) competition, $245 million is available as a one-time opportunity, and it is expected that $10 million will be the average grant.[45]

In addition to federal efforts to spur the establishment of state longitudinal data systems, philanthropies such as the Lumina Foundation and the Bill and Melinda Gates Foundation have invested significant resources in creating "cultures of evidence" on community-college campuses by teaching administrators how to use data. In the last five years, state longitudinal data systems have improved substantially in terms of having a unique statewide student identifier in place, collecting enrollment, demographic and program participation information and test score data, and recording graduation and dropout data. At this time, six states have all ten elements the Data Quality Campaign considers essential, and forty-eight states have at least five elements in place. Areas that the Data Quality Campaign has identified as in need of further improvement include data on course taking, grades, and college-readiness test scores.[46] These are steps in the right direction, and they are necessary. The main goal should be to link academic transcripts and wage records, enabling an analysis of what kinds of wage premiums are generated by what number and type of courses.

Uses of Information

Again drawing on lessons from the Achieving the Dream initiative, colleges should be encouraged to develop organizational cultures of assessment, committing to data-based decision making, and openly sharing data results. By helping community-college administrators analyze their own data on student achievement and identify disparities in student success, theory indicates that they will in turn work to develop new effective strategies to improve their institutions. To date, surveys indicate that colleges participating in the initiative are more likely to use and discuss data on student outcomes, though there remains widespread variation among Achieving the Dream colleges in these practices. Moreover, while establishing a culture of evidence may be a necessary condition to improving student success, it is unlikely to be sufficient because adoption of new practices by administrators do not always follow.[47]

The Community College Research Center recently issued several recommendations for how to encourage wider use of performance data, including providing additional assistance to facilitate regular analysis of that data, and providing professional development and training to help both college and state officials figure out ways to integrate data into their decision making.[48]

For an example of how community colleges respond to accountability regimes that do not provide adequate support in terms of data systems and reporting, we only need to look back to the implementation of the 1998 Workforce Investment Act (WIA). In my coauthored book, *Putting Poor People to Work: How Work-First Policies Eroded College Access for the Poor*, my colleagues and I documented the effects of WIA's inadequate accountability system on the participation rates of community-college in-job training, a function they have long served. WIA set unrealistic standards for reporting; for example, by requiring colleges to report on the outcomes for all students in a class, if even one student was receiving WIA funding, and not providing resources for colleges to revamp their data systems to collect those outcomes. As reported both in our research and by the Government Accountability Office, this led some colleges to conclude it was more efficient to opt out of the system entirely. This sharply reduced the number of training providers in the public two-year sector, and while it is difficult to know for certain, likely reduced access to training for certain disadvantaged populations as well.[49] It is therefore imperative that any new accountability system include realistic supports for compliance costs and a period of training for colleges to learn precisely how it is supposed to operate and to begin to improve performance.

Another concern has to do with whether and how accountability is tied to funding. The nation's history of funding-based higher-education policy has moved from a focus on adequacy funding, in which state governments gave institutions what they needed to continue programs, to progressively aggressive state interventions into the performance of higher-education institutions, shifting from emphasis on quality and value to assessment and accountability.[50] In some cases accountability has been tied to base funding, while in others it is linked to small amounts of incentive funding. In neither case has it been particularly effective, possibly because the amount of incentive funding provided was too small, or because institutions do not respond to accountability not tied to their base funding. In fact, an assessment of the reasons why ten of the twenty-six states that have used performance funding for higher education since the 1970s have subsequently done away with it reveals that one main challenge is stalled or insufficient funding.[51] Keeping funding stable so that colleges can plan on it is essential to maintaining political support and therefore effectiveness.

Washington State is leading an effort to introduce accountability to community colleges through the use of incentive funding rather than straight performance funding, and I think this is a promising approach.[52] Resources should not decline (at least not immediately) under a new regime, and therefore measures should not be tied to base funding, at least not immediately. We need to take into account the existing levels of funding (underfunding) at the baseline of accountability implementation, otherwise we simply set up colleges to fail. Moreover, while accountability has the potential to create communities among colleges that are working toward similar goals and encourage sharing of successes and failures to the benefit of all, if they perceive a strong likelihood that accountability will rapidly result in decreases in resources, they will likely act against it.

It would be best if accountability were tied to collaboration among key partners, requiring K-12 and higher education to work together to improve college completion rates, and for partnerships among community colleges to benefit the entire sector within a state. One community-college president raised this issue in my survey, saying that "more emphasis on accountability could create unfair competition between community colleges, and unhealthy finger-pointing at K-12 partners that will not improve opportunity and success for our students." This would be an unfortunate outcome and one likely to emerge if states do not reward productive partnerships. We could encourage collaboration as part of the performance plan; the activities of the community colleges (at least within regions) are intertwined. Resources could be leveraged. In Kentucky and Virginia, accountability goals are set for the entire community-college system; this could effectively help colleges work together rather than in competition, though it does rely on a centralized community-college governance structure, which many states lack.[53]

Moving Forward

The purposes of new accountability frameworks must be made clear from the start, and they should rest on establishing goals for performance, high standards for data and the measurement of results, and meaningful evaluation of programs and practices. Virginia is an example of a state that has adopted, in coordination with institutional leadership, a set of student-success metrics that will serve as the basis for the system's strategic plan. There is inherent accountability in the state's approach, but the colleges were involved in developing the measures.

In the end the hope is that, given a fair opportunity to succeed, community colleges will easily demonstrate their accountability and show that they are deserving of a much greater share of federal and state funding than they currently receive. This would indeed be transformative.

Notes

The author would like to thank the many community-college presidents, trustees, and other leaders who responded to her request for input on the viability and design of an accountability system. As I promised them, specific comments and suggestions are not attributed here, for they are not meant to illustrate the needs or views of specific colleges or individuals but rather broader perspectives. I also thank Kevin Carey and Mark Schneider for their input and guidance as I wrote this chapter.

1. Jennifer O'Day, "Complexity, Accountability, and School Improvement," *Harvard Educational Review* 72, no. 3 (2002).
2. W. B. Devall, "Community Colleges: A Dissenting View," *Educational Record* 49 no. 2 (1968).
3. Sara Goldrick-Rab et al., *Transforming Community Colleges* (Washington, DC: Brookings Institution, 2009).
4. Steven Brint and Jerome Karabel, *The Diverted Dream: Community Colleges and Educational Opportunity in America, 1900–1985* (New York: Oxford University Press, 1989); Burton Clark, "The 'Cooling-out' Function in Higher Education," *American Journal of Sociology* 65, no. 6 (1960).
5. Goldrick-Rab et al., *Transforming Community Colleges*.

6. Barack Obama, "Remarks by the President on the American Graduation Initiative," White House, July 14, 2009, http://www.whitehouse.gov/the_press_office/Remarks-by-the-President-on-the-American-Graduation-Initiative-in-Warren-MI/.

7. Frederick M. Hess, "Obama's \$12B plan will slow community college reform," *New York Daily News*, July 15, 2009, Opinions section, http://www.nydailynews.com/opinions/2009/07/15/2009–07–15_obamas_12b_plan_will_slow_community_college_reform.html.

8. Given this "snowball" approach I cannot calculate a response rate (since I do not know precisely how many leaders were invited by friends to participate), and given that demographic information was not collected, I cannot assess the profile of these leaders compared to their counterparts. This survey was intended as a pilot one, a precursor to a larger, more rigorous survey of presidents' perspectives on accountability.

9. Kevin Dougherty, Rachel Hare, and Rebecca Natow, *Performance Accountability Systems for Community Colleges: Lessons for the Voluntary Framework of Accountability for Community Colleges* (New York: Community College Research Center, 2009); John Immerwahr, Jean Johnson, and Paul Gasbarra, *The Iron Triangle: College Presidents Talk about Costs, Access, and Quality* (San Jose: National Center for Public Policy and Higher Education, 2008). Because the publicly available version of the report did not distinguish respondents based on their type of institution, I obtained that data directly from the authors.

10. My projects have included a six-state study of the effects of welfare reform and the Workforce Investment Act, a multicampus study of contextualized learning practices in community colleges, and interviews involved in the writing and dissemination of a Brooking Institution blueprint on "transforming community colleges."

11. Thomas Bailey, Davis Jenkins, and D. Timothy Leinbach, "Is Student Success Labeled Institutional Failure? Student Goals and Graduation Rates in the Accountability Debate at Community Colleges" (New York: Community College Research Center, 2006).

12. Author's calculations using NCES QuickStats.

13. For example, 28 percent of BA recipients earn their degrees more than six years after first beginning college (though this statistic isn't limited to community colleges). See Paul Attewell and David Lavin, "Distorted Statistics on Graduation Rates," *Chronicle of Higher Education*, July 6, 2007.

14. This is true after setting aside research support and student financial aid, both of which primarily accrue to four-year institutions and their students. See Goldrick-Rab et al., *Transforming Community Colleges*.

15. John Bound, Michael Lovenheim, and Sarah Turner, "Why Have College Completion Rates Declined? An Analysis of Changing Student Preparation and Collegiate Resources" (Working Paper 15566, National Bureau of Economic Research, Cambridge, MA, December 2009).

16. Elaine H. El-Khawas and Linda Knopp, *Campus trends* (panel report, Higher Education Panel, American Council on Education, Washington, DC, 1996).

17. Goldrick-Rab et al., *Transforming Community Colleges.*

18. For recent reflections on these issues by a number of community-college experts, see the commentary associated with this article: Jennifer Epstein, "Taking Aim at the Supply Side," *Inside Higher Ed*, December 8, 2009, http://www.insidehighered.com/news/2009/12/08/attainment.

19. Dougherty, Hare, and Natow, *Performance Accountability Systems.*

20. For examples of this line of research, see Mariana Alfonso, "The impact of community college attendance on baccalaureate attainment," *Research in Higher Education* 47, no. 8 (2006); W. R. Doyle, "The Effect of Community College Enrollment on Bachelor's Degree Completion," *Economics of Education Review* 28, no. 2 (April 2009): 199–206; D. E. Leigh, and A. M. Gill, "Do Community Colleges Really Divert Students from Earning Bachelor's Degrees?" *Economics of Education Review* 22, no. 1 (February 2003): 23–30; Bridget Terry Long and Michael Kurlaender, "Do Community Colleges Provide a Viable Path to the Baccalaureate Degree?" *Educational Evaluation and Policy Analysis* 31, no. 1 (2009): 30–53; Cecilia Rouse, "Democratization or diversion? The effect of community colleges on educational attainment," *Journal of Business and Economic Statistics* 13, no. 2 (April 1995): 217–224; Cecilia Rouse, "Do Two-Year Colleges Increase Overall Educational Attainment? Evidence from the States," *Journal of Policy Analysis and Management* 17, no. 4 (Fall 1998): 595–620; Jennifer L. Stephan, James E. Rosenbaum, and Ann E. Person, "Stratification in College Entry and Completion," *Social Science Research* 38, no. 3 (September 2009): 572–593.

21. Stephan, Rosenbaum, and Person, "Stratification in College Entry and Completion."

22. Juan Carlos Calcagno et al., *Stepping Stones to a Degree: The Impact of Enrollment Pathways and Milestones on Community College Students* (New York: Community College Research Center, 2006); Colleen Moore, Nancy Shulock, and Jeremy Offenstein, *Steps to Success: Analyzing Milestone Achievement to Improve Community-College Student Outcomes* (Sacramento: Institute for Higher Education Leadership and Policy, 2009).

23. Timothy Bailey and Jim Jacobs, "Can Community Colleges Rise to the Occasion?" *American Prospect*. October 26, 2009.

24. Jobs for the Future, *Test Drive: Six States Pilot Better Ways to Measure and Compare Community College Performance* (report prepared for Achieving the Dream: Community Colleges Count initiative, Boston: Jobs for the Future, July 2008).

25. Ibid.

26. The author thanks Robert Kelchen of the University of Wisconsin-Madison for computing these figures using the IPEDS Data Center.

27. Margaret E. Goertz, "Standards-based Accountability: Horse Trade or Horse Whip?" in *From the Capitol to the Classroom: Standards-based Reform in the States*, ed. Susan Fuhrman (Chicago: National Society for the Study of Education, 2001).

28. Indeed, two of America's top thirty community colleges, as identified by Carey (2007), have graduation rates of 10 percent. Carey's rankings are based primarily on CCSSE data rather than graduation rates.
29. Immerwahr, Johnson, and Gasbarra, *The Iron Triangle*.
30. Chad Aldeman and Kevin Carey, *Ready to Assemble: Grading State Higher Education Accountability Systems* (Washington, DC: Education Sector, 2009).
31. Darrell M. West, Grover J. Whitehurst, and E. J. Dionne, *Invisible: 1.4 Percent Coverage for Education is Not Enough* (Washington, DC: Brookings Institution, 2009).
32. Immerwahr, Johnson, and Gasbarra, *The Iron Triangle*, 30.
33. Goldrick-Rab et al., *Transforming Community Colleges*.
34. Douglas N. Harris and Sara Goldrick-Rab, "The (Un)Productivity of American Colleges: From 'Cost Disease' to Cost-Effectiveness" (paper presented at the American Education Finance Association meetings, Richmond, Virginia, March 19, 2010).
35. These indicators come from Richard Alfred, Christopher Shults, and Jeffrey Seybert, *Core Indicators of Effectiveness for Community Colleges*, 3rd ed. (New York: Community College Press, 2007).
36. Davis Jenkins, Todd Ellwein, and Katherine Boswell, "Formative Evaluation of the Student Achievement Initiative 'Learning Year'" (New York: Community College Research Center, 2009).
37. See Kevin Carey, "America's Best Community Colleges," *Washington Monthly*, June 2007; Kevin Carey, "Rankings Help Community Colleges and Their Students," *Inside Higher Ed*, August 27, 2007.
38. "Community Colleges to Create New Accountability System to Improve Graduation Rates," news release, October 6, 2009, http://www.luminafoundation.org/newsroom/news_releases/2009-10-06.html.
39. Wendy Erisman and Lan Gao, *Making Accountability Work: Community Colleges and Statewide Higher Education Accountability Systems* (Washington, DC: Institute for Higher Education Policy, 2006).
40. Dougherty, Hare, and Natow, *Performance Accountability Systems*.
41. Thomas Bailey, Juan Carlos Calcagno, Davis Jenkins, Timothy Leinbach, and Gregory Kienzl, "Is Student Right-to-Know All You Should Know? An Analysis of Community College Dropout Rates" *Research in Higher Education* 47, no. 5 (August 2006).
42. Of course, some argue that a *virtue* of a good accountability system is creating a fear of negative press (or other publicity) which spurs institutional leaders to improve their performance and avoid such negative attention. This is the assumption of ratings systems, for example. See Carey, "America's Best Community Colleges" and Carey, "Rankings Help Community Colleges and Their Students." This theory of change, however, is likely less effective in motivating the work of a sector that is on the bottom of the totem pole, demoralized, and underfunded. It is also less likely to work in a sector that lacks much competition for enrollment; students simply do not choose among community colleges the way they do among four-year institutions.

43. Immerwahr, Johnson, and Gasbarra, *The Iron Triangle*, 22.
44. "Test Drive: Six States Pilot Better Ways to Measure and Compare Community College Performance."
45. U.S. Department of Education, "Statewide Longitudinal Data System Grant Program: Request for Applications-84.384 (FY09 ARRA)," http://www.dataqualitycampaign.org/files/FY09_ARRA_WebEx_for_Labor.pdf.
46. Data Quality Campaign, "10 Essential Elements of a State Longitudinal Data System," http://www.dataqualitycampaign.org/survey/elements.
47. Davis Jenkins, "Institutional Effectiveness and Student Success: A Study of High- and Low-Impact Community Colleges," *Journal of Community College Research and Practice* 31, no. 12 (December 2007): 945–962; Davis Jenkins and Monica Reid Kerrigan, "Faculty and Administrator Data Use at Achieving the Dream Colleges: A Summary of Survey Findings" (New York: Community College Research Center, 2009); Elizabeth Zachry and Genevieve Orr, "Building Student Success from the Ground Up: A Case Study of an *Achieving the Dream* College" (New York: MDRC, 2009).
48. Dougherty, Hare, and Natow, *Performance Accountability Systems*.
49. For more, see Government Accountability Office, "Workforce Investment Act: States and Local Areas Have Developed Strategies to Assess Performance, but Labor Could Do More to Help" (Washington, DC: GAO, June 1, 2004); "Workforce Investment Act: Additional Actions Would Further Improve the Workforce System" (Washington, DC: GAO, June 28, 2007); "Workforce Development: Community Colleges and One-Stop Centers Collaborate to Meet 21st Century Workforce Needs" (Washington, DC: GAO, May 2008).
50. Kevin J. Dougherty and Esther Hong, "State Systems of Performance Accountability for Community Colleges: Impacts and Lessons for Policymakers" (Boston: Jobs for the Future, 2005).
51. Kevin J. Dougherty and Rebecca Natow, "The Demise of Higher Education Performance Funding Systems in Three States" (working paper, Community College Research Center, May 2009).
52. Jenkins, Ellwein, and Boswell, "Formative Evaluation."
53. Erisman and Gao, *Making Accountability Work*.

10

Scaling Back Tenure: How Claims of Academic Freedom Limit Accountability in Higher Education

Naomi Schaefer Riley

If you ask a professor why he needs tenure, the first words out of his mouth will undoubtedly be some variation of this phrase: "to guarantee academic freedom." Believe me. I've tried this dozens, if not hundreds, of times. I have asked professors on both ends of the political spectrum and those whose work falls squarely in the middle.

They have all given me the same response—at least to start. If professors don't have a guaranteed job for life (or what usually amounts to it), the argument goes, they will not be able to speak or write freely. Those with unpopular views, or views that upset the administration or the trustees or other members of the faculty, will be run off campus.

But many Americans might wonder just why academic freedom is a principle worthy of defending anyway. Don't some radical faculty members deserve to be run off campus? Why aren't college faculty subject to the same kind of scrutiny by customers (that is, parents) and the general public that other sorts of professionals are?

The institution of tenure has experienced a severe decline in recent years. Today, fewer than half of American college faculty members hold tenure or tenure-track jobs. Some might reasonably ask why now would be the time to have a debate about the worth of this academic perk. Tenure's fate, though, is hardly sealed. Currently, powerful unions such as the American

Federation of Teachers are pushing to mandate that a certain percentage of public university faculty (they mention the figure 75 percent often) be tenured or put on the tenure track. And if these mandates are written into bargaining contracts, tenure could be ubiquitous for the long haul.

In addition, lately, more attention has been paid to the plight of non-tenured "contingent" faculty, many of whom make minimum wage, work at multiple institutions, and have no job security at all and little chance of advancement in the profession. The solution, these contingent faculty and their advocates argue, is more tenured positions. Some studies by scholars like Cornell's Ronald Ehrenberg and the University of Iowa's Paul Umbach have shown better learning outcomes for students and higher graduation rates for students taught by tenured professors when compared with those taught by contingent faculty. And there are reasons to believe these findings are correct. Contingent faculty generally have less time to spend with students outside class, for instance. But tenure and adjunct status are not the only two options out there for the academic labor system. The American professional landscape is filled with employees who have neither the complete security of tenure nor the poor working conditions of adjuncts.

Finally, the budget crunches at both public and private universities created by the current recession invite all of us to examine more closely how colleges use their resources—that is, their tax and tuition dollars. Is tenure so fundamental to the identity of academic institutions and the functioning of college professors that it is worth the expense? Does tenure really protect academic freedom? And, if we may be so bold: How important is academic freedom to the duties that most academics today perform?

The idea that tenure protects academic freedom is "an article of faith," says David Kirp, professor of public policy at the University of California, Berkeley. "It needs to be justified."[1] Let me add to Mr. Kirp's challenge. It is not simply that tenure needs to be justified. We must first answer the question of just who is entitled to academic freedom in the first place.

For example, the extension of academic freedom to people teaching even the most basic courses, such as freshman composition, produces a lack of consistency and quality control. But there are also professors teaching in the physical sciences, in a variety of vocational areas, and in area, ethnic, and gender studies for whom academic freedom is not at all necessary. Granting it to them anyway only invites trouble.

The Early Days

Tenure was really a de facto arrangement until the early twentieth century. It had little to do with academic freedom and was intended mostly to protect the economic security of a group of people who devoted long years to training for a job that did not provide much remuneration. For that matter, tenure was not a particularly unusual arrangement. In 1950 most people worked for the same company for their entire lifetime. It did not seem unreasonable for professors to have a similar deal.

Professors did not really need tenure to protect their academic freedom because academic freedom wasn't much of an issue. There is no doubt that some intellectuals found themselves on the wrong side of public sentiment, but they were the exceptions.

In the early days of America, most colleges were religious. Sometimes they were devoted specifically to training clergy. Many simply took a religious vision as the foundation for studies of the secular world. The goals of such schools were well illustrated in a 1643 brochure explaining Harvard's purpose: "To advance Learning and perpetuate it to Posterity; dreading to leave an illiterate Ministry to the Churches."[2]

If this is the stated mission of a school, then the question of who deserves to teach there is not a particularly open-ended one. When lines were crossed—that is, when faculty engaged in one sort of heresy or another—they were dismissed. The rules were made abundantly clear from the beginning.

Who Is Paying the Piper?

In the nineteenth century, the conflicts between scholars and university benefactors began to grow. A few factors drove this trend. First, religious institutions began to receive a smaller percentage of their funding from denominational churches, and university scholars and administrators sought to compete with secular schools by shedding their parochial identities. Second, more and more universities saw money coming in from business interests that were hoping to see scientific advances that would bear fruit for the American economy. And third, President Lincoln signed the Morrill Act in 1862, which provided the basis for "land-grant universities," making the state and federal governments major benefactors of higher education in a way they hadn't been before.

Despite the money they poured into the system, neither America's clergy, its businessmen, nor its politicians were altogether happy with the results. The faculty had their own ideas about what they wanted to study and how, and they didn't much care for the outside interference. As Bruce Smith, Jeremy Mayer, and A. Lee Fritschler note in their recent book, *Closed Minds: Politics and Ideology in American Universities*, the universities "wanted patronage, but found it difficult to live with the patrons."[3]

The first significant conflict along these lines occurred in 1894. Richard Ely, who was the director of the University of Wisconsin's School of Economics, Politics and History, found himself accused by the state superintendent of education of inciting agitation through organized labor and encouraging people who were not unionized to get cracking. Ely, who was studying what we might now call the "root causes" of violent labor unrest, was tried in a three-day hearing that was later dramatized on Profiles in Courage, the 1960s television series. Ely was absolved of the charges, and the university regents concluded: "In all lines of academic investigation it is of utmost importance that the investigator should be absolutely free to follow the indications of truth wherever they may lead."[4]

It was John M. Olin who insisted that the regents' conclusion be used "to do the University a great service."[5] A plaque at the school now reads: "Whatever may be the limitations which trammel inquiry elsewhere, we believe that the great state University of Wisconsin should ever encourage that continual and fearless sifting and winnowing by which alone the truth can be found."[6]

Ely's case is still celebrated today, not only for those inspirational lines, but also for its rarity. Despite the simmering tensions between patrons and professors, few faculty members in the nineteenth or early twentieth century ever suffered dismissal as a result of controversial scholarship. And few politicians or members of the public demanded it.

Edward Ross, a Stanford University economist, was not as lucky as Ely. Ross, who favored a ban on Asian immigration, pushed for municipally owned utilities, and supported socialist Eugene Debs for president, found himself on the wrong side of the school's benefactor, Mrs. Leland Stanford. Her husband had made his money in railroads and gave the seed money to start the university. In 1900 she penned a letter to the university's president, David Starr Jordan: "When I take up a newspaper...and read the utterances of Professor Ross," she wrote, "and realize that a professor of the Leland Stanford Junior University thus steps aside, and out of his sphere, to associate with the political demagogues of this city...it brings tears to my eyes. I must confess I am weary of Professor Ross, and I think he ought not to be retained by Stanford University."

Unlike some of its cousins back east, Stanford was not originally a religious institution. It was founded on the German model of a "research university." The new model, which came to the American shores in the nineteenth century, had two distinct features. One was that its faculty were tasked with pursuing knowledge free from any "proprietary" strictures. According to this theory, no benefactor of the institution, whether he was a religious leader or a businessman or a politician, could determine the direction of the faculty's scholarship. In other words, the founders of this system seemed to build a lack of accountability into it.

The second feature of the research university was that professors were no longer simply educating students in classical texts with a view to making them good people or good citizens. Rather, faculty at these new institutions were conceived of as experts. They were supposed to add to the general pool of knowledge available to mankind and use that knowledge to improve society.

The research university made some sense for professors studying the physical sciences. The nineteenth century began with the invention of the steam locomotive and the stethoscope and ended with the development of the internal combustion engine and germ theory. Scientific knowledge was becoming more specialized and more difficult for the average person to understand. Under the old model of the proprietary institution, of course, the school administrators could still decide what sorts of research and teaching fell afoul of the institutional mission. But under the new model, only faculty colleagues familiar with a particular discipline could determine the bounds for research.

The implications of the new research university for professors in the social sciences and humanities were harder to comprehend. After all, what did it mean that professors of sociology or history or English were supposed to add to the store of society's knowledge? Is our twenty-first century understanding of Shakespeare inherently superior to the seventeenth-century one? Should we count on modern professors of political science to improve American government? Do they understand our politics better than, say, the authors of the Federalist Papers?

The answer of the era's progressives was an unqualified "yes." Herbert Croly, for example, wrote of the need in government for a "permanent body of experts in social administration" whose task would be to "promote individual and social welfare."[7] For our own good, the progressives argued, we needed to protect the rights of these professors to engage in any kind of scholarship that they and their fellow experts deemed necessary. It was their expertise that meant these men could not be held accountable by the public who knew nothing of these complex matters.

In firing Edward Ross, Stanford had plainly violated the new rules of the higher-education game. A year later, seven Stanford professors resigned in protest of the university's actions. Among them was Arthur O. Lovejoy, a philosophy professor.

Fifteen years later, Lovejoy, along with famed progressive educator John Dewey, formed the American Association of University Professors. The "Declaration of Principles" they issued remains a sort of biblical document among academics today. Here, for Dewey and his colleagues, was the crux of the matter: "To the degree that professional scholars, in the formation and promulgation of their opinions, are, or by the character of their tenure appear to be, subject to any motive other than their own scientific conscience and a desire for the respect of their fellow-experts, to that degree the university teaching profession is corrupted; its proper influence upon public opinion is diminished and vitiated; and society at large fails to get from its scholars, in an unadulterated form, the peculiar and necessary service which it is the office of the professional scholar to furnish."[8]

As far as Dewey and his colleagues were concerned, if faculty find their teaching or writing or "outside" statements are being influenced by, say, their desire to hold on to their jobs, then they don't have much academic freedom. The AAUP issued a restatement of this idea in 1940.[9]

What Does Academic Freedom Mean Today?

In the second half of the twentieth century, the AAUP has come to represent most of the country's faculty in one way or another, and the organization's pronouncements on academic freedom and tenure have come to be the law of the academic land. But there is still a lot of confusion about what academic freedom means. "The commentary on these AAUP statements is like the Talmud," jokes Martin Finkelstein, a professor of higher education at Seton Hall University. "So many people have attempted to do an exegesis on this or that aspect of the statement. But, for all of our discussion in the academy, I think we do a terrible job of articulating what we mean by academic freedom."[10] Even Robert O'Neill, director of the Thomas Jefferson Center for the Protection of Free Expression at the University of Virginia and a member of the AAUP's Committee on Academic Freedom and Tenure, agrees that the organization has not done a very good job of explaining what all this means.

"Is it academic freedom," Mr. Finkelstein asks, "to teach anything you want when giving a course in freshman English?" What if the department has a syllabus that all the instructors are required to follow? "Is this an issue of academic freedom?" he wonders.[11] This is a particularly important question for widely offered courses like freshman composition.

Indeed, Mr. Finkelstein's questions bring to mind the controversy a few years ago over a University of California, Berkeley course offering called "The Politics and Poetics of Palestinian Resistance." Listed as a "composition" class in the English department, the instructor explained, "This class takes as its starting point the right of Palestinians to fight for their own self-determination" and "Conservative thinkers are encouraged to seek other sections."[12] As Erin O'Connor explained in her blog, Critical Mass,

> Politics seems to interest Cal's fall writing instructors more than writing does. Roughly twice as many courses promise to address politics—which they define, predictably and uniformly, in terms of race, class, gender, nation, ethnicity, ideology—than promise to address the craft and technique of writing. Many instructors seem to have forgotten entirely that they are teaching writing courses, and make no mention of writing at all in their descriptions of what students who take their class will do.[13]

Is it academic freedom to stray so far from the job you were hired to do? Even the legal definition of academic freedom is in flux. As it pertains to private universities, the courts have traditionally considered that professors and administrators have a contract. And like any other employer, the university is required to live up to the terms of it. But if the contract says the institution is an evangelical Christian one and faculty should not say things that violate a particular church's teachings, then those who do, whether or not they have tenure, can be fired. There are, of course, professors who decide to run afoul of the rules anyway, and the AAUP has censured innumerable religious institutions, such as Brigham Young University, for restricting the activities of its faculty members. Overall, though, these institutions seem to have plenty of autonomy from a legal perspective.

At public institutions, however, the matter is significantly more complex. Oddly enough, the current precedent for determining what professors can say seems to be a 2006 Supreme Court case (*Garcetti et al. v. Ceballos*) about a Los Angeles deputy district attorney, Richard Ceballos, who recommended dismissing another member of his office for misrepresenting information in an affidavit. He claimed his supervisors retaliated by firing him, thereby violating his First Amendment rights. The court held, though, "that when public employees make statements pursuant to their official duties, the employees are not speaking as citizens for First Amendment purposes, and the Constitution does not insulate their communications from employer discipline."[14]

So what happens at a public university? Is speech protected in a classroom? Is it protected when a faculty member is criticizing the school's provost or his department chair? What if he is railing against American foreign policy? Surely the jobs of a professor and that of other public employees are somewhat different.

Professors are not simply hired for the purpose of being government mouthpieces or to carry out the government's bidding the way, say, a bureaucrat in a municipal department of public health might be asked to do. In other words, professors are not supposed to be instruments of the state. (There are some libertarians who would reasonably argue that this is the problem with public universities in the first place.) And if they are not instruments of the state, to whom are the professors accountable? Can taxpayers reasonably complain when public university faculty go off the rails?

The court briefly acknowledged the dilemma in applying the public employee standard to university professors when it wrote: "We need not, and for that reason do not, decide whether the analysis we conduct today would apply in the same manner to a case involving speech related to scholarship or teaching."

But as it stands, the court has not clarified what the decision means for professors. Rachel Levinson, the general counsel for the American Association of University Professors notes one significant problem with the way the court has drawn the lines. "The paradox of *Garcetti* is that the more you know about something, the less you are protected for speaking about it." Ms. Levinson believes that this is "problematic for the faculty and the public interest as well." If a constitutional law professor wants to write a controversial op-ed about constitutional law, he won't be protected from retaliation by his employer, but if he wants to write one about the scientific proof for the existence of UFOs, the university has no claim against him. Ms. Levinson argues that this decision actually means that professors' speech is protected less than that of the average American. "Do you give up the basic rights of being a citizen when you become government employee?"[15]

While the Supreme Court has left things vague, some lower courts have taken up the issue of academic freedom. In 2003 five professors at the Metro College of Denver sued, claiming that changes in the school handbook significantly altered the terms of their employment by making it easier to fire tenured professors. The state district court ruled for the trustees. The decision was appealed, with the American Association of University Professors filing an amicus brief, and in 2007 a state appeals court ordered a new trial.

The AAUP argued in its brief that "depriving the tenured faculty of a preference in retention places the tenured faculty at greater risk of being singled out" because of an administrator's or trustee's dislike for his teaching or research, or for positions taken on issues off campus.[16]

The results of that new trial came down in June 2009. Rather than simply deciding that the change in the handbook altered what was a "vested right" of the professors, Judge Norman D. Haglund ruled that, "the public interest is advanced more by tenure systems that favor academic freedom over tenure systems that favor flexibility in hiring or firing." He also noted that "by its very nature, tenure promotes a system in which academic freedom is protected."[17] In this ruling, Judge Haglund purports to know the best governance policies for universities; he is also cementing in law the relationship between academic freedom and tenure.

Finding a New Way to Think about Academic Freedom

So in the course of the past hundred years or so we've gone from tenure as a de facto system that gives poor academics a little economic security to a system where tenure is actually deemed by our courts to be in the public interest because it protects academic freedom. And despite all this, we are still without a very good definition of academic freedom.

Perhaps the best way to proceed is by using a little common sense. Most Americans would probably agree that there are some courses in some subjects at some universities that require professors to go out on a limb. Those faculty members will have to question accepted truths. They might say things that their colleagues don't agree with. They might write things in newspapers or academic journals that challenge the theories of their disciplines. We should not fire those people for saying such things.

Perhaps, but higher education today looks a lot different than it did in John Dewey's time. Do all of the new additions to our university menu mean we need to extend the protections of academic freedom to a whole bunch of new chefs?

Tenure, as Stanley Fish explains in his book, *Save the World on Your Own Time*, was not meant to protect off-the-cuff political statements outside the classroom, but merely the freedom to teach and conduct research in one's own discipline without administrative interference. When all is said and done, writes Mr. Fish in *The Chronicle of Higher Education*, "academic freedom is just a fancy name for being allowed to do your job, and it is only because that job has the peculiar feature of not having a prestipulated goal that those who do it must be granted a degree of latitude and flexibility not granted to the practitioners of other professions... That's why there's no such thing as 'corporate-manager freedom' or 'shoe-salesman freedom' or 'dermatologist freedom.'"[18]

But here is the truth of the matter: more college teachers resemble dermatologists and corporate managers and shoe salesmen than ever before. I do not say this to insult them, but merely to acknowledge this fact. The landscape of higher education has changed and most courses have exactly what Mr. Fish calls a "prestipulated goal."

The Rise of Vocational Education

The total number of four-year degrees awarded during the 1970–71 school year was 839,730.[19] In 2005–06, that number jumped to 1,485,242,[20] an increase of 77 percent. (The U.S. population grew by about half during the same time.) We are a wealthier country now. More of the American population can afford college. And more of us need it too. As factory jobs became a less reliable source of lifetime income, high-school graduates looked to college to train themselves both for our information economy and our service economy. It is also true that K-12 education in America has experienced a decline. Some of the knowledge that young people used to receive in high school is now only gained through a college degree. And finally, apprenticeships are less common. That is, job skills that people used to learn under the watchful eye of a single skilled craftsman are now only offered in a formal setting.

The bottom line is that people who never used to go to college now find that they have to in order to train for good jobs. And so, not surprisingly, a significant portion of those additional degrees colleges have added in the past few decades came in vocational areas. Degrees in agriculture and natural resources doubled. Degrees in communications and related fields increased sevenfold. The number of degrees awarded in health sciences tripled. Parks, recreation, leisure, and fitness studies went from 1,621 degrees in 1971 to 25,490 in 2006.[21] As a percentage of degrees awarded, these vocational categories went from making up 10 percent of all four-year degrees to 22 percent.[22] In fact, vocational degrees made up 38 percent of the overall increase in four-year degrees in the past 25 years.[23]

There is no doubt that young people with these vocational degrees have contributed significantly to American prosperity. But these fields simply do not engage students in the search for ultimate truths. They all have "prestipulated goals" that are immediately obvious. And so one must ask, do we need to guarantee the academic freedom of professors engaged in teaching and studying transportation and materials moving, a field in which more than 5,000 degrees were awarded in 2006?[24]

Of course, there are also plenty of what one might call vocational courses within nonvocational fields. Freshman composition, a requirement at almost every four-year institution in the country, does not require faculty members to ask existential questions. Some will say that making judgments about the quality of writing is inherently subjective. But most college freshmen have yet to master even the most basic principles of thesis statements, rules of grammar and style, and research citations. If these courses are not fundamentally rigorous exercises in "how to" rather than "why," then the faculty teaching them haven't done their jobs. Yet it is increasingly common to hear disgruntled junior faculty complain that sticking to a required curriculum for these types of courses is a violation of their academic freedom. Of course, they would rather teach Derrida, but that's not the purpose of the course.

In the "Declaration of Principles," Dewey wrote that "if education is the cornerstone of the structure of society and progress in scientific knowledge is essential to civilization, few things can be more important than to enhance the dignity of the scholar's profession."[25]

There is no need to belittle or demean teachers of vocational subjects, but we would be kidding ourselves if we suggested that degrees in "family and consumer sciences" (20,775 degrees) are "essential to civilization."[26] We don't have to treat the people who teach them badly, of course, but we also don't need to "enhance the dignity" of their positions by offering them special job perks such as tenure.

Many of the courses offered at the Metro College of Denver fall into exactly this vocational category. Some of the courses taught this year by the five professors who sued include American baseball history and business statistics. The school even offers a nutrition major. These are all fields of study that have fairly definitive answers. Faculty members don't really need the freedom to ask controversial questions in discussing them.

When we tie ourselves in knots to make sure that professors of these vocational subjects are guaranteed their academic freedom, we are only asking for trouble. Do professors of "security and protective services" (35,319 degrees)[27] really need to be granted the freedom to make controversial statements in the interests of creating a better learning environment? As Peter Berkowitz of the Hoover Institution rightly notes, "The more a college education is vocational, the less you need tenure."[28] And the more we give people tenure when they don't need it, the more times we will end up defending the perfectly outrageous.

Take the case, for instance, of Arthur Butz, who has been teaching electrical engineering at Northwestern University for more than three decades now. In 1976, he published *The Hoax of the Twentieth Century: The Case Against the Presumed Extermination of European Jewry*, shortly after he received tenure. A couple of years ago, in interviews with the Iranian press, Mr. Butz was asked about Iranian president Mahmoud Ahmadinejad's views on the Holocaust: "I congratulate him on becoming the first head of state to speak out clearly on these issues and regret only that it was not a Western head of state."[29]

Northwestern has been tacitly defending Mr. Butz's Holocaust denial as within the bounds of his "academic freedom" for years now. But why?

Why does a professor of electrical engineering need protection in the first place? Was he going to go out on a limb with some untested idea about integrated circuit design and be subject to persecution at the hands of the university administration or board of trustees? No. The only occasions on which people in disciplines with "prestipulated goals" make use of their academic freedom is to stray from their field.

But, critics will ask, doesn't Mr. Butz have rights as a citizen of the United States to say whatever he wants? Sure, but he doesn't have the right to his job. If Mr. Butz were running a *Fortune* 500 company, do you think he'd be allowed to spout this nonsense? The board of directors would fire him in an instant. They couldn't revoke his citizenship, but they sure wouldn't have to pay him a salary. That's the kind of accountability that exists in the private, for-profit sector of our economy.

Selling Academic Freedom

In its 1915 statement, the AAUP founders discussed the case of "a proprietary school or college designed for the propagation of specific doctrines prescribed by those who have furnished its endowment."[30] The writers were referring to the institutions of the time, those controlled by religious denominations, or the case of "a wealthy manufacturer [who] establishes a special school in a university in order to teach, among other things, the advantages of a protective tariff." In these cases, the authors conclude "the trustees have a right to demand that everything be subordinated to that end."[31]

The AAUP authors express no opinion about the "desirability of the existence of such institutions." If someone wants to fund a university for a particular end, that's fine. "But," they write, "it is manifestly important that they should not be permitted to sail under false colors. Genuine boldness and thoroughness of inquiry, and freedom of speech, are scarcely reconcilable with the prescribed inculcation of a particular opinion upon a controverted question."[32]

The return of the proprietary institution is also evident in university life today. Research scientists are increasingly entering into multimillion-dollar contracts with corporations. Unlike Edward Ross, the professor at Stanford who was fired for his political views, these faculty members are directly selling their services to drug companies or firms engaged in biomedical research. The university itself often gets a cut of the deal, but the faculty are definitely at the bargaining table. And the corporations are often engaged in determining whether the results of the research are released and how.

If academic freedom means the ability not only to question the assumptions of a particular discipline, but also the free flow of information gained from research and writing, then many faculty members seem to be selling their cherished principles.

Take, for example, the University of California. As Jennifer Washburn documents in her book, *University, Inc.*, "From 1993 to 2003...industry-sponsored research at the University of California system grew 97 percent in real terms (from $65 million to $155 million). In 1998 the University of California, Berkeley signed a $25 million agreement with the pharmaceutical company Novartis. Under the agreement, Ms. Washburn writes, "Berkeley granted Novartis first right to negotiate licenses on roughly one-third of the [College of Natural Resources'] discoveries, including the results of research funded by Novartis, as well as projects funded by state and federal resources. It also granted the company unprecedented representation—two of five seats—on the department's research committee, which determined how the money would be spent."[33]

There were faculty objections, of course, to this arrangement. After all, it basically gave a private corporation a vested interest in, not to mention proprietary rights, to the research that was supposedly being conducted by impartial scientists. Still, 41 percent of the faculty, according to Ms. Washburn, "supported the agreement as signed."[34]

And why wouldn't they? If they agree to the corporations' terms, these professors will see the resources for their departments expanded, their prominence rise, and presumably, a nice bump in their salaries too. But how far are they willing to go in acceding to the industry's terms? Ms. Washburn's research is eye-opening.

A team at the University of California, San Francisco signed a contract with the Immune Response Corporation to test the company's newly developed AIDS drug Remune. Three years into the testing, the researchers determined that the drug was ineffective, according to Ms. Washburn. When they went to write up the results, however, they noticed a clause in their contract with IRC saying that they couldn't use in publications any of the raw data from their study.[35]

This is not uncommon. One Harvard survey found that 88 percent of life-science companies often require students and faculty to keep information confidential.[36]

Professor Donald Downs at the University of Wisconsin began to notice this tension between academic freedom and the desire of universities and professors themselves to gain corporate sponsors a few years ago. His own university was about to sign a contract with Reebok. The company would supply all of the athletic attire for the university's teams. And the university faculty would promise not to say anything negative about Reebok.

Mr. Downs recalls going to the chancellor and demanding that he excise this clause. "Once you have a gag order between a university and someone outside, you're playing with the devil," says Mr. Downs.[37]

Some observers of higher education would come away with the impression that it is only the administrators engaged in this kind of solicitation. But as Ms. Washburn notes, there are plenty of professors these days who are playing the role of corporate interest as well. They own their own companies and often use their undergraduate and graduate students as employees. *The Wall Street Journal* reported one MIT student who refused to hand in a homework assigned to one professor because he feared doing so would violate his employment agreement with a company founded by another of his professors.[38]

It is also important to note here that research scientists, unlike many academics, are not hurting for money. The AAUP's original desire to ensure that academics have a degree of economic security to "enhance the dignity" of their profession is not a concern of this group. One need only look at recent reports on the apparently widespread practice of ghostwriting articles for journals among some research scientists to realize how many professors seem to forget that their primary employers are universities, not drug companies. As an editorial in the *Public Library of Science Medicine* journal explained the problem: "While readers expect and assume that the named academic authors on a paper carried out the piece of work and then wrote up their article or review informed by their professional qualifications and expertise, instead we see . . . 'ghostwriting': a writing company was commissioned to produce a manuscript on a piece of research to fit the drug company's needs and then a person was identified to be the 'author.'"[39]

If professors and students want to enter into commercial agreements with corporations, there is no law preventing them from doing so. Schools will have to negotiate for themselves whether they understand their faculty to be acting ethically. As the AAUP founders said, there is nothing wrong with these proprietary agreements, per se. But they do reveal a great deal about the value that university faculty place on academic freedom. If the price is right, they are happy to give it up. (One could imagine that humanities professors might feel the same, if only someone were willing to pay so much for a study of Chaucer). Given this attitude among many research scientists, why should the public take their claims to academic freedom seriously? If they're voluntarily giving it up, should we really worry about taking it away?

Unlike the professors of vocational studies and "area studies," it turns out that professors in the physical sciences are subject to some standards of accountability. The market compensates the competent ones, not the incompetent ones. But these professors still don't seem to be answerable to the parents and taxpayers funding their academic salaries. Many of these faculty have simply arranged their workload and their careers in order to please their highest corporate bidders. But if their jobs as faculty members are not their priority, we don't need to offer them special protections as such.

When the Answers Are Political

Another change in the face of higher education over the past thirty years has been the expansion of "area, ethnic, cultural and gender studies." Only 2,579 degrees were awarded in these areas in 1971.[40] Today, that number has tripled to 7,879.[41] Unlike the vocational degrees, this increase was felt most at the country's most elite institutions. At universities that ranked in the top twenty-five in the *U.S. News and World Report* survey, degrees in these disciplines went from an average of thirty-five per school in 1987 to seventy-three per school in 2006.[42]

Like the vocational disciplines, the missions of these academic pursuits also have predetermined outcomes. As Mark Bauerlein of Emory University explains, in many cases, "ideological content has drifted down to the fundamental norms of the discipline."[43] Whether it is women's studies or black studies or queer studies, the entire premise of the discipline is often a political agenda. While the cases of departments with political agendas may be more difficult to sort out, they are certainly worth considering in the grand scheme of this "academic freedom creep." Just as with the vocational disciplines, there is, in these areas, a growing sense that projects that are not strictly academic are deserving of academic protections.

One need only read the mission statements of these departments to see what Mr. Bauerlein means. At Berkeley, the African American Studies department's mission "emerges out of a conviction that a sound understanding of the realities of the life and culture of persons of African descent in the United States cannot but take into account the legacies of colonialism, enslavement, the plantation, and migration."[44] And at SUNY New Paltz, the Black Studies department "seeks to define the Black experience from an African and Afro-American centered perspective rather than Euro-centric perspective."[45] Courses include "Psychology of the Black Child" which "assumes that Black children are, in general, subject to forces that cause their psychological development to differ from that of the middle-class American child studied in traditional child psychology courses."[46]

"Political correctness represented the return of proprietary universities," says Professor Downs.[47] They may not have religious or industrial goals, but they are prestipulated nonetheless. It is not merely that these departments approach African American studies from a particular perspective: an African-centered one, and one in which blacks residing in America today are still deeply hobbled by the legacy of slavery. Indeed, course and department descriptions often seem as if they are a series of axes that faculty members would like to grind. These departments must also ensure that their professors are engaged in a particular political project.

Take the mission of Ohio State's department where the faculty "contributes ideas for the formulation and implementation of progressive public policies with positive consequences for the black community."[48] The distinction between academic researcher and policymaker has been lost in these disciplines. The emphasis on "service learning," which has recently become all the rage in higher education, contributes to this trend. It means that faculty members are no longer simply engaged in teaching, learning, and research. Rather, professors are supposed to lead students into the field to accomplish particular "progressive public policies."

A similar trend can be seen in the women's studies departments (many of which have become gender studies departments in recent years to include queer studies and the study of sexuality generally). At Columbia College in South Carolina, the women's studies program "encourages students to advocate for social justice for women."[49] At Iona College in New York, the department is supposed to "promote social justice for women through the practical application of theory... [and]... develop proactive responses to the differential impact of gender-based bias in the lives of women from diverse backgrounds and experiences."[50]

And just as in the case of African American Studies, professors are not simply supposed to be engaged in policymaking. The endpoint of their academic study is also predetermined. Take, for example, the University of Rhode Island where

> the discipline of Women's Studies has a vision of a world free from sexism. By necessity, freedom from sexism must include a commitment to freedom from nationalism; class, ethnic, racial, and heterosexual bias; economic exploitation; religious persecution; ageism; and ableism. Women's Studies seeks to identify, understand, and challenge ideologies and institutions that knowingly or unknowingly oppress and exploit some for the advantage of others, or deny fundamental human rights.[51]

At Penn State, the department "analyzes the unequal distribution of power and resources by gender."[52] The department of Sexuality Studies at Duke has as its "central emphasis" the "social construction" of sexuality—that is, how sexuality is shaped by historical, social, and symbolic contexts."[53]

But what if you believe, as many Americans do, that gender is not purely a "social construct," that biology does mean something for the way that men and women act in relation to each other and their children? Or what if you think that power is not unequally distributed among men and women? For that matter, what if you don't believe that it is the job of a professor to free your students from "nationalism"? These various departments at institutions both large and small, with students both elite and average, are advertising their lack of a need for academic freedom.

There are a few schools on the other end of the political spectrum that offer courses with clear political agendas. Patrick Henry College in Purcellville, Virginia, for example, is an evangelical college mostly geared toward children from homeschool backgrounds. The school purports to be a sort of political training ground for young conservatives headed into fields such as government service. A cursory glance at the school's Web site would suggest that professors do not have much wiggle room at all when it comes to asking big questions of their students. But then Patrick Henry doesn't offer tenure at all. If a school's goal is to be a political boot camp of sorts, there is little reason to allow for much inquiry or protection for those who deviate from the party line.

Many universities want to play host to disciplines in which almost no "inquiry" is actually required." That's fine. But these departments should not be able to "sail under false colors" either. They needn't deceive themselves or the public by making a claim to the protections of academic freedom.

Conclusion

If you count faculty in vocationally oriented departments, those who teach area, ethnic, cultural and gender studies, as well as a significant chunk of the country's research scientists, you will arrive at number that is more than half of the tenured faculty in the United States.

Obviously we can't revoke the contracts of these professors now, but going forward, there is no justification for continuing to offer life-time contracts to people in these fields. Whether because they have a political agenda or their subjects do not necessitate the freedom to ask big questions or because many seem happy to voluntarily give up their right to ask big questions for the right price, these professors do not need their academic freedom protected. And they don't need tenure.

So what can be done to build accountability back into the academic profession? In the growing world of for-profit colleges and universities, tenure is virtually nonexistent. Whatever the criticisms of this sector of higher education, it is surely among the most accountable to its students.

For-profit colleges are among the least subsidized by taxpayers, and students are paying for the classroom experience, not for any of the campus-life extras offered by many other public and private institutions.

Short of doing away with tenure altogether, universities could return to the original idea of tenure, one that protected only professors' speech in the classroom, as it related to discipline, instead of the one that has recently evolved to protect outrageous political activism on campus.

A different kind of tenure agreement could be written, one that allowed for serious posttenure review. It would ensure that even if there were some ideological eccentricities, at least the basic competence of professors could be monitored and some quality control could be enforced.

There are a number of "carrots and sticks" that exist under the current system, but are rarely employed by university administrations. Administrators do generally have some amount of discretion when it comes to faculty raises, but the difference in salary between underperforming and overperforming tenured professors is often negligible. As for those cushy academic schedules, there is no reason that good teaching and strong research can't be rewarded with afternoon classes three days a week.

Tenure could be considered a fringe benefit and treated as such. Professors should be given the option at some point early in their careers: Do you want tenure or a higher salary? Do you want tenure or the more expensive health-insurance package? Tenure or a nicer office? Tenure or a better parking space? The idea would be that people who knew they were good teachers and smart researchers would take the chance on more money instead of job security. And the people who decided they preferred what one faculty observer calls the "statism" of the university could have tenure. It would also protect dissenting voices. If you know you're the type of person who is going to say controversial things, you can opt into the tenure system. But there will be a cost.

At the very least, there is no reason that tenure shouldn't be abolished at the vast majority of the 4,000 degree-granting colleges and universities in the United States where academic freedom is an almost irrelevant concept. When professors are engaged in imparting basic literacy skills, or even classes on how to cook or how to start a business, there is no reason that their academic freedom has to be protected. At that point professors are just like any other employee. They have the right to speak freely, as guaranteed by the Constitution, but they don't have the right to say whatever they want in their role at the university.

Administrators, faculty, and parents might disagree about which disciplines are vocational, which ones have "prestipulated" political goals, and which professors have already sold their academic freedom to the highest bidder. The goal of this chapter is not to make determinations about each faculty member or department. Rather, it is to suggest that the burden of proof should be on professors. They should have to show parents and tax-payers that there is some reason that academic freedom is necessary for them to do the job they have taken on.

There are, it's important to note, a number of universities out there that don't offer tenure. The military academies don't. Neither do some religious schools. Colleges such as Grove City, in Pennsylvania, which has a decidedly conservative curriculum, and Hampshire, in Massachusetts, with a liberal one, also don't have tenure. What do these schools all have in common? Very clear missions. The goal of eliminating tenure is not to fire people more often. Instead, getting rid of the academic jobs for life might make colleges think more seriously about their missions, hire professors who will carry them out, and show parents that what they are paying for is what they will get.

Notes

1. David Kirp, interview with the author, Spring 2009.
2. Harvard Divinity School, "History and Mission," http://www.hds.harvard.edu/history.html.
3. Bruce L. R. Smith, Jeremy D. Mayer, and A. Lee Fritschler, *Closed Minds?: Politics and Ideology in American Universities* (Washington, DC: Brookings Institution, 2008), 46.
4. Theodore Herfuth, "Sifting and Winnowing," University of Wisconsin Library, http://www.library.wisc.edu/etext/WIReader/WER1035-Chpt1.html.
5. Harry Miller, "Sifting and Winnowing: Academic Freedom and Ely Trial," Wisconsin Stories, http://www.wisconsinstories.org/2002season/school/closer_look.cfm.
6. Ibid.
7. Herbert Croly, Progressive Democracy (Memphis, TN: General Books LLC, 1914), 359.
8. American Association of University Professors, *1915 Declaration of Principles on Academic Freedom and Academic Tenure*, http://www.aaup.org/AAUP/pubsres/policydocs/contents/1915.htm.
9. American Association of University Professors, *1940 Statement of Principles on Academic Freedom and Tenure*, http://www.aaup.org/AAUP/pubsres/policydocs/contents/1940statement.htm.
10. Martin Finkelstein, interview with the author, Spring 2009.
11. Ibid.
12. University of California, Berkeley, English 1A course syllabus, "The Politics and Poetics of Palestinian Resistance," http://berkeley.edu/news/mideast/syllabus.html.

13. Erin O'Connor, "Snehal Shingavi's controversial course," *Critical Mass* blog, May 12, 2002, http://www.erinoconnor.org/archives/2002/05/snehal_shingavi.html.

14. *Garcetti et al. v. Ceballos*, 547 U.S. 410 (2006).

15. Rachel Levinson, interview with the author, Spring 2009.

16. Naomi Schaefer Riley, "Tenure and Academic Freedom: College campuses display a striking uniformity of thought," *Wall Street Journal*, June 23, 2009, Opinion section, http://online.wsj.com/article/SB124571593663539265.html.

17. Scott Jaschik, "Tenure's Value...to Society," *Inside Higher Ed*, June 8, 2009, http://www.insidehighered.com/news/2009/06/08/metro.

18. Stanley Fish, "Academic Freedom Is Not a Divine Right," *Chronicle of Higher Education*, September 5, 2008, http://chronicle.com/article/Academic-Freedom-Is-Not-a-D/10461.

19. National Center for Education Statistics, Table 268, "Degrees conferred by degree-granting institutions, by level of degree and sex of student: Selected years, 1869–79 through 2018–19," *Digest of Education Statistics: 2009*, http://nces.ed.gov/programs/digest/d09/tables/dt09_268.asp?referrer=list.

20. Ibid.

21. National Center for Education Statistics, Table 271, "Bachelor's degrees conferred by degree-granting institutions, by field of study: Selected years, 1970–71 through 2007–08," *Digest of Education Statistics: 2009*, http://nces.ed.gov/programs/digest/d09/tables/dt09_271.asp?referrer=list.

22. Author's calculations based on data from Table 271.

23. Ibid.

24. National Center for Education Statistics, Table 271.

25. AAUP, *1915 Declaration of Principles*.

26. National Center for Education Statistics, Table 271.

27. Ibid.

28. Peter Berkowitz, interview with the author, Spring 2009.

29. Arthur R. Butz, "Revisionists only deny one aspect of Holocaust story," *Mehr News*, January 25, 2006, http://www.mehrnews.com/en/NewsPrint.aspx?NewsID=282535.

30. AAUP, *1915 Declaration of Principles*.

31. Ibid.

32. Ibid.

33. Jennifer Washburn, *University, Inc.: The Corporate Corruption of Higher Education* (New York: Basic Books, 2006), 3.

34. Ibid., 4.

35. Ibid., 107.

36. Ibid., 86.

37. Donald Downs, interview with the author, Fall 2009.

38. Amy Dockser Marcus, "Class Struggle: MIT Students, Lured to New Tech Firms, Get Caught in a Bind," *Wall Street Journal*, June 24, 1999.

39. The *PLoS Medicine* Editors, "Ghostwriting: The Dirty Little Secret of Medical Publishing That Just Got Bigger," *PLoS Medicine* 6, no. 9 (September 8, 2009): http://www.plosmedicine.org/article/info%3Adoi %2F10.1371%2Fjournal.pmed.1000156.
40. *Digest of Education Statistics*, Table 271.
41. Ibid.
42. Author's calculations based on *Digest of Education Statistics: 2009* data.
43. Naomi Schaefer Riley, "When Academic Freedom Lost its Meaning," *Wall Street Journal*, October 24, 2008, Opinion section, http://online.wsj.com/article/SB122480129356364639.html.
44. University of California, Berkeley, Department of African American Studies, http://africam.berkeley.edu/history.htm.
45. State University of New York, New Paltz, Black Studies, www.newpaltz.edu/blackstudies.
46. Ibid.
47. Donald Downs, interview with the author, Fall 2009.
48. Ohio State University, Department of African American and African Studies, http://aaas.osu.edu/aboutus/mission.cfm.
49. Columbia College, Women's Studies Program, http://www.columbiacollegesc.edu/academics/womensstudies.asp.
50. Iona College, Women's Studies Program, www.iona.edu/academic/artsscience/departments/womenstudies/mission.cfm.
51. University of Rhode Island, Women's Studies, www.uri.edu/assessment/uri/outcomes/Undergraduate/arts_sciences/majors/women%27s_studies/outcomes.html.
52. Pennsylvania State University, Department of Women's Studies www.womenstudies.psu.edu.
53. Duke University, Women's Studies, http://web.duke.edu/womstud/about.html.

II

Policy Barriers to Postsecondary Cost Control

Burck Smith

And so tonight, I ask every American to commit to at least one year or more of higher education or career training. This can be community college or a four-year school; vocational training or an apprenticeship. But whatever the training may be, every American will need to get more than a high school diploma.

—*President Barack Obama, February 24, 2009*

The cost of a private four-year college runs about $25,143 (up 5.9 percent from last year). The cost for a public four-year, $6,585 (up 6.4 percent from last year). When adding in living costs, and books several recent studies present an overall price tag of $30,000.

—*College Board, 2009*

Introduction

What if we took President Obama's challenge seriously? Could we afford it as a nation? Is it a good value? In today's higher education system, I think the answers are "no" and "not as much as we think." In 2008, 2.2 million or 68 percent of students who graduated in the previous year were enrolled in college.[1] To achieve Obama's goal for high-school graduates only, one million more students would need to be absorbed into the system in the first year. The average tuition, not including room and board, of a year of college to individuals is about $10,000.[2] Further, in 2007 states spent an additional $5,353 per student enrolled in public higher education.[3] In today's higher-education system, it might cost about $15 billion to provide one year of college to these remaining students. Since many of these students would stay in the system, the annual cost would likely approach $20 billion or more. Even if everyone did have a year of college, studies show the true return on a college degree at less selective institutions is about $250,000 over the course of a lifetime.[4] Presumably, the return on a single year of college would be less than a quarter of this. Further, this was calculated before the nation's economic slump and without the glut of newly degreed individuals that an obligatory year in college would create.

At the same time, there is little doubt that the economic prospects of our nation hang on our ability to build a better skilled workforce. The only way to reconcile our national needs with the current higher education system is to create a higher-education system that is more accountable. In education, accountability usually means holding colleges accountable for the learning outcomes produced. While this is a critical component, colleges also must have market accountability. Are students, states, and the nation getting the most for their dollar? Are colleges sufficiently subject to the discipline of competition to ensure efficient and effective operations? To have market accountability, the market must work. There must be opportunities for innovation, for market winners and for market losers. Today, the market does not work. There are significant barriers to innovation, and existing institutions have insufficient incentives to be innovative, cost conscious, and customer focused. To meet our nation's educational goals, we need to foster innovation in higher education on a scale never before seen. The good news is that the tools and technology are available to do this. The bad news is the systems and policies of our existing higher-education system are not.

Barriers to Innovation

All industries have barriers to innovation. Sometimes the barriers are created by the product itself. For instance, cell-phone service delivery requires an extraordinary fixed investment to build a network of cell-phone towers. Sometimes the barriers are erected to protect consumers. For instance, pharmaceutical and financial services are regulated to prevent consumer injury and fraud. Other barriers are created by market participants. For instance, software companies can generate proprietary code to integrate with their software or a digital camera maker may require a specific chip or charger only produced by that company. The government may decide that it is in the nation's interest to distort competition by giving grants and selectively subsidizing providers or levying taxes on other companies. Natural barriers to innovation such as industries characterized by high fixed costs and proprietary specifications usually give way to technological change and the demands of the market-place. Artificial barriers to change such as regulation and price subsidies require governmental action. Today, higher education, particularly public higher education, is protected by a range of mostly artificial barriers to innovation. These barriers prevent consumers from realizing the cost savings and product evolution possible from technology.

The task for policymakers is to determine whether artificial regulations have outlived their usefulness and then to summon the political will to change them. Frequently, regulatory obsolescence, as in the telecommunications industry, is caused by the creation or adoption of new technologies that dramatically disrupt the marketplace. Today, in higher education, technology has transformed the cost structure of content creation and distribution and individual and group communication. The tools exist for a variety of new education formats and price points. Further, online education has removed barriers to competition enabling students to make education choices at the course level as opposed to the institutional level. However, higher education's regulatory, accountability, and financial structures are tied to institutions. Technology has created the necessary tools for innovation, yet the policy structures are not sufficient to allow innovation to emerge.

Higher Education Barriers to Innovation

Because higher education is believed to create a variety of public benefits such as economic development, technological breakthroughs, and an informed citizenry, federal and state governments subsidize higher education through direct grants to schools, direct grants to students, and subsidized loans. Prospective students prefer to rely on some combination of these subsidies when enrolling in postsecondary education. Accordingly, access to these funding streams is critical to the success of new postsecondary providers. The only way students can get access to these grants and loans is to enroll in a nationally or regionally accredited institution. However, attaining and keeping accreditation has created a regulatory structure that inhibits innovation. Barriers to innovation in higher education include:

1. *Start-up Costs*: The basic elements of a course or college are easy to compile: faculty, content, facilities and a few others. This is even easier in an online environment when most course elements are available for license and geography is not a constraint. However, it typically takes two or more years to receive accreditation from the point of an initial application, and an initial application can

only be filed after the school has been in operation for several years. Further, only full degree programs, not individual courses, can be accredited. This creates a catch-22 for would-be school operators. It is difficult to attract students without access to financial aid, but access to financial aid cannot be provided until you have attracted students. Further, by only accrediting degree programs, academic innovations at the course level are discouraged. By extending the start-up period to 3–5 years—the years of initial operation plus the time necessary to receive accreditation—the return on an investment takes longer to realize, thereby further suppressing innovation and increasing end-user costs.

2. *Regulatory Burdens*: Government-imposed regulations are necessary to insure product safety, protect public finances from fraud, and to diminish the opportunity for consumer exploitation. Indeed the accreditation process is often justified as a way to protect consumers from "diploma mills"—entities that will confer a degree without academic rigor—and to insure quality. However, the price of safety and quality assurance are higher costs for the regulated industry that are then passed on to consumers. Such a price may be worth it if the regulatory infrastructure is effective. Unfortunately, today's accrediting system—the system responsible for most college regulation—does not seem to provide the promised quality assurance. In higher education the presence or absence of accreditation has very little correlation with college quality. A recent report found wide variations in six-year college graduation rates among schools with similar admission standards, track records and test scores. Indeed, finding accredited colleges with six-year graduation rates below 20 percent that have stayed that way for years is distressingly easy.[5]

3. *Ambiguous Quality Standards*: Despite the fact that accreditation provides little information about the quality of an education provided by a college, consumers still must choose a college to attend. Without meaningful data on education quality, students use proxies to make these decisions. So, price, selectivity, rankings, location, and other factors not related to the educational process dramatically affect selection. This provides incentives to innovate in non-academic areas such as the provision of climbing walls, better dormitories, sports teams, student centers, recreation facilities, and more. Also, similar to the consumer purchasing patterns of wine, price can often be confused with quality because consumers have little other data on which to base decisions.

4. *Proprietary Specifications*: Any product composed of interoperable parts must have specifications that allow them to fit together.

The producer of that product can use open specifications such that other providers can build or attach parts to his product, or closed specifications such that the provider controls all the pieces. Closed specifications typically inhibit innovation, but may improve an overall product. For instance, Apple uses closed specifications for products wishing to run on its system. This has resulted in far fewer programs available for Apple computers. However, many will argue that Apple's system is more reliable and better designed because it keeps tight control of its specifications. While it may seem strange to talk about interoperability with regard to higher education, the earning and transfer of credit is a specification that allows "parts" earned at one college to be fit into another. Despite having an accreditation process that is supposed to assure a minimum level of quality, articulation—the process by which one college agrees to accept another college's credits—is famously incomplete and confusing. Not only will a college only accept a patchwork of credits from a patchwork of colleges, but information about what will and what will not be accepted is difficult to obtain. Further, the process of transferring credit can be cumbersome and time-consuming for the student. Lastly, government subsidies in the form of federal grants, subsidized loans and sometimes in-state tuition can only be applied to the student's home institution, not to a course provider from a third party that would count at the home institution. The lack of easy interoperability stifles the demand for course-level innovation and keeps students at individual colleges.

5. *Distorted Industry Economics*: One of the most obvious ways to undermine innovation is for government to "pick" the provider of a product by offering the service itself, or by offering price subsidies in the form of tax breaks or grants. This creates a situation in which the new entrant to the market simply is not on a level playing field with the existing entrants. State governments fund most of public higher education. Further, nonprofit universities benefit from preferred tax status. Lastly, the federal government only allows federal grants and subsidized loans to be provided to students enrolled in accredited institutions.

Given the magnitude of the regulatory barriers, the time needed to start new colleges, the difficulty of transferring credits among schools, the unlevel playing field, and the lack of performance information, it is not surprising that the price of higher education continues to rise. Further, despite the growth in price, the amount spent on academics has actually declined. From 2002 to 2006 total spending on education and related services declined for all types of institutions except research universities. Additionally, the share of educational spending dedicated to classroom instruction declined at all types of institutions from 2002 to 2006.[6] It would seem that, despite all our new technology and new educational capabilities, educational quality has gone down and prices have gone up.

It Is Easier to Change the Course of History than Change a History Course

Unnatural barriers to competition have two pernicious impacts on consumers. First, prices are higher than they should be. Second, product quality is usually lower than it should be. While it is hard to show examples of stifled innovation (because they have been stifled), it is possible to point to market excesses caused by the lack of innovation. In general, the areas of higher education that have a high degree of standardization across colleges and that have few, if any, hands-on or geographic requirements are the ones ripe for dramatic cost reductions and competition. In figure 11.1, the upper right quadrant is the area that is most ripe for disruption. The bottom left quadrant is the area that is least ripe for disruption.

Not only are courses in the upper right quadrant easily taught online and applicable across the entire industry, but the online versions are usually dramatically overpriced in today's higher-education system. For instance, general education courses such as college algebra, microeconomics,

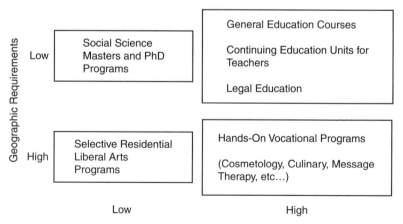

Figure 11.1   Standardization of Content across Colleges.

history 101, and other prerequisite courses, typically have a large number of students and are taught by adjuncts or graduate assistants making only slightly more than minimum wage. Though few in number, these courses account for nearly one-third of all enrollment in higher education,[7] making them a significant driver of cost and quality. The National Center for Academic Transformation (NCAT) ran a grant program that asked colleges to redesign high-enrollment introductory courses in ways that would reduce cost and improve quality. A requirement for participation was to estimate the cost per student before and after redesign. Using data from the thirty initial colleges (all of whom were public), it cost on average $170 per student before redesign and $111 per student after redesign.[8] These figures specifically exclude fixed costs such as classroom space and Internet access and administrative costs. These colleges charge about $1,000 per course and they receive state subsidies to boot. While it is impressive that colleges were able to reduce their cost per student and, in almost all cases, improve performance, the difference between the unit cost to deliver a course and the unit price charged for that course is extreme. At most colleges this overhead, tacked onto high-enrollment courses, is used to subsidize other parts of the university, such as low-enrollment courses, less popular degree programs, new buildings, sports teams, and other features. However, many students—particularly commuters, adult students and distance education students—neither want nor benefit from these amenities. These nontraditional students are the fastest growing segment of higher education. At many colleges these formerly nontraditional students have become the majority of enrollments. In a better functioning market new entrants would dramatically reduce this extreme and widening profit margin.

Another example of market imperfection is how online courses are priced. Despite some arguments to the contrary, online courses are dramatically cheaper to offer than face-to-face courses. Online courses need far less infrastructure, rely more on individuals moving at their own pace, and allow greater scale. However, these cost savings are not reflected in prices to students. Online courses typically have the same tuition as face-to-face courses. Adding insult to injury, additional fees are often charged to take these courses. Universities frequently treat these programs as revenue centers rather than applying the same subsidies to them as are applied to face-to-face courses.

These barriers to competition are particularly relevant as the unit of a student's educational selection is increasingly at the course level rather than the institutional level. For instance, Fort Hays State University, a fairly typical four-year public university located in western Kansas, conducted an internal study to find out where its students' credits had come from. It found that 75 percent of students had credits from two or more places, and

25 percent of students had credits from five or more places.[9] These credits came from other colleges, dual enrollment from high schools, CLEP, AP, life-skills awards, American Council of Education-recommended courses, and elsewhere. This credit diversity exists despite the barriers to intercollege articulation and the inability to use financial aid at colleges outside the one in which a student is enrolled. Increasingly, students are making their educational choices at the course level, yet accreditation and financial-aid disbursement are focused at the institutional level. Accreditors do not review courses; they review the inputs and outputs of institutions. This mismatch between current student behavior and legacy regulatory structures generates many of the internal contradictions of higher education. For instance, accreditors want to review college graduation and completion rates. However, this is only truly relevant where students are taking almost all of their courses from that institution. Also, the cost of higher education is usually quoted as institutional tuition, not course-level costs. Such a cost structure enables subsidies that mask the true cost of a college's activities. Lastly, when financial aid is driven through an institution, students must pay for courses from other providers with out-of-pocket money. Such a practice discourages course-level competition.

Proinnovation Policies

Everyone wants to make higher education more affordable. Recent policy proposals suggested increasing loans and grants to students, penalizing tuition increases, "shaming" colleges that raise tuition by publishing their names and tuition raises, or a combination of the above. None of these proposals are likely to work. Increasing loans and grants simply pours more money into an inefficient system and may result in higher prices as colleges raise prices to match loan limits. Artificially capping tuition increases creates scarcity in some markets, which will lead to further market distortions. Lastly, a "shame" list will have little bearing because students more often pay net tuition rather than full tuition. To truly make education more affordable, "education" (or at least some elements of it) must be objectively defined by the regulatory apparatus and the market for higher education must more accurately reflect the costs of providing it at the course level.

The first priority is to create an objective and comparable measurement of minimum college outcomes. Dozens of more specialized fields such as nursing, accounting, medical assisting, law, teaching, and others require basic tests to enter a profession. It should not be too much to ask of general education to create a similar basic test. Even liberal arts colleges that will resist subject-matter assessments could be held to standards of critical-thinking improvement among their students that can be measured by tests such as the College Learning Assessment (CLA)[10] and others. Such testing requires agreement on what constitutes the elements of minimum success. Efforts are underway in Europe through the Bologna Process and via a Lumina Foundation-funded project in Indiana, Utah, and Minnesota to identify core standards across institutions in selected disciplines.

The second priority is to require that colleges take each other's credits. Once there is some agreement on minimum standards, as there already is among several state systems, then all colleges should at least accept credits in these courses from other colleges. International travelers know the hassle of preparing for different electrical standards in different countries. What if that were magnified a hundredfold? What if it were magnified a hundredfold and a traveler might not be able to determine the standards before traveling? With colleges' byzantine credit transfer system, postsecondary students are like these twilight-zone travelers. According to a 2005 General Accounting Office study, "institutions vary in how they evaluate credits, who makes the decisions to accept credits, and when credit transfer decisions are made. For example, some institutions evaluate transfer credits prior to student transfer, while others make final credit transfer decisions after student enrollment... A student's inability to transfer credit may result in longer enrollment, more tuition payments, and additional federal financial aid."[11] While it would seem that colleges regulated by a common entity with supposedly objective standards would be able to easily compare similar courses, this is not the case. Once basic quality measurements are established and accepted, it should be a requirement that any accredited college must accept any other accredited college's credits just as they would accept their own and without additional fees or hassles. Many courses, particularly general education courses, such as college algebra, economics, chemistry, and others are commodities. They should be treated as such.

The third priority is that colleges and educational entities should be regulated based on their students' performance on common assessments. Today, receiving accreditation is more like joining a country club than achieving a certain standard of success. If you are funded by the state, you are certain to get in. If you are a nonprofit institution, you have a very good shot. If you are a for-profit institution, your actions will be scrutinized much more closely. Once in, it is very difficult to be kicked out. With a subjective regulation system, innovation must come in a structure that is acceptable to those already approved. However, innovation is much more likely to take completely different forms. For instance, educational specialists might emerge who focus on specific courses or subsets of courses. New educational practices might emerge that can only be achieved at scale. So long as the student meets a common outcome, it should not matter who provides the education.

The fourth priority is to create a level economic playing field. Imagine going to several car dealerships to purchase a car. The first dealership gives you the lowest price, and it is based on where you live. The second gives you a price that is much more expensive, but professes to fit your needs better. The third one gives you a price, but only has a limited supply and cannot guarantee that you will get a car. The second and third dealers also insinuate that if you buy a car from them, they will cut you a special deal. Lastly, you know that all the cars must be pretty similar, but you are not allowed to look prior to buying. While this is perplexing to the consumer; it wreaks havoc on new-car sellers. If I want to be a new-car seller, I would not improve the car because the customer is not making the purchasing decision based on the product. The customer is making the purchasing decision based on ambiguous pricing, location, and marketing. To allow innovation to flourish, policymakers not only need to create common objectives and evaluative practices, they must tie these to the true cost of delivery. This brings market discipline to the delivery of education. Specifically, states should stop funding colleges directly. Assuming states believe higher education is a public good worth subsidizing, it would be much more efficient to create a voucher system such that the market determined pricing and the state subsidized a portion of it. A variety of conditions could be attached to these vouchers to achieve policy goals. For instance, as in the existing financial aid system, students could be means tested to insure that the neediest received vouchers. Further, to keep state dollars and college graduates in state, states could require college attendance in state, postgraduation residency requirements, or both. Given the dramatic organizational change that a voucher system would entail, most states are not likely to implement it in the short term. Short of a voucher system, states should let each public college set its own tuition. For private colleges, states should consider giving all institutions tax exemptions or giving tax exemptions to none.

Objective Evaluation

In 2007 the Spellings Commission—a commission appointed by the U.S. Department of Education in the Bush administration—examined issues of access, affordability, accountability, and quality in higher education. Their findings were highly critical of the higher-education system. In an article written after his time at the commission, Charles

Miller, the commission's chair said, "If the academy does not find ways to measure and assess its productivity and outcomes, that will be done for it. The evidence is clear, particularly because of financial pressures, that outside intervention is going to occur if higher education does not respond to the need to change."[12] This was met with severe resistance from the higher-education community. Existing accrediting bodies argued that the extraordinary diversity of missions within postsecondary education made it impossible to prescribe a single model of evaluation. Instead, accreditors and colleges argued for the status quo and voluntary quality-assurance efforts.

It is true that one of American higher education's strengths is its diversity of institutions. Would it be fair to measure a college that deliberately serves struggling students on student success? Some liberal arts colleges argue that their academic offerings cannot be separated from the academic culture created by a resource-intensive residential college. Should this college be penalized because it is necessarily expensive? What might a common assessment system look like?

Though finding a common assessment system to compare all aspects of all colleges will be impossible, there are at least four principles that can guide the creation of a sufficient assessment system. Because no single measure will accurately evaluate colleges, multiple methods of evaluation need to be combined. Some are:

1. *Assess Minimum Commonalities Only*: Despite the arguments to the contrary, much of the general education core is more or less the same across colleges. If what a student learns in calculus at one college is truly different from what a student learns at another college, then our bridges would not meet in the middle and our buildings would fall down. Admittedly, some subjects—particularly the liberal arts—are more subjective across colleges. However, where there are common standards—math, science, economics, accounting, statistics, basic composition—they should be assessed.

2. *Results Must Be Tied to Price*: Knowing that more students pass a calculus course at College A than at College B does not tell me much about that course. If I am buying a car, a Mercedes might be nice, but I might rather buy a Ford and use the rest of the money on something else. Assuming objective standards, schools could publish price-per-pass information, which would be the price per course divided by the percentage of students that passed it. For instance, a course that cost $1000 and had a 90 percent pass rate would have a cost per pass of $1,111. A course that cost $150 and had a 50 percent pass rate would have a cost per pass of $300. Which is

the better course? In conjunction with other measures, this can give some sense of the value of the course.

3. *Student Opinions Matter*: While studies have shown that lenient graders get better student-survey results, student opinions about their overall education, particularly within a decade of graduation, do matter. It is an indicator of the student perception of value of the educational experience and whether it provided what he or she expected it to provide in the workforce.

4. *Transparency Is Critical*: Assuming objective standards, interoperability and a level economic playing field, pass rates, price figures, and student opinions should be sufficient to allow students to pick the college experience that best meets their needs. However, this information needs to be publicly accessible and current.

Innovations That Aren't

Many of the points made in this article are not new to higher education. Policymakers and higher education administrators wring their hands about price escalation. They are aware that their ability to demonstrate and compare effectiveness is insufficient. Institutions spend a large and increasing amount of money on new technologies with which they intend to save money and increase access to education. There are many, many efforts underway within higher education to address these problems. Unfortunately, most of these efforts serve to perpetuate existing structures or to respond to critics. Like more open markets, market disruption that dramatically changes product make-up and cost structures almost never originates from those who would be disrupted. Existing players tend to make incremental changes that will appeal to their individual customers. Here are some of the innovations that are not likely to change the cost and accountability problems of higher education.

1. *Statewide Collaborations*: In international trade, countries are happy to exchange the things that neither has. The United States is happy to import sushi and the Japanese are happy to import hamburgers. However, when both Japan and the United States want to send the other its cars, negotiations get tense. Suddenly, tariffs, regulations, and motivated constituencies restrict trade. Similarly, colleges in collaborations are happy to accept courses and programs not provided at their own college, but are much less likely to allow students to take courses already offered by the home institution. It is telling that many states have distance-learning collaboratives, but most are structured as distance-learning catalogs for the member

institutions. Such an arrangement preserves college autonomy without creating competition among individual departments or courses. A more cost-effective structure would be the aggregation of an entire state's demand for online courses and letting a single public entity fulfill that demand. Such a structure would take advantage of economies of scale to derive pricing advantages and amortization efficiencies. It would also avoid the duplicative online efforts offered by a state's many public colleges.

2. *Voluntary Quality-Assurance Programs*: In response to increased pressure on higher education to demonstrate accountability, several voluntary accountability programs that allow cross-institutional comparisons have emerged.[13] While these programs represent an improvement over the current lack of comparable data, they still suffer from several critical problems. First, these programs are voluntary. The participants are few in number and, presumably, are the ones with little to hide. Second, the information is usually self-provided, creating an incentive to provide biased information.

3. *Content Collaboratives and Open Courseware*: In 2002 the Massachusetts Institute of Technology (MIT) made headlines by announcing that it intended to put all of its course materials online and make them available to anyone for free. In the last fifteen years this evolved into the OpenCourseWare Consortium with well over one hundred members across the globe. With such materials available, everyone would be able to benefit from MIT's world class educational content. By providing free materials, the cost of education should decline. Classic economics states that the price of a good should equal its marginal cost of production. In other words, in a perfect market, the price of an item should equal the amount that it costs to produce one more unit of that item. Rightly, like MIT, states have taken note of the fact that the marginal cost of electronic content is effectively zero. Therefore, electronic content produced by their institutions can be shared at almost no cost. In theory, this should reduce course development costs, textbook costs, and speed the development of new courses. Several collaboratives have been created to take advantage of this. For instance, MERLOT is a collaboration of fifteen state college systems that contribute to a database of educational content objects, combinations of content and software that provide a lesson or explanation. Unfortunately, while there are many states and individuals who are willing to contribute to MERLOT, college-governance structures, course-development procedures, textbook-adoption processes, and tuition policies conspire to

limit the demand for free content. For instance, a professor has limited incentive to develop a course more cheaply. Further, even if the professor does develop a course more cheaply, that savings will not be passed on to the student. Similarly, for open courseware and free content to reduce the price of a course, it must be composed of a significant portion of that course's price structure. For most colleges, online content comprises a negligible portion of that course's cost to deliver and price to the student.

4. *Technology Adoption*: Colleges are eager to adopt new technologies. Most colleges offer some form of learning management system for both distance education and face-to-face classes. Most make extensive use of administrative tools to manage student data, grades, payments, and other necessary services. Overhead projectors, smartboards, "clickers," and other in-classroom technologies are extremely common. Most colleges offer some form of distance education. However, despite the presence of all of these technologies, costs continue to rise. Without changes in the business processes in which these technologies are embedded, the potential for cost and quality improvements will not be realized.

Signs of Change

Despite the significant policy barriers to innovation, the postsecondary market is poised for dramatic transformation. The cost savings of electronic content and communication are so significant that they can allow new entrants to overcome the pricing advantages enjoyed by public and nonprofit colleges. Further, and more importantly, by making postsecondary education time and place independent, online education removes the biggest barriers to competition. Instead of having a few postsecondary options, the prospective student now has dozens. Online enrollments continue to grow at rates far in excess of the total higher-education student population. Over 3.9 million students were taking at least one online course during the fall 2007 term; a 12 percent increase over the number reported the previous year. The 12 percent growth rate for online enrollments far exceeds the 1.2 percent growth of the overall higher-education student population. Over 20 percent of all U.S. higher-education students were taking at least one online course in the fall of 2007.[14] Eduventures, an education market research firm, estimates that the market for online education was $6.2 billion in 2005, $11.7 billion in 2008, and will grow to $26 billion by 2013.[15]

With increased competition between distance-education providers *and* between distance-education providers and face-to-face providers, colleges seeking to enroll new students must compete on the features of their offering, price, their marketing efforts, or some combination. Not willing to compete on price, so far, online colleges have differentiated themselves primarily on educational features such as course flexibility, access to potential employers, and degree specialization, while increasing marketing expenses. The marketing cost to enroll a new student continues to rise, though the recent global recession has decreased the cost of advertising, which has temporarily slowed the overall marketing-cost increase. In 2005 private not-for-profit colleges spent $2073 to enroll a student.[16] In 2008 for-profit colleges spent about 25 percent of their annual revenue on marketing, resulting in a median cost-per-start of $2,615.[17] Public colleges spend substantially less because their pricing advantage allows them to enroll students without as much marketing effort. However, as the online education market gets even more crowded, many colleges will no longer be able to afford to spend more on marketing and will be forced to look to other ways to attract students, such as lower prices and differently packaged courses and degrees.

So far, price competition has been constrained because the low-cost provider is almost always the public university or community college. However, as public college tuition and fees continue to rise, the difference between their pricing and private and for-profit college pricing will decrease despite the government subsidies enjoyed by public colleges. Further, private and for-profit colleges will likely engage in fierce price competition bringing their costs even closer to public college tuitions. Also, to attract students, less selective colleges are increasingly willing to allow students to "import" credits from elsewhere, creating de facto interoperability among less selective colleges.

Concurrent with colleges showing signs of being subject to newly competitive market dynamics, students are displaying characteristics of retail consumers. Enabled by technology, they are submitting significantly more college applications than ever before. In 1991 about 59 percent of high-school seniors applied to three or more colleges. In 2006 that number had skyrocketed to 71 percent, and about 18 percent of seniors applied to seven or more institutions.[18] The economic crisis is increasing their interest in low-cost college options such as public four-year universities and community colleges.[19] They are increasingly emboldened to switch their college mid-stream for one that has better value. The number of "swirlers," students who attend two or more institutions prior to graduation, is growing rapidly. As of 2001, 40 percent of students who first enrolled in college had attended more than one postsecondary institution. As of 2004, 20 percent of all four-year college enrollments were comprised of transfer students.[20] Because selective institutions are far less likely to have a large transfer population, this likely dramatically understates transfers for less selective institutions. Additional information on transfer students is difficult to find as it is not routinely collected by the U.S. Department of Education. However, anecdotal information suggests rapid growth. Other methods of alternative credit generation are accelerating as well. For instance, dual enrollment, the fulfillment of college credits while taking high-school courses, has become a fixture of public secondary and postsecondary education in dozens of states. Also, the number of students taking Advanced Placement courses continues to rise. In 2008, 1.6 million high-school teens sat for 2.7 million AP exams, a 45 percent increase in students from 2004.[21] Interestingly, this may be causing more selective schools to limit the number of courses for which it will grant exemptions. For instance, Tufts, following the lead of Williams College, restricted the number of courses that a student could exempt out of with AP scores.[22] This, of course, requires the student to spend more for a selective education.

Also, a variety of controversial business models have emerged that combine private-sector marketing and efficiency with the public college accreditation to offer students lower-cost courses. These models take aim at the high profit margins inherent in the market niches that are easily delivered online, have common standards across schools, and tuition does not reflect the cost of delivery. For instance, Higher Ed Holdings, a for-profit company run by an established education entrepreneur, has partnered with Lamar University in Texas to offer graduate degrees in education through Lamar at half the price of Lamar's existing programs. Higher Ed Holdings provided the marketing expertise, student services, content, and other resources in exchange for a significant percentage of the tuition revenue. The partnership yielded record enrollment. However, a similar program at the University of Toledo generated enough opposition from University of Toledo's faculty to prevent the program's implementation. StraighterLine, a company that I founded and run, offers general education courses that can be taken by students for $99 per month plus $39 per course started and can be transferred into regionally accredited colleges. These courses receive no state or federal subsidies. Multiple regionally accredited colleges agreed to award credit upon enrollment to students who had completed these courses. Further, the Distance Education and Training Council (DETC), a nationally recognized accreditor, said that these courses met all of their standards of quality. Despite these assertions of quality, the model has generated strident opposition from faculty members and the media. In addition to Higher Ed Holdings and StraighterLine, a variety of other for-profit and not-for-profit entities provide turn-key online courses that include content, infrastructure, and instruction using an accredited university's brand name and accreditation. For instance, Bisk Education provides finance, nursing, and education programs that are "private labeled" by partner colleges. Ed2Go provides noncredit courses through community colleges. Regis College's New Ventures program provides adult-education curricula and expertise to other Catholic colleges. The Institute for Professional Development owned by the University of Phoenix provides similar adult-focused programming for colleges. The potential impact of online learning on the cost structure of course delivery combined with the ever-increasing prices charged by public colleges and the dramatic decrease in the ability of the population to afford postsecondary education is poised to overcome the legacy structural barriers to innovation in higher education.

Conclusion

U.S. higher education, whether for-profit, nonprofit, or public, is big business. To maintain national competitiveness and meet the new administration's policy goals, the number of students served must increase. However, given the state of the economy and the national debt, we cannot afford to spend more to do this. The only way to educate more students without breaking the bank will be to improve the effectiveness, efficiency, and accountability of higher education. This requires us to rethink the regulatory structure of higher education to create conditions more favorable for academic and price innovation. Allowing a more efficient education market, one that allows price competition, new entrants, winners, and losers, could impose far greater market accountability. In turn, market accountability can create a stronger relationship between product quality and price paid.

Fortunately, technological change and the resulting competition plus the emergence of new business models are pulling a reluctant higher-education edifice into conversations about reform. However, without supportive policy makers, new business models will continue to be forced to perform unnatural acts to succeed. For instance, why must Higher Ed Holdings partner with an accredited college if it is providing the lion's share of the educational experience? Why must StraighterLine's credits be limited to only those regionally accredited colleges where the faculty is willing to accept its credits? What value does a university provide in a "private labeled" relationship with a third party that is providing all of the educational resources? What other business models might emerge if the pricing advantage enjoyed by public universities did not prevent competitors from entering the market?

From the residential liberal-arts experience to vocational training to online baccalaureate degrees to cutting-edge research, postsecondary education provides an extraordinarily diverse set of experiences to an extraordinarily diverse set of students. This has served the United States well. However, with a growing student population looking to be served using new mediums and competition now existing at the individual course level, the regulatory and financing structures of the past need to be revisited. It is time to build a provider-neutral, objectively assessed, higher-education system.

Notes

1. Bureau of Labor Statistics, *College Enrollment and Work Activity of 2008 High School Graduates*, news release, April 28, 2009.
2. While net tuition is about half of published tuition, the difference is typically composed of grants, scholarships, and low-interest loans. These remain costs, but simply come from another source. College Board, Trends in College Pricing, Trends in Higher Education Series, http://www.collegeboard.com/html/costs/pricing/3_1_net_prices.html; and Laura G. Knapp, Janice E. Kelly-Reid, and Scott A. Ginder, *Enrollment in Postsecondary Institutions, Fall 2007; Graduation Rates, 2001 & 2004 Cohorts; and Financial Statistics, Fiscal Year 2007: First Look* (Washington, DC: National Center for Education Statistics, Institute for Education Sciences, U.S. Department of Education, March 2009).
3. James Palmer, Table 2, "One-Year (FY08 to FY09) and Two-Year (FY07 to FY09) Percent Changes in State Tax Appropriations for Higher Education, by Region," in *Grapevine*, ed. James Palmer (Normal, IL: Center for the Study of Education Policy, Illinois State University, 2009), www.grapevine.ilstu.edu/tables/; and Laura G. Knapp, Janice E. Kelly-Reid, and Scott A. Ginder, *Enrollment in Postsecondary Institutions, Fall 2007; Graduation Rates, 2001 & 2004 Cohorts; and Financial Statistics, Fiscal Year 2007* (Washington, DC: National Center for Education Statistics, Institute for Education Sciences, U.S. Department of Education, March 2009).
4. Mark Schneider, "How Much Is That Bachelor's Degree Really Worth? The Million Dollar Misunderstanding," (Washington, DC: American Enterprise Institute, May 2009).
5. Frederick Hess, Mark Schneider, Kevin Carey, and Andrew Kelly, *Diplomas and Dropouts* (Washington, DC: American Enterprise Institute, June 2009).
6. Jane Wellman, Donna Desrochers, and Colleen Lenthan, *Trends in College Spending* (Washington DC, Delta Project on Postsecondary Education Costs, Productivity, and Accountability, 2009).
7. Carol Twigg, "The One Percent Solution," *Educom Review*, December 1995.
8. National Center for Academic Transformation, *Program in Course Redesign (PCR): Outcomes Analysis*, http://www.thencat.org/PCR/Outcomes.htm
9. From e-mail correspondence with Dr. Larry Gould, Provost, Fort Hays State University, December 4, 2009.
10. Roger Benjamin and Marc Chun, *Returning to Learning in an Age of Assessment* (New York: Council for Aid to Education, May 2009), http://www.collegiatelearningassessment.org/files/ReturningToLearning.pdf.

11. U.S. Government Accountability Office (GAO), *Transfer Students* (Washington DC: Government Accountability Office, 2005)

12. Charles Miller, "The Spellings Commission Report: The Chair's Perspective," in *Forum Futures, 2008* (papers of the 2007 Aspen Symposium of the Forum for the Future of Higher Education).

13. Examples include Transparency by Design funded by the Lumina Foundation and run by the Western Council on Education and Technology (WCET), and the Voluntary System of Accountability (VSA) sponsored by the American Association of State Colleges and Universities (AASCU) and the National Association of State Universities and Land-grant Colleges (NASULGC).

14. I. Elaine Allen and Jeff Seaman, *Staying the Course—Online Education in the United States, 2008* (Needham, MA: Sloan Consortium, November 2008).

15. Richard Garrett, *Online Higher Education Market Update, 2008: National and New York Data* (Boston: Eduventures, 2009) www.slideshare.net/ alexandrapickett/richard-garretts-online-higher-education-market-update-2008-national-new-york-data.

16. Noel-Levitz, "*Cost of Recruiting Report: Summary of Findings for Two-Year and Four-Year Institutions*," National Research Study (Iowa City, IA: Noel-Levitz, 2006), http://www.noellevitz.com/NR/rdonlyres/B3EB8C48–8886–4457–9B9E-514E30B88A3E/0/CostofRecruitingReport.pdf.

17. Jeffrey Silber, *Education and Training*, BMO Capital Markets Equity Research (NewYork: BMO Financial Group, September, 2009), 186.

18. Glenn Altshuler, " It Only Gets Worse From Here," *Forbes.com*, August 13, 2008.

19. David A. Hawkins and Melissa E. Clinedinst, *2008 State of College Admission* (Arlington, VA: National Association of College Admission Counseling, 2009).

20. Lutz Berkner and Susan Choy, *Descriptive Summary of 2003–04 Beginning Postsecondary Students: Three Years Later* (Washington, DC: National Center for Education Statistics, Institute of Education Sciences, U.S. Department of Education, July 2008).

21. Eddy Ramirez, "Teachers Offer Conflicting Views on AP Program's Rapid Growth," *US News and World Report*, April 30, 2009, www.usnews.com/ blogs/on-education/2009/04/30/teachers-offer-conflicting-views-on-ap-programs-rapid-growth.html.

22. Dave Moltz, "Professors and Students Split on AP Credits," *Inside Higher Ed*, February 10, 2009.

Contributors

Maurice Black earned his B.A. in English and economics from the National University of Ireland, Maynooth, and his Ph.D. in English from the University of Pennsylvania. He has worked as an editor at major New York book publishers, and has been a writer and editor for the Foundation for Individual Rights in Education and the Human Rights Foundation. He is currently Director of Programs and Development at the Moving Picture Institute and a Research Fellow with the American Council of Trustees and Alumni.

Kevin Carey is Education Sector's policy director. Carey came to the organization in September 2005. In addition to managing Education Sector's policy team, he regularly contributes to the Quick and the Ed blog, and has published Education Sector reports on topics including a blueprint for a new system of college rankings, how states inflate educational progress under NCLB, and improving minority college graduation rates. He has published magazine articles and op-eds in publications including *Washington Monthly, The American Prospect, Phi Delta Kappan, Change, Education Week, Washington Post, Los Angeles Times, New York Daily News*, and *Christian Science Monitor*. He also writes a monthly column on higher-education policy for *The Chronicle of Higher Education*. In 1995, Carey worked as an education finance analyst for the state of Indiana where he developed a new formula for setting local property taxes and distributing state education aid. He subsequently served as a senior analyst for the Indiana Senate Finance Committee, writing legislation and advising the Democratic caucus on fiscal policy. From 1999 to 2001, he served as Indiana's Assistant State Budget Director for Education, where he advised the governor on finance and policy issues in K–12 and higher education.

In 2001 Carey moved to Washington DC and became an analyst for the Center on Budget and Policy Priorities, a nonprofit research organization focused on policies that serve low- and moderate-income families. There he published new research on state poverty-based education funding programs. Carey subsequently worked at The Education Trust, where he was director of policy research. He wrote articles and publication on topics including: implementation of the No Child Left Behind Act; value-added measure of teacher effectiveness; state education funding disparities; using state education data systems to analyze minority participation in science and mathematics; improving the distribution of quality teachers to low-income and minority students; and increasing college graduation rates. He also designed and implemented www.collegeresults.org, the graduation rate Web site.

Peter T. Ewell is vice president of the National Center for Higher Education Management Systems (NCHEMS). A member of NCHEMS's staff since 1981, Mr. Ewell's work focuses on assessing institutional and higher-education system effectiveness and the outcomes of postsecondary education. He has directed many projects on this topic, including initiatives funded by the W.K. Kellogg Foundation, the National Institute for Education, the Consortium for the Advancement of Private Higher Education, the Lumina Foundation, and the Pew Charitable Trusts. In addition, Mr. Ewell has consulted with over 375 colleges and universities and twenty-four state systems of higher education on topics related to performance indicators and the assessment of student learning. He has authored seven books and numerous articles on the topic of improving undergraduate instruction through the assessment of student outcomes.

Sara Goldrick-Rab is assistant professor of educational policy studies and sociology at the University of Wisconsin-Madison. She is also the senior scholar at the Wisconsin Center for the Advancement of Postsecondary Education and an affiliate of the Institute for Research on Poverty, the La Follette School of Public Affairs, and the Consortium for Chicago School Research. Mrs. Goldrick-Rab received the William T. Grant Scholars Award in 2010 for her project, Rethinking College Choice in America. In 2009 she was lead author of a Brookings Institution blueprint on "Transforming Community Colleges," and in 2006–2007 was a National Academy of Education/Spencer Foundation postdoctoral fellow. Her work appears in academic journals such as Sociology of Education and the Future of Children as well as on her blogs (The Education Optimists and *The Chronicle of Higher Education*'s Brainstorm). Currently Mrs. Goldrick-Rab is codirecting the Wisconsin Scholars Longitudinal Study, an experimental evaluation of the impact of need-based financial aid on college graduation, and also launching a randomized trial of an early-commitment aid program for Wisconsin high-school students.

Lawrence B. Martin is dean of the graduate school, associate provost, director of the Turkana Basin Institute, and professor of anthropology and of anatomical sciences at Stony Brook University. He is also the founder and president of Academic Analytics, LLC, which produces an annual database on faculty scholarly productivity for university clients. Mr. Martin has analyzed faculty productivity data from the National Research Council's 1995 *Study of Research Doctorate Programs in the United States* to determine which variables serve as useful predictors of a program's reputation. He served on the Scholarly Advisory Board for the Association of American Universities' Assessment of Quality of University Education and Research project and was a member of the National Research Council's Committee to Study the Methodology for the Assessment of Research-Doctorate Programs.

Anne D. Neal is a founder and the president of the American Council of Trustees and Alumni (ACTA), which communicates regularly with more than 10,000 college and university trustees around the country. She has authored or coauthored numerous ACTA studies and a chapter in the volume, *Reforming the Politically Correct University* (AEI Press, 2009), and has directed higher-education programs for the Philanthropy Roundtable. She regularly gives lectures and expert testimony with past venues including the U.S. Senate, the Foreign Policy Association, the Association of American Colleges and Universities, the Council for Higher Education Accreditation, and the U.S. Secretary of Education's Commission on the Future of Higher Education. Before joining ACTA, Ms. Neal served as a First Amendment and communications lawyer and as general counsel and congressional liaison of the National Endowment for the Humanities. She is a member of the Department of Education National Advisory Committee on Institutional Quality and Integrity and serves on the governing boards of many cultural and civic organizations.

Erin O'Connor received her B.A. in English from the University of California, Berkeley, and earned her Ph.D. in English language and literature at the University of Michigan. From 1995 to 2008, she taught English at the University of Pennsylvania. She is currently Director of Programs and Development at the Moving Picture Institute and Research Fellow at the American Council of Trustees and Alumni. Since 2002, she has written "Critical Mass," a blog about the state of higher education.

Naomi Schaefer Riley is an affiliate scholar with the Institute for American Values. Until recently she was the deputy editor of the *Wall Street Journal*'s Taste page where she wrote extensively about higher education, religion, and philanthropy. Prior to joining the *Journal*, she was the editor of *In Character*, as well as an adjunct fellow at the Ethics and Public Policy Center. Her articles and essays have appeared in the *New York Times*, *Los Angeles Times*, *Boston Globe*, *Chronicle of Higher Education*, *Commentary*, *Public Interest*, and *First Things*. In January 2005 Ms. Riley published *God on the Quad: How Religious Colleges and the Missionary Generation Are Changing America* (St. Martin's, 2005). She is currently writing a book on the future of tenure and the academic labor market to be published by Rowman and Littlefield.

Mark Schneider is a vice president for new education initiatives at the American Institutes for Research and a visiting scholar at the American Enterprise Institute. From 2005 to 2008 Mr. Schneider served as the commissioner of the U.S. Department of Education's National Center for Education Statistics and as deputy commissioner from 2004 to 2005. Previously, Mr. Schneider was a professor, department chairman, and director of graduate studies in the political-science department of Stony Brook University. He is the author and coauthor of numerous scholarly books and articles, including, with Jack Buckley, *Charter Schools: Hope or Hype* (Princeton University Press, 2007) and the award-winning *Choosing Schools: Consumer Choice and the Quality of American Schools* (Princeton University Press, 2000).

Burck Smith is the CEO and founder of StraighterLine. Before launching StraighterLine, he was the founder and CEO of SMARTHINKING, the dominant online tutoring provider for schools and colleges. In addition to building StraighterLine, Burck is writing chapters for two books on education policy for the American Enterprise Institute (AEI). He is a member of the American Enterprise Institute's Higher Education Working Group. Burck worked as an independent consultant who contracted with for-profit and nonprofit educational organizations, including clients such as the Gates Foundation; Microsoft's Computer Curriculum Corporation; the CEO Forum on Education and Technology; the Milken Exchange on Education and Technology; Teaching Matters, Inc.; *Converge* magazine; and others. As a writer on education and technology issues, Burck has been published by *Wired* magazine, *Wired* news, *Converge* magazine, *University Business*, and the National School Boards Association. In the early 1990s he wrote articles on a variety of subjects including creating community telecommunication networks, electronic access to political information, telecommunications deregulation, and the ability of utilities to serve as telecommunications service providers. Burck holds an MA in Public Policy from Harvard University's John F. Kennedy School of Government and a BA from Williams College.

Jeffrey Steedle is a measurement scientist at the Council for Aid to Education where he manages research and development projects and assists in operational aspects of administering the Collegiate Learning Assessment. Current projects include redesigning scoring rubrics for extended, open-ended tests of critical thinking and writing skills; managing the calibration of human scorers and the development of machine scoring models; and implementing value-added models for use by institutional assessment programs in higher education. His research interests include value-added modeling, diagnostic assessment, psychometrics, and science education. Dr. Steedle holds a PhD in educational psychology and an MS in statistics from Stanford University. Before his doctoral studies, he taught high-school physics in Baton Rouge while earning his MEd in middle and secondary science education through the Alliance for Catholic Education's Service Through Teaching Program. He currently teaches item-response theory as an adjunct assistant professor at New York University.

Bridget Terry Long is professor of education and economics at the Harvard Graduate School of Education. Her work focuses on college access and choice, factors that influence student outcomes, and the behavior of postsecondary institutions. Dr. Long's current and past projects examine the role of information and simplification in college decisions, the effects of financial-aid programs, and the impact of postsecondary remediation on student outcomes. She is also a faculty research associate of the National Bureau of Economic Research and a research affiliate of the National Center for Postsecondary Research. She has received the National Academy of Education/Spencer Postdoctoral Fellowship, was named one of the new voices in higher education by *The Chronicle of Higher Education*, and was awarded the Robert P. Huff Golden Quill Award for excellence in research and published works on student financial assistance.

Ben Wildavsky is a senior fellow in research and policy at the Kauffman Foundation and a guest scholar at the Brookings Institution. He is the author of *The Great Brain Race: How Global Universities Are Reshaping the World* (Princeton University Press, 2010). Prior to his work at the Kauffman Foundation, Mr. Wildavsky spent eighteen years as a writer and editor specializing in education and public policy. Most recently he was education editor of *U.S. News & World Report* where he was the top editor of *America's Best Colleges* and *America's Best Graduate Schools* and oversaw several award-winning cover stories. Previously, he was economic policy correspondent for the *National Journal*, higher-education reporter for the *San Francisco Chronicle*, and executive editor of *The Public Interest*. As a consultant to national education reformers, Wildavsky has written and edited several influential reports, including the final report of the Secretary of Education's Commission on the Future of Higher Education.

Index